Yamada-kun AND THE Seven Witches

4

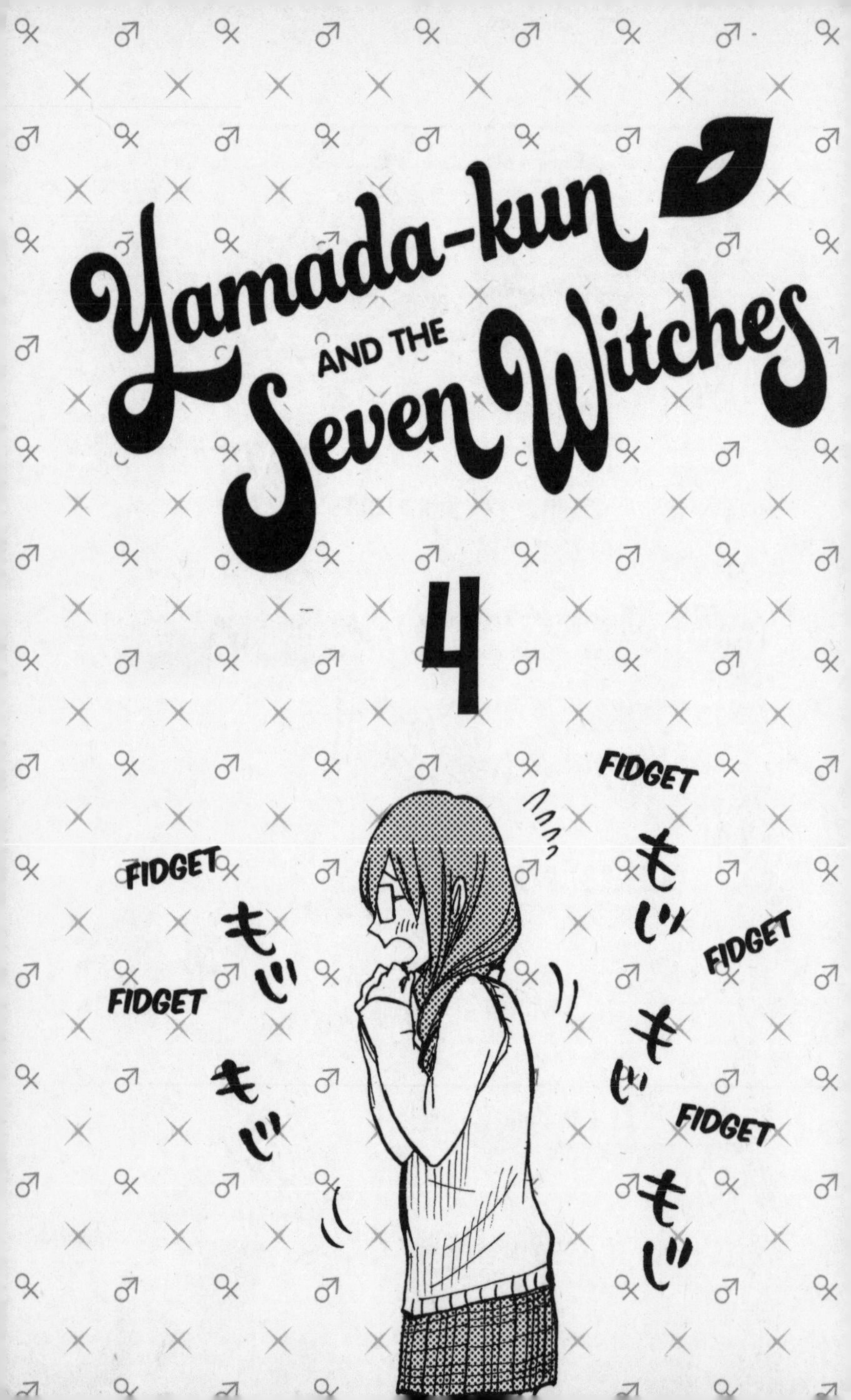
FIDGET
もじ
FIDGET
もじ
FIDGET
もじ
FIDGET
もじ
FIDGET
もじ

CONTENTS

CHAPTER 26: What did you dooo?! 003

027 Chapter 27: Dejected

Chapter 28: Lather Lather 047

067 Chapter 29: Time to whip you into shape, Yamada!!

Chapter 30: Boobs. 087

107 CHAPTER 31: Odagiri's Breasts.

CHAPTER 32: Fsshhh! Pop! Pop! 127

CHAPTER 33: A hot guy is here!

147 167

CHAPTER 34: Pay you with my body?

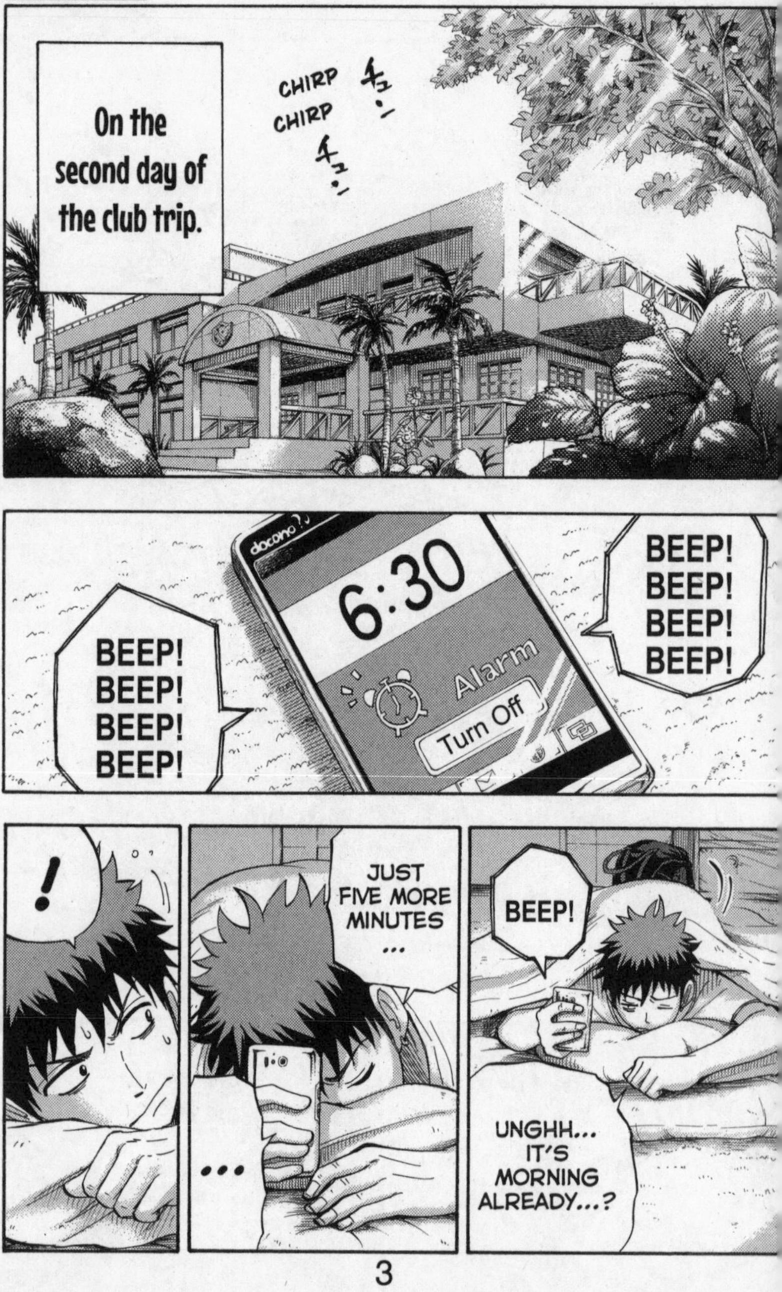
On the second day of the club trip.
CHIRP
CHIRP
BEEP! BEEP! BEEP! BEEP!
6:30
Alarm
Turn Off
BEEP! BEEP! BEEP! BEEP!
BEEP!
UNGHH... IT'S MORNING ALREADY...?
JUST FIVE MORE MINUTES ...
...
!

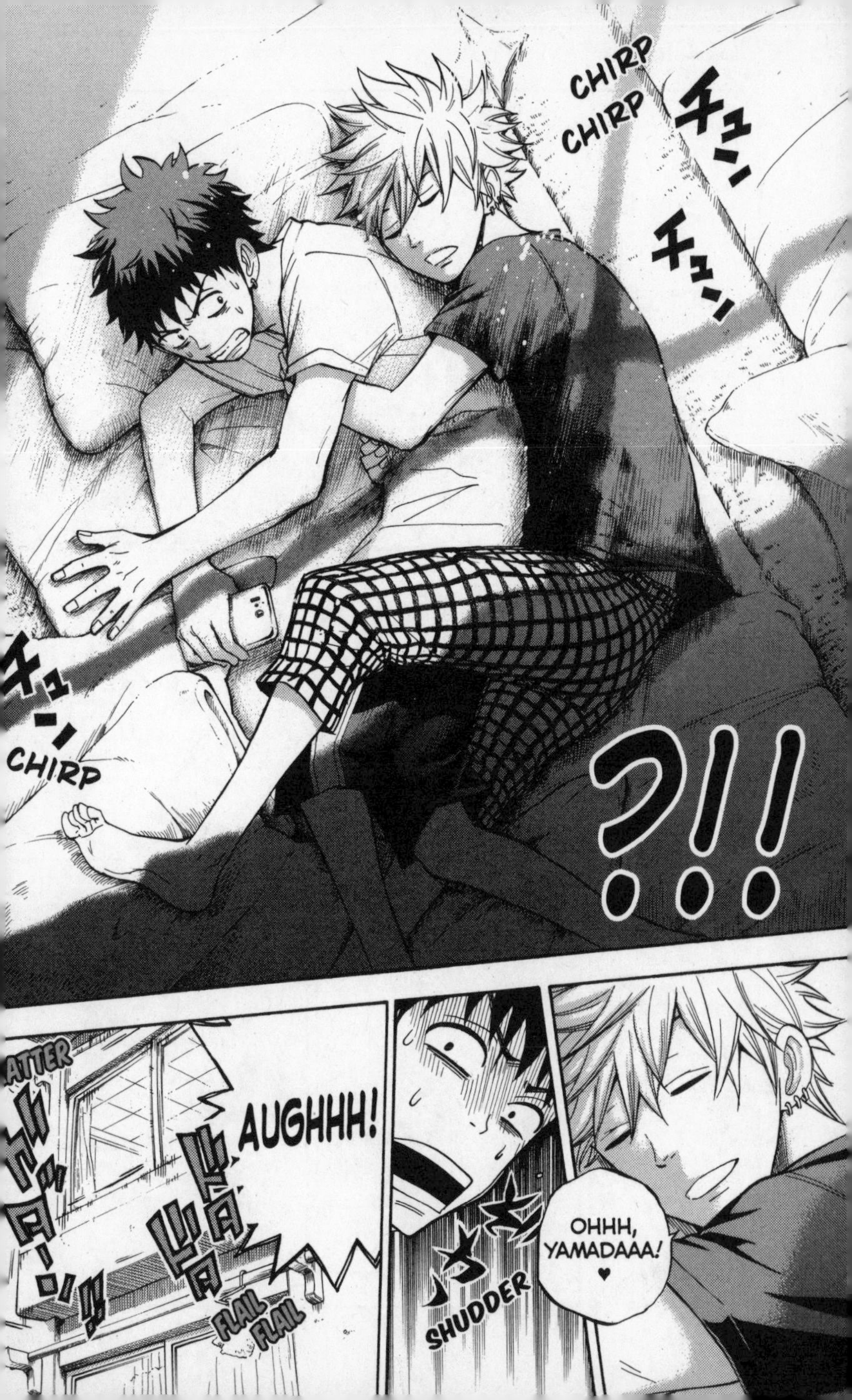
CHIRP CHIRP
チュン
チュン
チュン
CHIRP
?!!
OHHH, YAMADAAA! ♥
SHUDDER
AUGHHH!
FLAIL FLAIL
ATTER

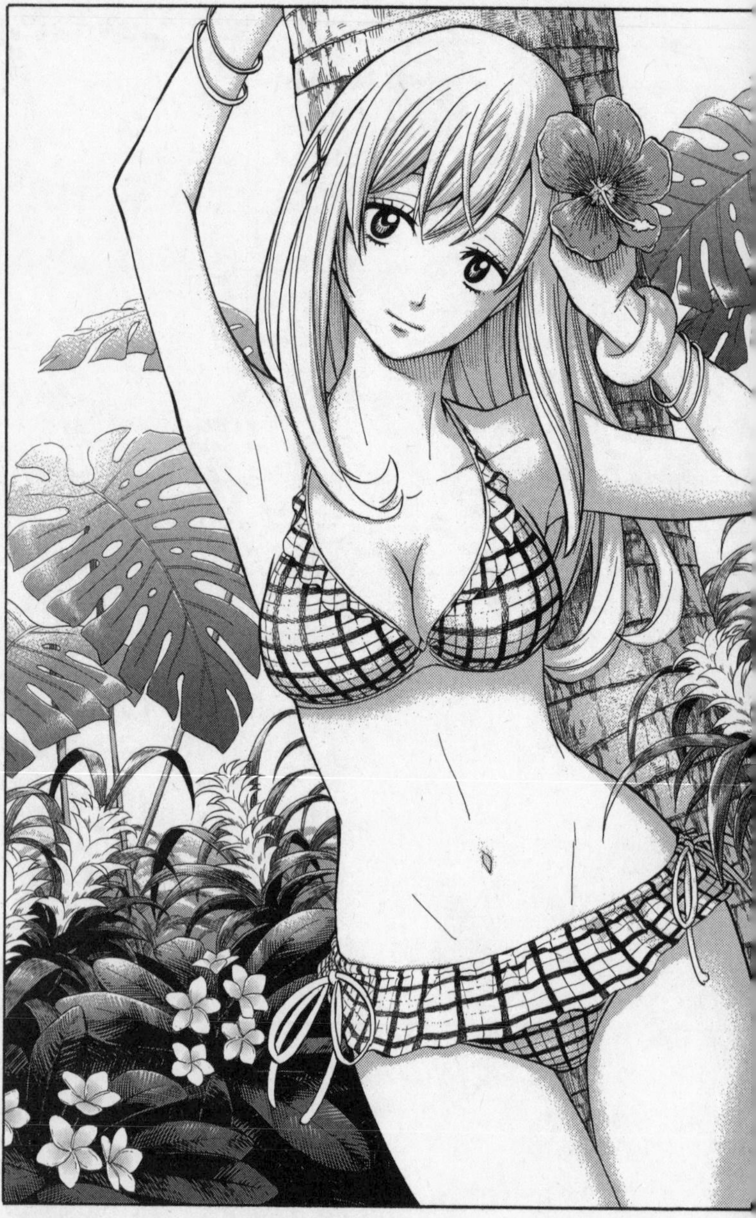

Chapter 26: What did you dooo?!

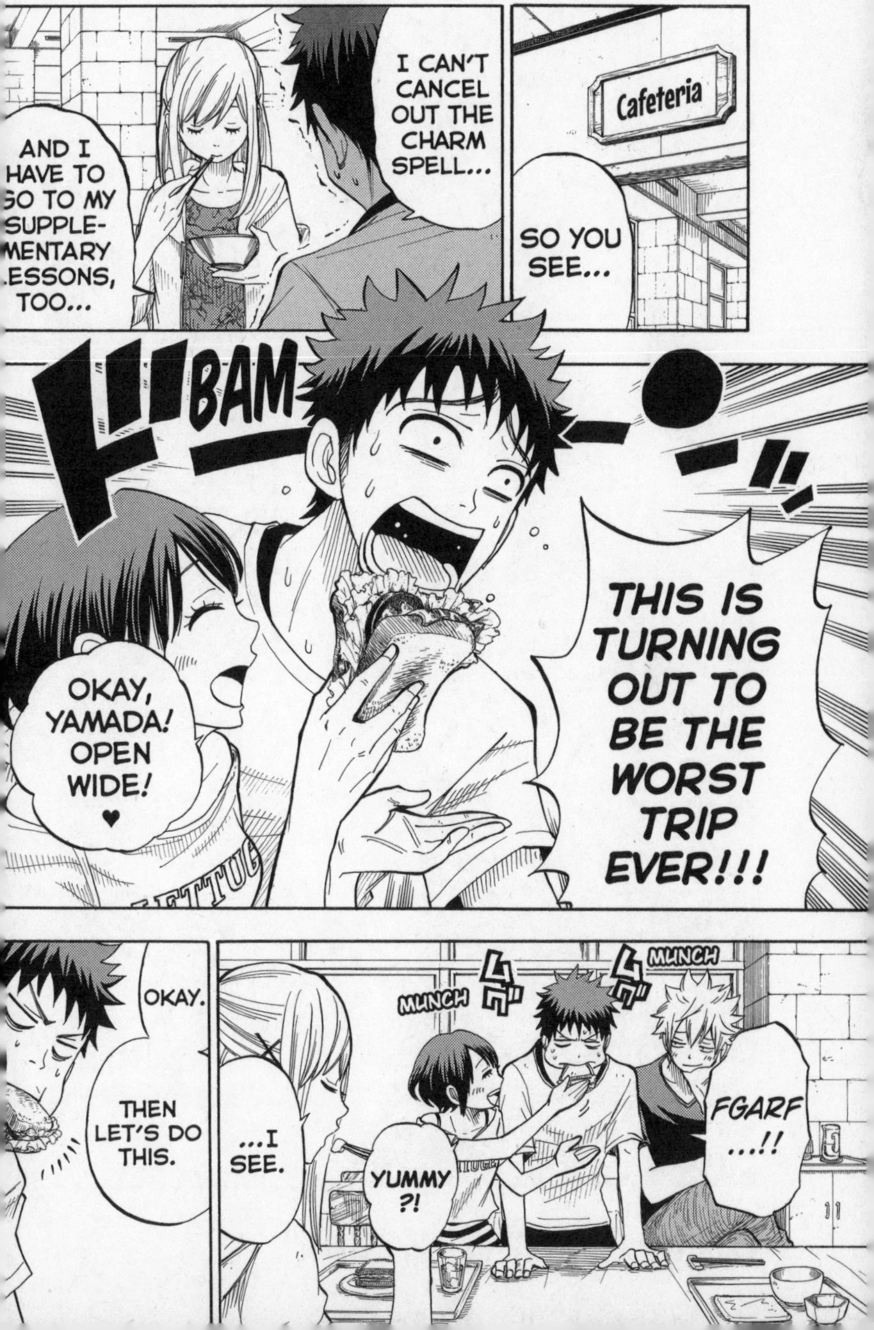
Cafeteria
SO YOU SEE...
I CAN'T CANCEL OUT THE CHARM SPELL...
AND I HAVE TO GO TO MY SUPPLE-MENTARY LESSONS, TOO...
BAM
THIS IS TURNING OUT TO BE THE WORST TRIP EVER!!!
OKAY, YAMADA! OPEN WIDE! ♥
MUNCH
MUNCH
FGARF ...!!
YUMMY ?!
...I SEE.
OKAY.
THEN LET'S DO THIS.

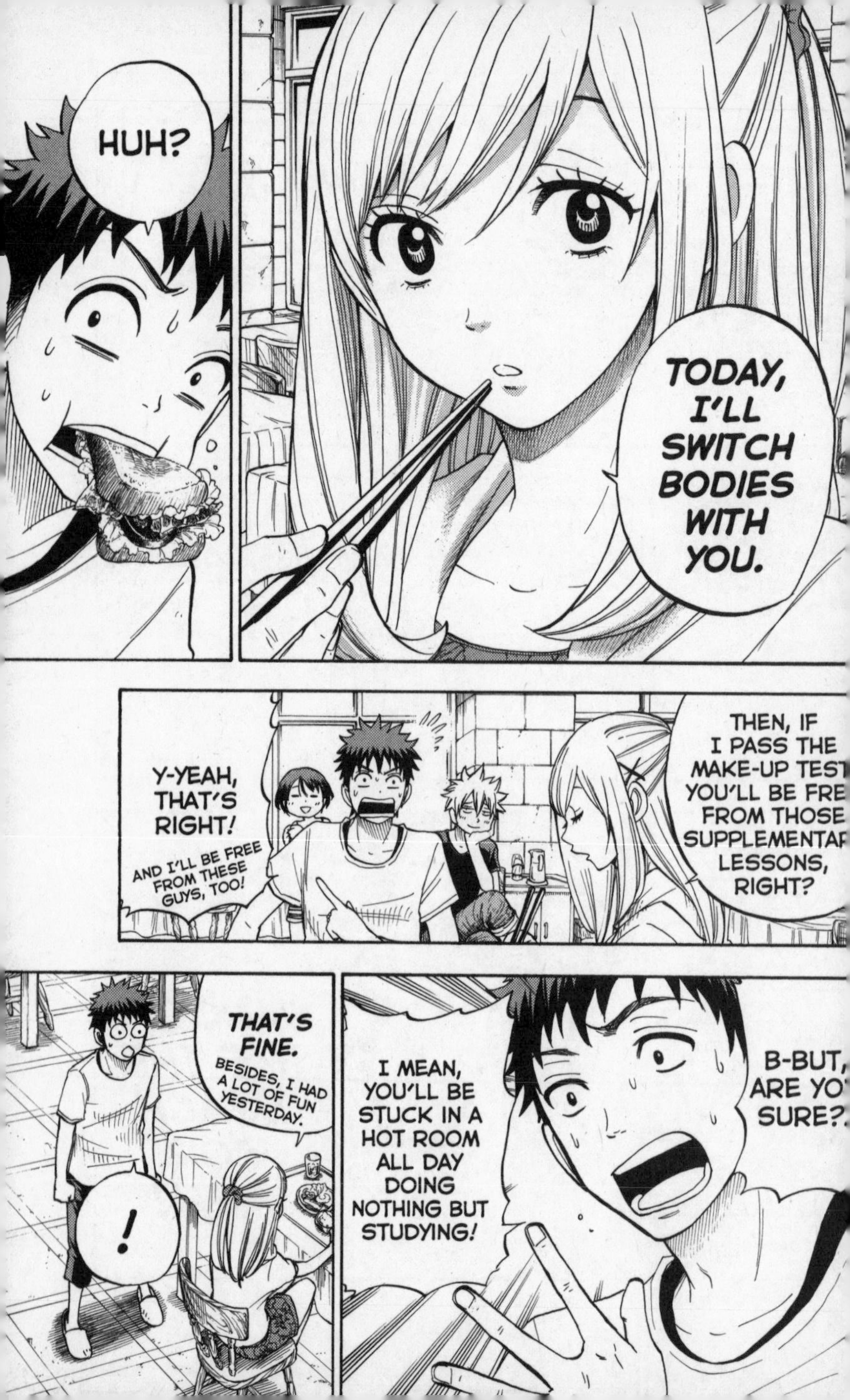
TODAY, I'LL SWITCH BODIES WITH YOU.
HUH?
THEN, IF I PASS THE MAKE-UP TES YOU'LL BE FRE FROM THOSE SUPPLEMENTAR LESSONS, RIGHT?
Y-YEAH, THAT'S RIGHT!
AND I'LL BE FREE FROM THESE GUYS, TOO!
B-BUT, ARE YO SURE?..
I MEAN, YOU'LL BE STUCK IN A HOT ROOM ALL DAY DOING NOTHING BUT STUDYING!
THAT'S FINE.
BESIDES, I HAD A LOT OF FUN YESTERDAY.
!

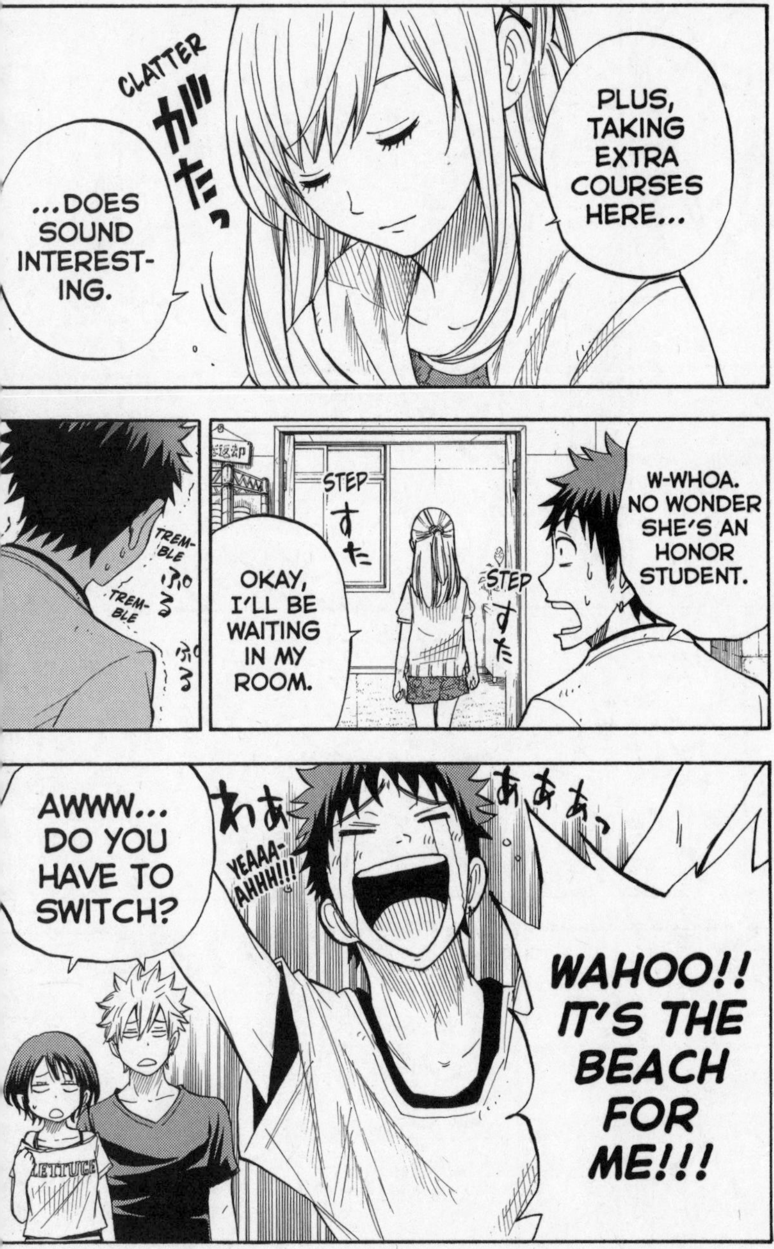
PLUS, TAKING EXTRA COURSES HERE...
CLATTER
がたっ
...DOES SOUND INTERESTING.
W-WHOA. NO WONDER SHE'S AN HONOR STUDENT.
STEP
すた
STEP
すた
OKAY, I'LL BE WAITING IN MY ROOM.
TREMBLE
ぷる
TREMBLE
ぷる
あああっ
WAHOO!! IT'S THE BEACH FOR ME!!!
わあ
YEAAA-AHHH!!!
AWWW... DO YOU HAVE TO SWITCH?
LETTUCE

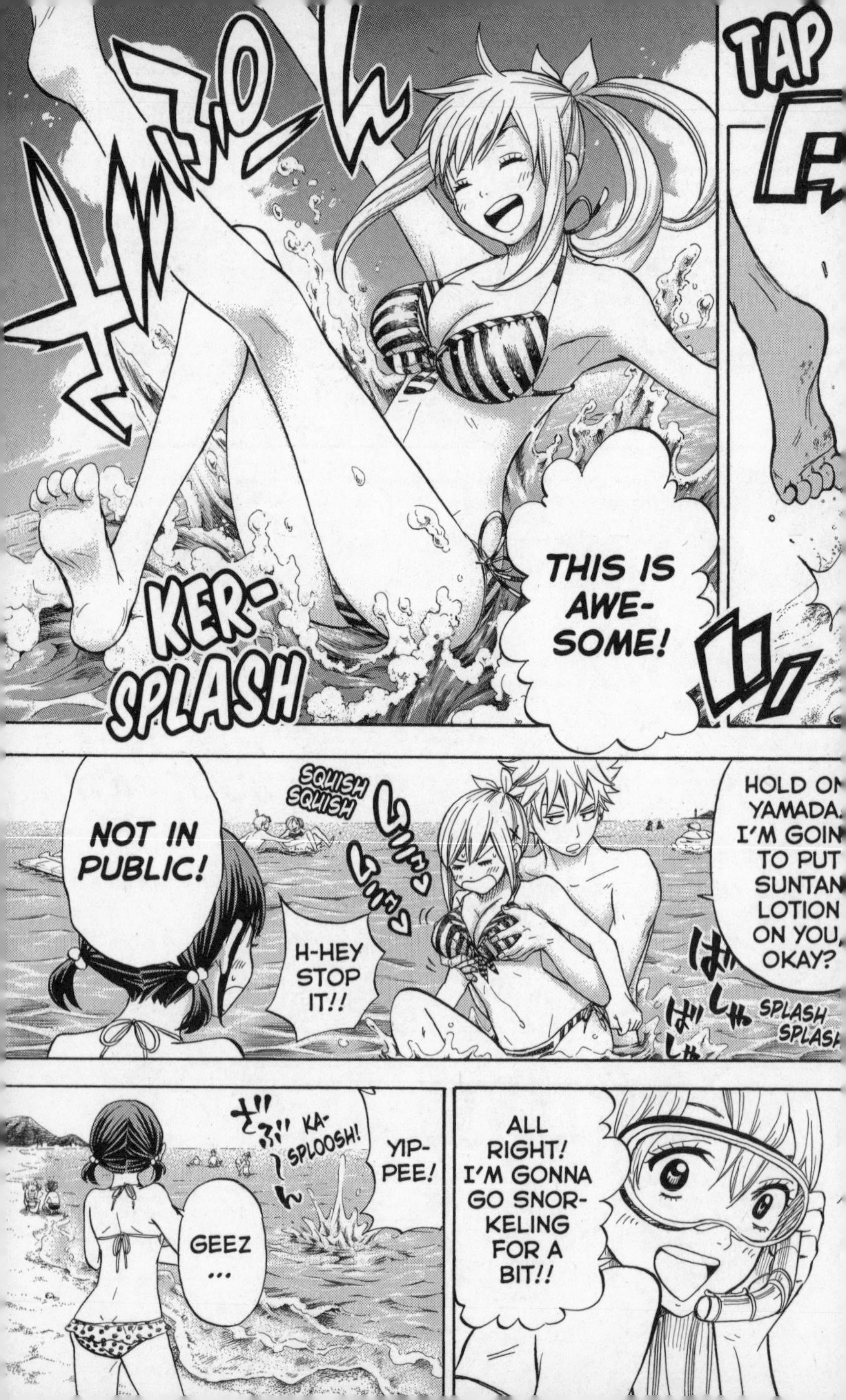
TAP
KER-SPLASH
THIS IS AWESOME!
HOLD ON YAMADA. I'M GOIN TO PUT SUNTAN LOTION ON YOU, OKAY?
SPLASH SPLASH
SQUISH SQUISH
H-HEY STOP IT!!
NOT IN PUBLIC!
ALL RIGHT! I'M GONNA GO SNORKELING FOR A BIT!!
YIP-PEE!
KA-SPLOOSH!
GEEZ ...

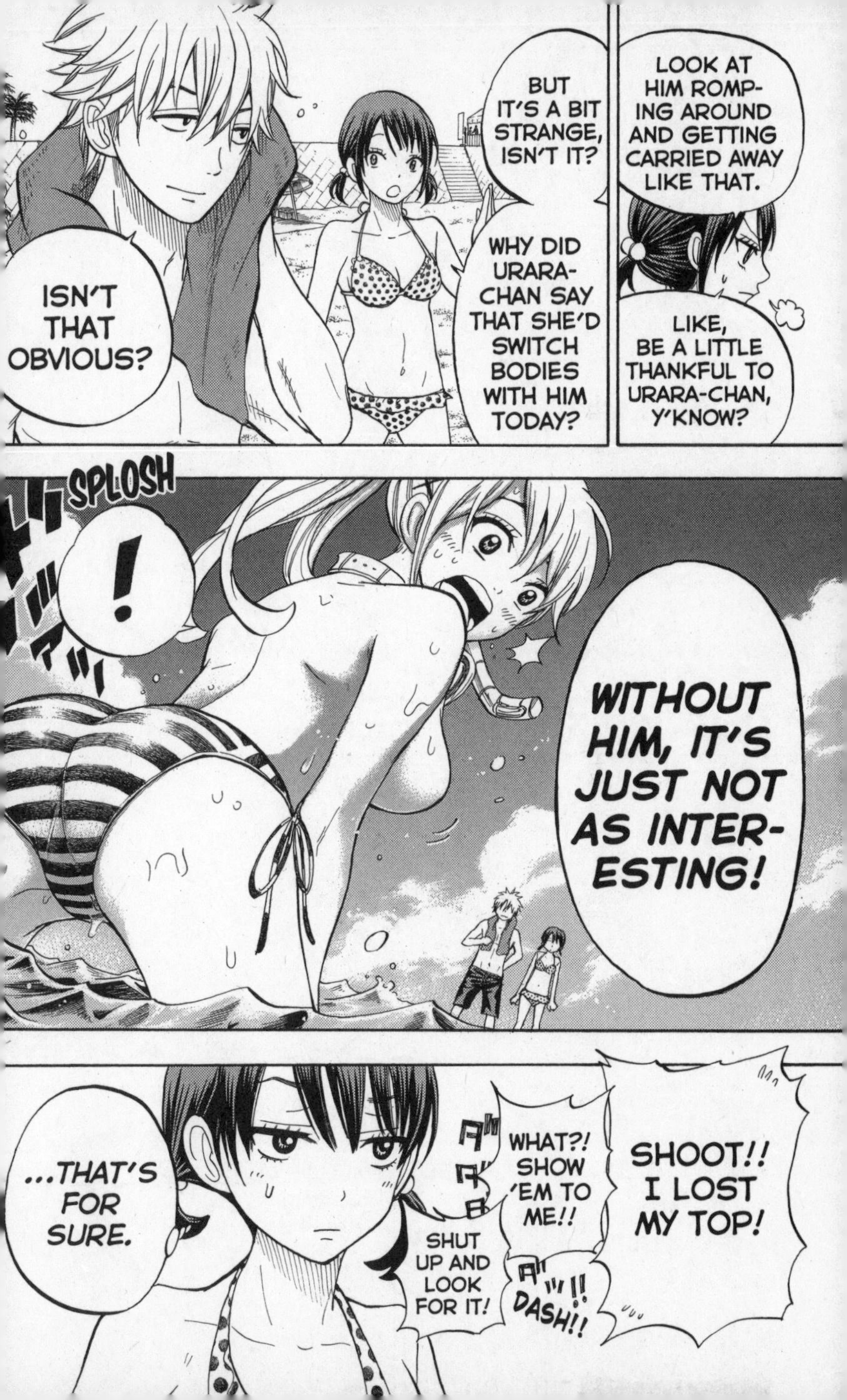

LOOK AT HIM ROMPING AROUND AND GETTING CARRIED AWAY LIKE THAT.
LIKE, BE A LITTLE THANKFUL TO URARA-CHAN, Y'KNOW?
BUT IT'S A BIT STRANGE, ISN'T IT?
WHY DID URARA-CHAN SAY THAT SHE'D SWITCH BODIES WITH HIM TODAY?
ISN'T THAT OBVIOUS?
WITHOUT HIM, IT'S JUST NOT AS INTERESTING!
SPLOSH
!
SHOOT!! I LOST MY TOP!
WHAT?! SHOW 'EM TO ME!!
SHUT UP AND LOOK FOR IT!
DASH!!
...THAT'S FOR SURE.

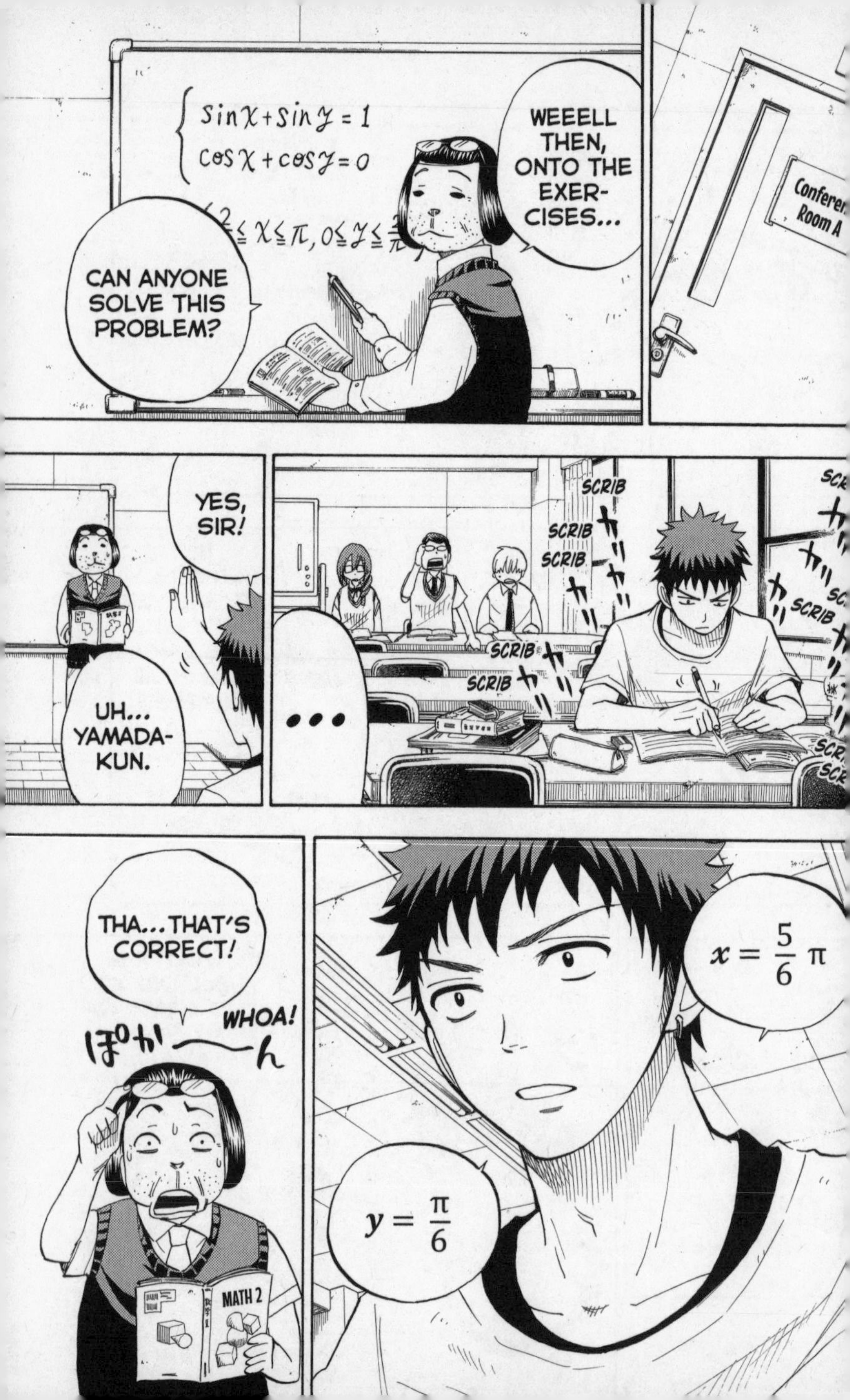
Conferen
Room A
sin x + sin y = 1
cos x + cos y = 0
WEEELL THEN, ONTO THE EXER-CISES...
CAN ANYONE SOLVE THIS PROBLEM?
SCRIB
SCRIB
SCRIB
SCRIB
SCRIB
SCRIB
SCRIB
...
YES, SIR!
UH... YAMADA-KUN.
$x = \frac{5}{6}\pi$
$y = \frac{\pi}{6}$
THA...THAT'S CORRECT!
WHOA!
ぽかーん
MATH 2

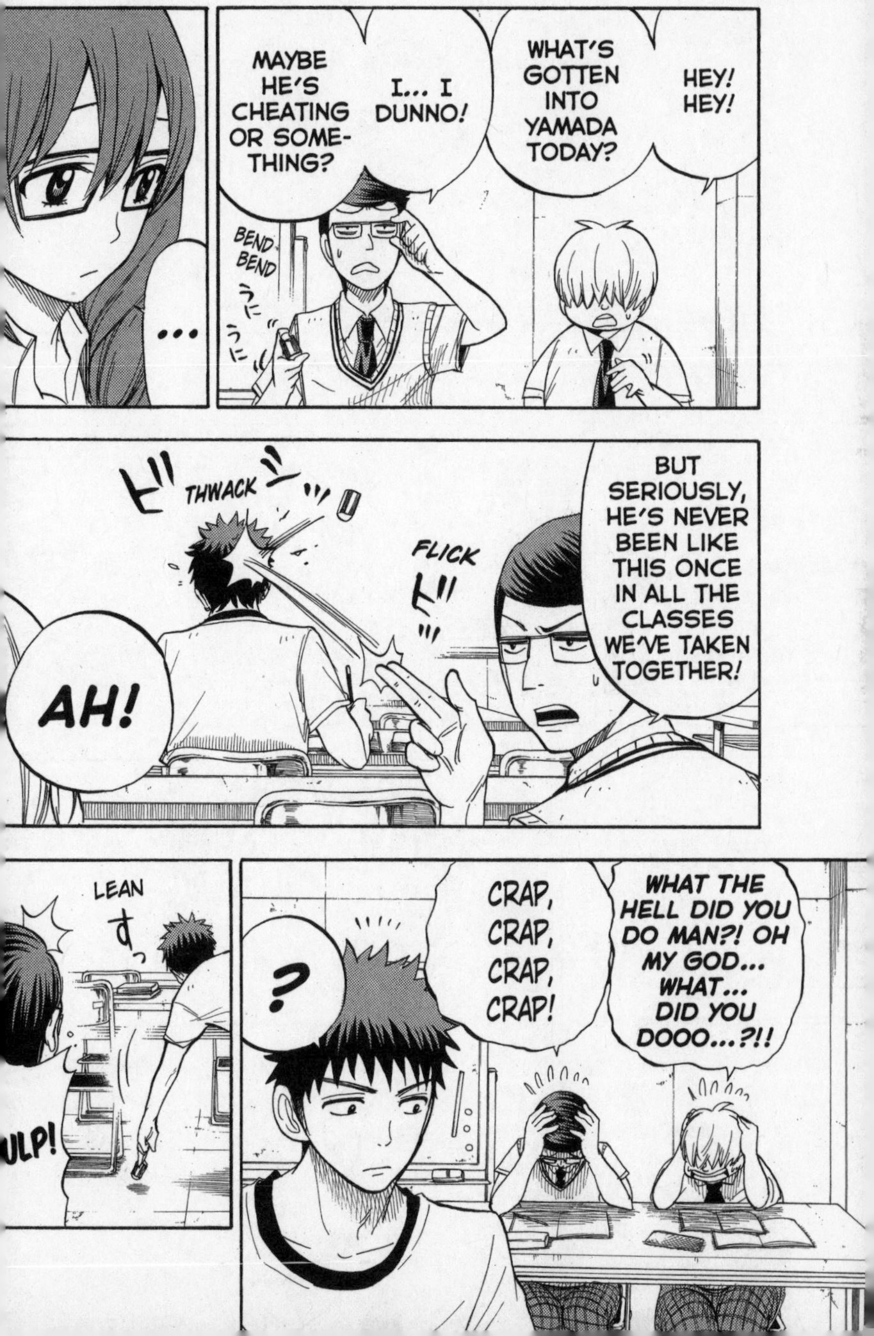
HEY! HEY!
WHAT'S GOTTEN INTO YAMADA TODAY?
I... I DUNNO!
MAYBE HE'S CHEATING OR SOME-THING?
BEND BEND
うに うに
...
BUT SERIOUSLY, HE'S NEVER BEEN LIKE THIS ONCE IN ALL THE CLASSES WE'VE TAKEN TOGETHER!
FLICK
THWACK
AH!
WHAT THE HELL DID YOU DO MAN?! OH MY GOD... WHAT... DID YOU DOOO...?!!
CRAP, CRAP, CRAP, CRAP!
?
LEAN
すっ
ULP!

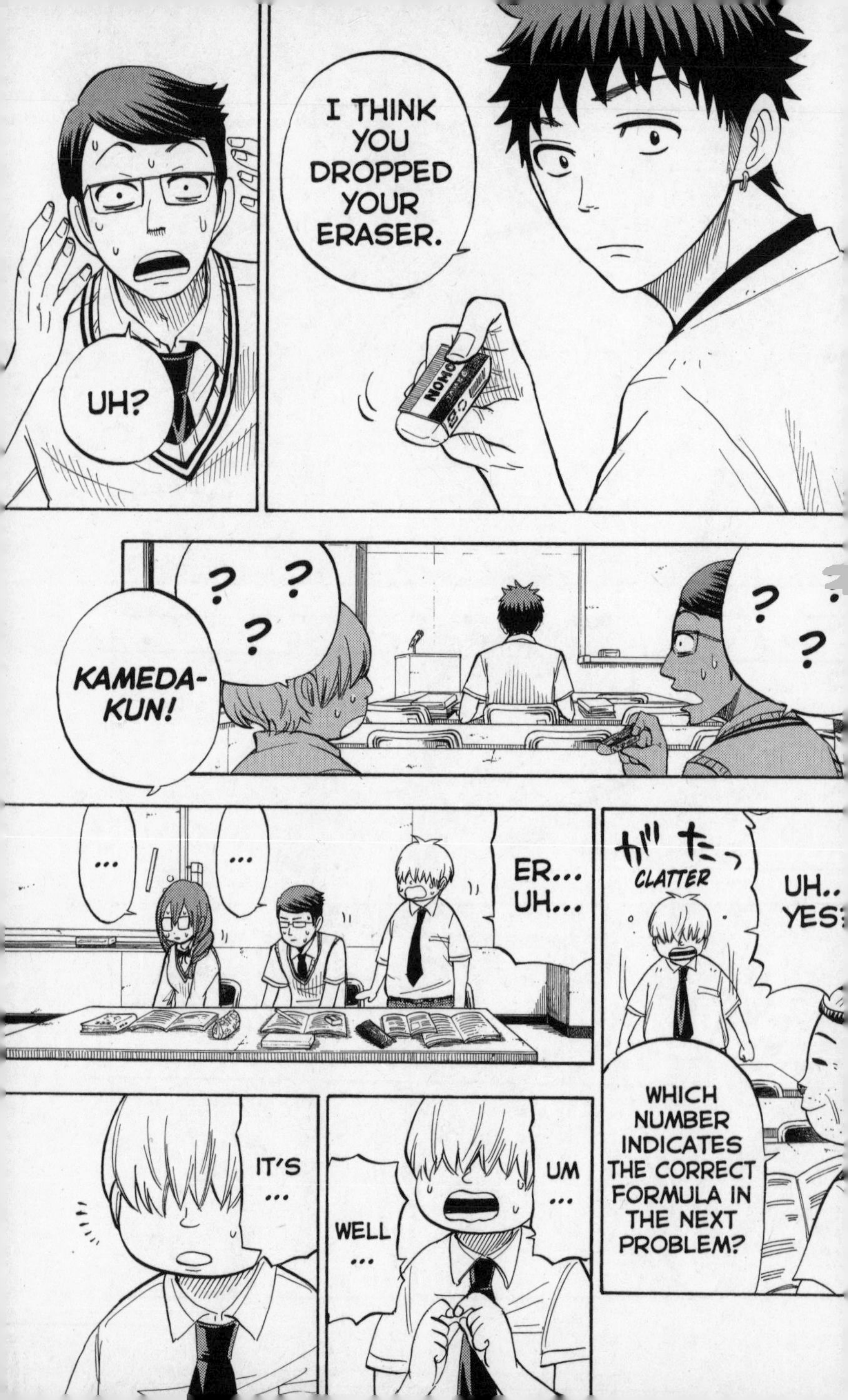

I THINK YOU DROPPED YOUR ERASER.
UH?
? ?
?
KAMEDA-KUN!
? ?
ガたっ
CLATTER
UH.. YES:
WHICH NUMBER INDICATES THE CORRECT FORMULA IN THE NEXT PROBLEM?
ER... UH...
...
...
UM ...
WELL ...
IT'S ...

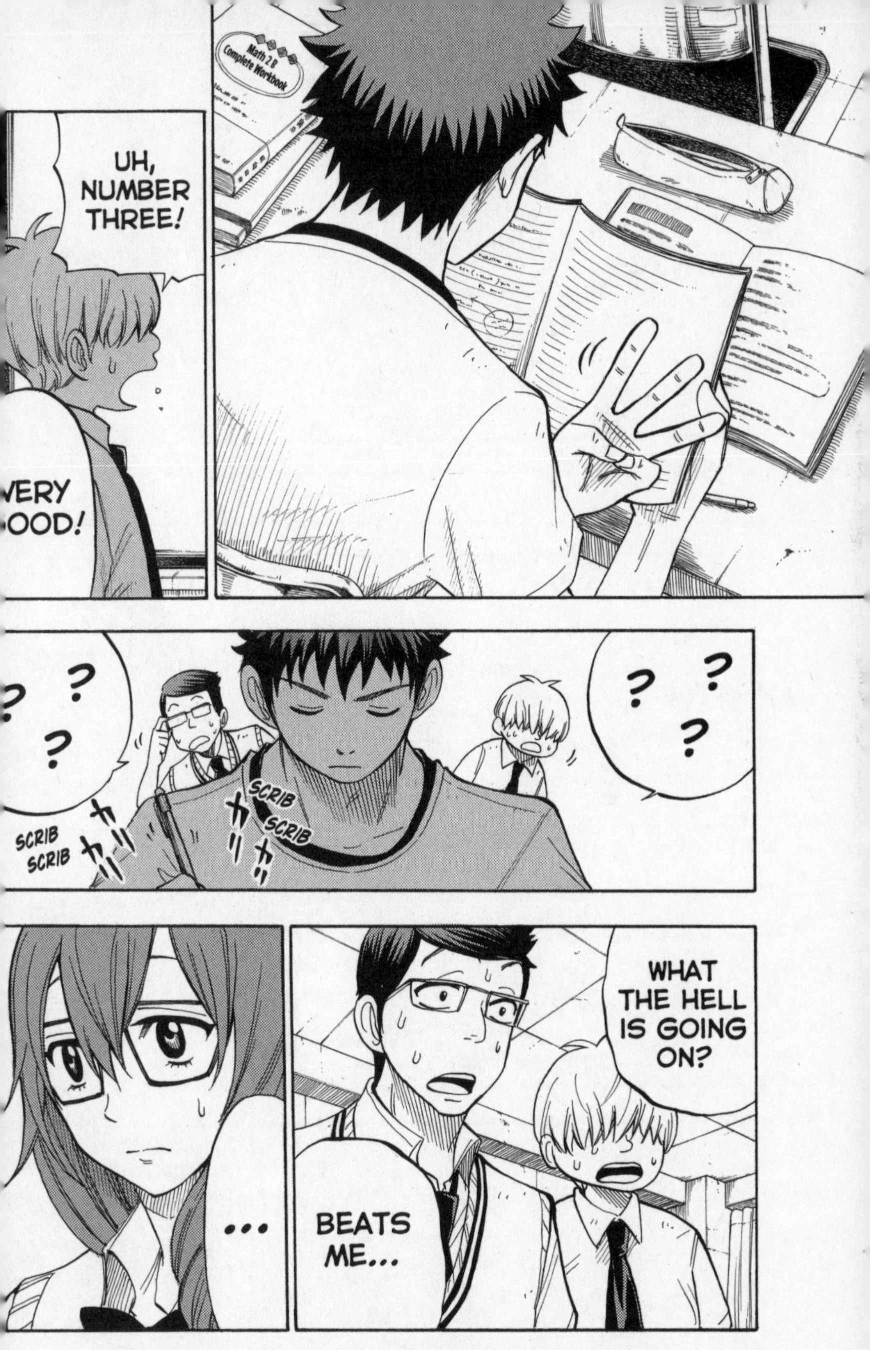

Math 2 B Complete Workbook
UH, NUMBER THREE!
ERY OOD!
? ? ?
SCRIB SCRIB
? ? ?
SCRIB SCRIB
WHAT THE HELL IS GOING ON?
BEATS ME...
...

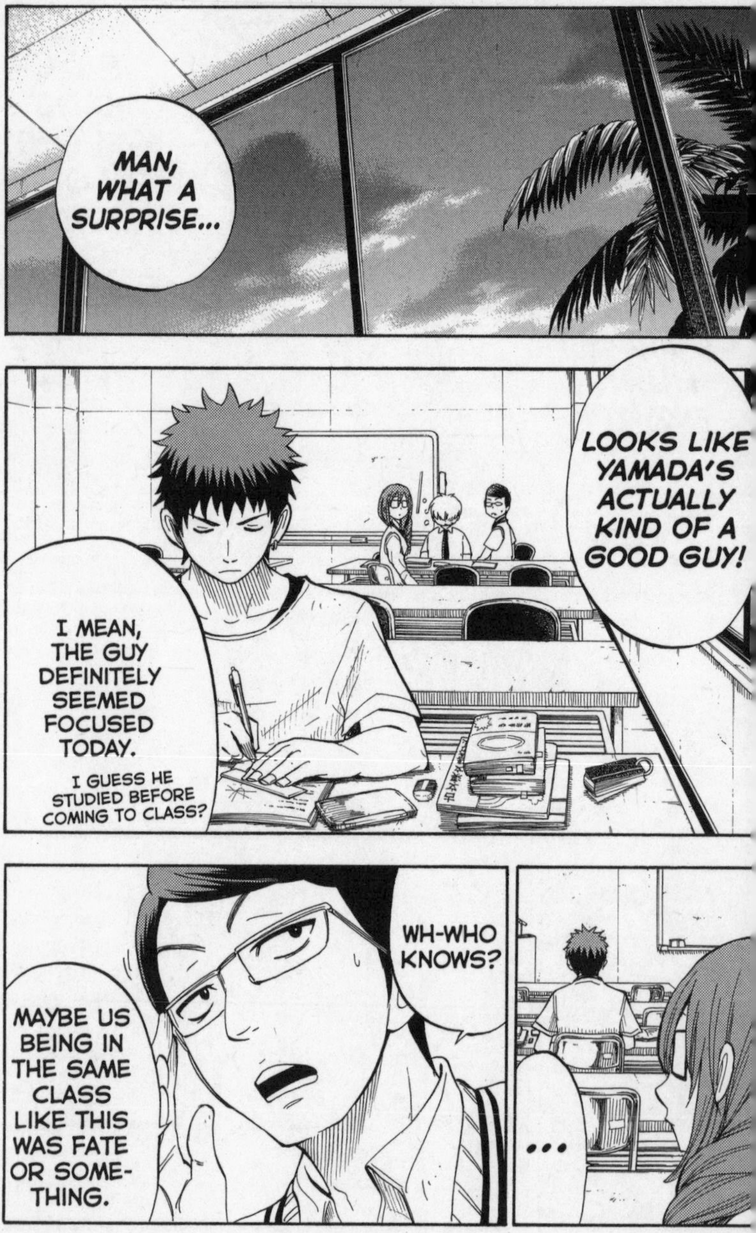
MAN, WHAT A SURPRISE...
LOOKS LIKE YAMADA'S ACTUALLY KIND OF A GOOD GUY!
I MEAN, THE GUY DEFINITELY SEEMED FOCUSED TODAY.
I GUESS HE STUDIED BEFORE COMING TO CLASS?
...
WH-WHO KNOWS?
MAYBE US BEING IN THE SAME CLASS LIKE THIS WAS FATE OR SOME-THING.

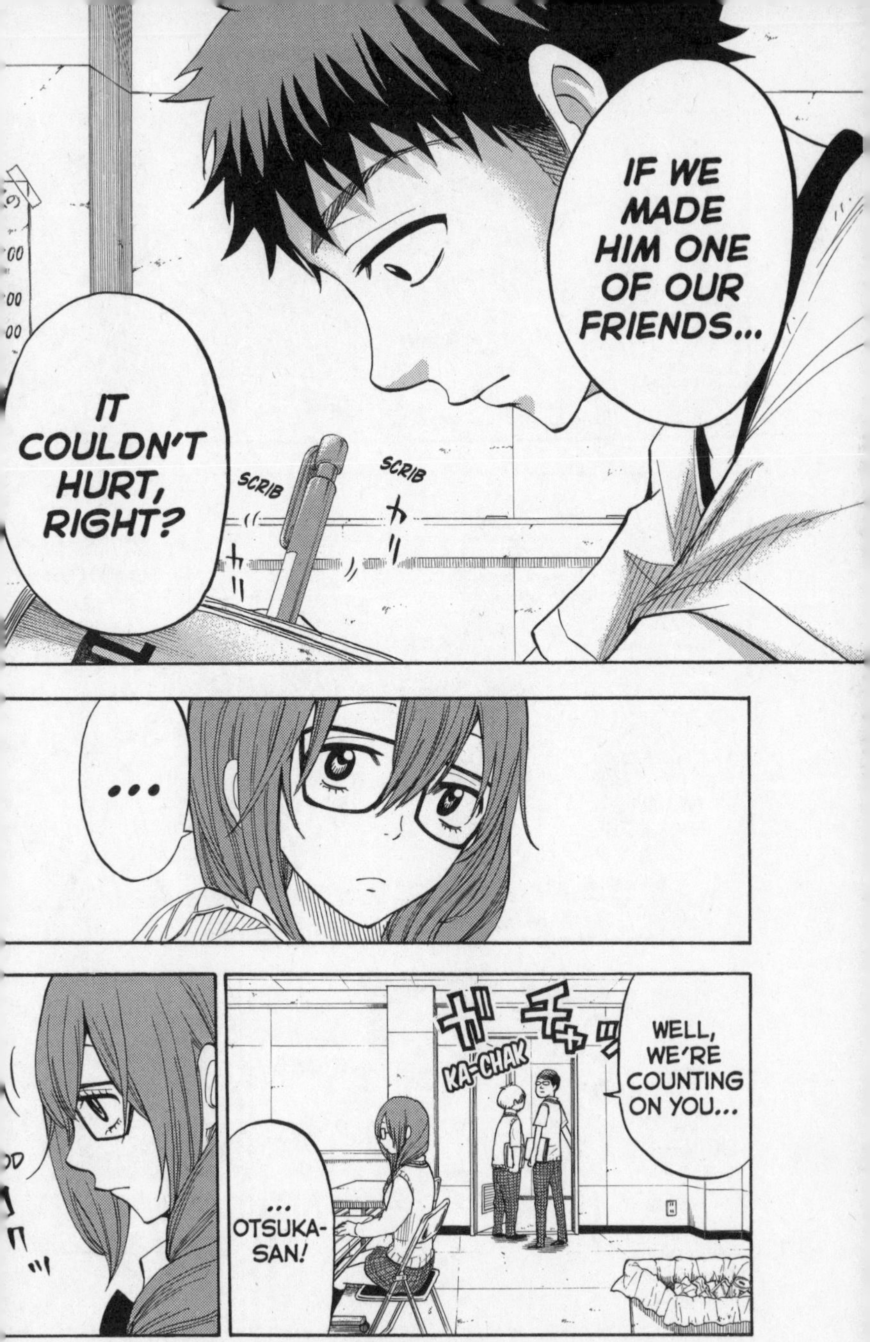
IF WE MADE HIM ONE OF OUR FRIENDS...
SCRIB
SCRIB
IT COULDN'T HURT, RIGHT?
...
KA-CHAK
WELL, WE'RE COUNTING ON YOU...
... OTSUKA-SAN!

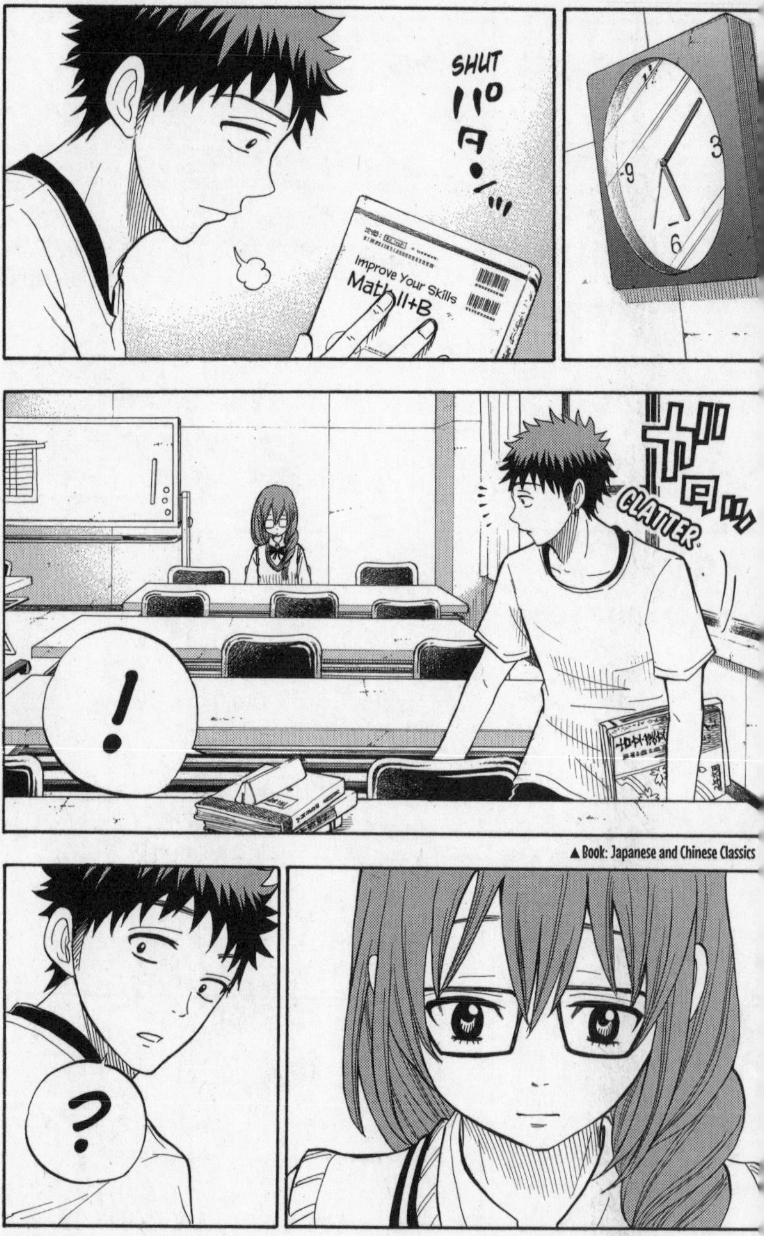
SHUT
パタン
Improve Your Skills
Math II+B
ガタッ
CLATTER
!
?
▲Book: Japanese and Chinese Classics

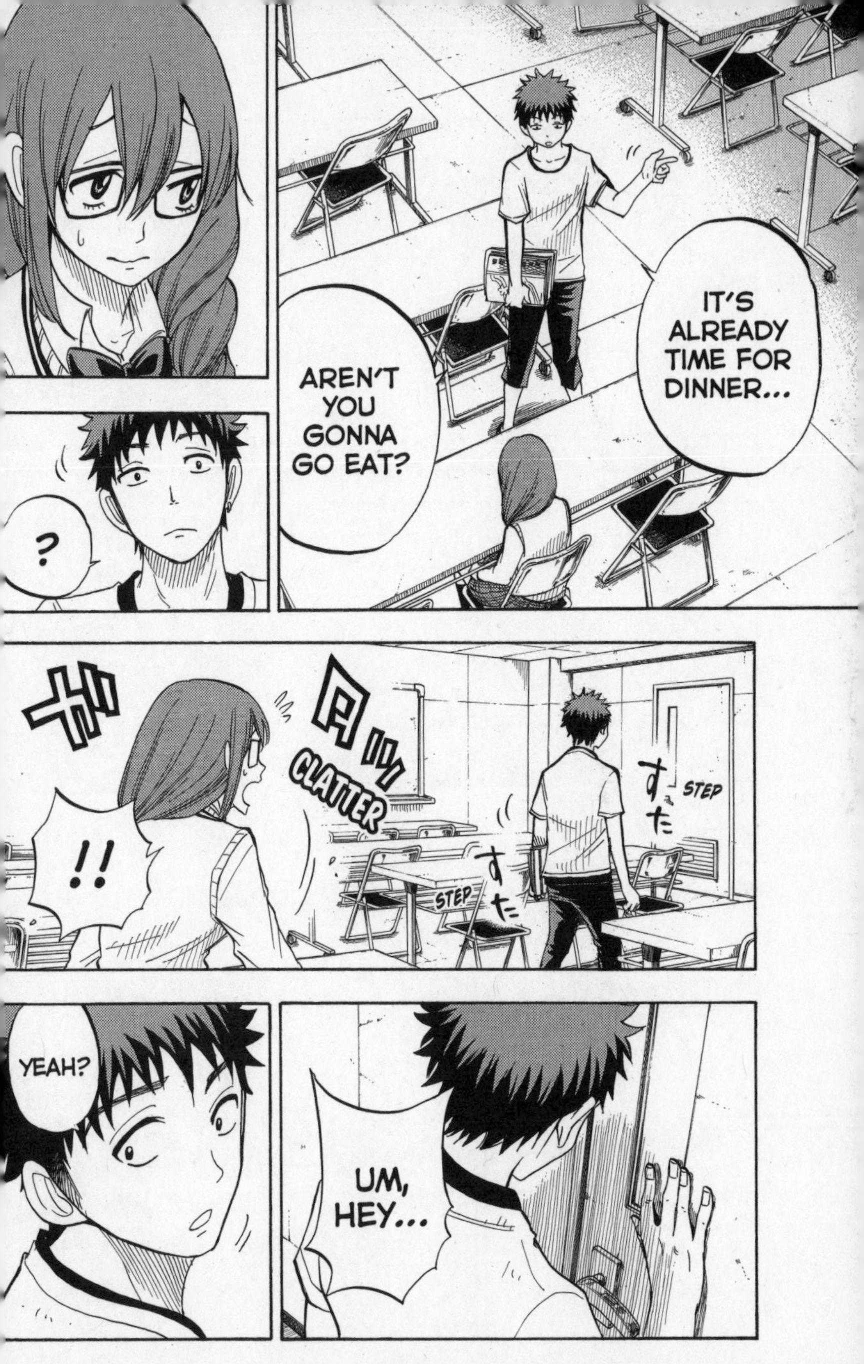
IT'S ALREADY TIME FOR DINNER...
AREN'T YOU GONNA GO EAT?
?
すた
STEP
すた
STEP
CLATTER
!!
UM, HEY...
YEAH?

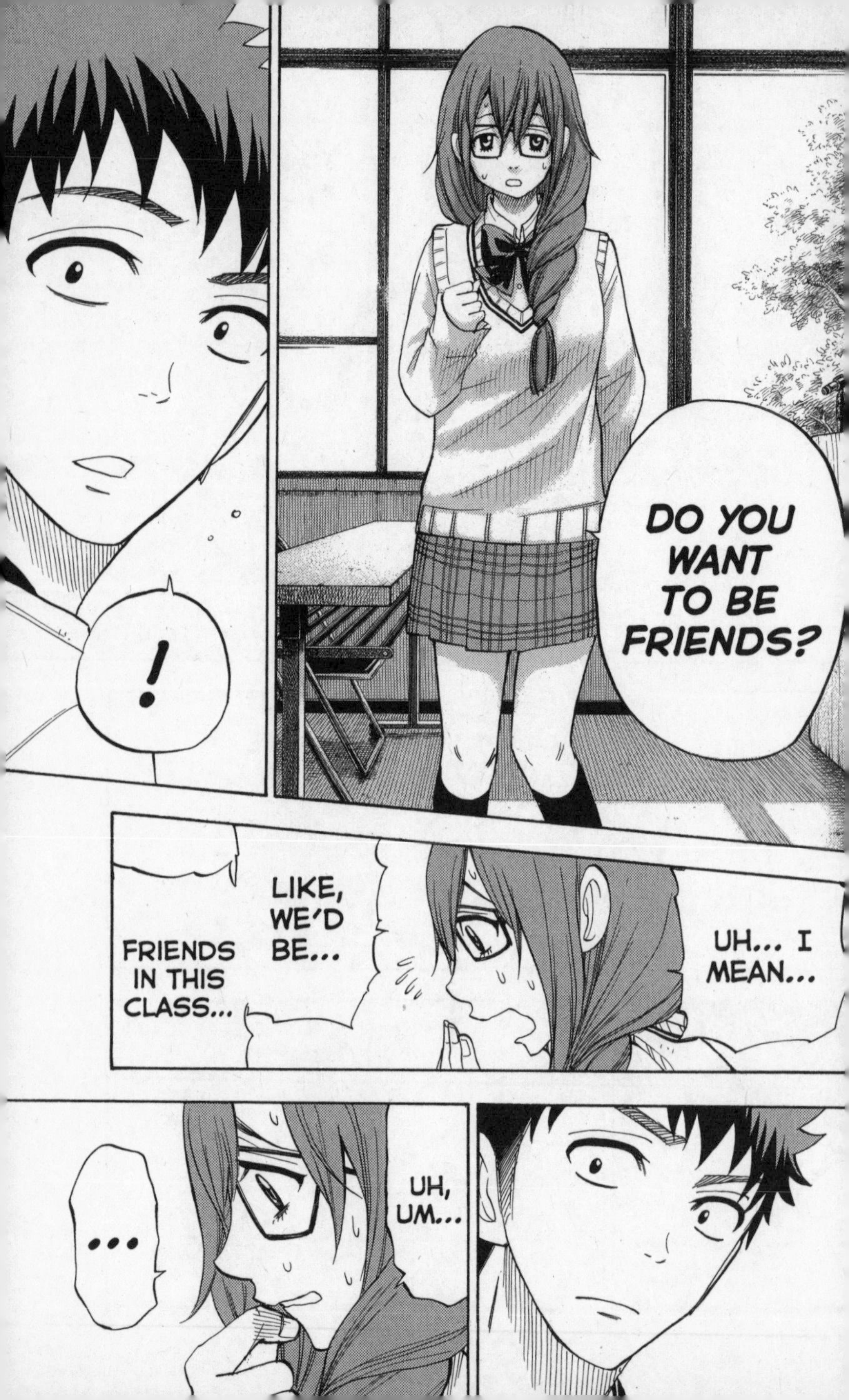
DO YOU WANT TO BE FRIENDS?
!
UH... I MEAN...
LIKE, WE'D BE...
FRIENDS IN THIS CLASS...
UH, UM...
...

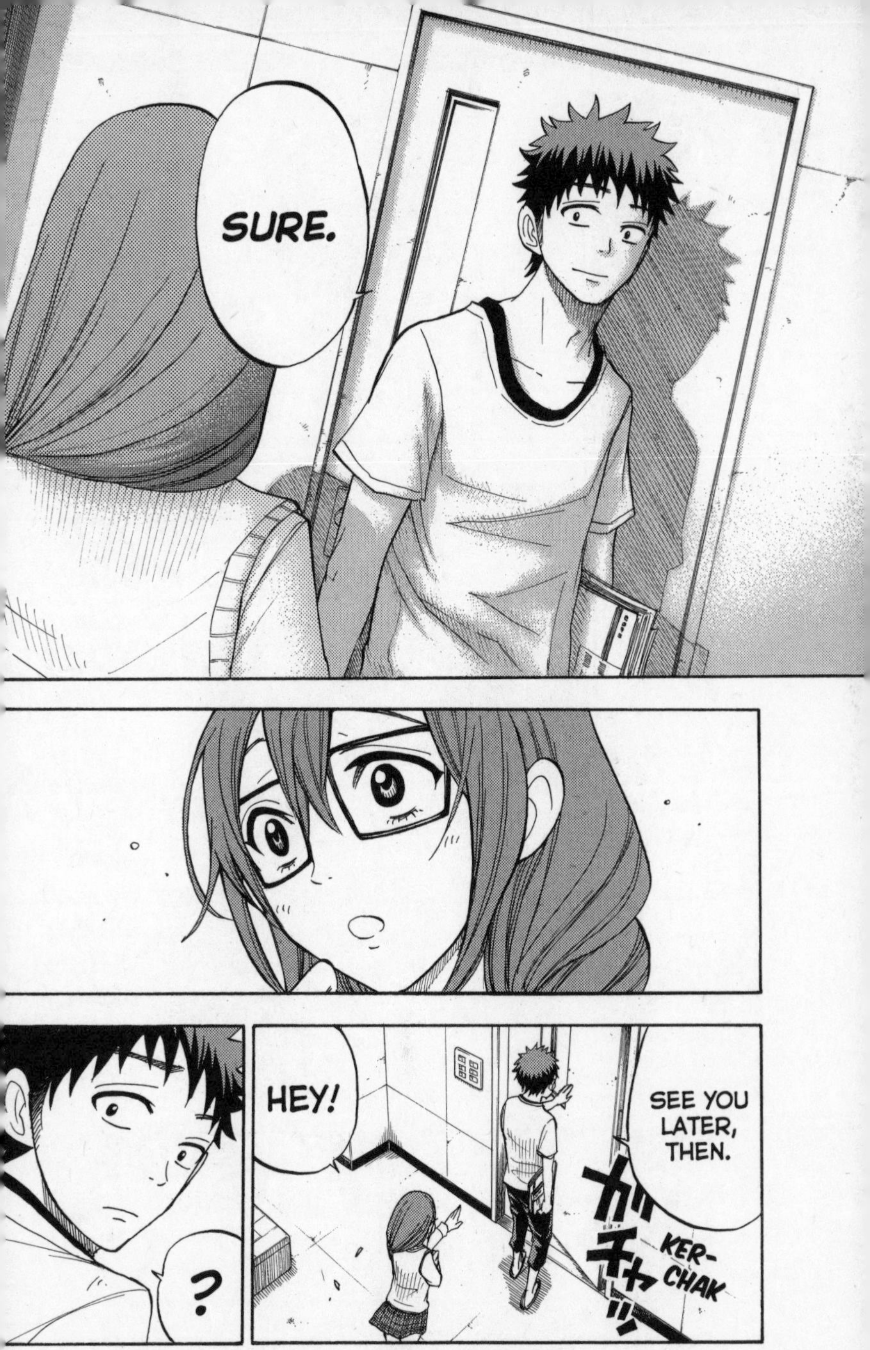
SURE.
SEE YOU LATER, THEN.
KER-CHAK
HEY!
?

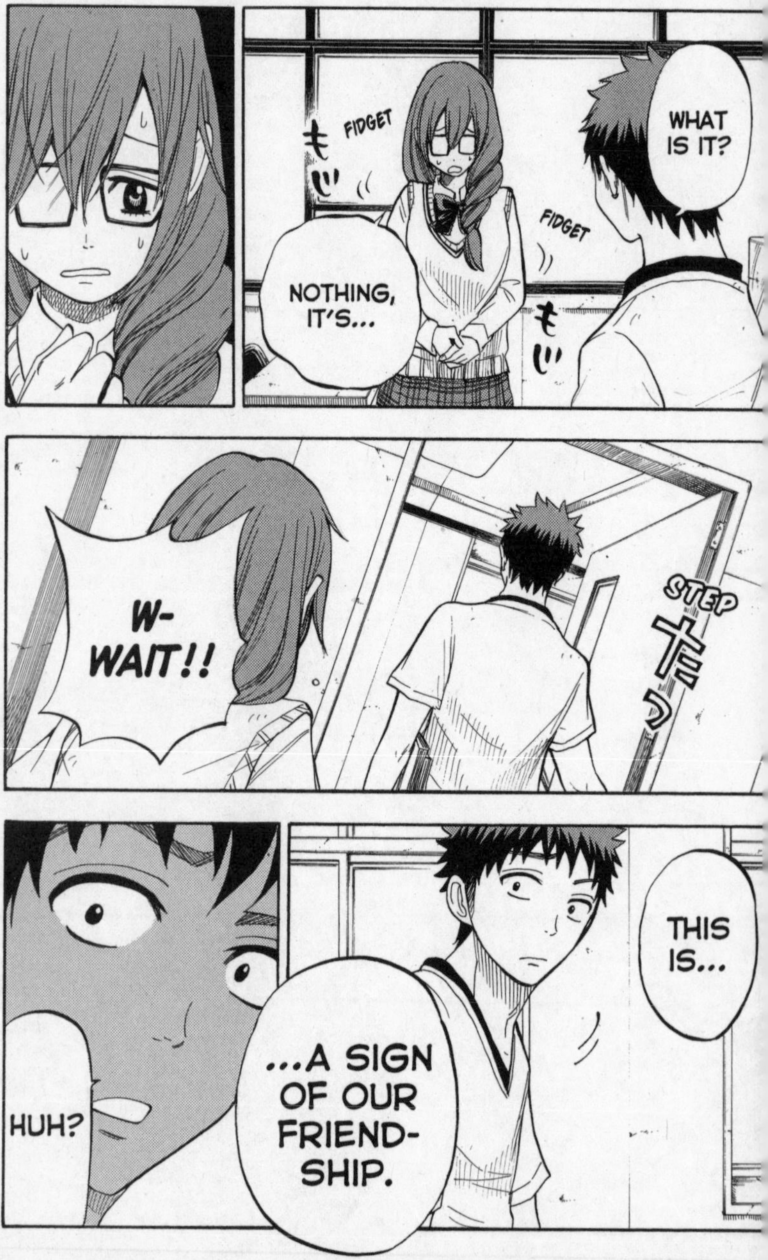
WHAT IS IT?
FIDGET
もじ
FIDGET
もじ
NOTHING, IT'S...
STEP
W- WAIT!!
THIS IS...
...A SIGN OF OUR FRIEND-SHIP.
HUH?

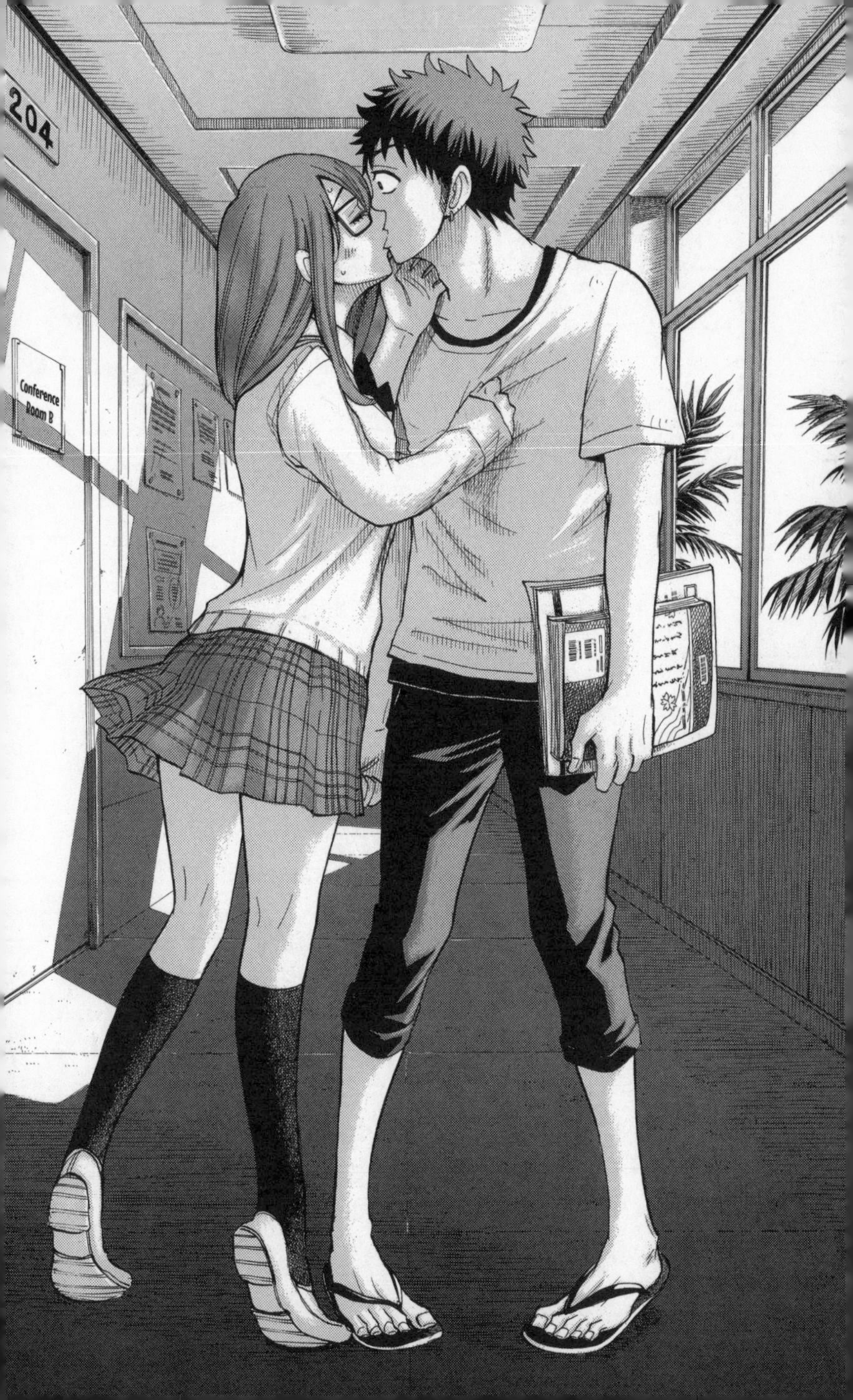
204
Conference
Room B

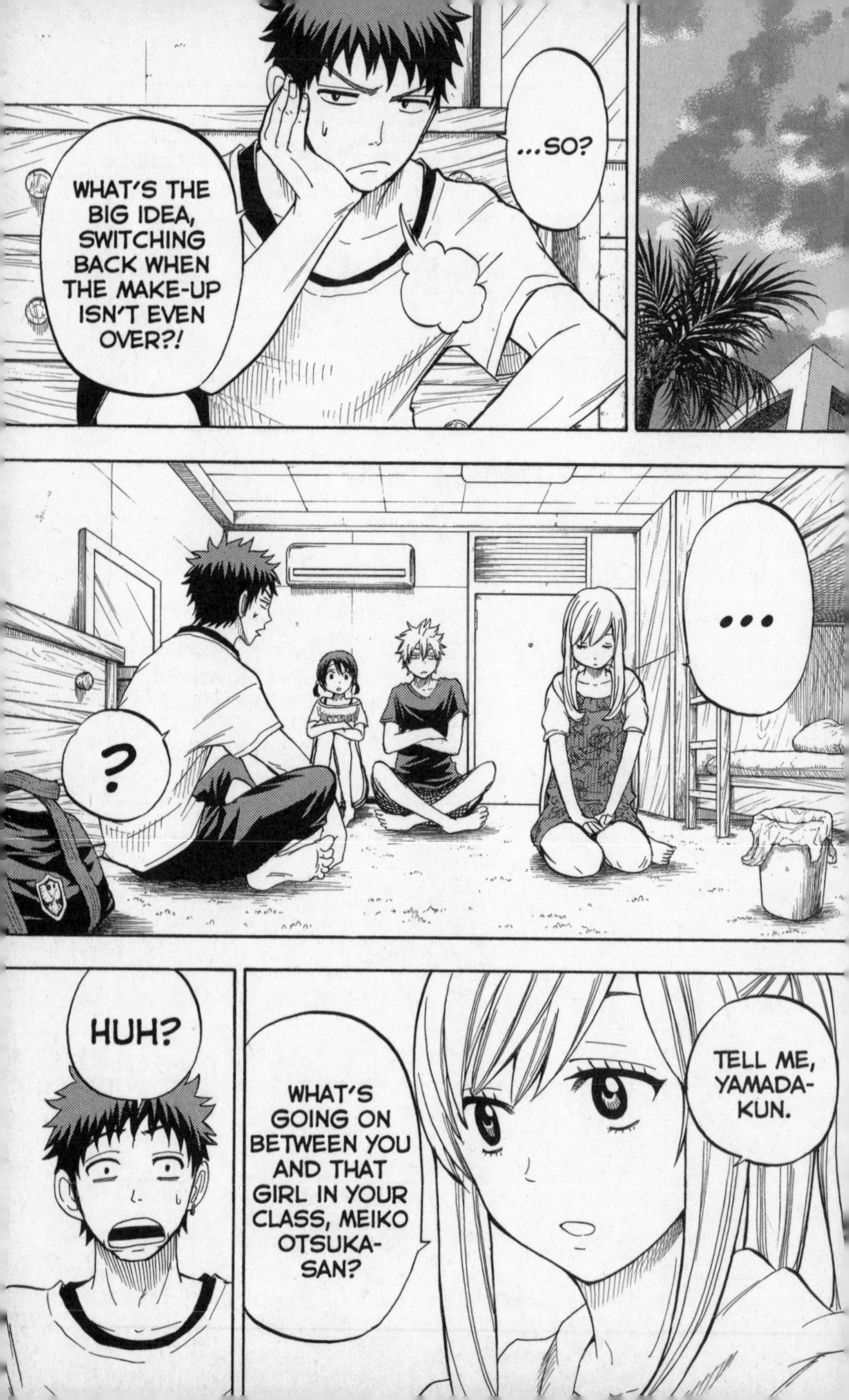
...SO?
WHAT'S THE BIG IDEA, SWITCHING BACK WHEN THE MAKE-UP ISN'T EVEN OVER?!
...
?
TELL ME, YAMADA-KUN.
WHAT'S GOING ON BETWEEN YOU AND THAT GIRL IN YOUR CLASS, MEIKO OTSUKA-SAN?
HUH?

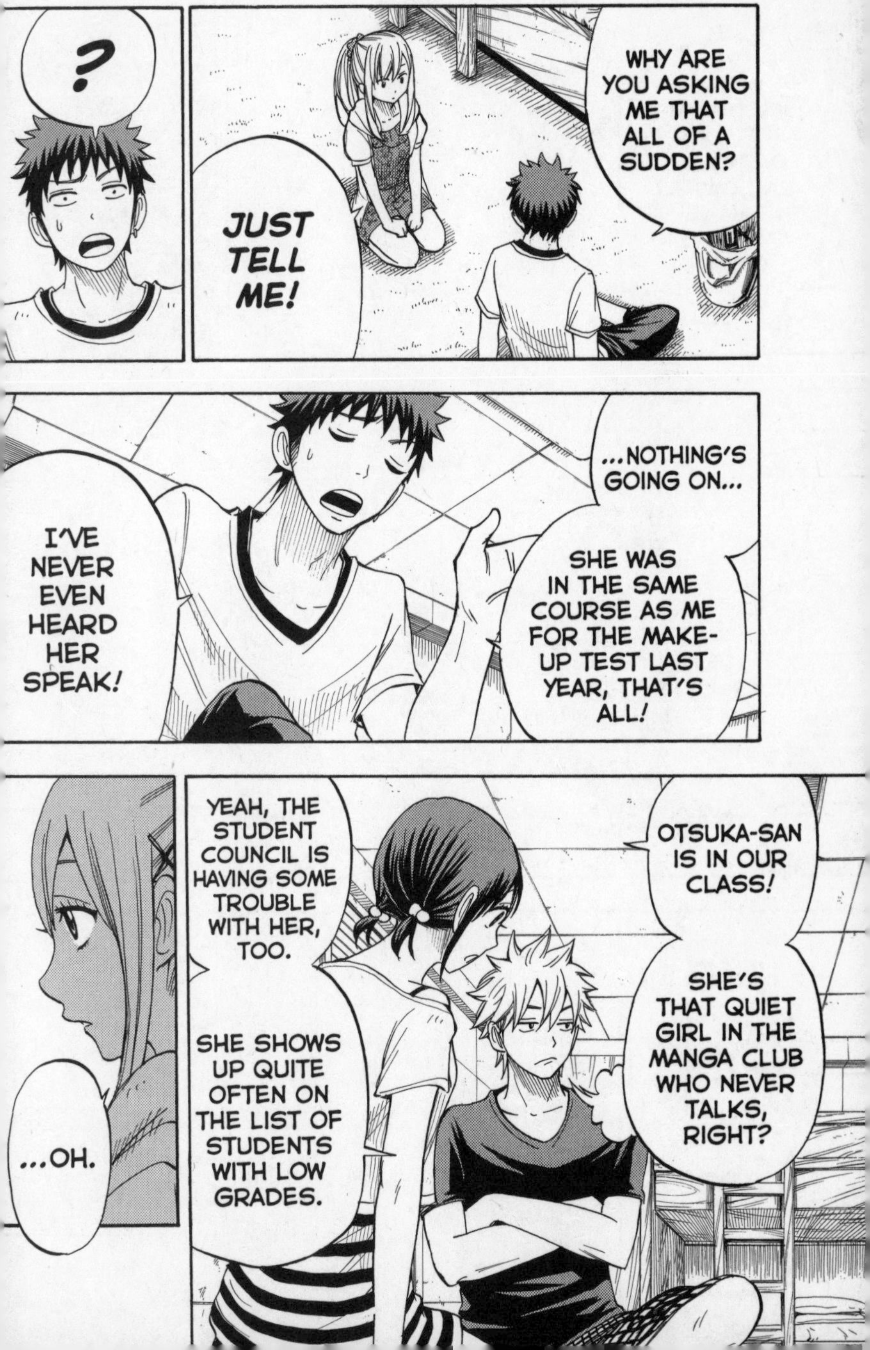
WHY ARE YOU ASKING ME THAT ALL OF A SUDDEN?
JUST TELL ME!
?
...NOTHING'S GOING ON...
SHE WAS IN THE SAME COURSE AS ME FOR THE MAKE-UP TEST LAST YEAR, THAT'S ALL!
I'VE NEVER EVEN HEARD HER SPEAK!
OTSUKA-SAN IS IN OUR CLASS!
SHE'S THAT QUIET GIRL IN THE MANGA CLUB WHO NEVER TALKS, RIGHT?
YEAH, THE STUDENT COUNCIL IS HAVING SOME TROUBLE WITH HER, TOO.
SHE SHOWS UP QUITE OFTEN ON THE LIST OF STUDENTS WITH LOW GRADES.
...OH.

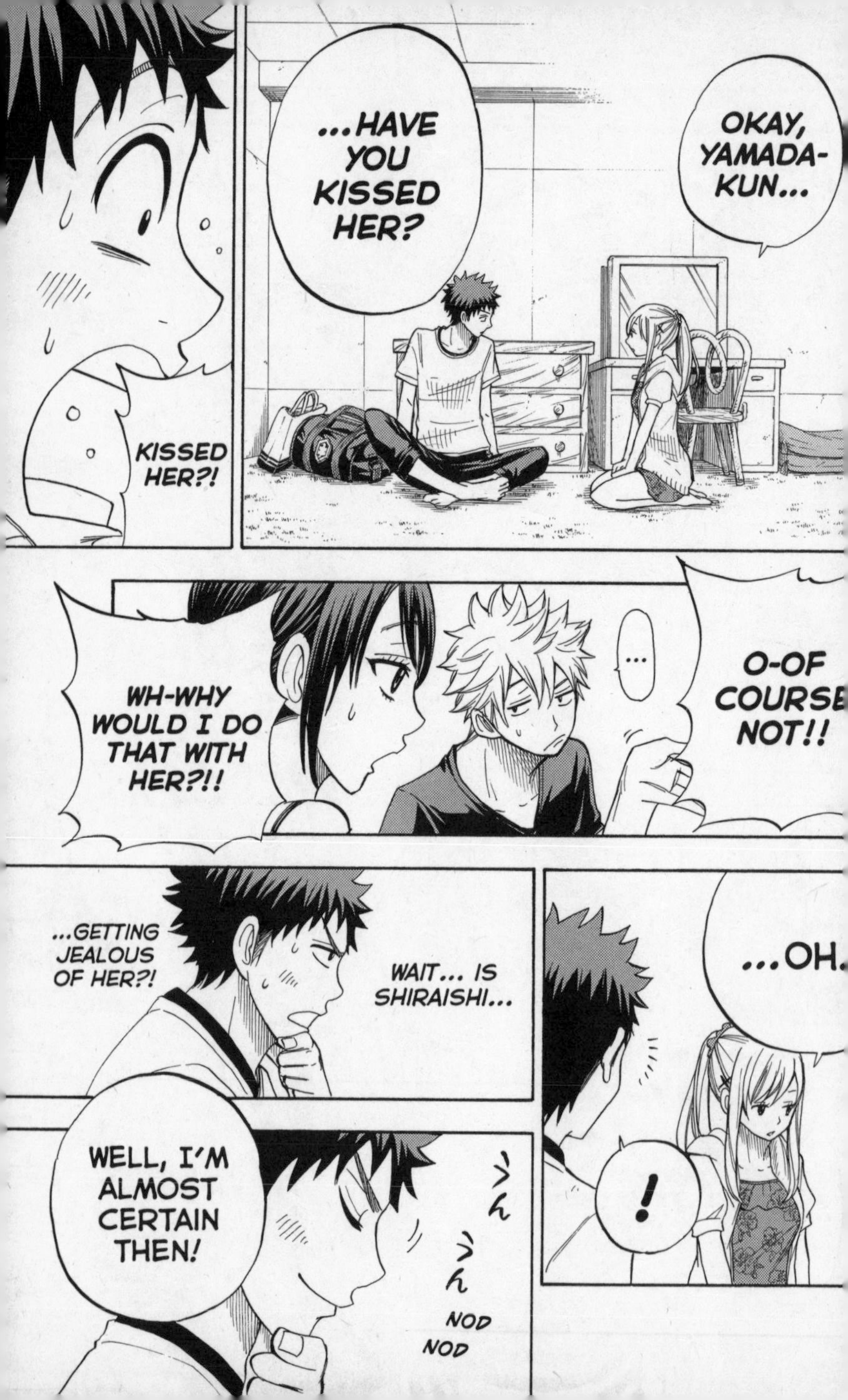
OKAY, YAMADA-KUN...
...HAVE YOU KISSED HER?
KISSED HER?!
O-OF COURSE NOT!!
...
WH-WHY WOULD I DO THAT WITH HER?!!
...OH.
!
WAIT... IS SHIRAISHI...
...GETTING JEALOUS OF HER?!
うん うん
NOD NOD
WELL, I'M ALMOST CERTAIN THEN!

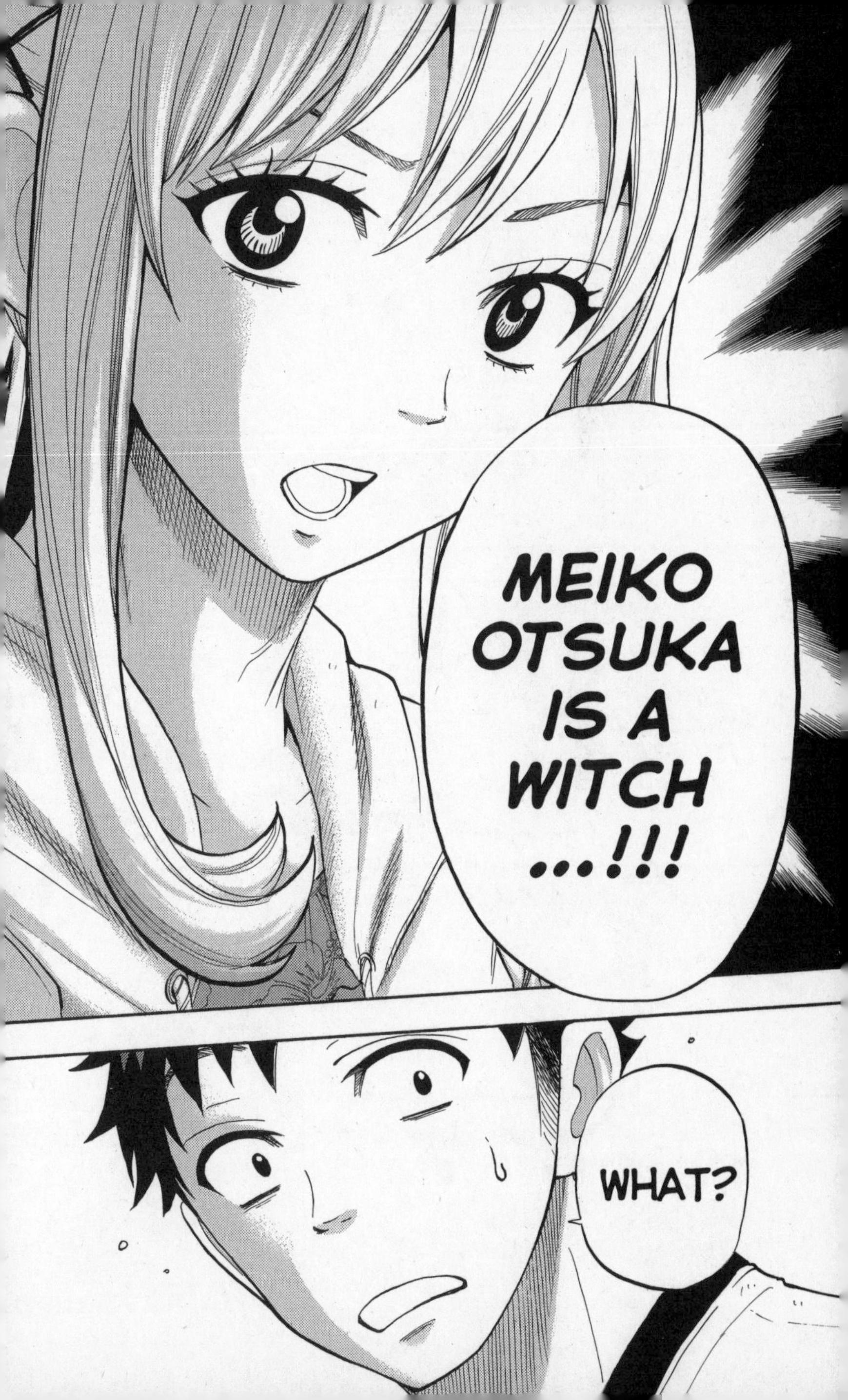
MEIKO OTSUKA IS A WITCH ...!!!
WHAT?

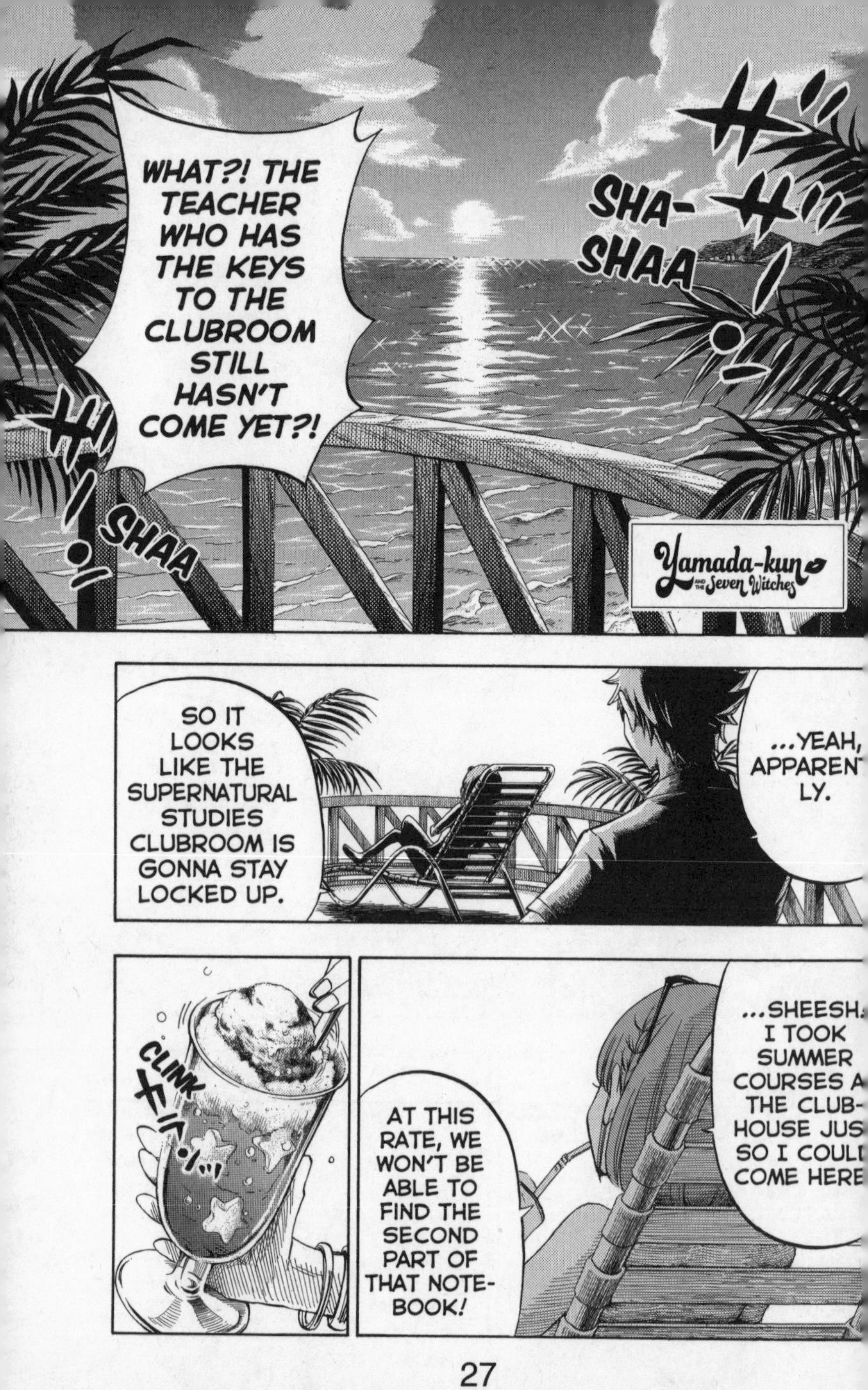
SHA-SHAA
WHAT?! THE TEACHER WHO HAS THE KEYS TO THE CLUBROOM STILL HASN'T COME YET?!
SHAA
Yamada-kun and the Seven Witches
...YEAH, APPAREN- LY.
SO IT LOOKS LIKE THE SUPERNATURAL STUDIES CLUBROOM IS GONNA STAY LOCKED UP.
...SHEESH. I TOOK SUMMER COURSES A THE CLUB-HOUSE JUS SO I COUL COME HERE
AT THIS RATE, WE WON'T BE ABLE TO FIND THE SECOND PART OF THAT NOTE-BOOK!
CLINK

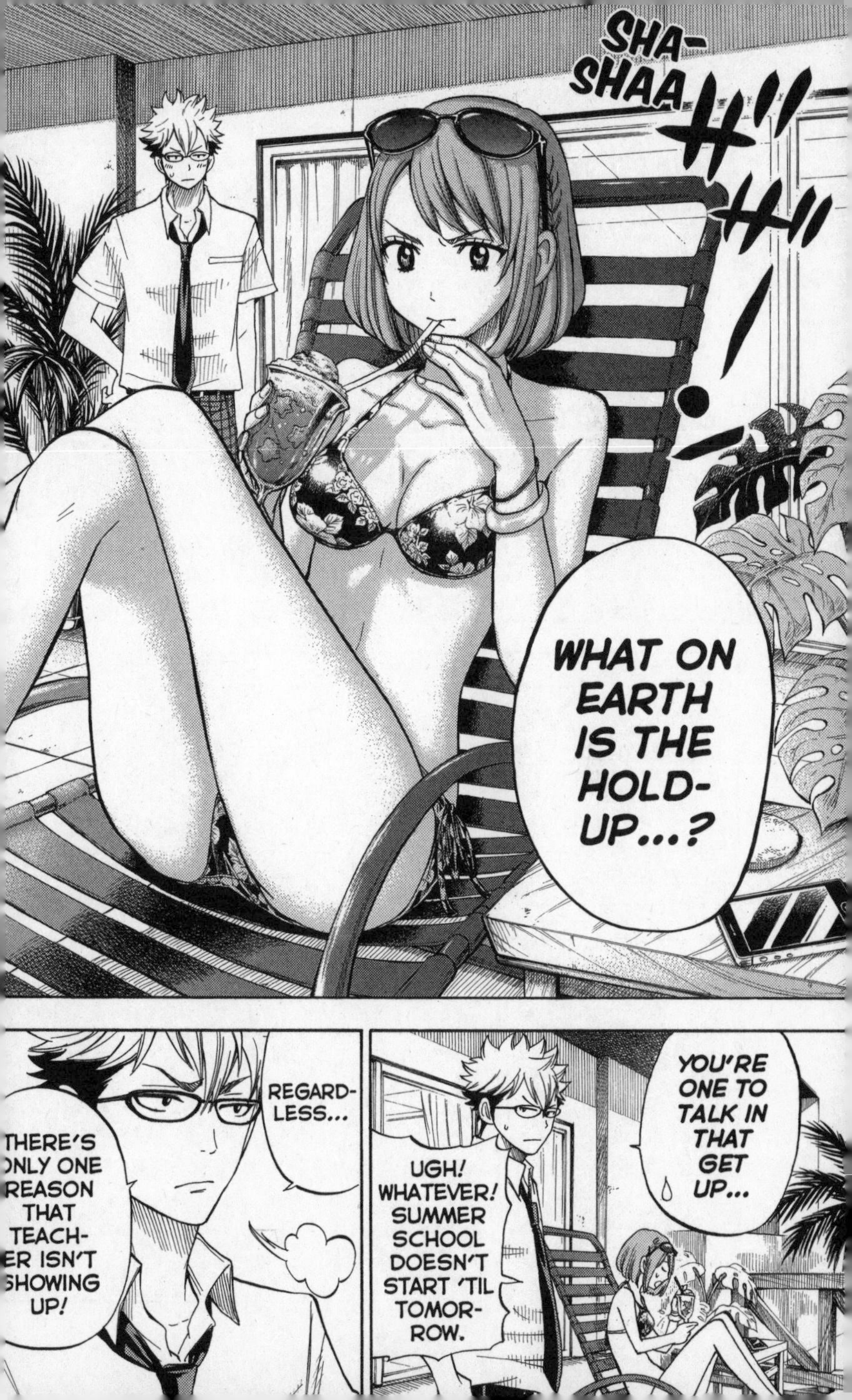
SHA-SHAA
WHAT ON EARTH IS THE HOLD-UP...?
YOU'RE ONE TO TALK IN THAT GET UP...
UGH! WHATEVER! SUMMER SCHOOL DOESN'T START 'TIL TOMORROW.
REGARDLESS...
THERE'S ONLY ONE REASON THAT TEACHER ISN'T SHOWING UP!

Chapter 27: Dejected

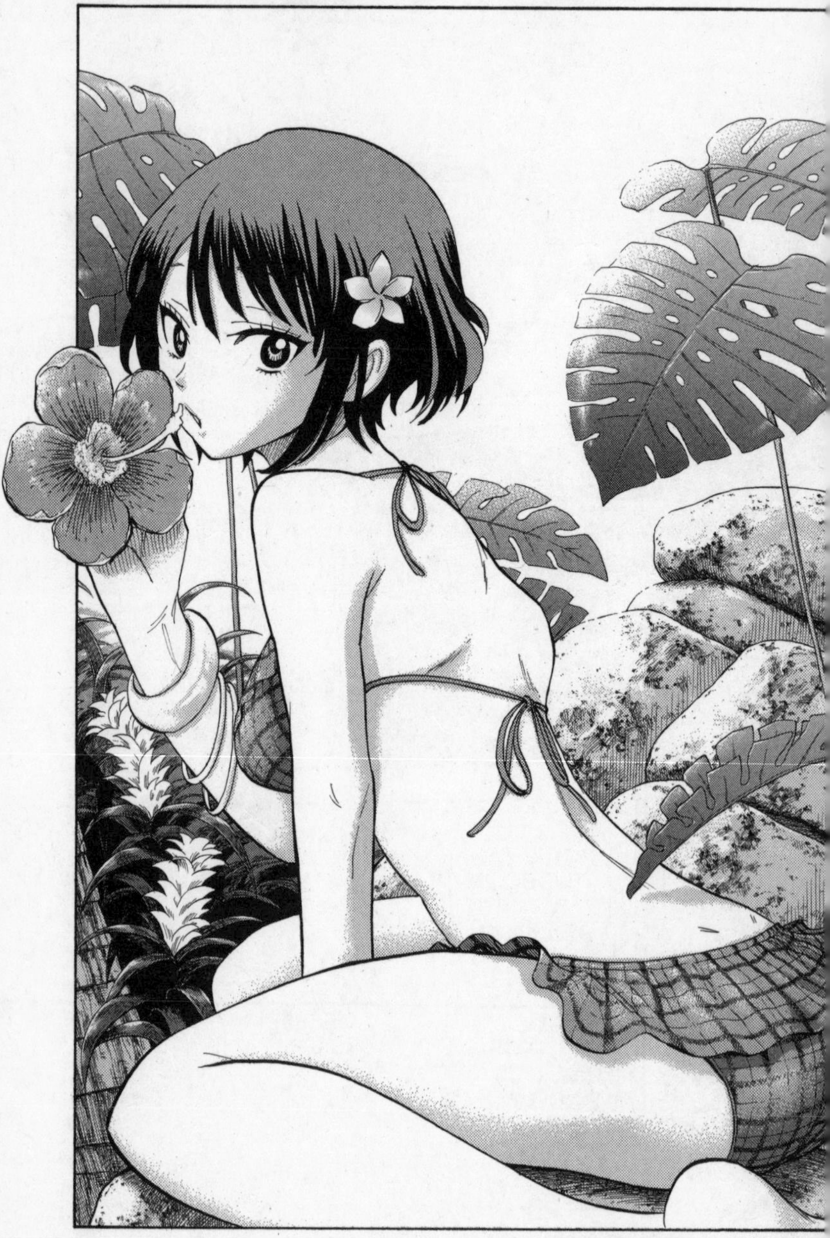

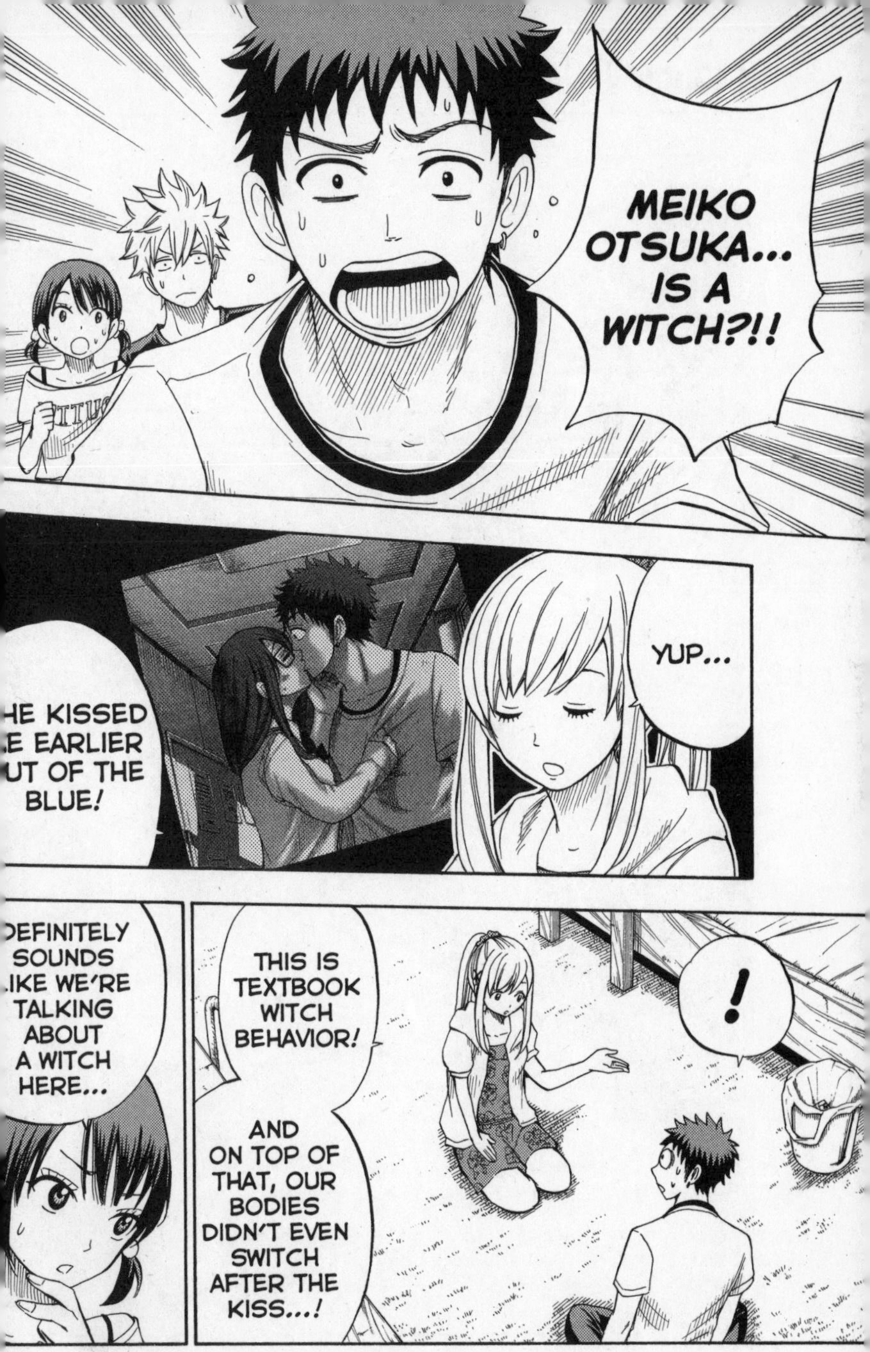
MEIKO OTSUKA... IS A WITCH?!!
YUP...
HE KISSED E EARLIER UT OF THE BLUE!
!
THIS IS TEXTBOOK WITCH BEHAVIOR!
AND ON TOP OF THAT, OUR BODIES DIDN'T EVEN SWITCH AFTER THE KISS...!
DEFINITELY SOUNDS IKE WE'RE TALKING ABOUT A WITCH HERE...

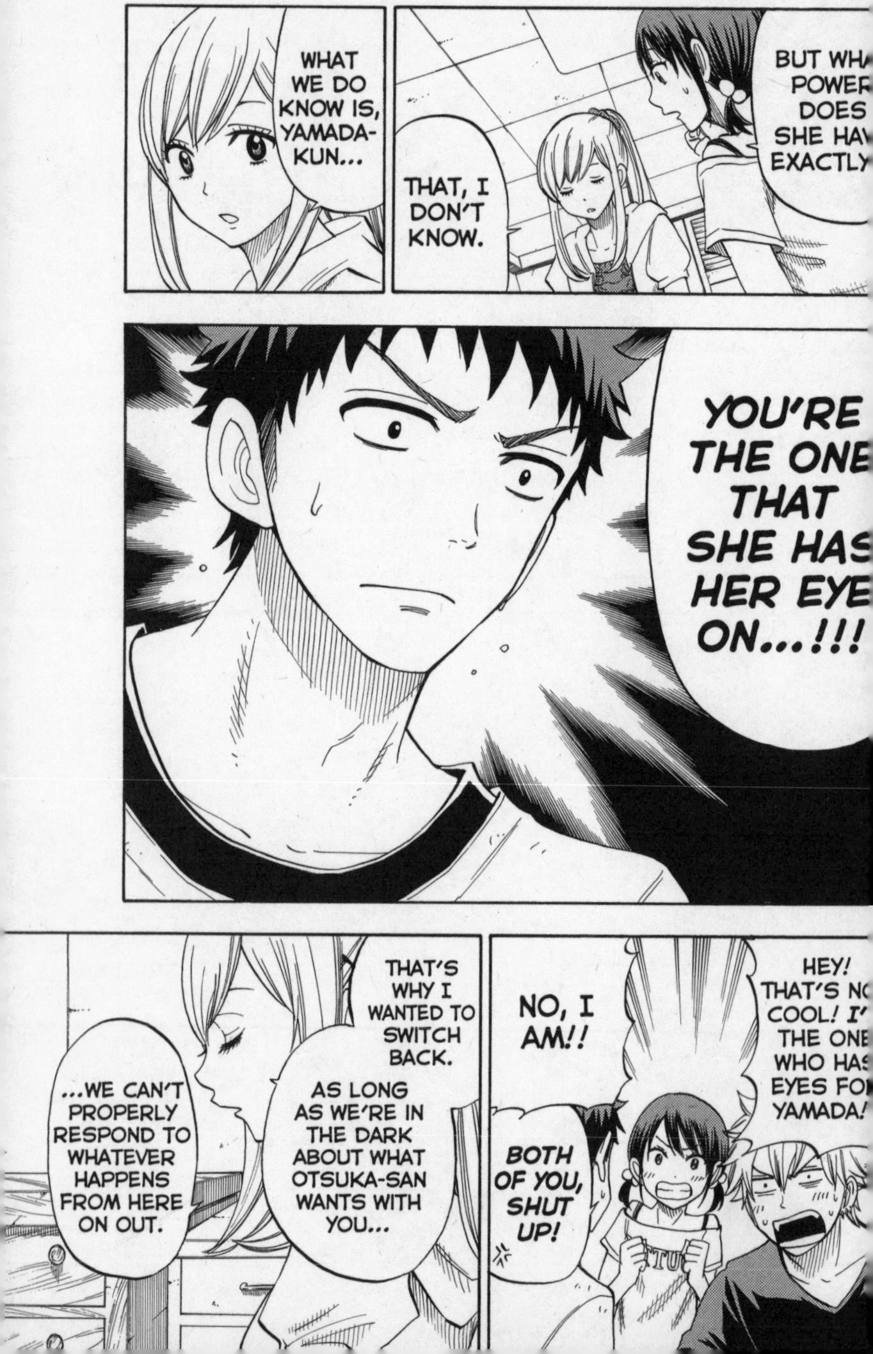
BUT WHA POWER DOES SHE HAV EXACTLY
THAT, I DON'T KNOW.
WHAT WE DO KNOW IS, YAMADA-KUN...
YOU'RE THE ONE THAT SHE HAS HER EYE ON...!!!
HEY! THAT'S NO COOL! I' THE ONE WHO HAS EYES FO YAMADA!
NO, I AM!!
BOTH OF YOU, SHUT UP!
THAT'S WHY I WANTED TO SWITCH BACK.
AS LONG AS WE'RE IN THE DARK ABOUT WHAT OTSUKA-SAN WANTS WITH YOU...
...WE CAN'T PROPERLY RESPOND TO WHATEVER HAPPENS FROM HERE ON OUT.

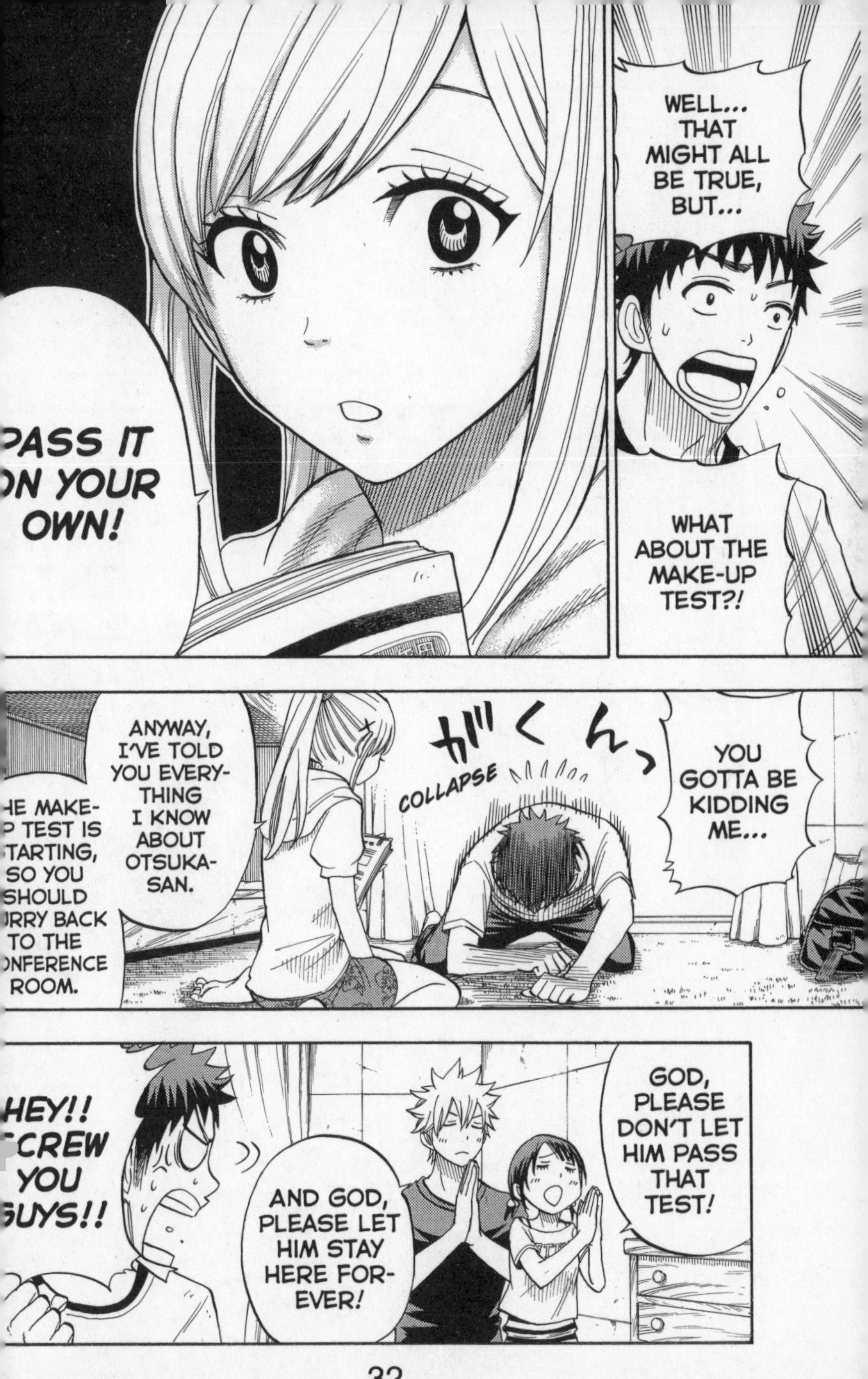
WELL... THAT MIGHT ALL BE TRUE, BUT...
WHAT ABOUT THE MAKE-UP TEST?!
PASS IT ON YOUR OWN!
YOU GOTTA BE KIDDING ME...
がくんっ
COLLAPSE
ANYWAY, I'VE TOLD YOU EVERYTHING I KNOW ABOUT OTSUKA-SAN.
HE MAKE-P TEST IS TARTING, SO YOU SHOULD URRY BACK TO THE ONFERENCE ROOM.
GOD, PLEASE DON'T LET HIM PASS THAT TEST!
AND GOD, PLEASE LET HIM STAY HERE FOREVER!
HEY!! CREW YOU UYS!!

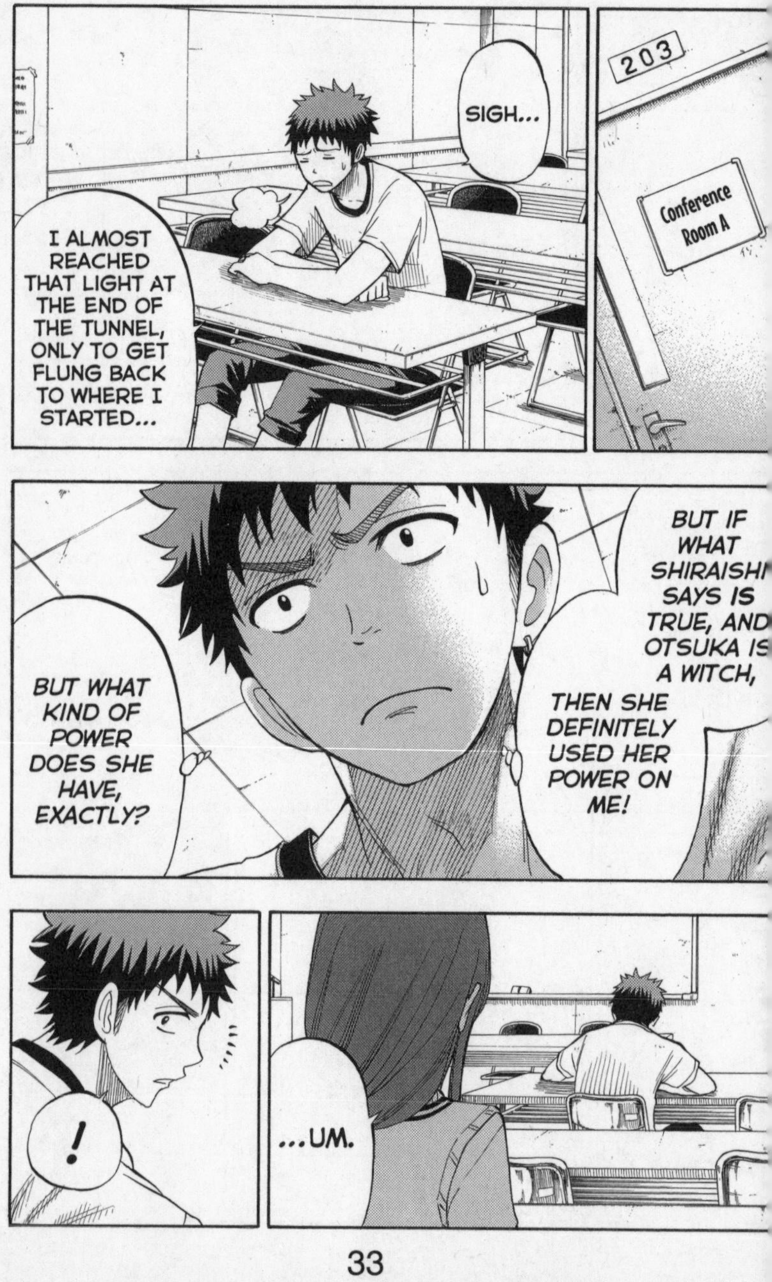
203
Conference Room A
SIGH...
I ALMOST REACHED THAT LIGHT AT THE END OF THE TUNNEL, ONLY TO GET FLUNG BACK TO WHERE I STARTED...
BUT IF WHAT SHIRAISHI SAYS IS TRUE, AND OTSUKA IS A WITCH,
THEN SHE DEFINITELY USED HER POWER ON ME!
BUT WHAT KIND OF POWER DOES SHE HAVE, EXACTLY?
...UM.
!

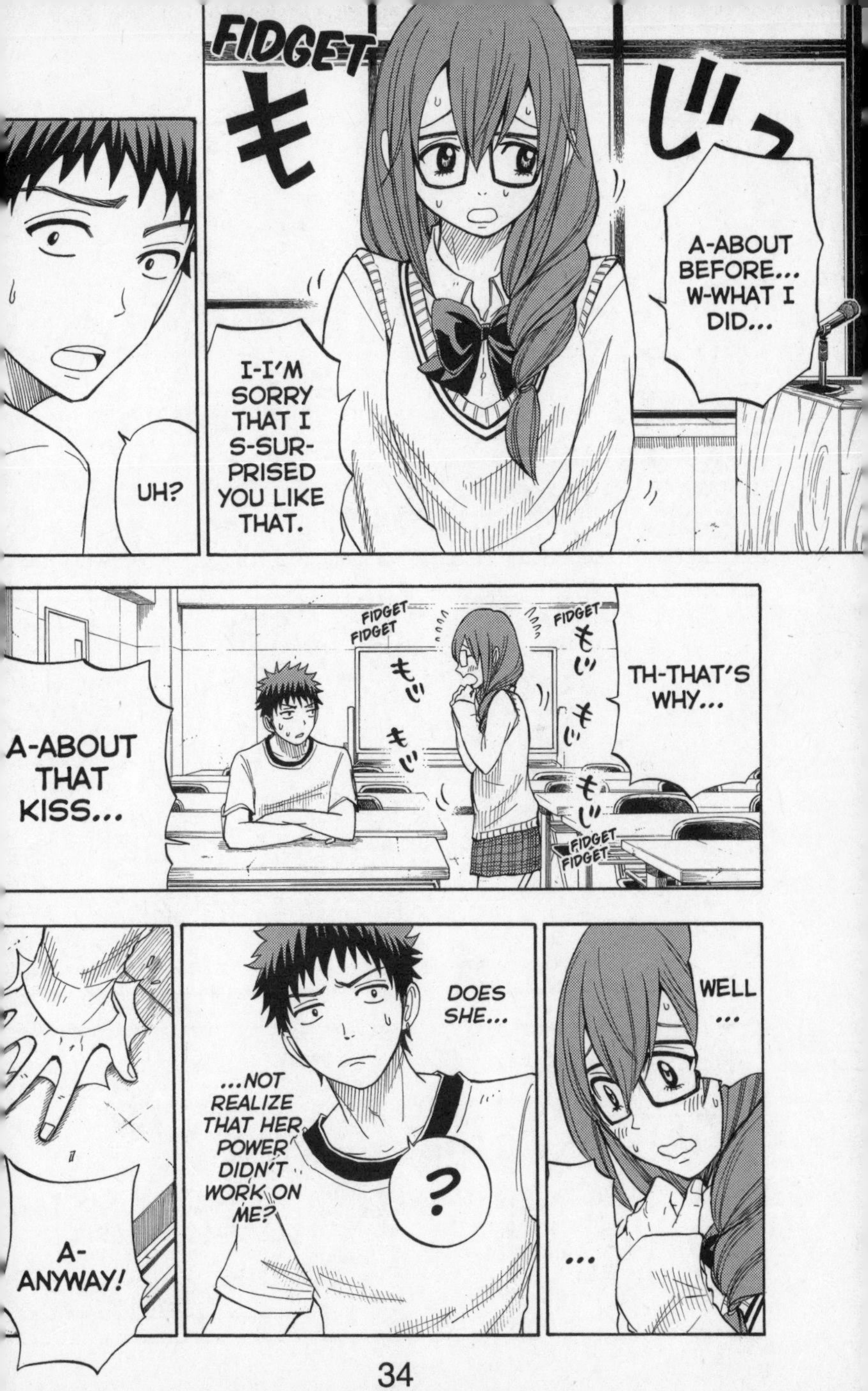
FIDGET
も
じっ
A-ABOUT BEFORE... W-WHAT I DID...
I-I'M SORRY THAT I S-SUR-PRISED YOU LIKE THAT.
UH?
FIDGET
もじ
TH-THAT'S WHY...
FIDGET FIDGET
もじ
もじ
FIDGET FIDGET
A-ABOUT THAT KISS...
WELL ...
...
DOES SHE...
...NOT REALIZE THAT HER POWER DIDN'T WORK ON ME?
?
A- ANYWAY!

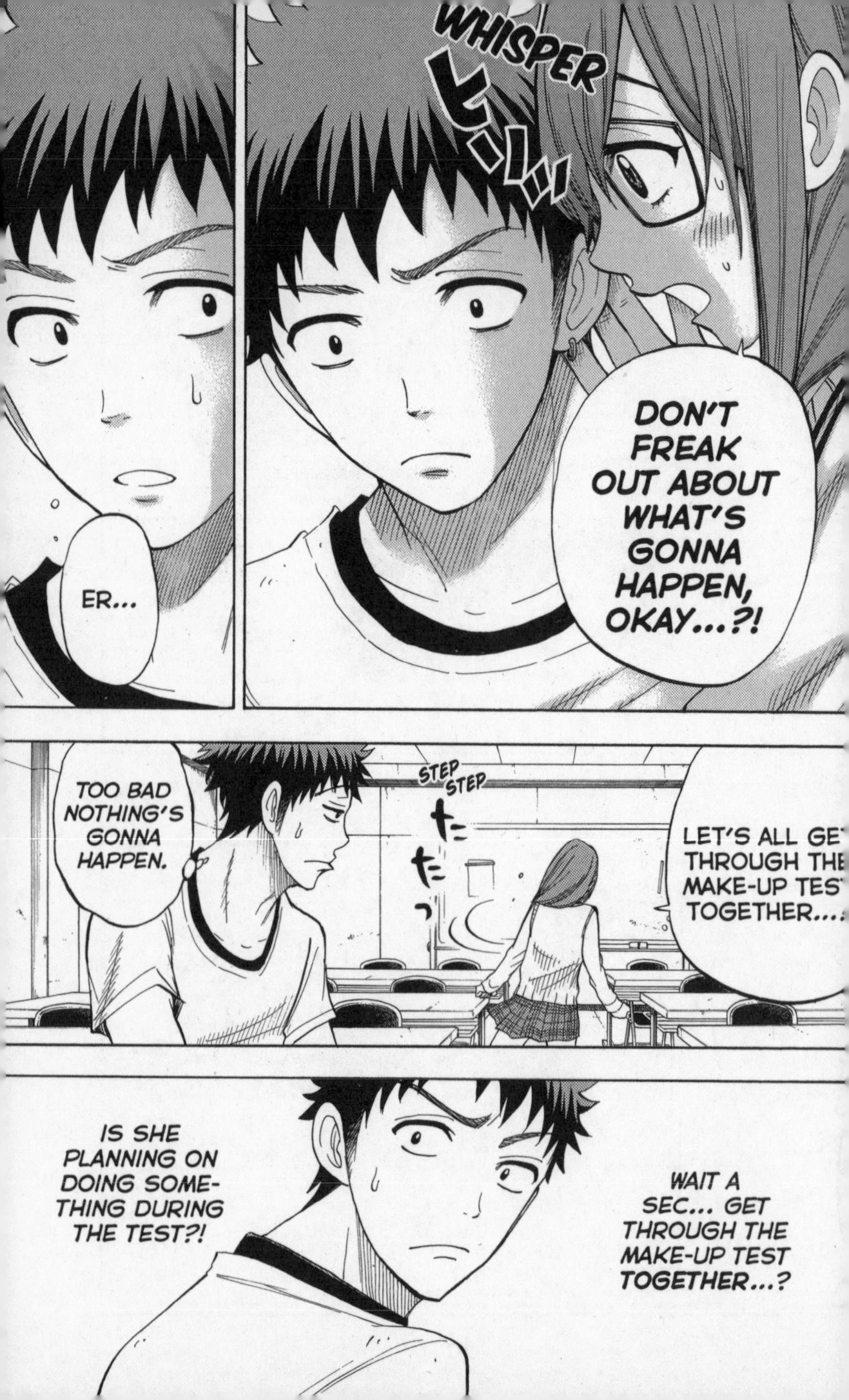
WHISPER
DON'T FREAK OUT ABOUT WHAT'S GONNA HAPPEN, OKAY...?!
ER...
LET'S ALL GET THROUGH THE MAKE-UP TEST TOGETHER....
STEP STEP
TOO BAD NOTHING'S GONNA HAPPEN.
WAIT A SEC... GET THROUGH THE MAKE-UP TEST TOGETHER...?
IS SHE PLANNING ON DOING SOME-THING DURING THE TEST?!

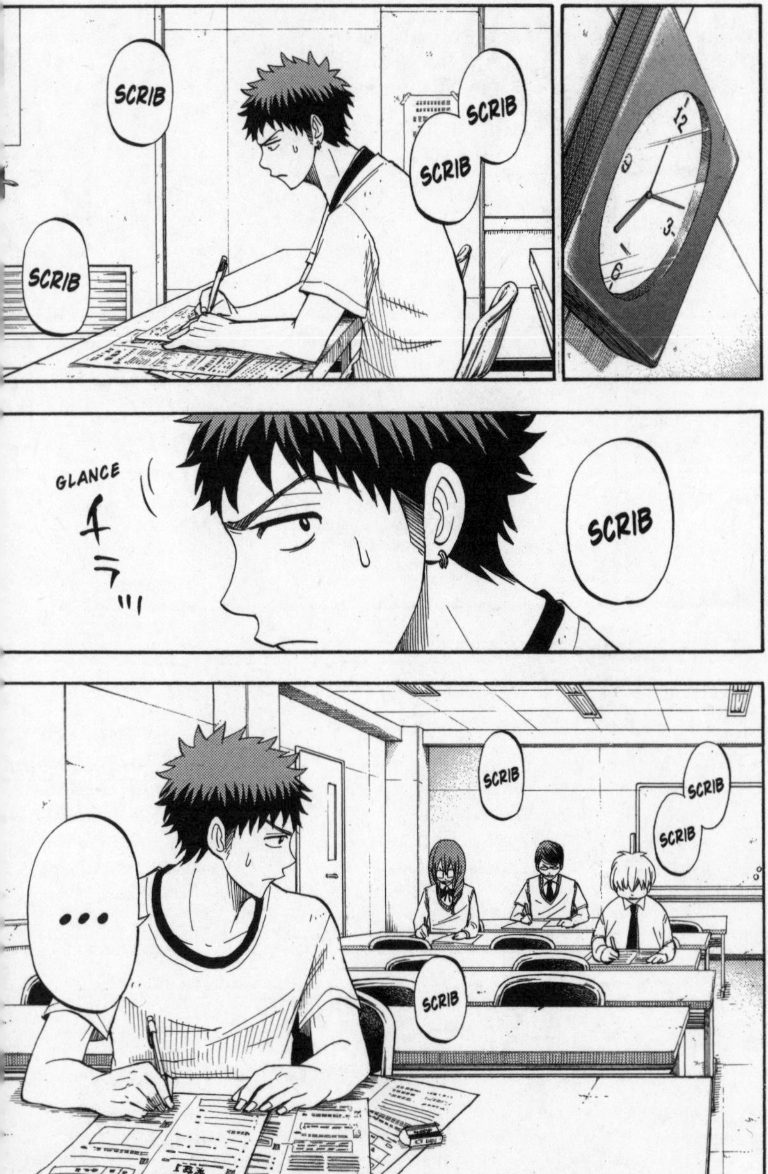
SCRIB
SCRIB
SCRIB
SCRIB
SCRIB
GLANCE
SCRIB
SCRIB
SCRIB
SCRIB
...

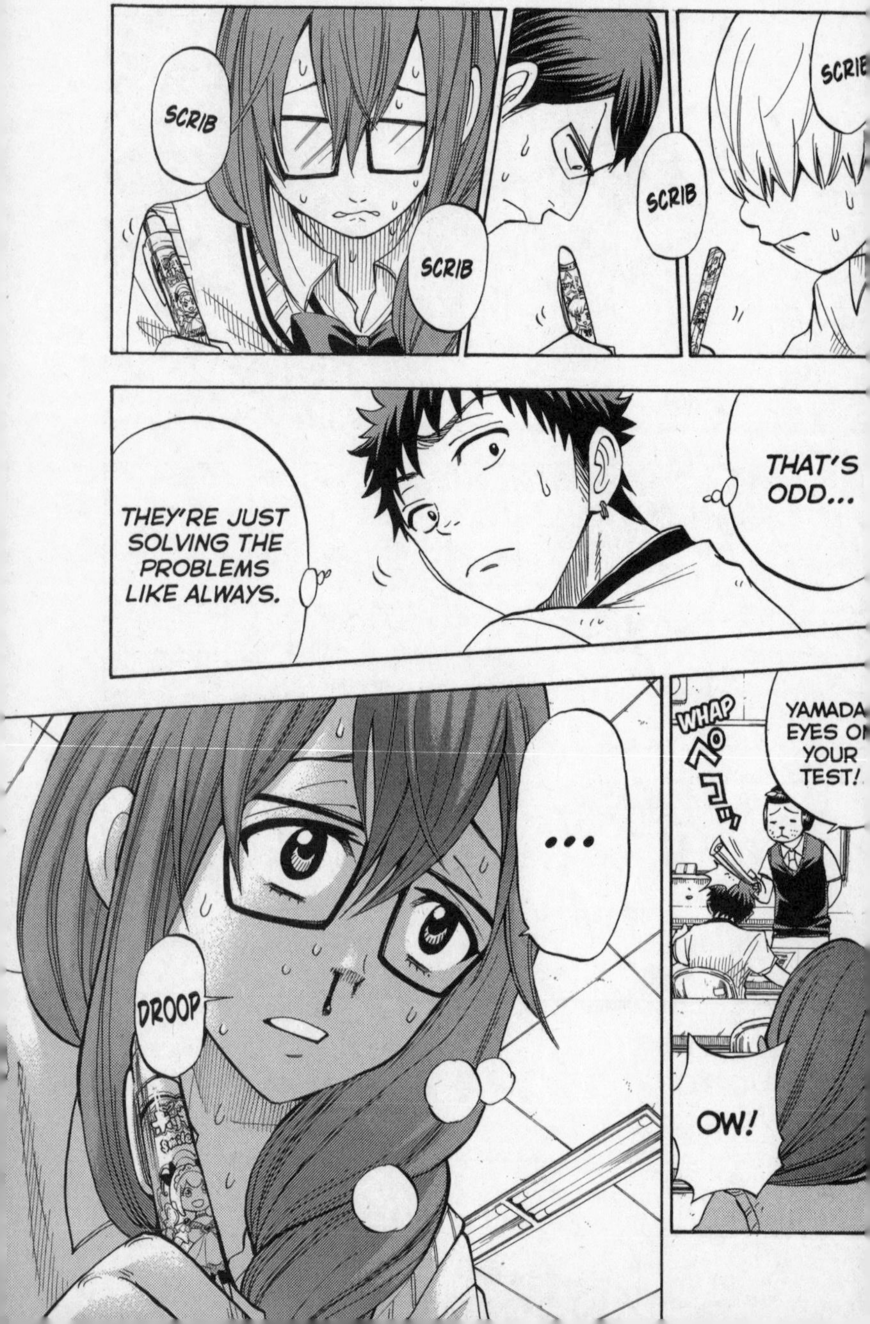
SCRI
SCRIB
SCRIB
SCRIB
THAT'S ODD...
THEY'RE JUST SOLVING THE PROBLEMS LIKE ALWAYS.
YAMADA EYES O YOUR TEST!
WHAP
OW!
...
DROOP

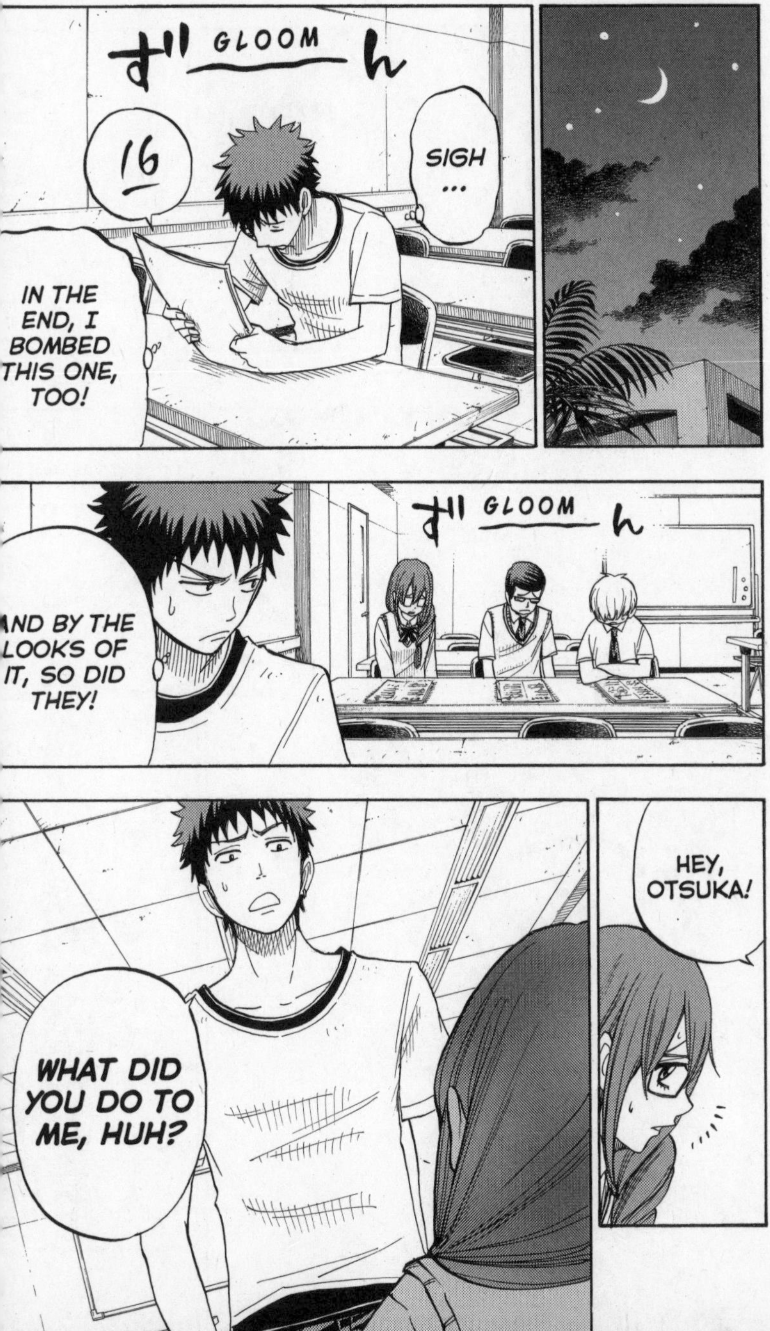
ず GLOOM ん
SIGH ...
16
IN THE END, I BOMBED THIS ONE, TOO!
ず GLOOM ん
AND BY THE LOOKS OF IT, SO DID THEY!
HEY, OTSUKA!
WHAT DID YOU DO TO ME, HUH?

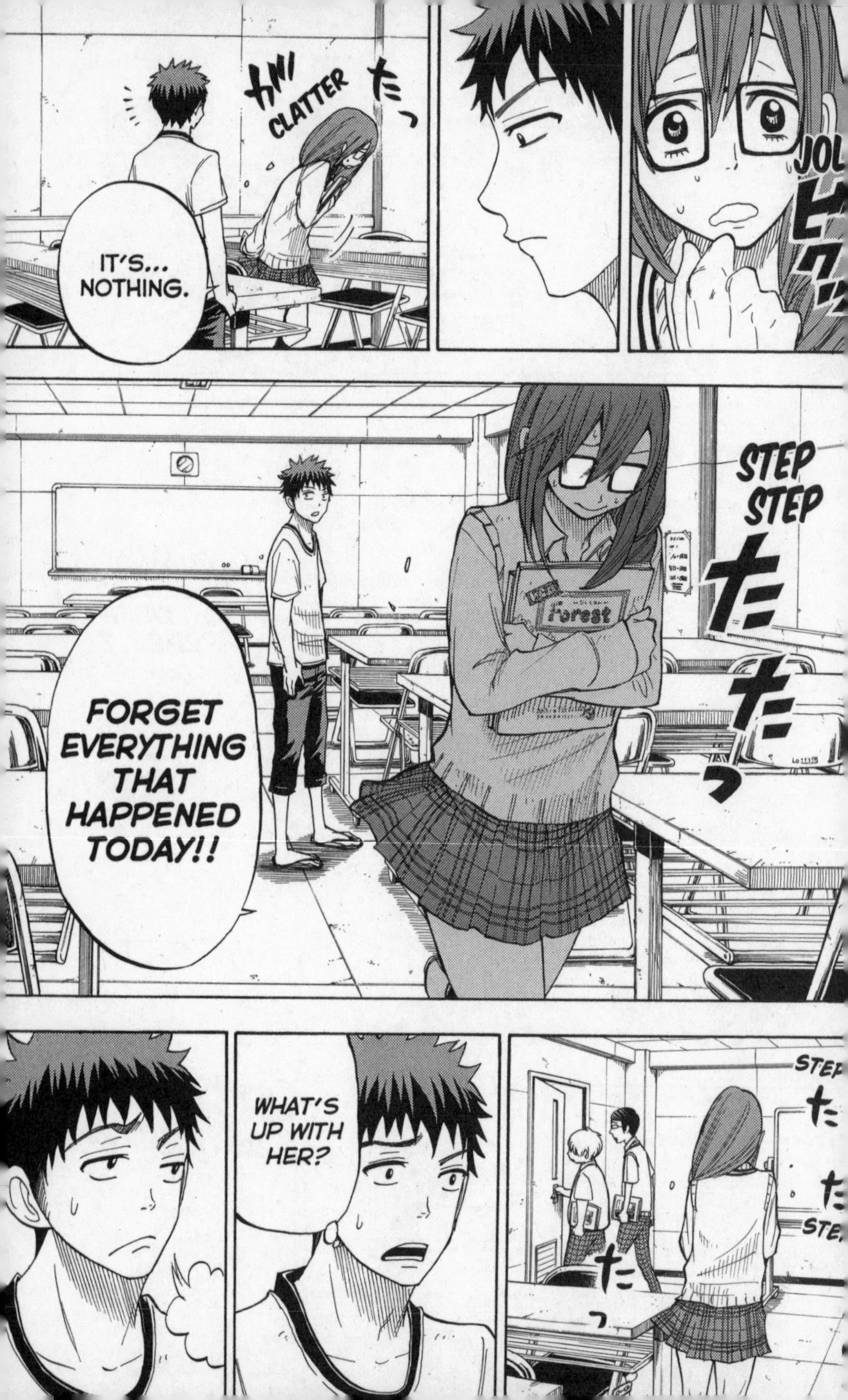

JOL
CLATTER
たっ
IT'S... NOTHING.
STEP STEP
たたっ
Forest
FORGET EVERYTHING THAT HAPPENED TODAY!!
STEP
STE
WHAT'S UP WITH HER?

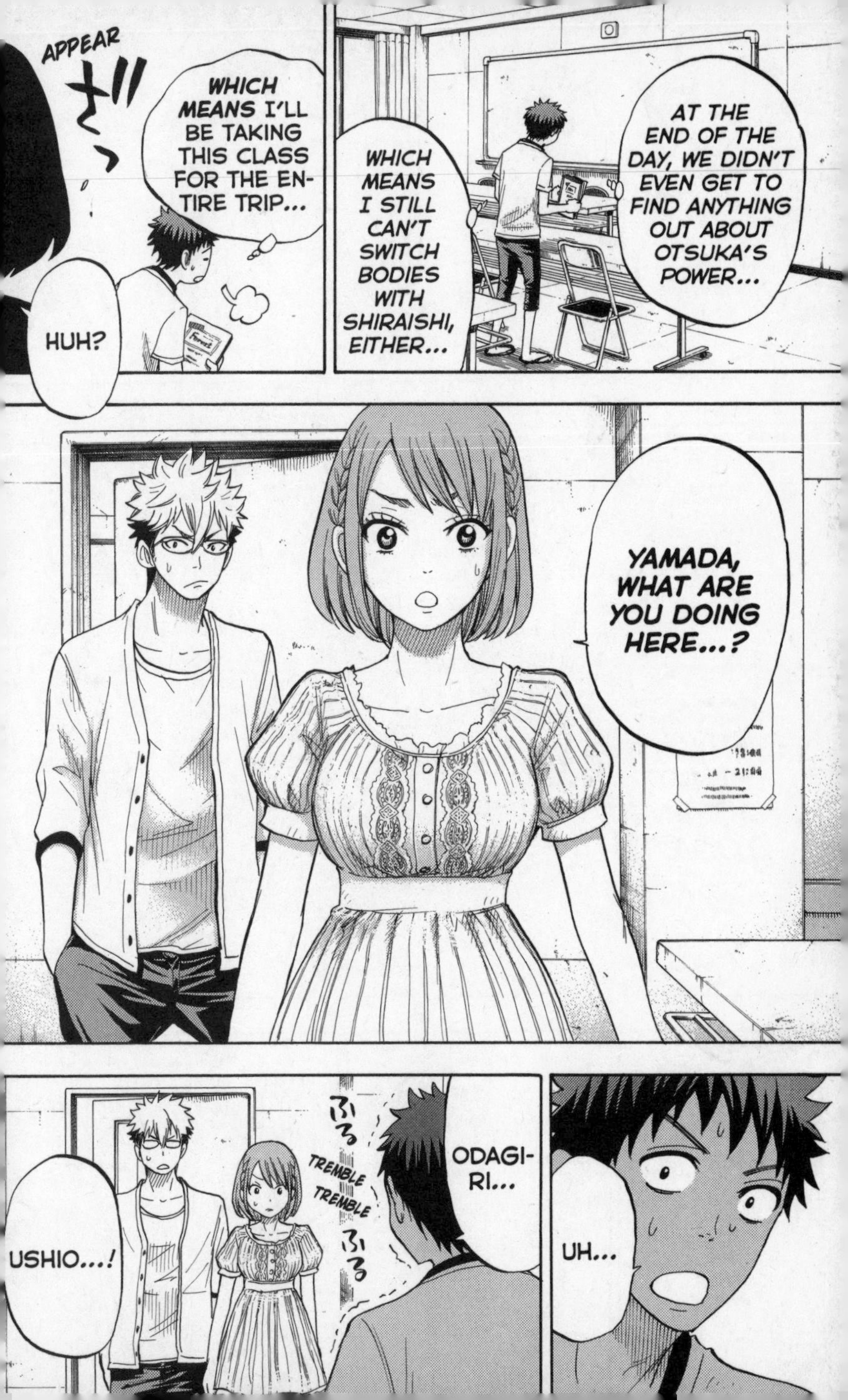
AT THE END OF THE DAY, WE DIDN'T EVEN GET TO FIND ANYTHING OUT ABOUT OTSUKA'S POWER...
WHICH MEANS I STILL CAN'T SWITCH BODIES WITH SHIRAISHI, EITHER...
WHICH MEANS I'LL BE TAKING THIS CLASS FOR THE ENTIRE TRIP...
APPEAR
ざっ
HUH?
YAMADA, WHAT ARE YOU DOING HERE...?
UH...
ODAGIRI...
ふる
TREMBLE TREMBLE
ふる
USHIO...!

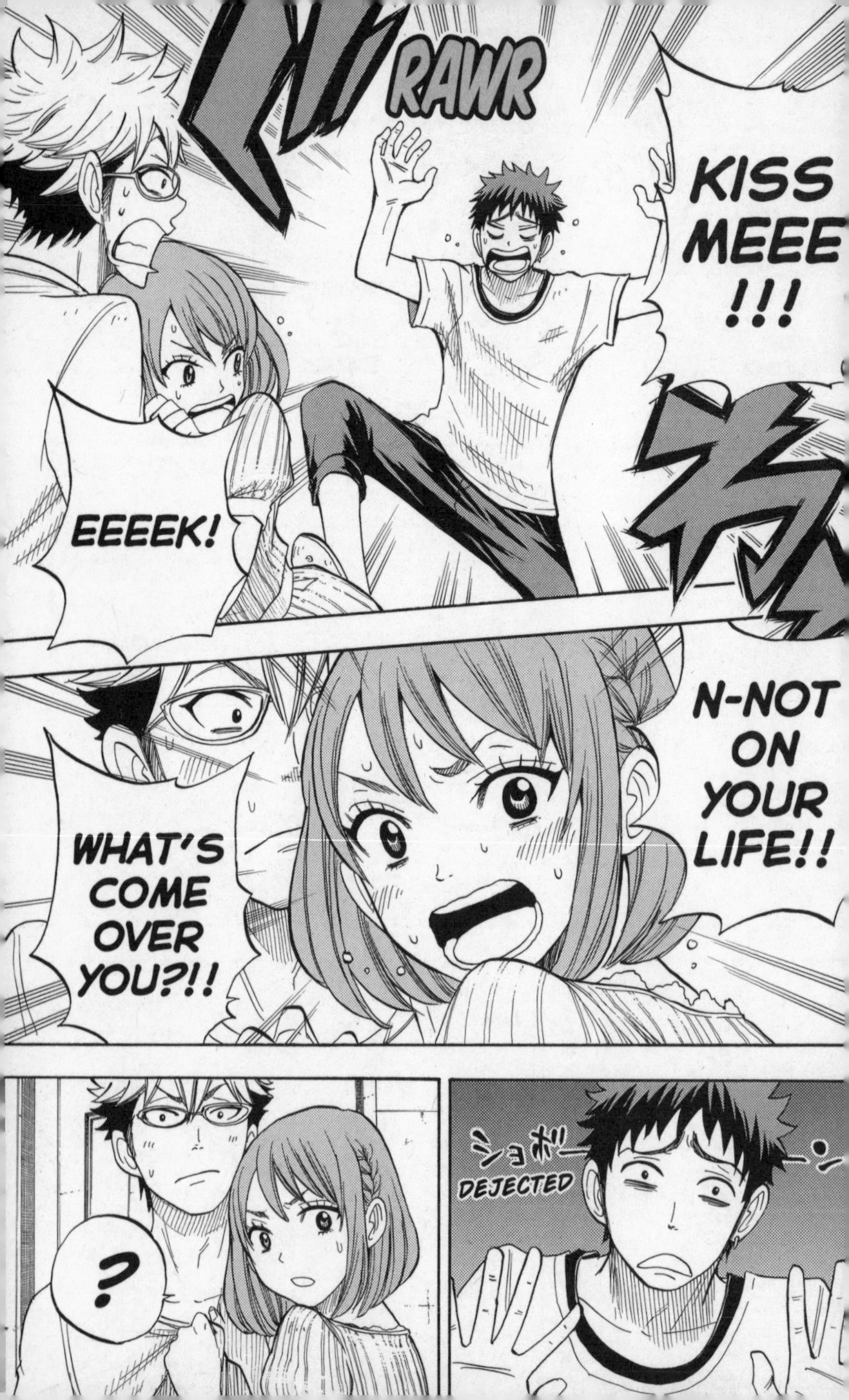
RAWR
KISS MEEE!!!
EEEEK!
N-NOT ON YOUR LIFE!!
WHAT'S COME OVER YOU?!!
ショボーーン
DEJECTED
?

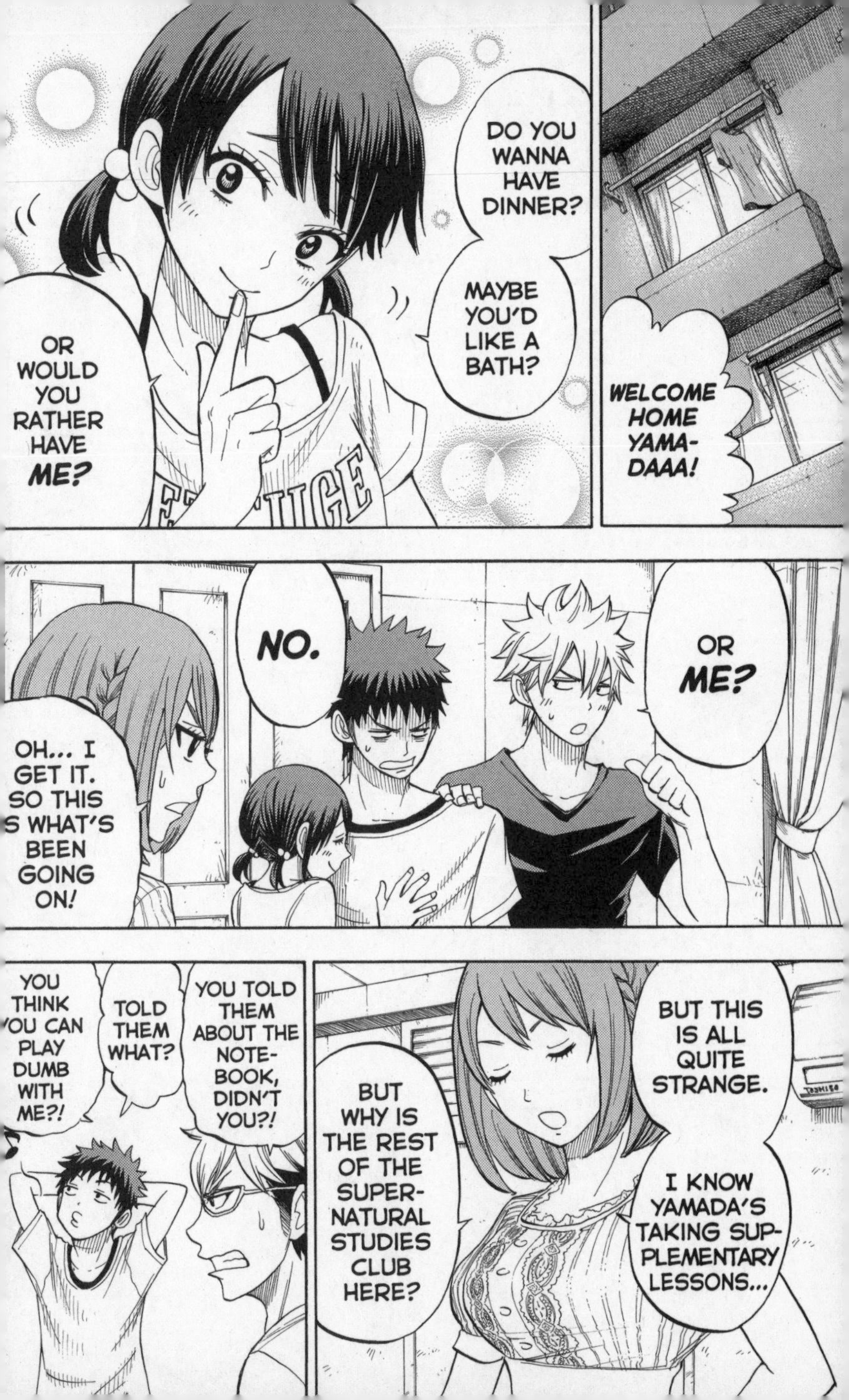
WELCOME HOME YAMA-DAAA!
DO YOU WANNA HAVE DINNER?
MAYBE YOU'D LIKE A BATH?
OR WOULD YOU RATHER HAVE *ME?*
OR *ME?*
NO.
OH... I GET IT. SO THIS S WHAT'S BEEN GOING ON!
BUT THIS IS ALL QUITE STRANGE.
I KNOW YAMADA'S TAKING SUP-PLEMENTARY LESSONS...
BUT WHY IS THE REST OF THE SUPER-NATURAL STUDIES CLUB HERE?
YOU TOLD THEM ABOUT THE NOTE-BOOK, DIDN'T YOU?!
TOLD THEM WHAT?
YOU THINK OU CAN PLAY DUMB WITH ME?!

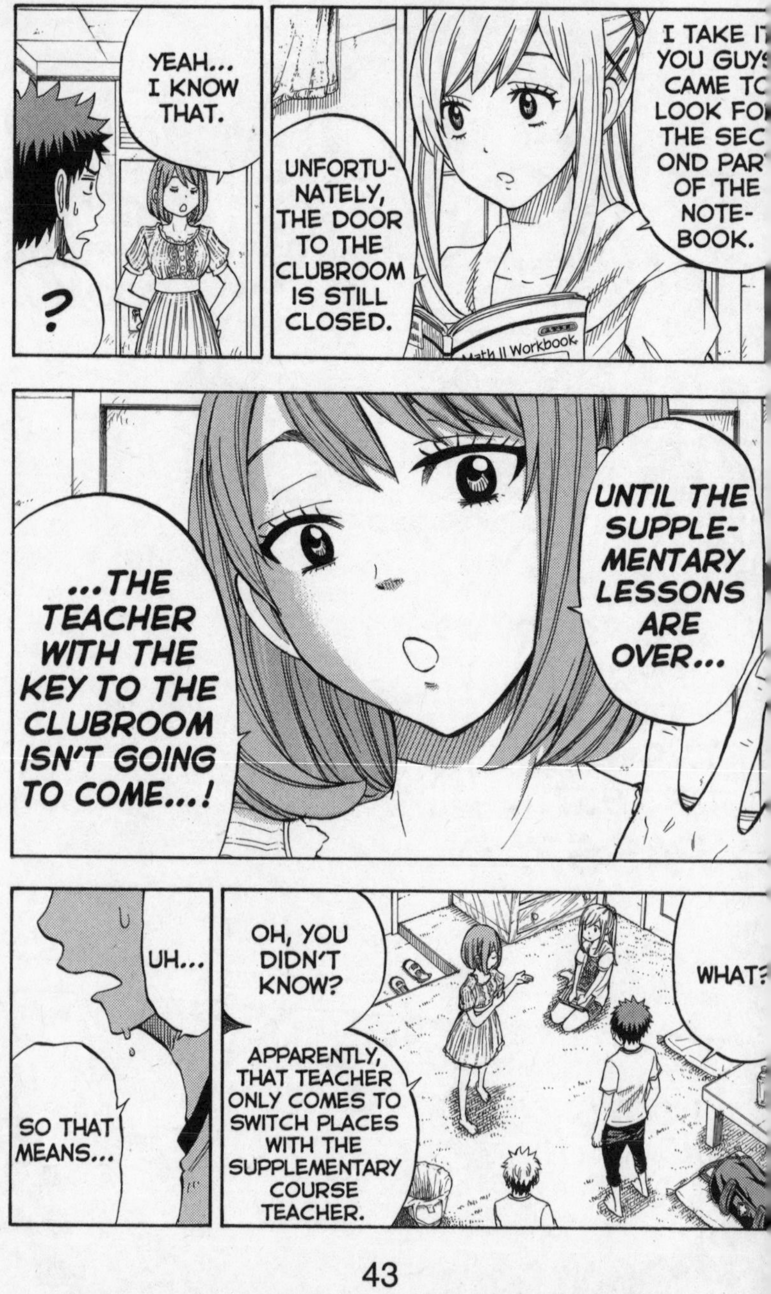

I TAKE IT YOU GUYS CAME TO LOOK FOR THE SECOND PART OF THE NOTEBOOK.
UNFORTUNATELY, THE DOOR TO THE CLUBROOM IS STILL CLOSED.
Math II Workbook
YEAH... I KNOW THAT.
?
UNTIL THE SUPPLEMENTARY LESSONS ARE OVER...
...THE TEACHER WITH THE KEY TO THE CLUBROOM ISN'T GOING TO COME...!
WHAT?
OH, YOU DIDN'T KNOW?
APPARENTLY, THAT TEACHER ONLY COMES TO SWITCH PLACES WITH THE SUPPLEMENTARY COURSE TEACHER.
UH...
SO THAT MEANS...

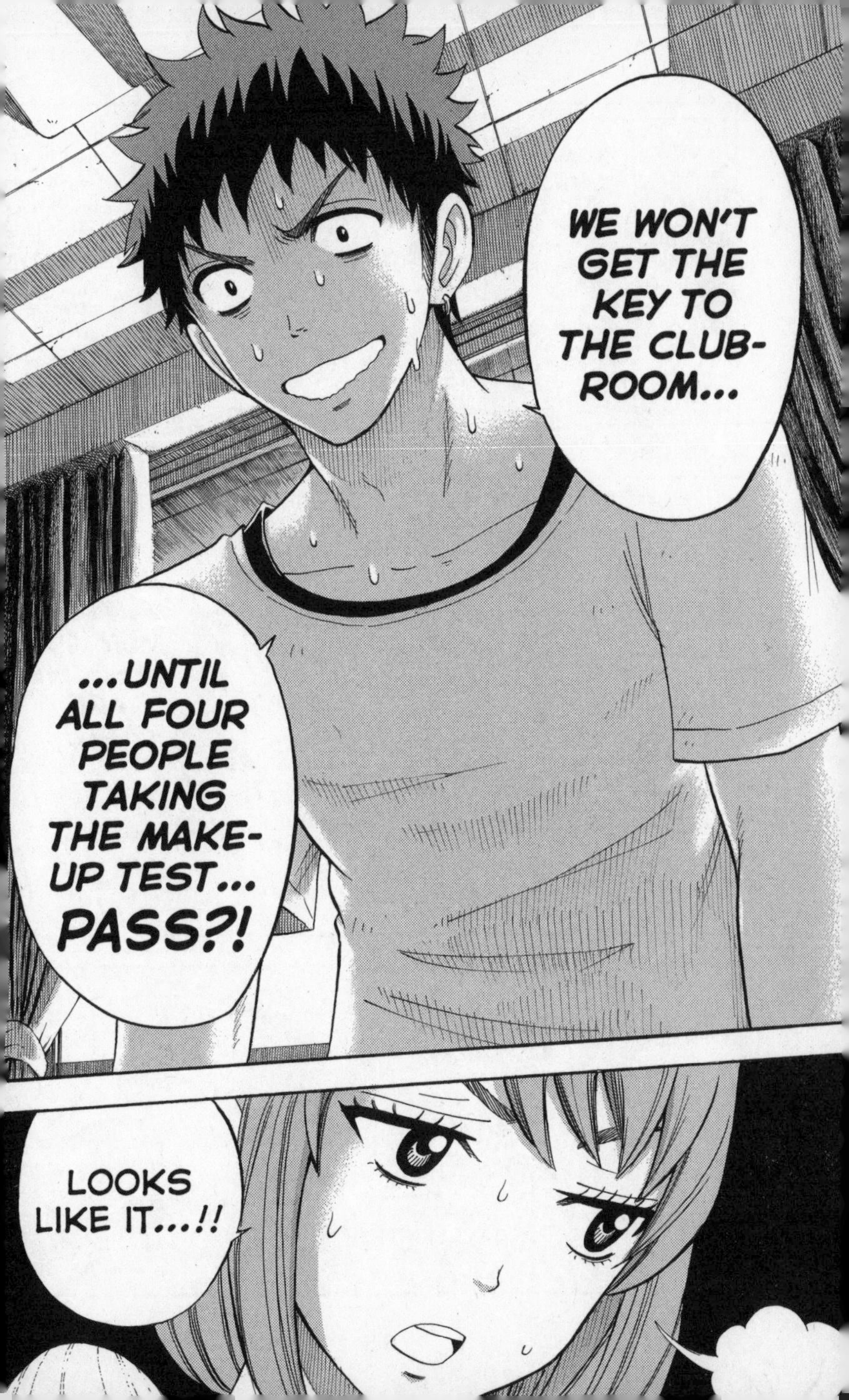
WE WON'T GET THE KEY TO THE CLUB-ROOM...
...UNTIL ALL FOUR PEOPLE TAKING THE MAKE-UP TEST... PASS?!
LOOKS LIKE IT...!!

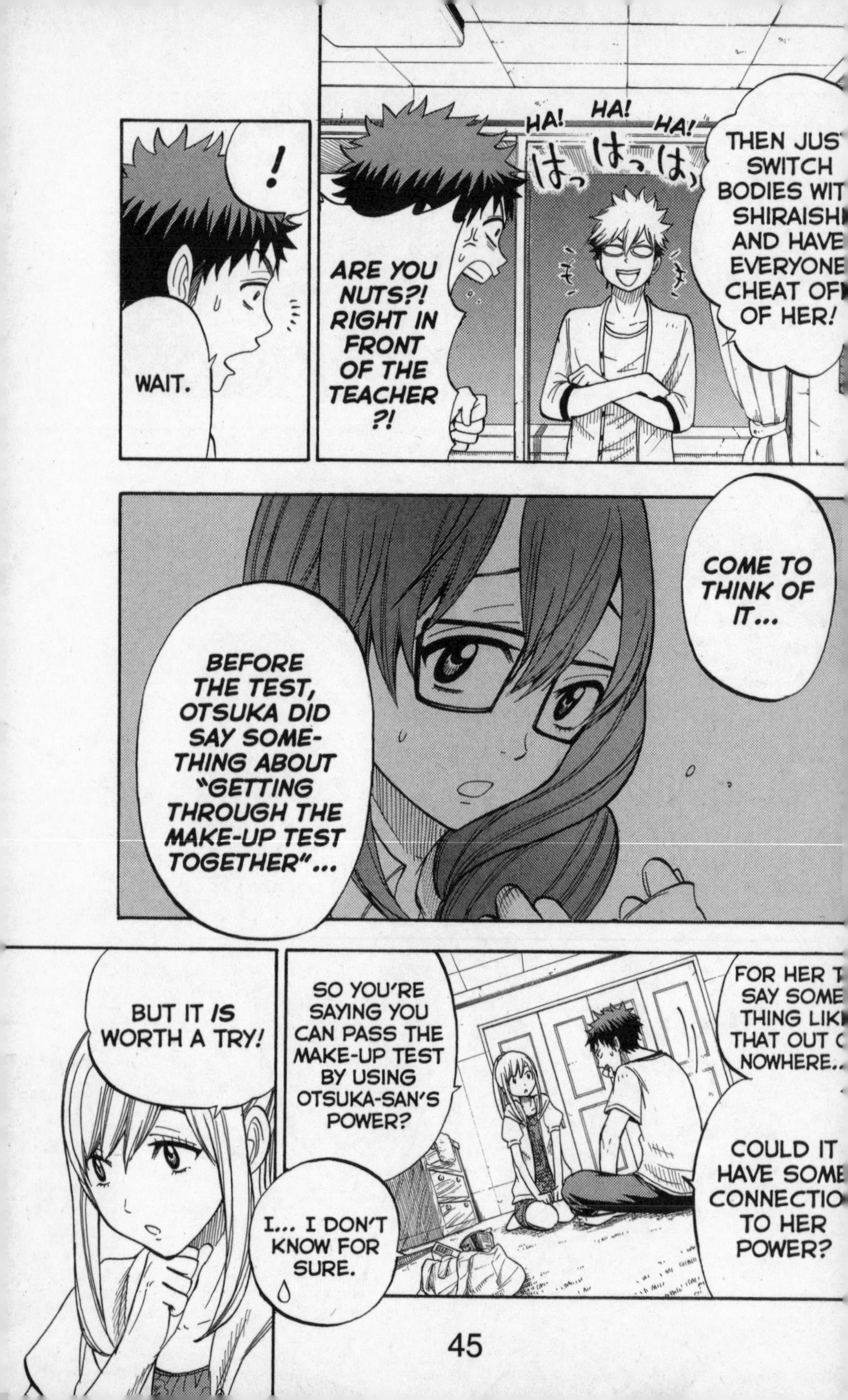
THEN JUST SWITCH BODIES WIT SHIRAISHI AND HAVE EVERYONE CHEAT OFF OF HER!
HA! HA! HA!
はっはっはっ
ARE YOU NUTS?! RIGHT IN FRONT OF THE TEACHER ?!
!
WAIT.
COME TO THINK OF IT...
BEFORE THE TEST, OTSUKA DID SAY SOME-THING ABOUT "GETTING THROUGH THE MAKE-UP TEST TOGETHER"...
FOR HER T SAY SOME THING LIK THAT OUT C NOWHERE...
COULD IT HAVE SOME CONNECTIO TO HER POWER?
SO YOU'RE SAYING YOU CAN PASS THE MAKE-UP TEST BY USING OTSUKA-SAN'S POWER?
I... I DON'T KNOW FOR SURE.
BUT IT *IS* WORTH A TRY!

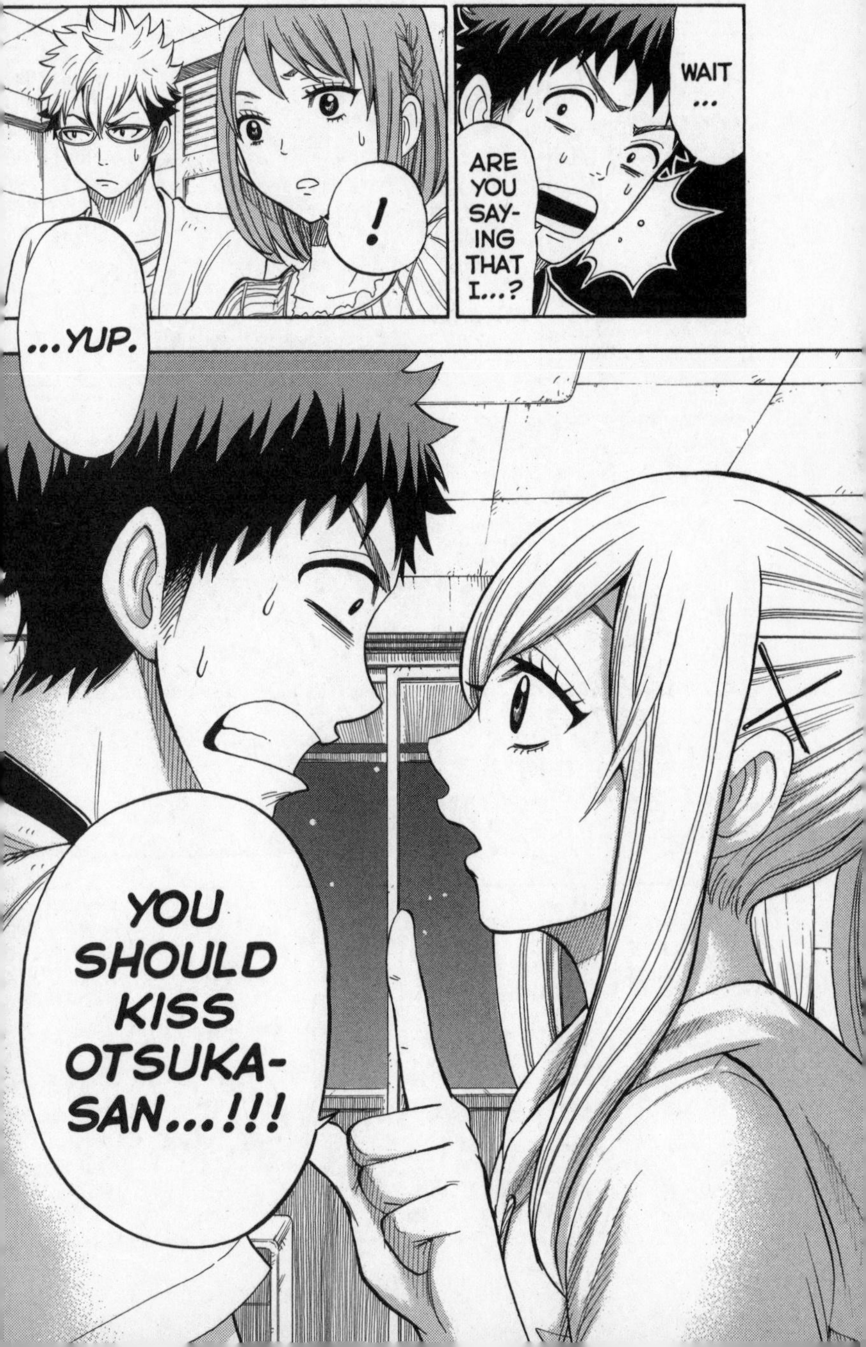
WAIT ...
ARE YOU SAY-ING THAT I...?
!
...YUP.
YOU SHOULD KISS OTSUKA-SAN...!!!

CHAPTER 28: Lather Lather

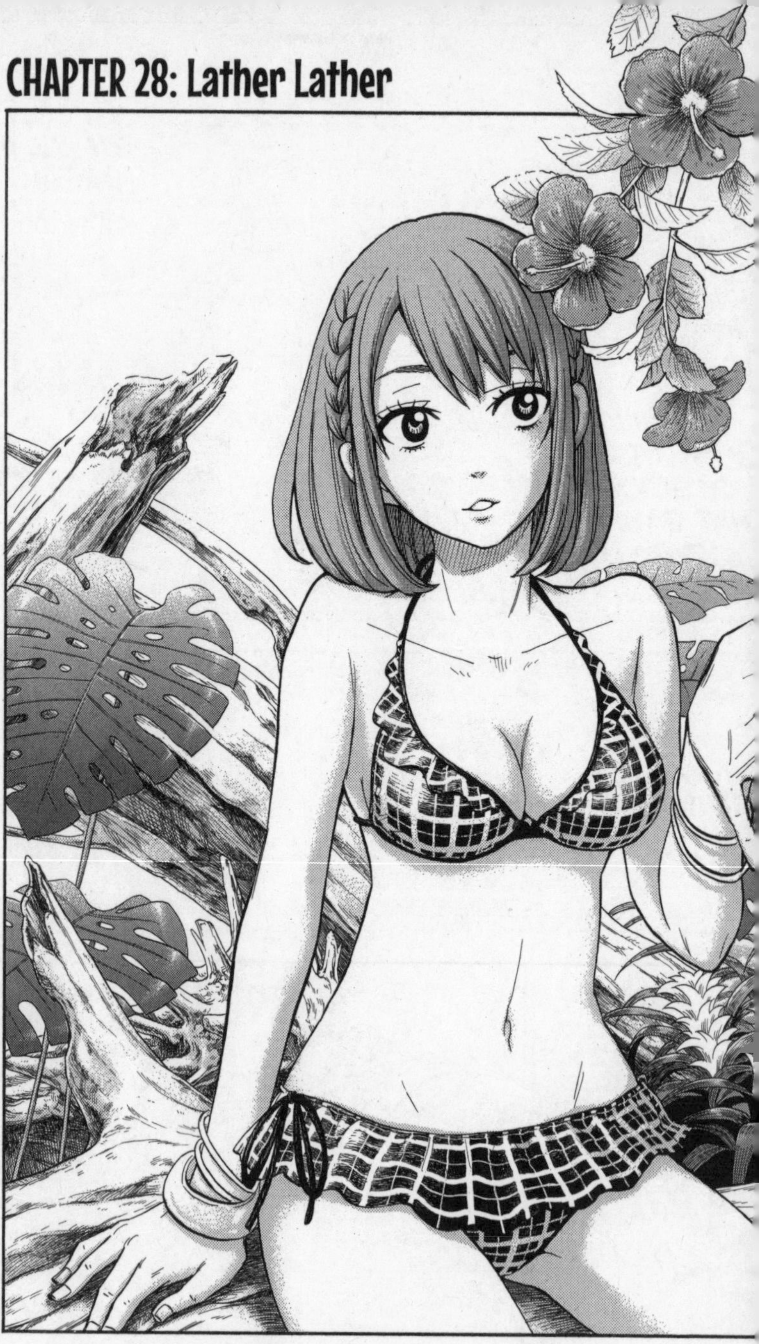

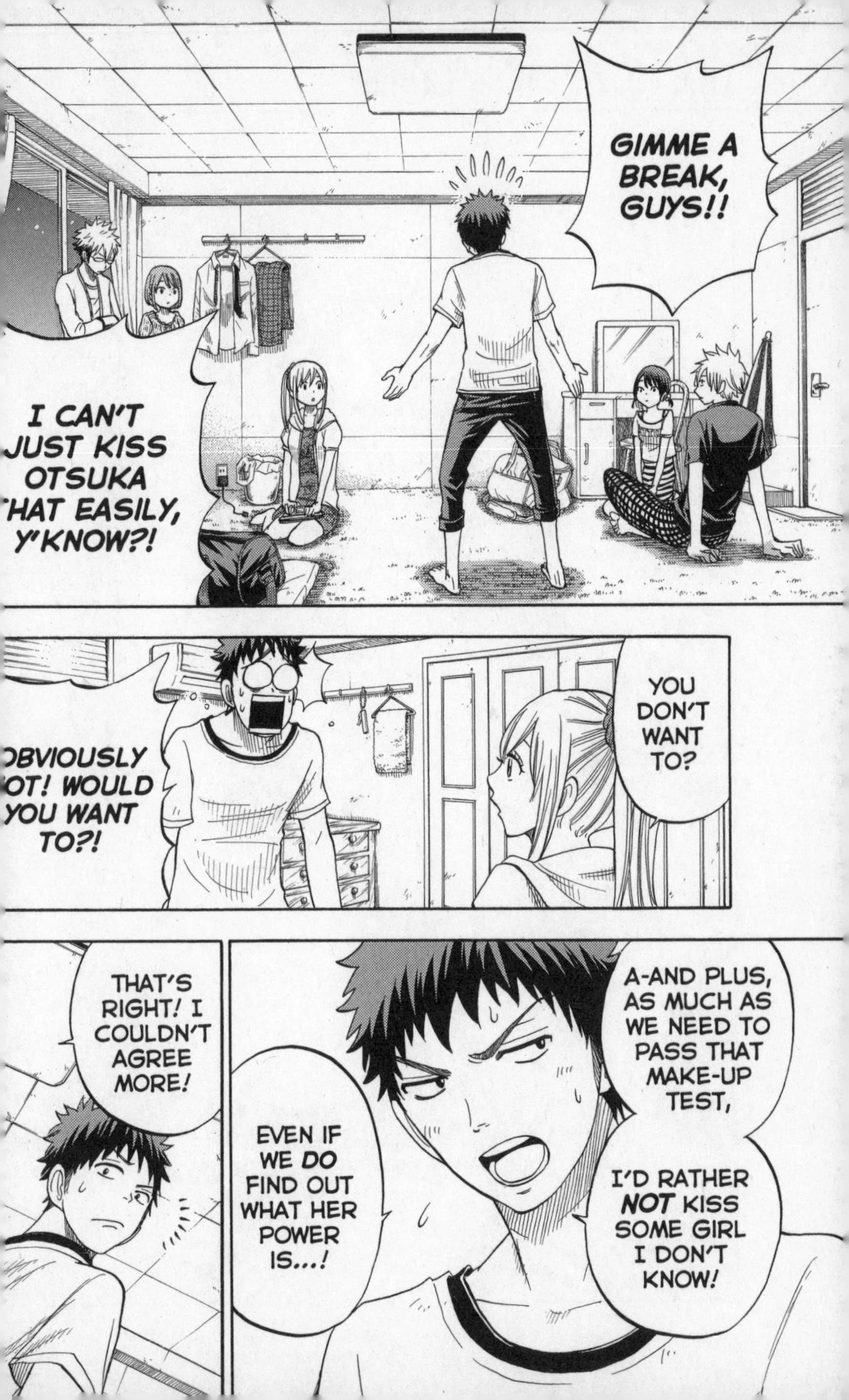

GIMME A BREAK, GUYS!!
I CAN'T JUST KISS OTSUKA 'HAT EASILY, Y'KNOW?!
YOU DON'T WANT TO?
BVIOUSLY OT! WOULD YOU WANT TO?!
A-AND PLUS, AS MUCH AS WE NEED TO PASS THAT MAKE-UP TEST,
I'D RATHER *NOT* KISS SOME GIRL I DON'T KNOW!
EVEN IF WE *DO* FIND OUT WHAT HER POWER IS...!
THAT'S RIGHT! I COULDN'T AGREE MORE!

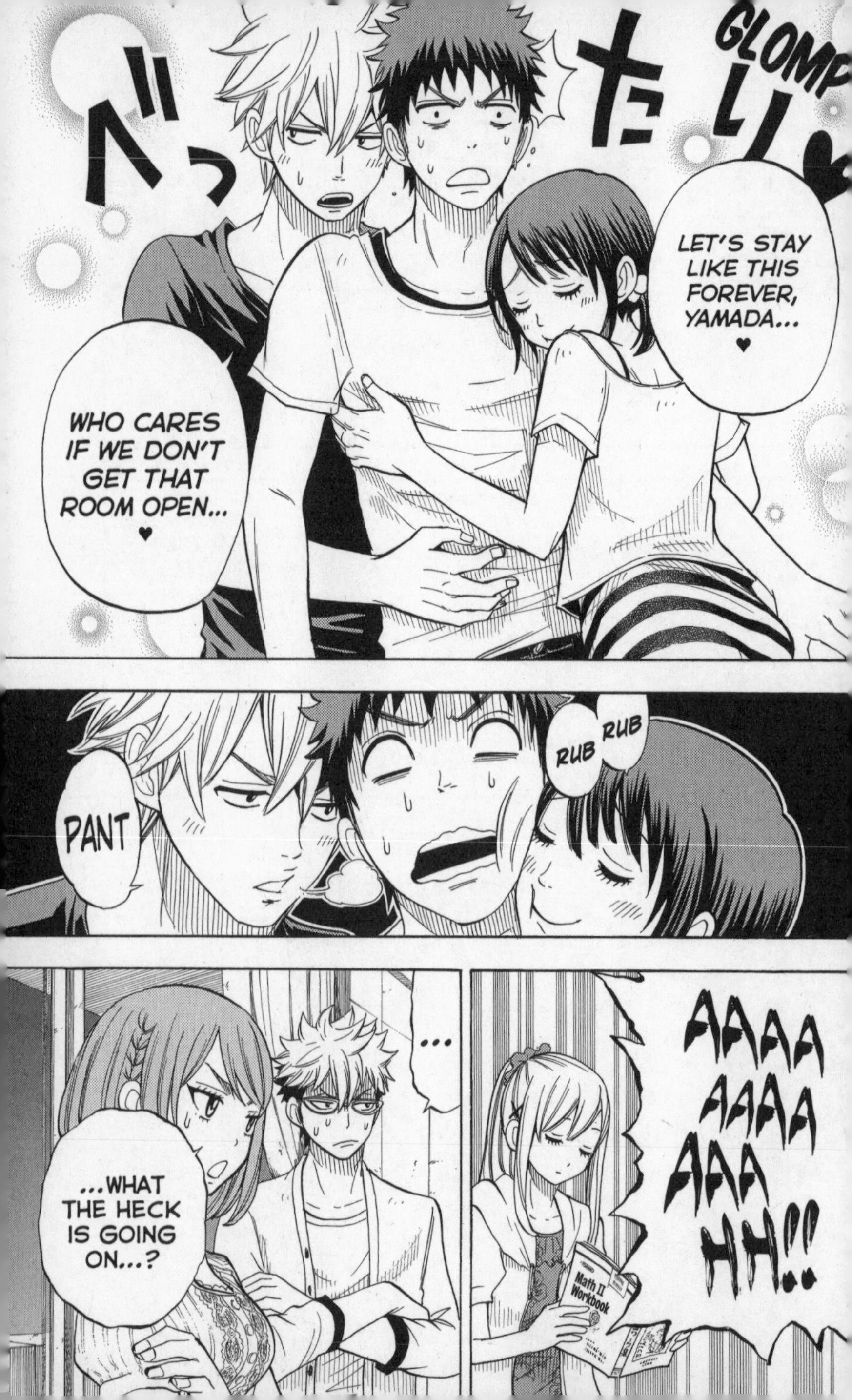
GLOMP
べったり♥
LET'S STAY LIKE THIS FOREVER, YAMADA... ♥
WHO CARES IF WE DON'T GET THAT ROOM OPEN... ♥
RUB RUB
PANT
AAAAAAAAAAAHH!!
...
...WHAT THE HECK IS GOING ON...?
Math II Workbook

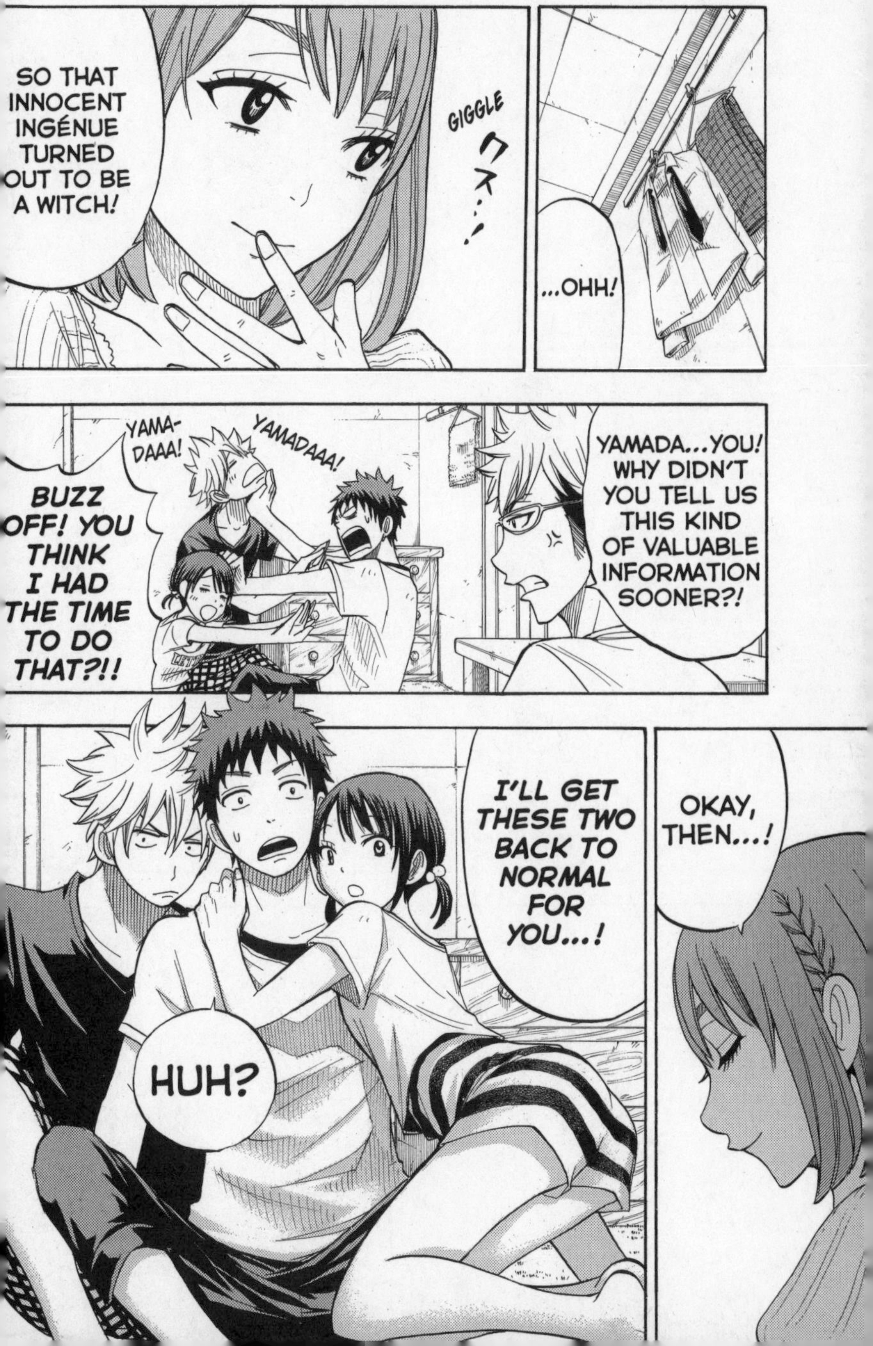
...OHH!
GIGGLE
クス…!
SO THAT INNOCENT INGÉNUE TURNED OUT TO BE A WITCH!
YAMADA...YOU! WHY DIDN'T YOU TELL US THIS KIND OF VALUABLE INFORMATION SOONER?!
YAMADAAA!
YAMA-DAAA!
BUZZ OFF! YOU THINK I HAD THE TIME TO DO THAT?!!
OKAY, THEN...!
I'LL GET THESE TWO BACK TO NORMAL FOR YOU...!
HUH?

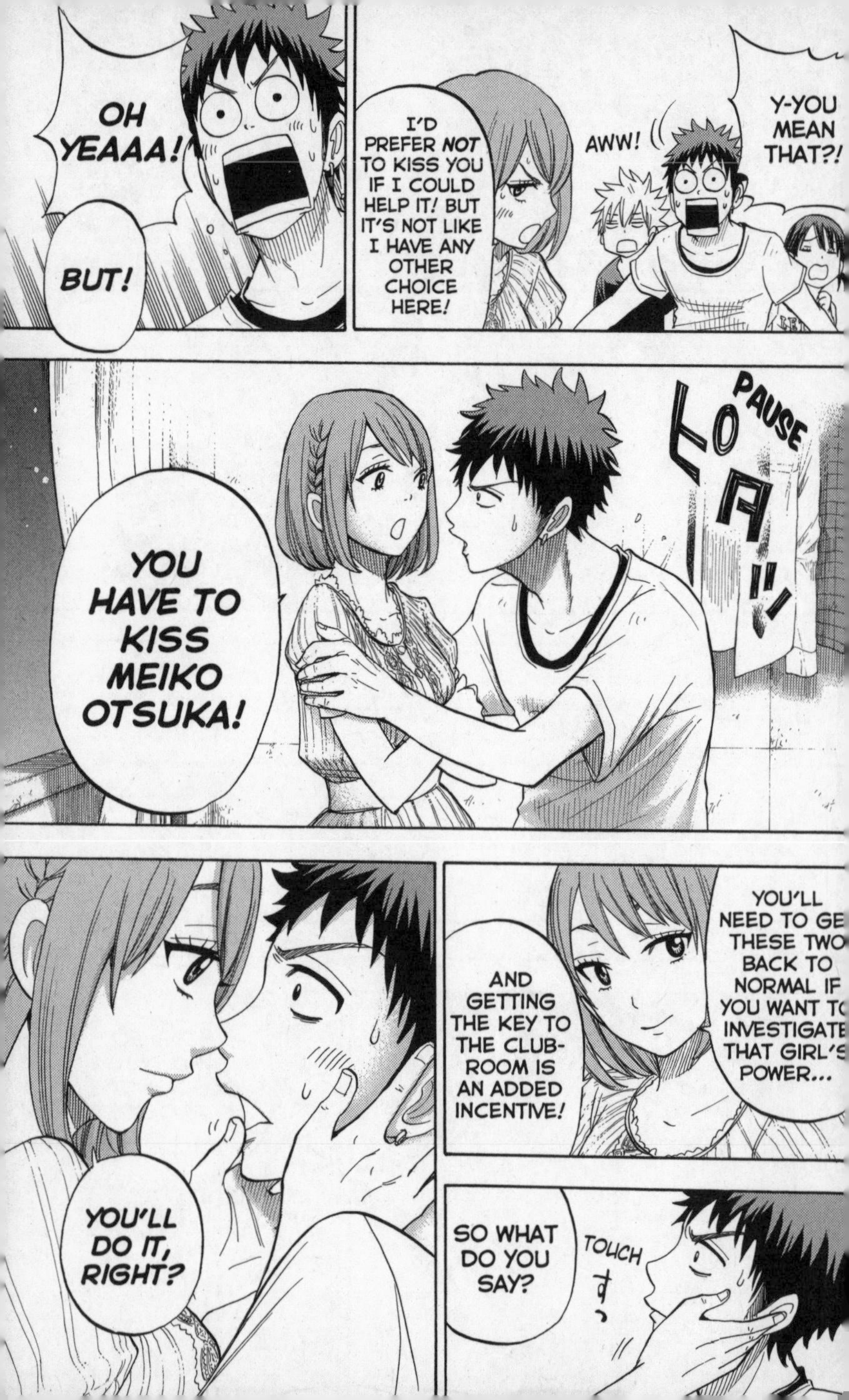
Y-YOU MEAN THAT?!
AWW!
I'D PREFER NOT TO KISS YOU IF I COULD HELP IT! BUT IT'S NOT LIKE I HAVE ANY OTHER CHOICE HERE!
OH YEAAA!
BUT!
PAUSE
YOU HAVE TO KISS MEIKO OTSUKA!
YOU'LL NEED TO GE THESE TWO BACK TO NORMAL IF YOU WANT TO INVESTIGATE THAT GIRL'S POWER...
AND GETTING THE KEY TO THE CLUB-ROOM IS AN ADDED INCENTIVE!
TOUCH
SO WHAT DO YOU SAY?
YOU'LL DO IT, RIGHT?

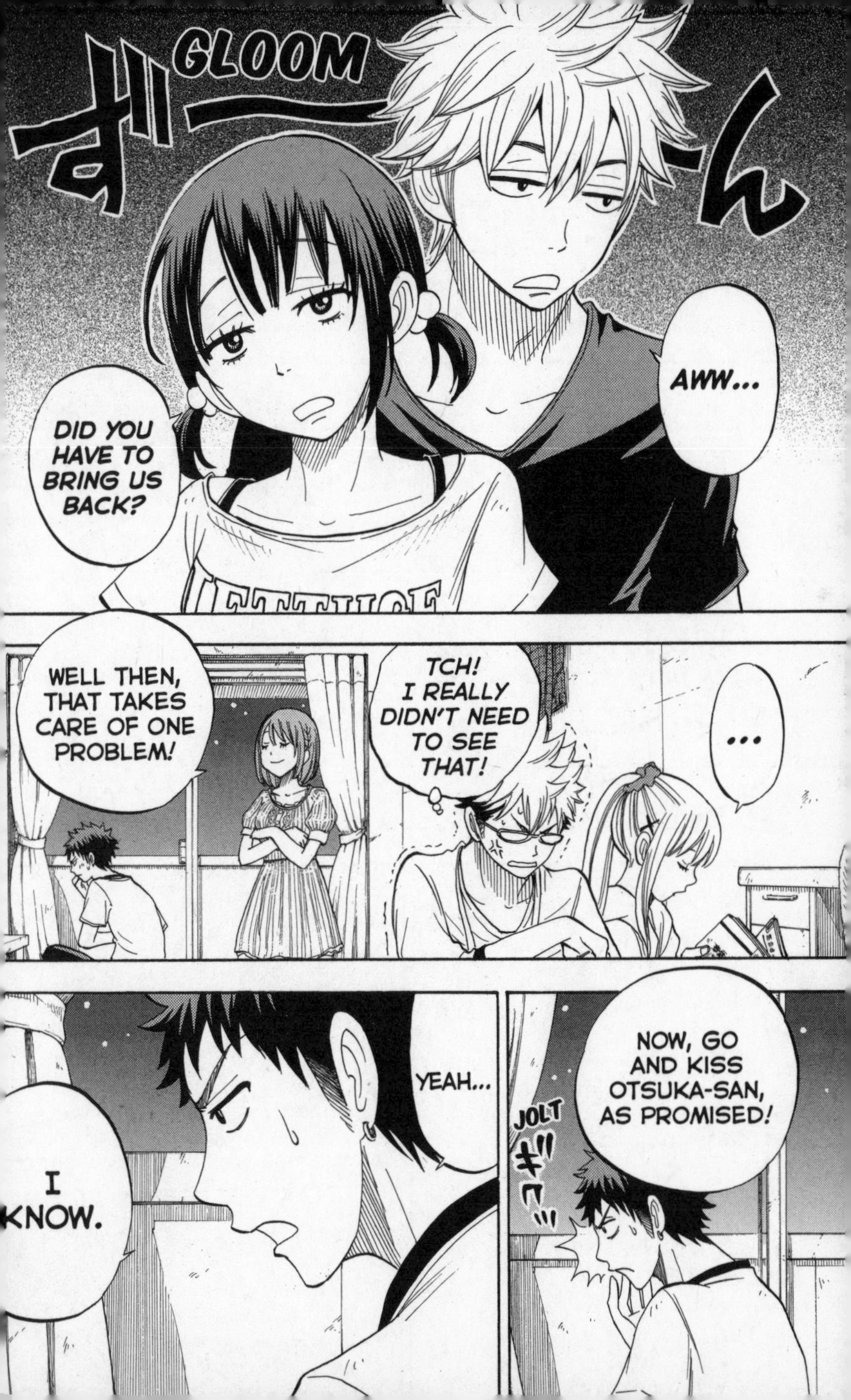
GLOOM
ずーーん
AWW...
DID YOU HAVE TO BRING US BACK?
...
TCH! I REALLY DIDN'T NEED TO SEE THAT!
WELL THEN, THAT TAKES CARE OF ONE PROBLEM!
NOW, GO AND KISS OTSUKA-SAN, AS PROMISED!
JOLT
ギクッ
YEAH...
I KNOW.

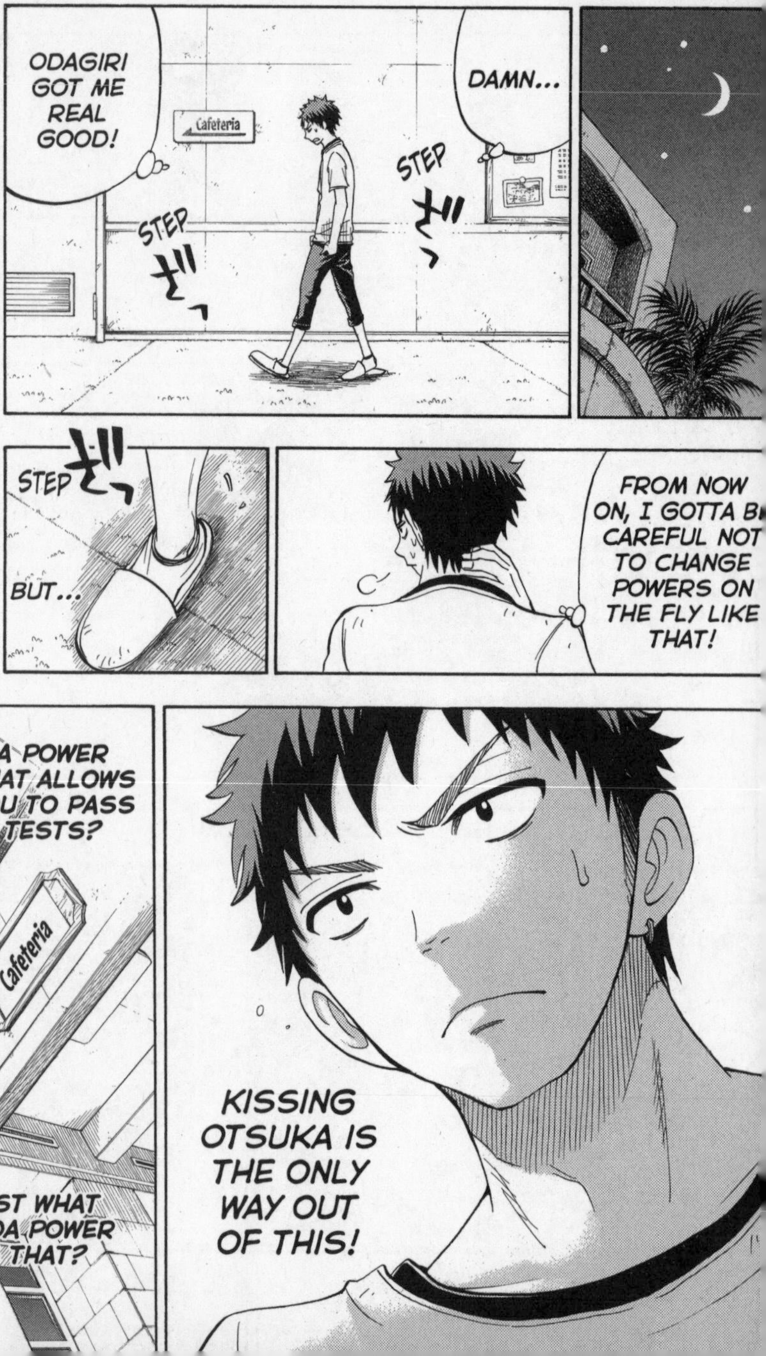
DAMN...
STEP
ODAGIRI GOT ME REAL GOOD!
Cafeteria
STEP
FROM NOW ON, I GOTTA B CAREFUL NOT TO CHANGE POWERS ON THE FLY LIKE THAT!
STEP
BUT...
KISSING OTSUKA IS THE ONLY WAY OUT OF THIS!
A POWER THAT ALLOWS YOU TO PASS TESTS?
Cafeteria
JUST WHAT KINDA POWER IS THAT?

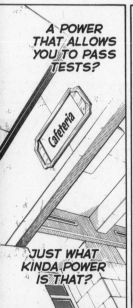

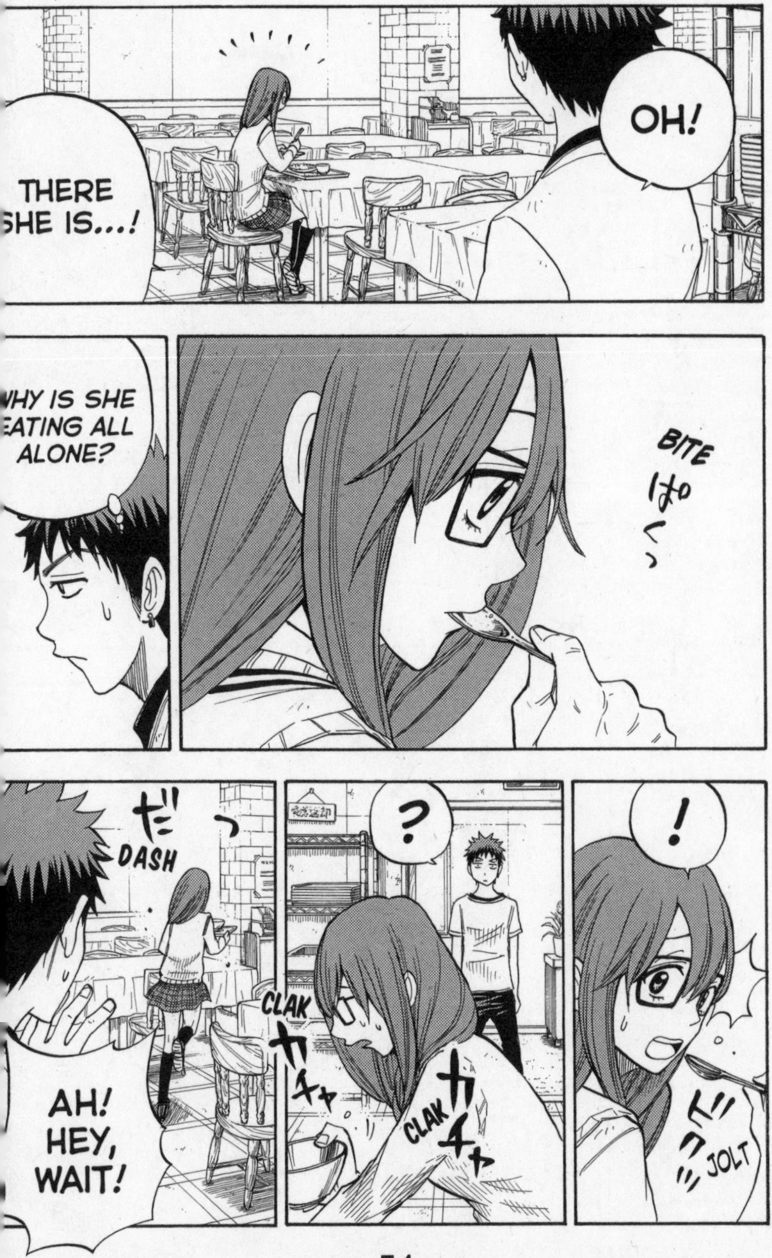
OH!
THERE SHE IS...!
BITE
ぱくっ
WHY IS SHE EATING ALL ALONE?
!
JOLT
?
CLAK
カチャ
CLAK
カチャ
だっ
DASH
AH! HEY, WAIT!

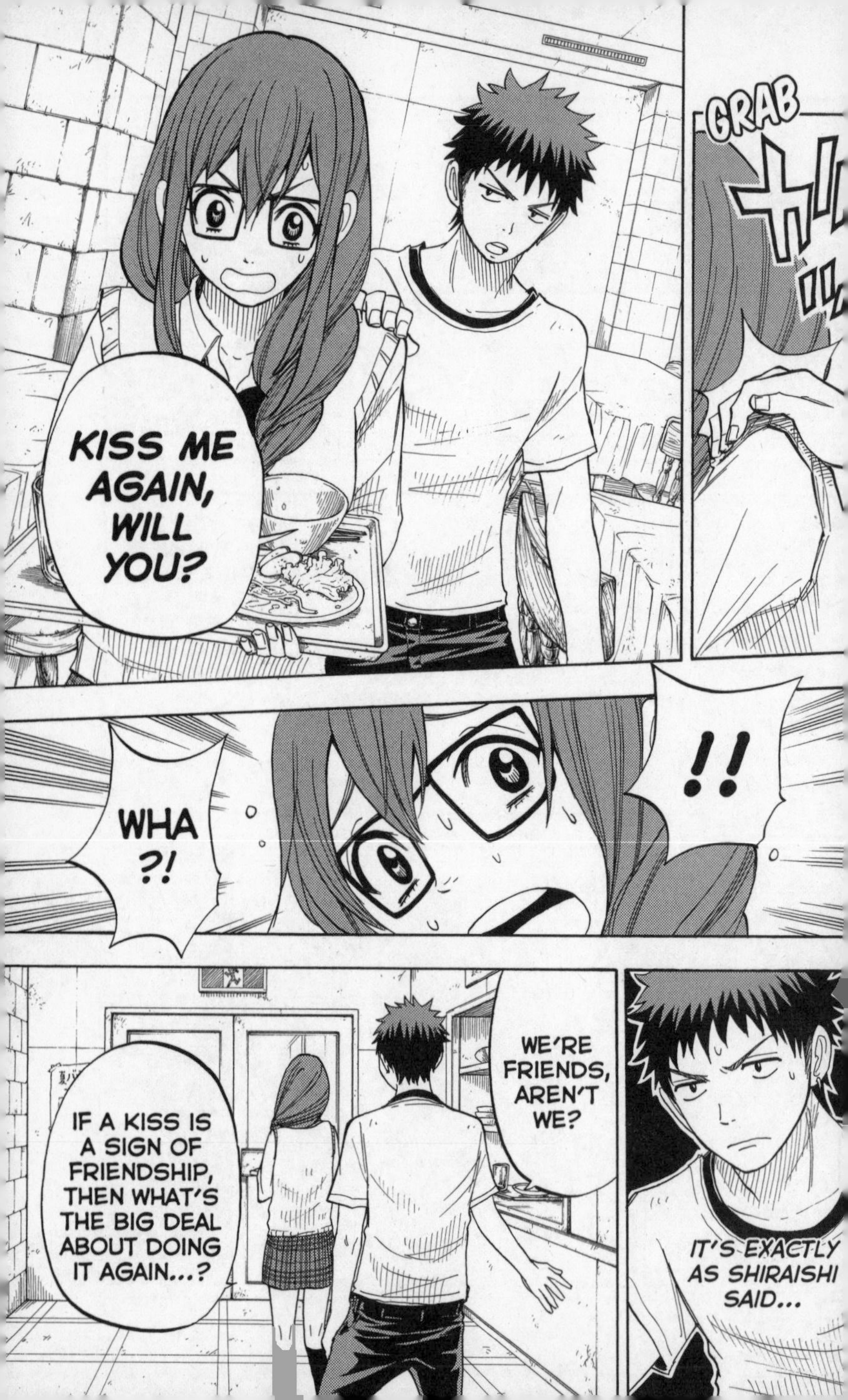
GRAB
KISS ME AGAIN, WILL YOU?
!!
WHA ?!
IT'S EXACTLY AS SHIRAISHI SAID...
WE'RE FRIENDS, AREN'T WE?
IF A KISS IS A SIGN OF FRIENDSHIP, THEN WHAT'S THE BIG DEAL ABOUT DOING IT AGAIN...?

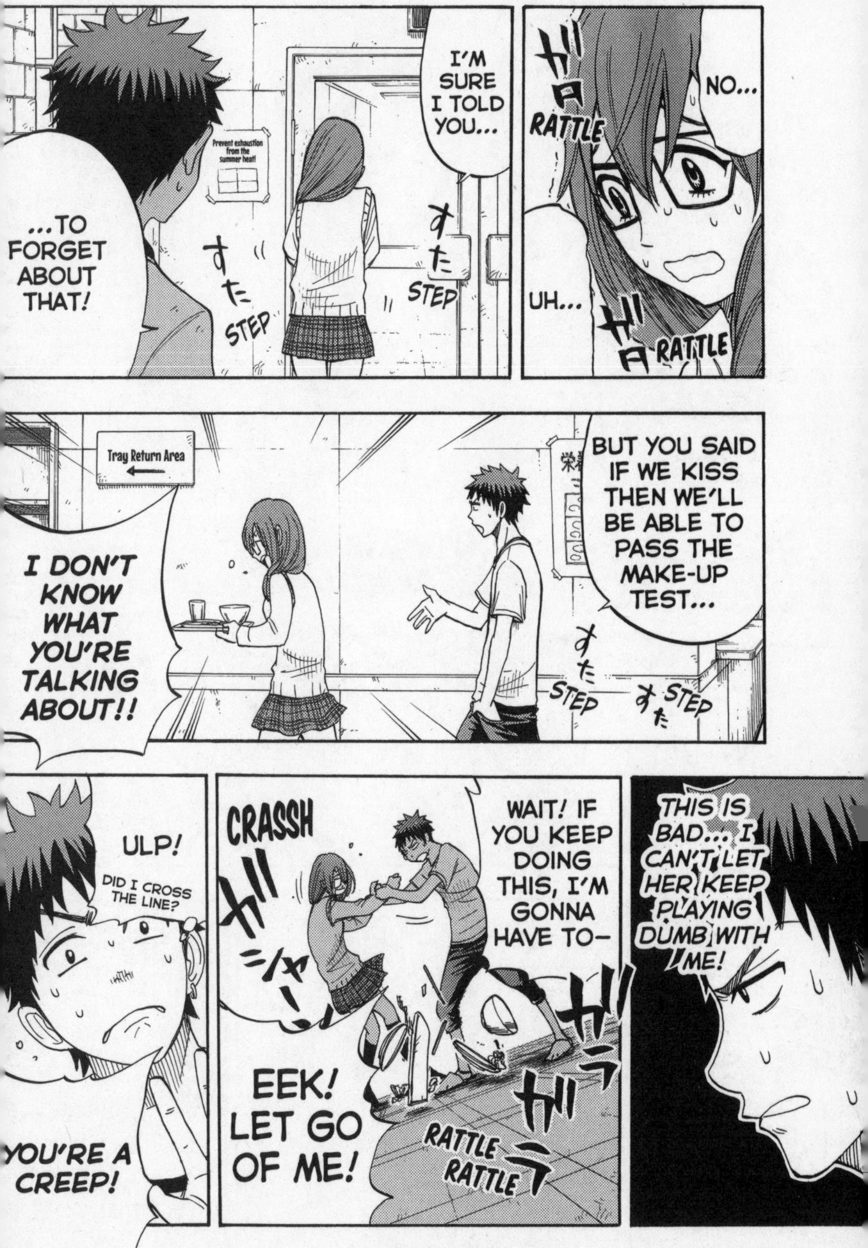

NO...
RATTLE
UH...
RATTLE
I'M SURE I TOLD YOU...
...TO FORGET ABOUT THAT!
Prevent exhaustion from the summer heat!
すた
STEP
すた
STEP
BUT YOU SAID IF WE KISS THEN WE'LL BE ABLE TO PASS THE MAKE-UP TEST...
I DON'T KNOW WHAT YOU'RE TALKING ABOUT!!
Tray Return Area
すた
STEP
すた
STEP
THIS IS BAD... I CAN'T LET HER KEEP PLAYING DUMB WITH ME!
WAIT! IF YOU KEEP DOING THIS, I'M GONNA HAVE TO—
CRASSH
EEK! LET GO OF ME!
RATTLE RATTLE
ULP!
DID I CROSS THE LINE?
YOU'RE A CREEP!

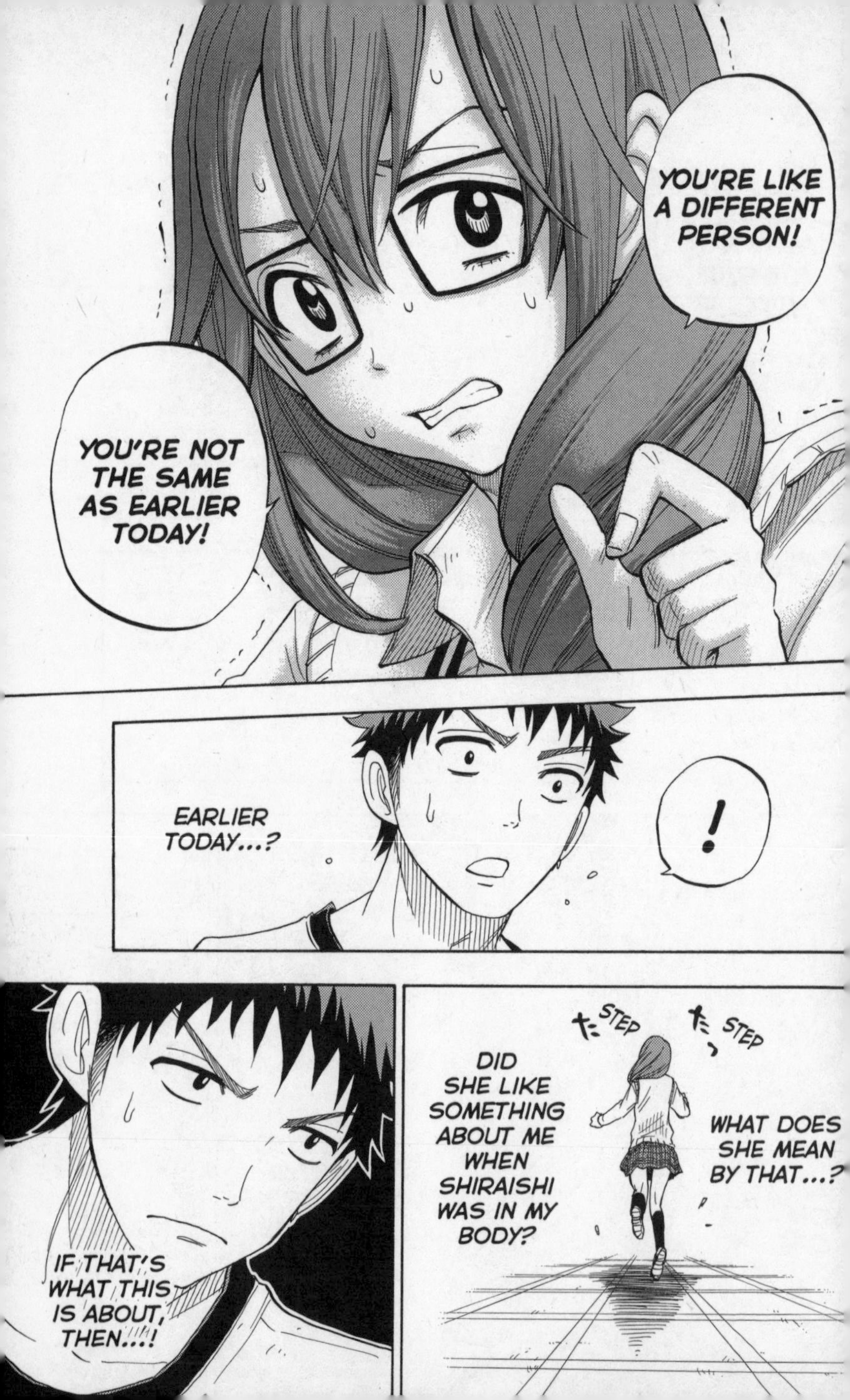
YOU'RE LIKE A DIFFERENT PERSON!
YOU'RE NOT THE SAME AS EARLIER TODAY!
!
EARLIER TODAY...?
STEP
STEP
WHAT DOES SHE MEAN BY THAT...?
DID SHE LIKE SOMETHING ABOUT ME WHEN SHIRAISHI WAS IN MY BODY?
IF THAT'S WHAT THIS IS ABOUT, THEN...!

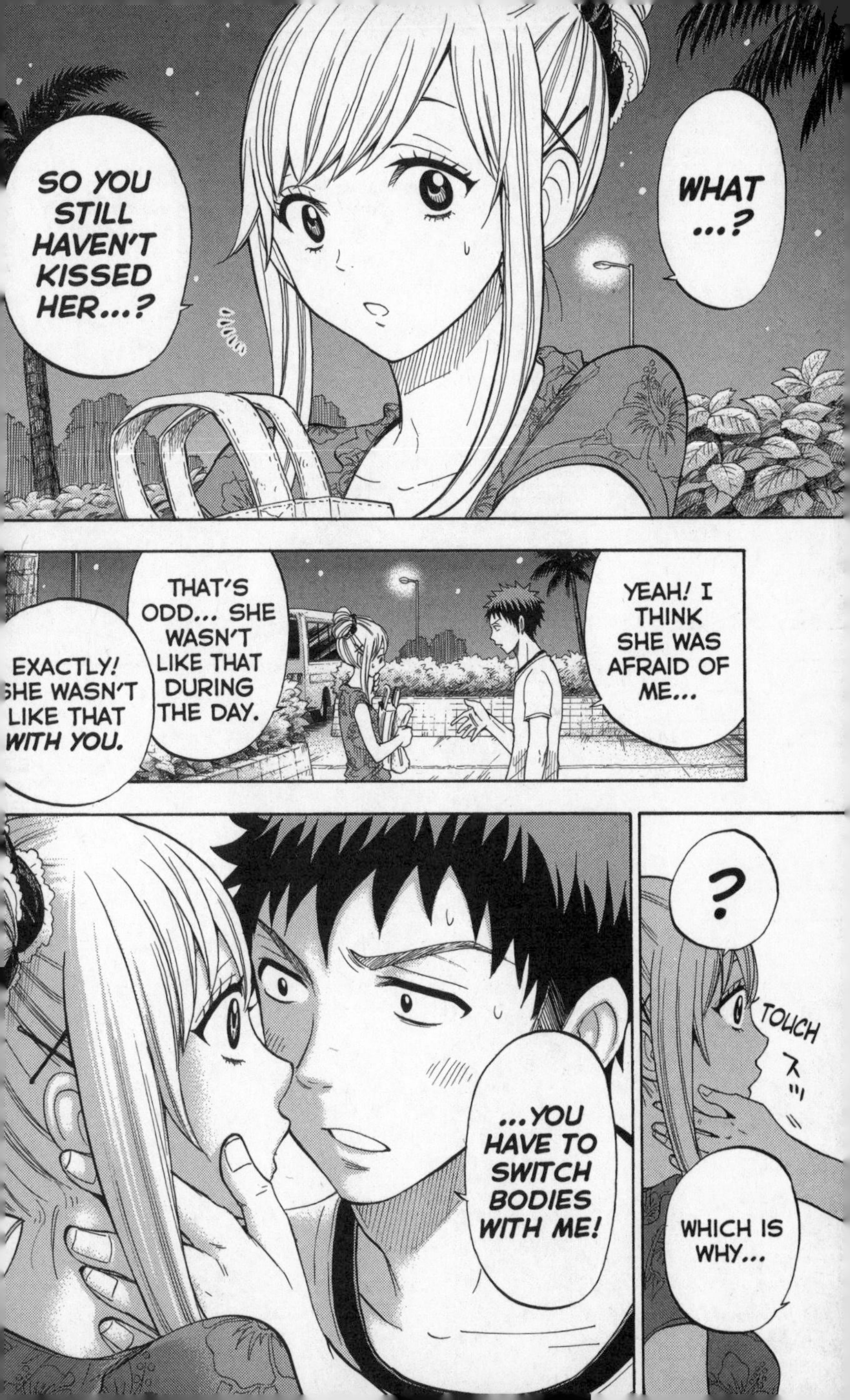
WHAT ...?
SO YOU STILL HAVEN'T KISSED HER...?
YEAH! I THINK SHE WAS AFRAID OF ME...
THAT'S ODD... SHE WASN'T LIKE THAT DURING THE DAY.
EXACTLY! SHE WASN'T LIKE THAT WITH YOU.
?
TOUCH
スッ
WHICH IS WHY...
...YOU HAVE TO SWITCH BODIES WITH ME!

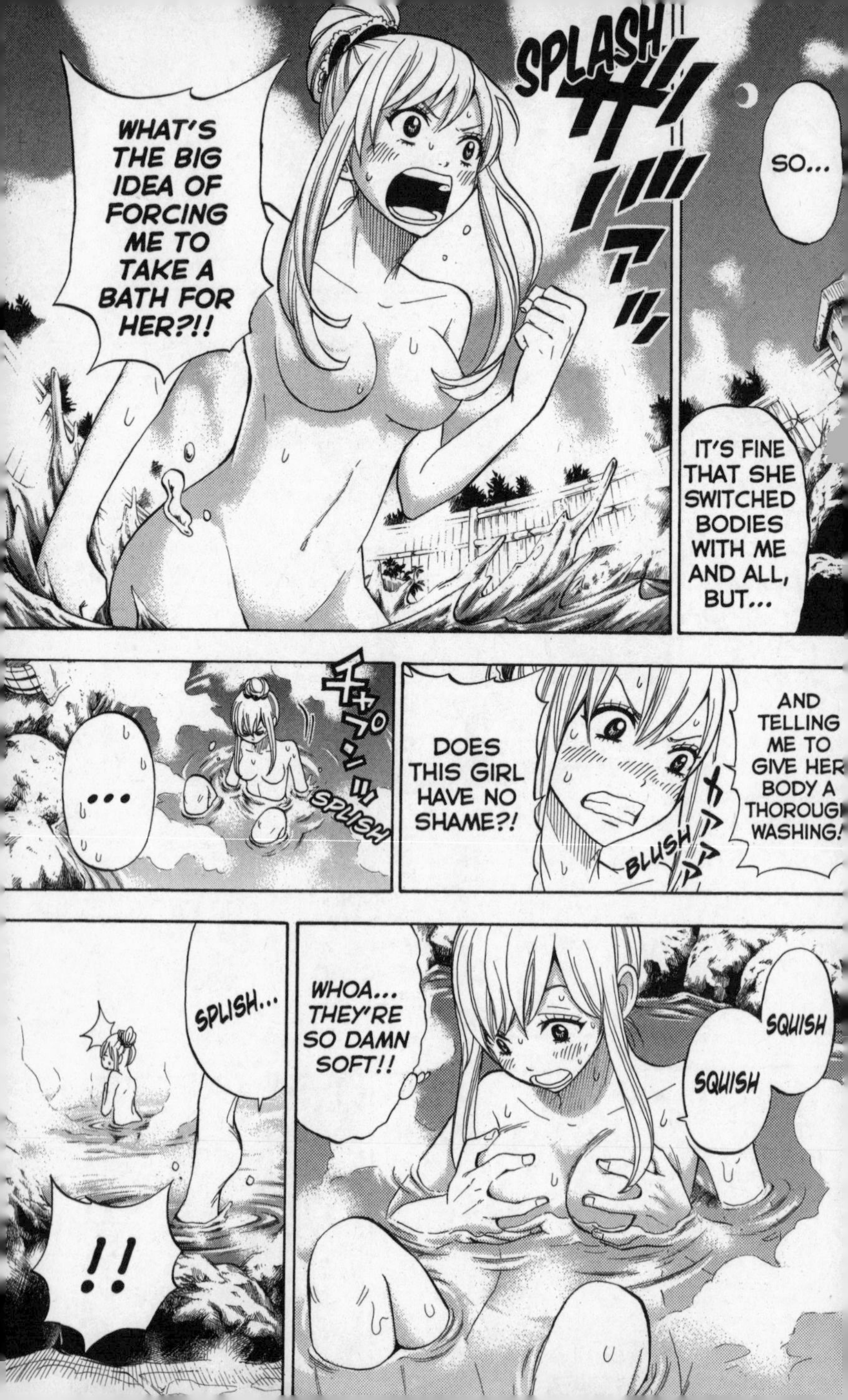
SO...
IT'S FINE THAT SHE SWITCHED BODIES WITH ME AND ALL, BUT...
SPLASH
WHAT'S THE BIG IDEA OF FORCING ME TO TAKE A BATH FOR HER?!!
AND TELLING ME TO GIVE HER BODY A THOROUG WASHING!
BLUSH
DOES THIS GIRL HAVE NO SHAME?!
SPLISH
...
SQUISH
SQUISH
WHOA... THEY'RE SO DAMN SOFT!!
SPLISH...
!!

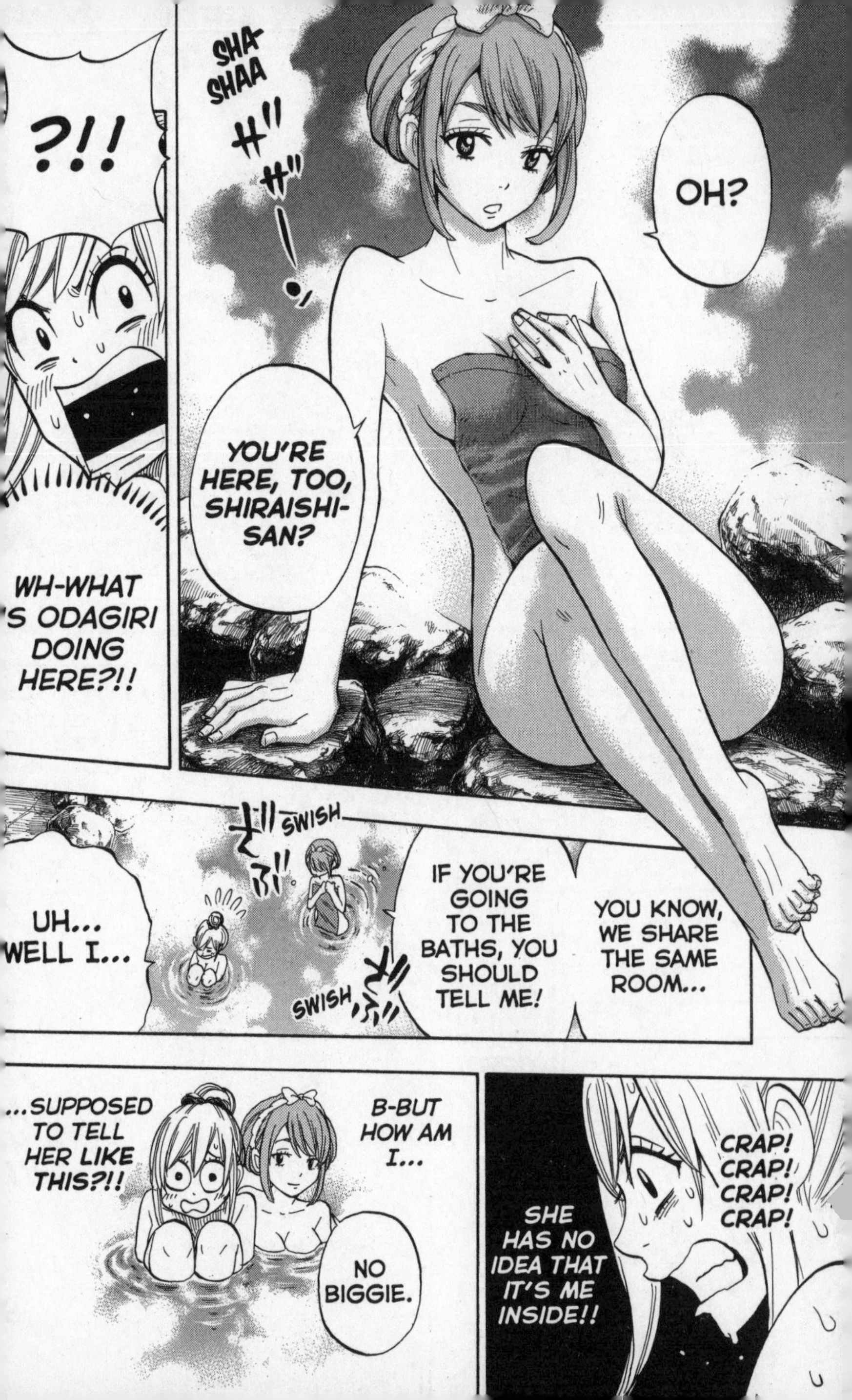
SHA SHAA
OH?
YOU'RE HERE, TOO, SHIRAISHI-SAN?
?!!
WH-WHAT 'S ODAGIRI DOING HERE?!!
YOU KNOW, WE SHARE THE SAME ROOM...
IF YOU'RE GOING TO THE BATHS, YOU SHOULD TELL ME!
SWISH
SWISH
UH... WELL I...
CRAP! CRAP! CRAP! CRAP!
SHE HAS NO IDEA THAT IT'S ME INSIDE!!
NO BIGGIE.
B-BUT HOW AM I...
...SUPPOSED TO TELL HER LIKE THIS?!!

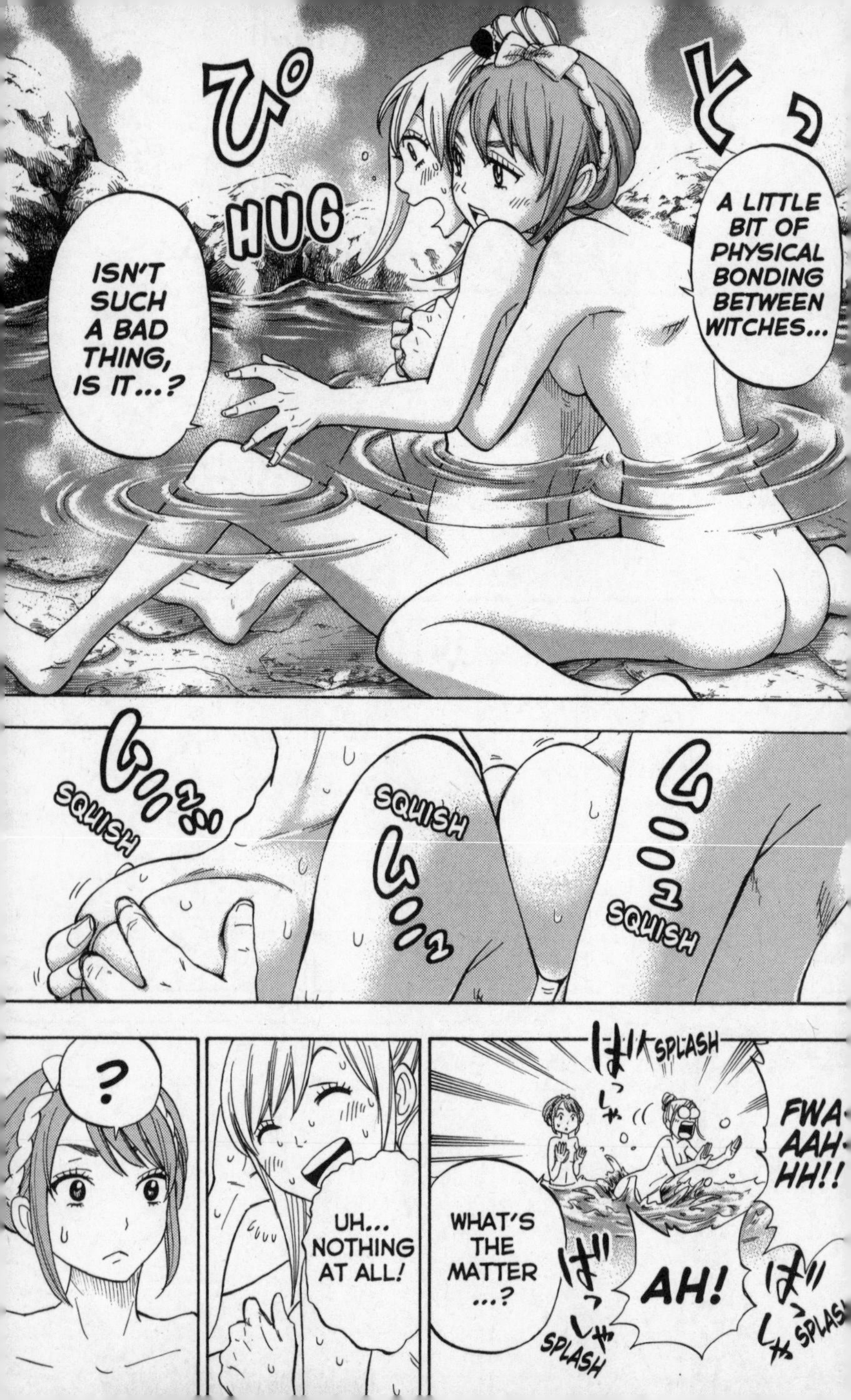
A LITTLE BIT OF PHYSICAL BONDING BETWEEN WITCHES...
HUG
ISN'T SUCH A BAD THING, IS IT...?
SQUISH
SQUISH
SQUISH
SPLASH
FWAAAHH!!
SPLASH
AH!
SPLASH
WHAT'S THE MATTER...?
UH... NOTHING AT ALL!
?

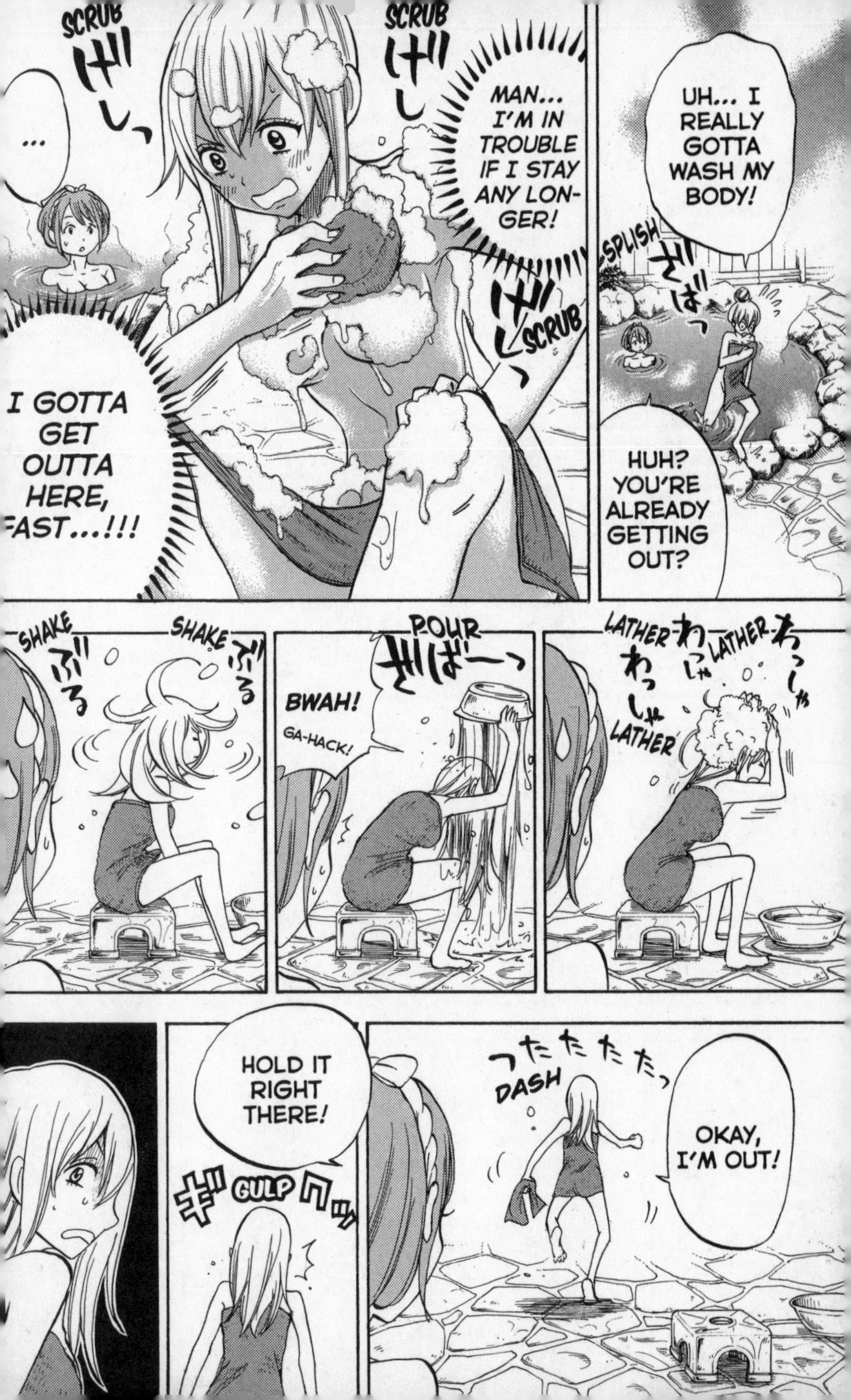

UH... I REALLY GOTTA WASH MY BODY!
SPLISH ざばっ
HUH? YOU'RE ALREADY GETTING OUT?
SCRUB げし
MAN... I'M IN TROUBLE IF I STAY ANY LONGER!
SCRUB げしっ
...
げしっ SCRUB
I GOTTA GET OUTTA HERE, FAST...!!!
LATHER わっしゃ
LATHER わっしゃ
LATHER わっしゃ
POUR ざばーっ
BWAH!
GA-HACK!
SHAKE ぶる
SHAKE ぶる
OKAY, I'M OUT!
つたたたたっ DASH
HOLD IT RIGHT THERE!
ギクッ GULP

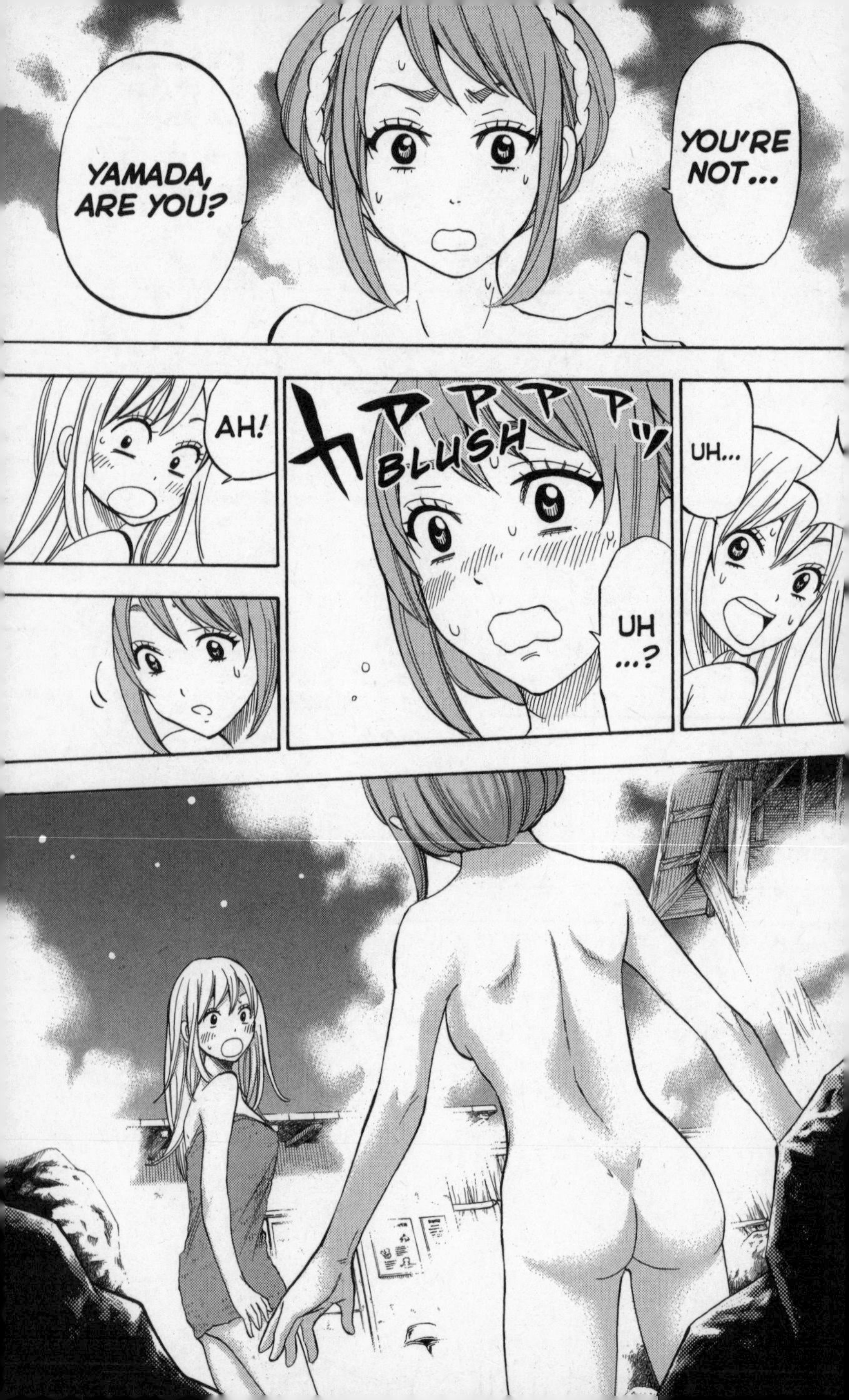
YOU'RE NOT...
YAMADA, ARE YOU?
UH...
カァァァァッ
BLUSH
UH ...?
AH!

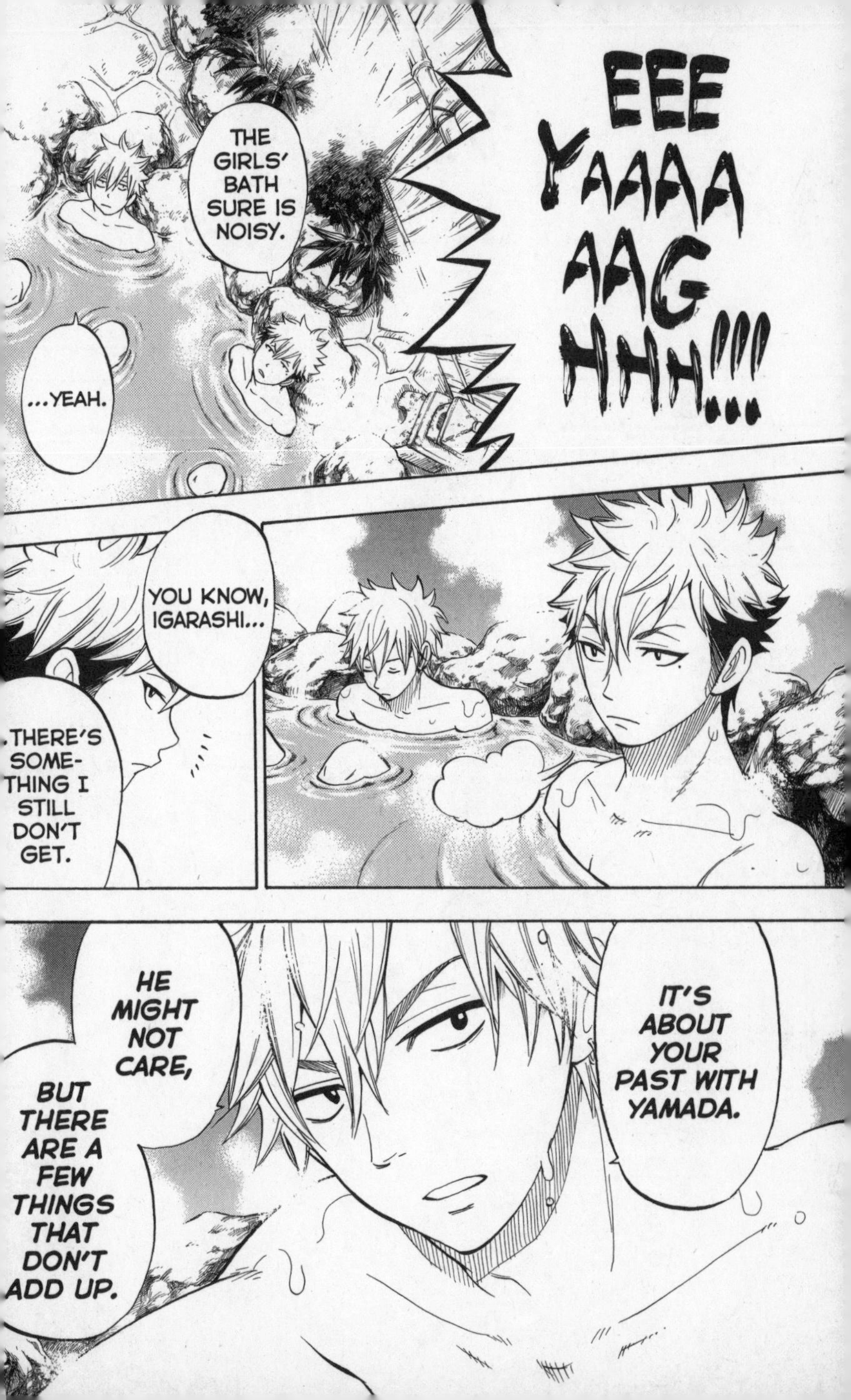
EEE YAAAA AAG HHH!!!
THE GIRLS' BATH SURE IS NOISY.
...YEAH.
YOU KNOW, IGARASHI...
...THERE'S SOME-THING I STILL DON'T GET.
IT'S ABOUT YOUR PAST WITH YAMADA.
HE MIGHT NOT CARE,
BUT THERE ARE A FEW THINGS THAT DON'T ADD UP.

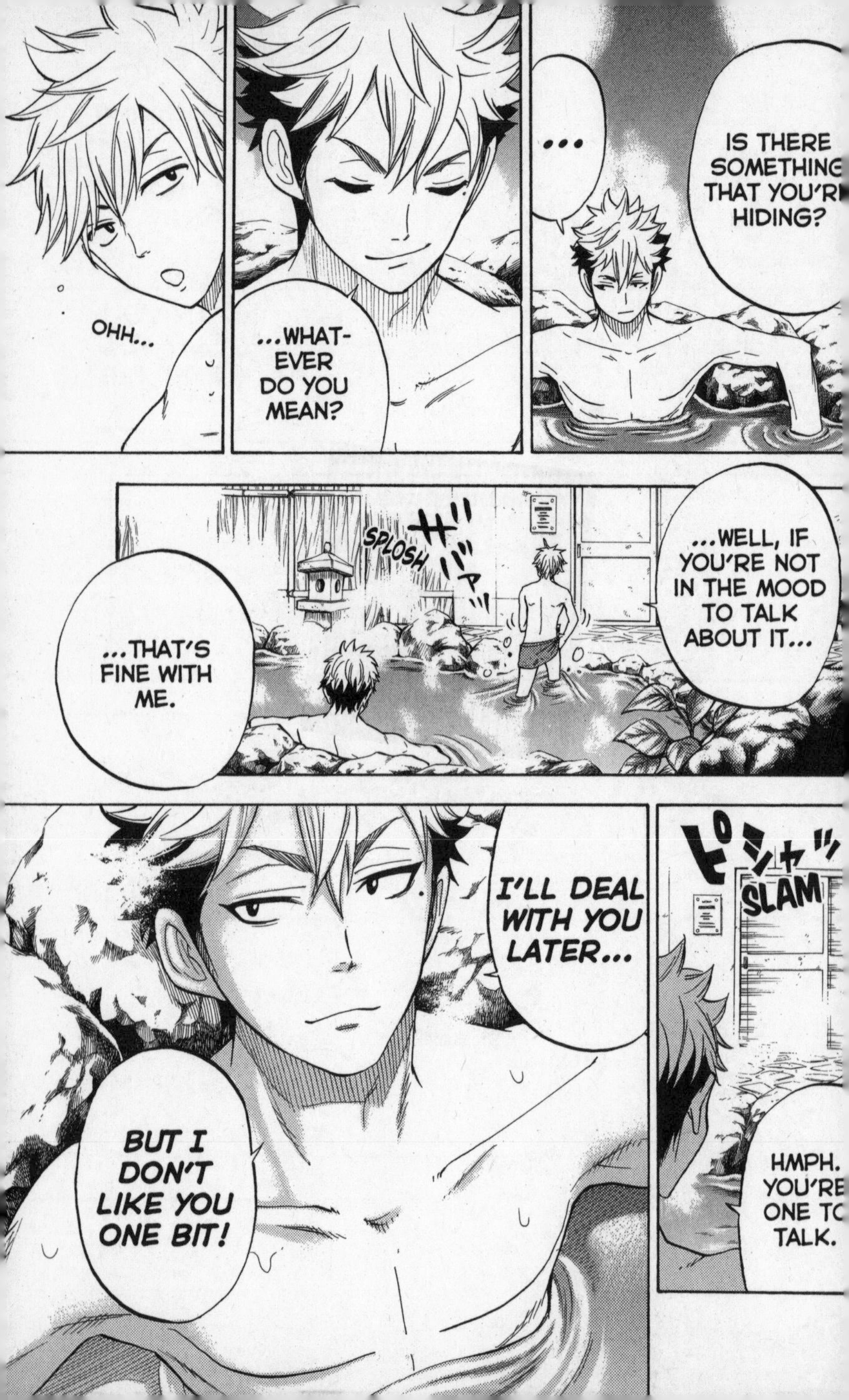
IS THERE SOMETHING THAT YOU'RE HIDING?
...
...WHAT-EVER DO YOU MEAN?
OHH...
...WELL, IF YOU'RE NOT IN THE MOOD TO TALK ABOUT IT...
ザバァッ
SPLOSH
...THAT'S FINE WITH ME.
ピシャッ
SLAM
HMPH. YOU'RE ONE TO TALK.
I'LL DEAL WITH YOU LATER...
BUT I DON'T LIKE YOU ONE BIT!

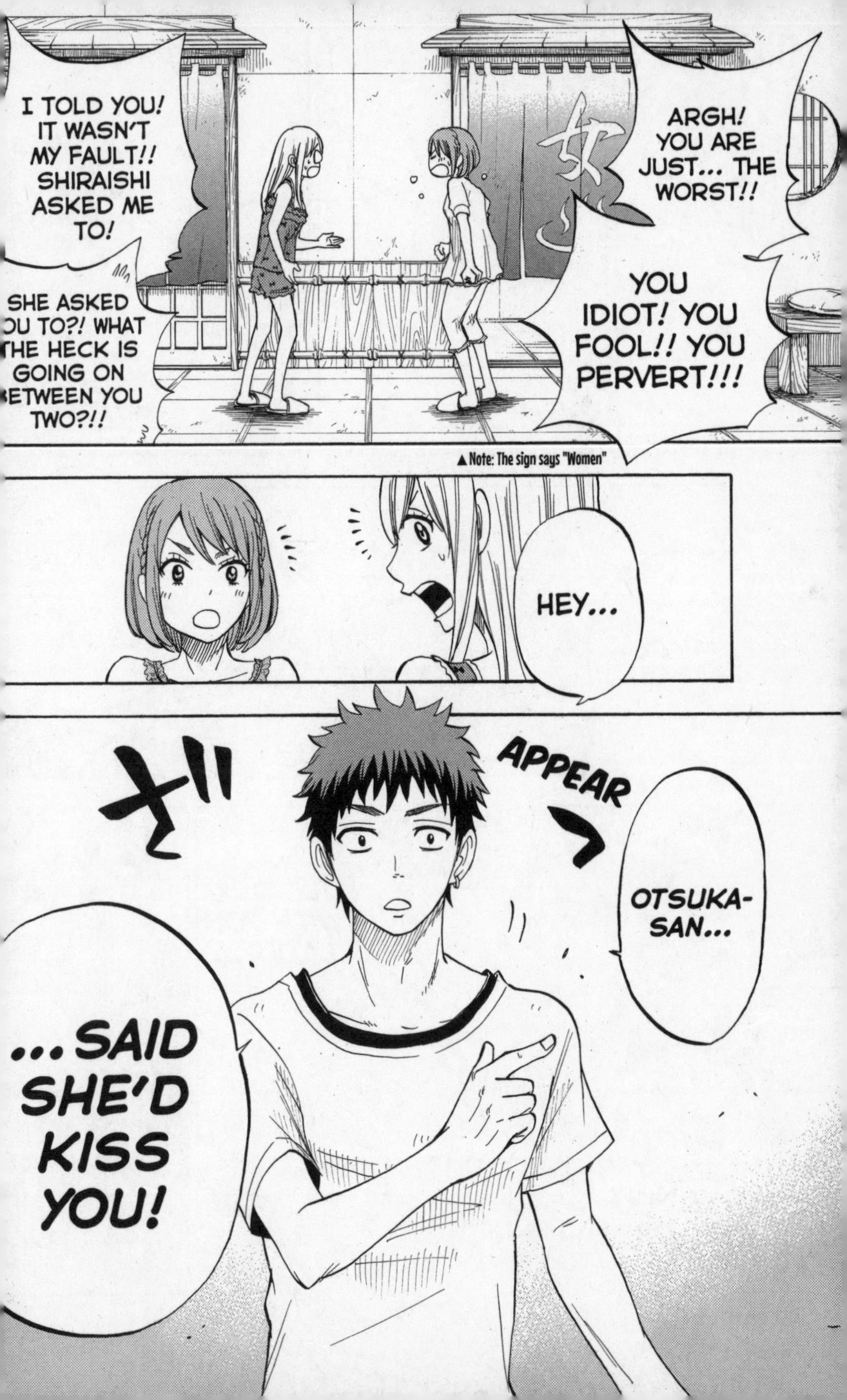
ARGH! YOU ARE JUST... THE WORST!!
YOU IDIOT! YOU FOOL!! YOU PERVERT!!!
I TOLD YOU! IT WASN'T MY FAULT!! SHIRAISHI ASKED ME TO!
SHE ASKED OU TO?! WHAT THE HECK IS GOING ON ETWEEN YOU TWO?!!
HEY...
APPEAR
OTSUKA-SAN...
...SAID SHE'D KISS YOU!
▲Note: The sign says "Women"

CHAPTER 29: Time to whip you into shape, Yamada!!

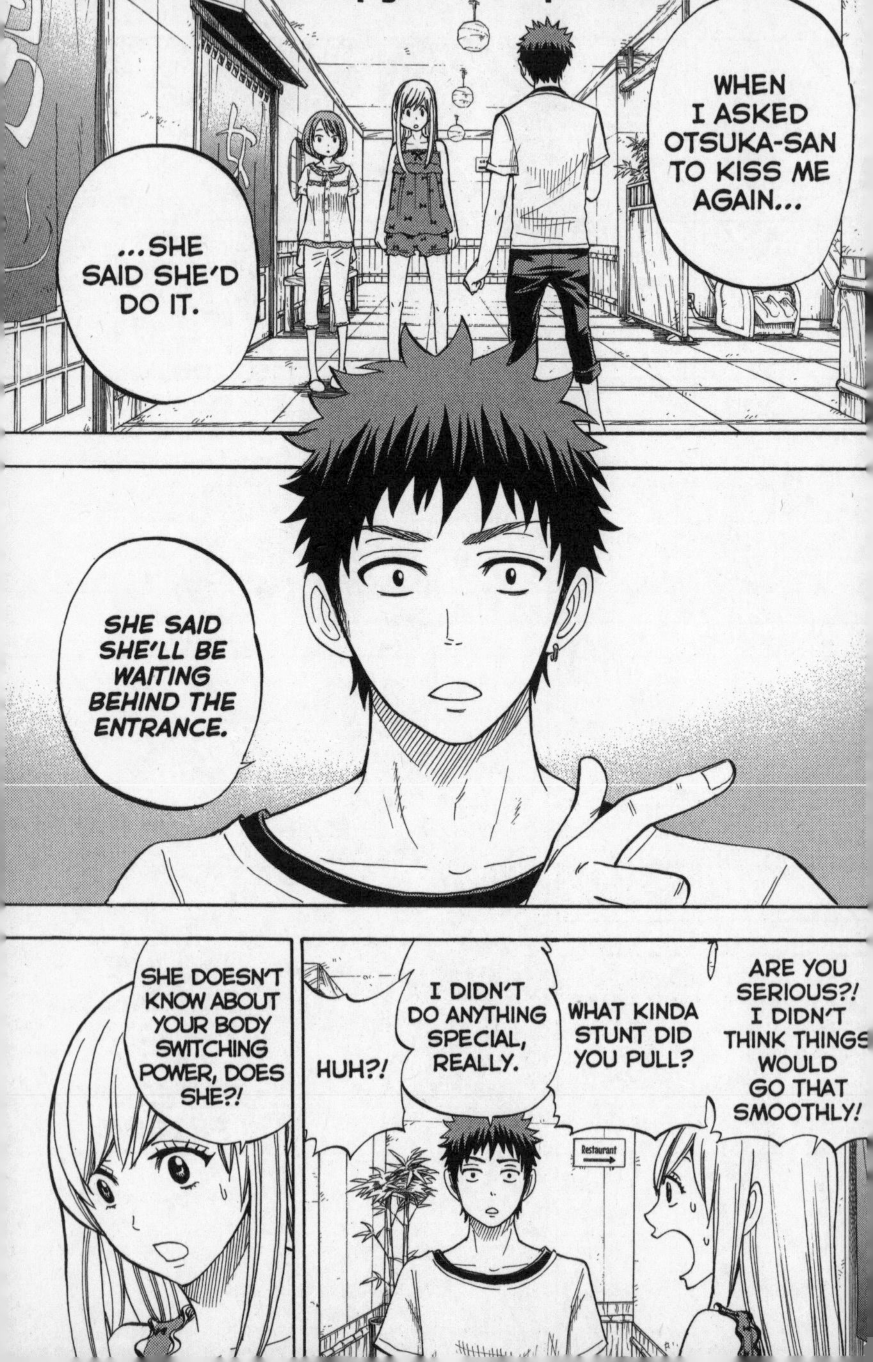
WHEN I ASKED OTSUKA-SAN TO KISS ME AGAIN...
...SHE SAID SHE'D DO IT.
SHE SAID SHE'LL BE WAITING BEHIND THE ENTRANCE.
ARE YOU SERIOUS?! I DIDN'T THINK THINGS WOULD GO THAT SMOOTHLY!
WHAT KINDA STUNT DID YOU PULL?
I DIDN'T DO ANYTHING SPECIAL, REALLY.
HUH?!
Restaurant
SHE DOESN'T KNOW ABOUT YOUR BODY SWITCHING POWER, DOES SHE?!

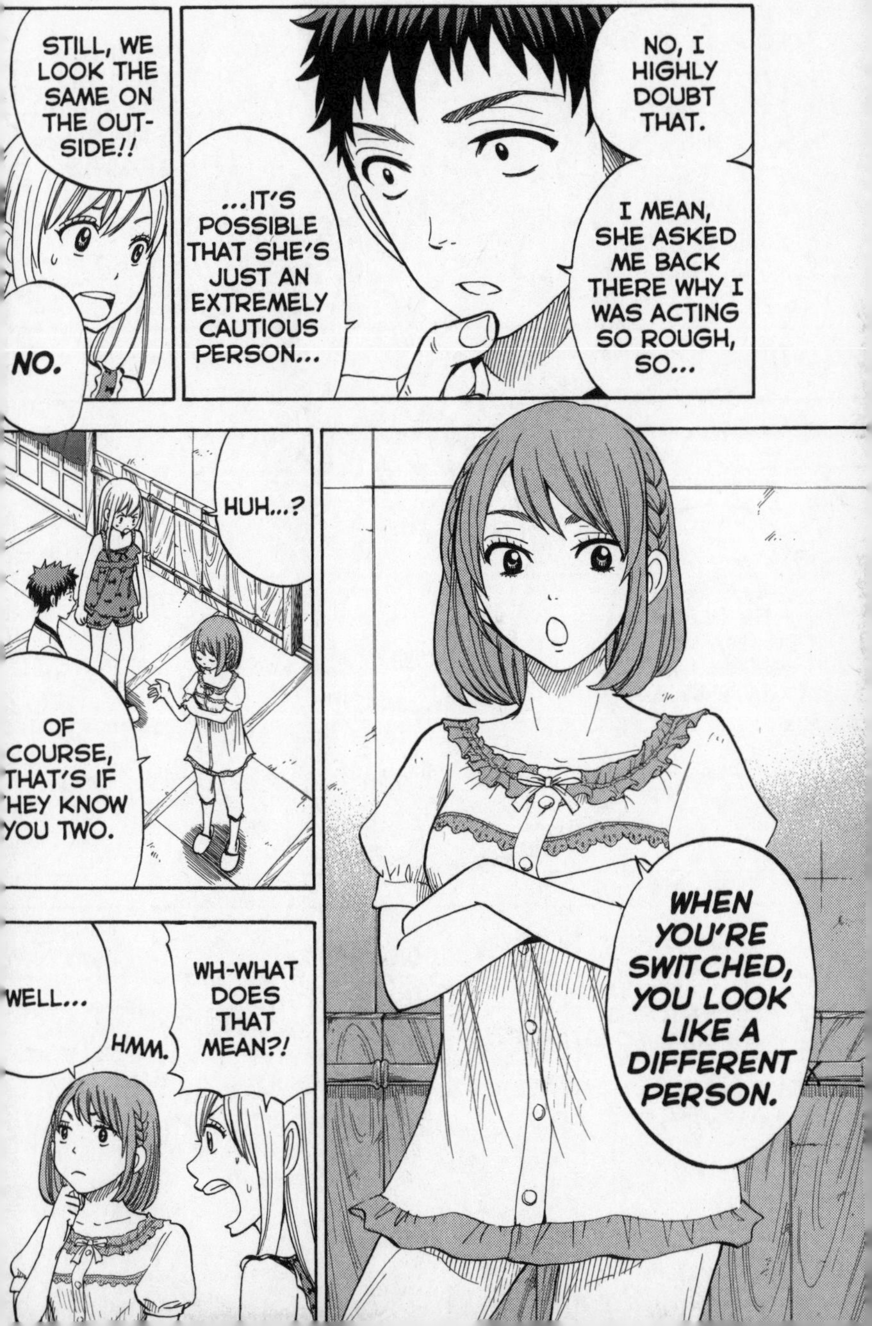
NO, I HIGHLY DOUBT THAT.
I MEAN, SHE ASKED ME BACK THERE WHY I WAS ACTING SO ROUGH, SO...
...IT'S POSSIBLE THAT SHE'S JUST AN EXTREMELY CAUTIOUS PERSON...
STILL, WE LOOK THE SAME ON THE OUT-SIDE!!
NO.
WHEN YOU'RE SWITCHED, YOU LOOK LIKE A DIFFERENT PERSON.
HUH...?
OF COURSE, THAT'S IF HEY KNOW YOU TWO.
WH-WHAT DOES THAT MEAN?!
HMM.
WELL...

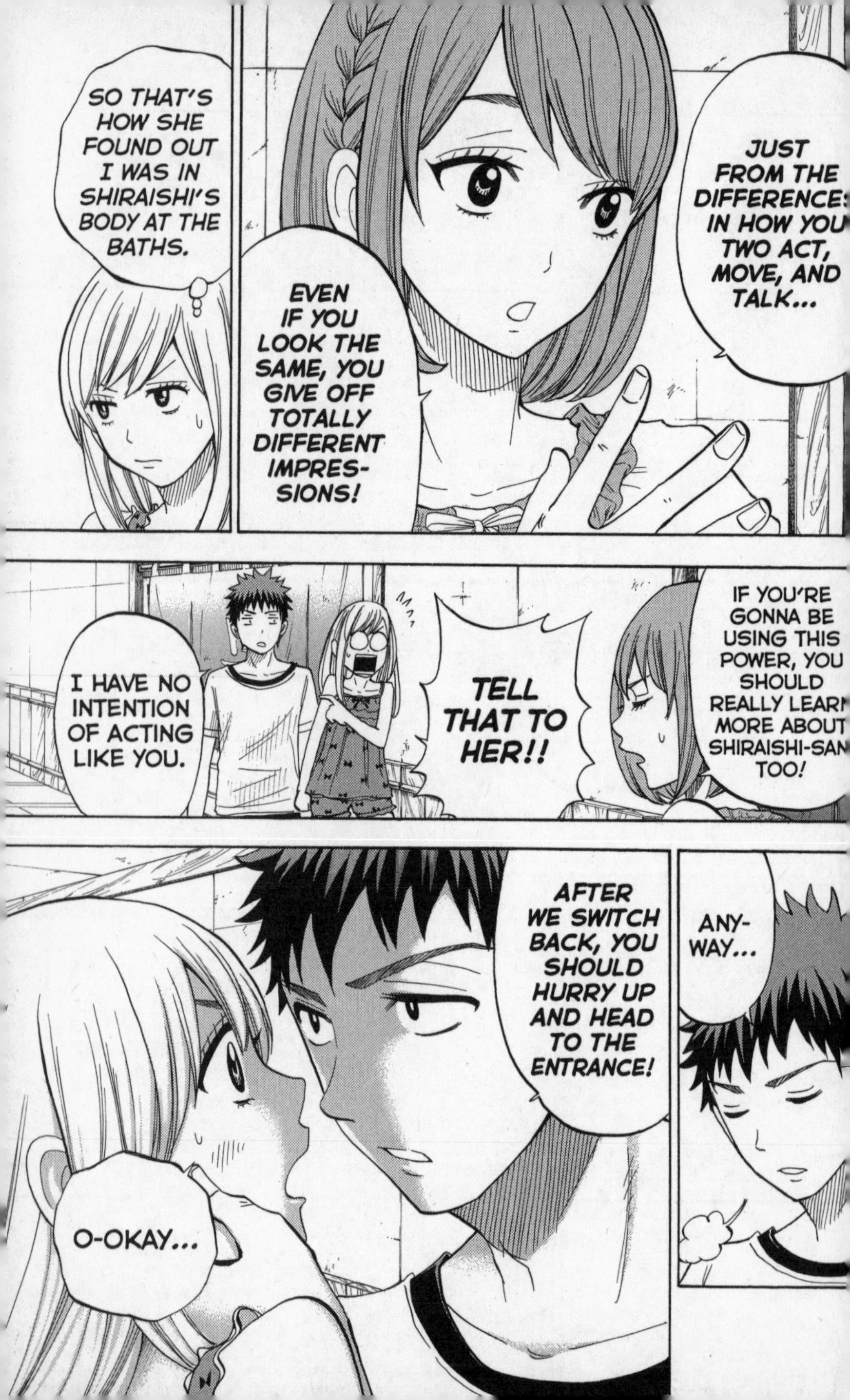
JUST FROM THE DIFFERENCES IN HOW YOU TWO ACT, MOVE, AND TALK...
EVEN IF YOU LOOK THE SAME, YOU GIVE OFF TOTALLY DIFFERENT IMPRES-SIONS!
SO THAT'S HOW SHE FOUND OUT I WAS IN SHIRAISHI'S BODY AT THE BATHS.
IF YOU'RE GONNA BE USING THIS POWER, YOU SHOULD REALLY LEARN MORE ABOUT SHIRAISHI-SAN TOO!
TELL THAT TO HER!!
I HAVE NO INTENTION OF ACTING LIKE YOU.
ANY-WAY...
AFTER WE SWITCH BACK, YOU SHOULD HURRY UP AND HEAD TO THE ENTRANCE!
O-OKAY...

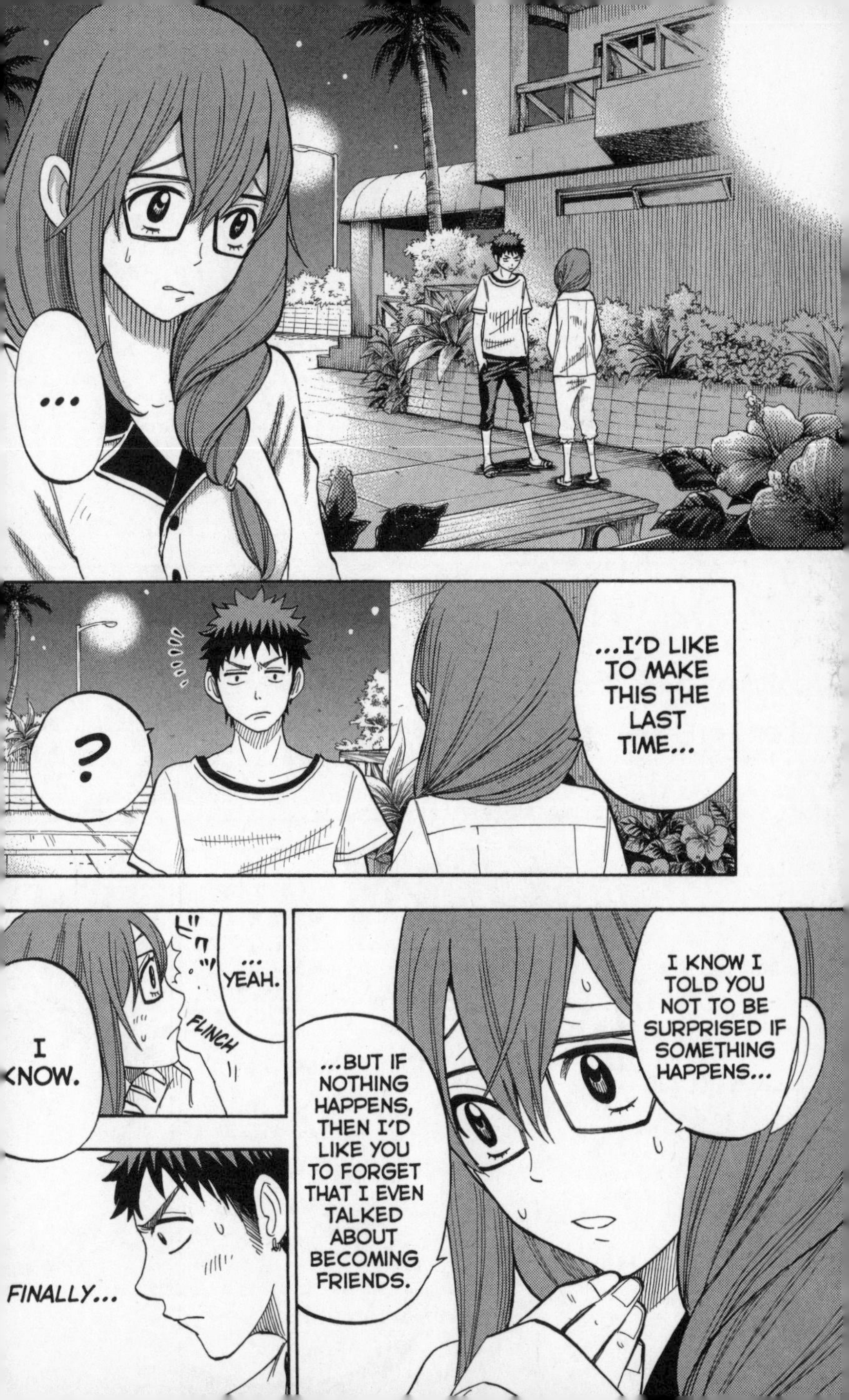
...
...I'D LIKE TO MAKE THIS THE LAST TIME...
?
I KNOW I TOLD YOU NOT TO BE SURPRISED IF SOMETHING HAPPENS...
...BUT IF NOTHING HAPPENS, THEN I'D LIKE YOU TO FORGET THAT I EVEN TALKED ABOUT BECOMING FRIENDS.
... YEAH.
FLINCH
I KNOW.
FINALLY...

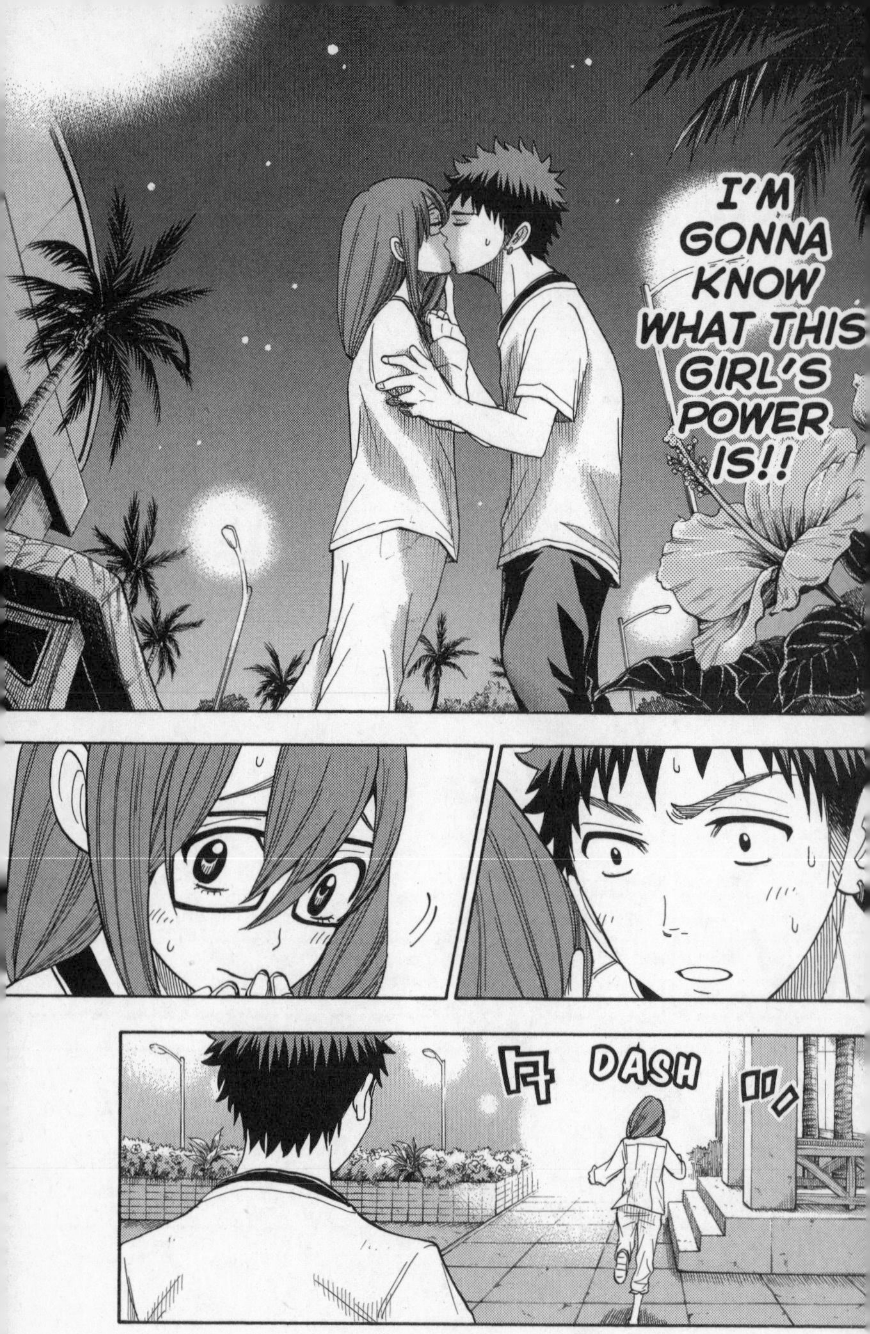
I'M GONNA KNOW WHAT THIS GIRL'S POWER IS!!
DASH

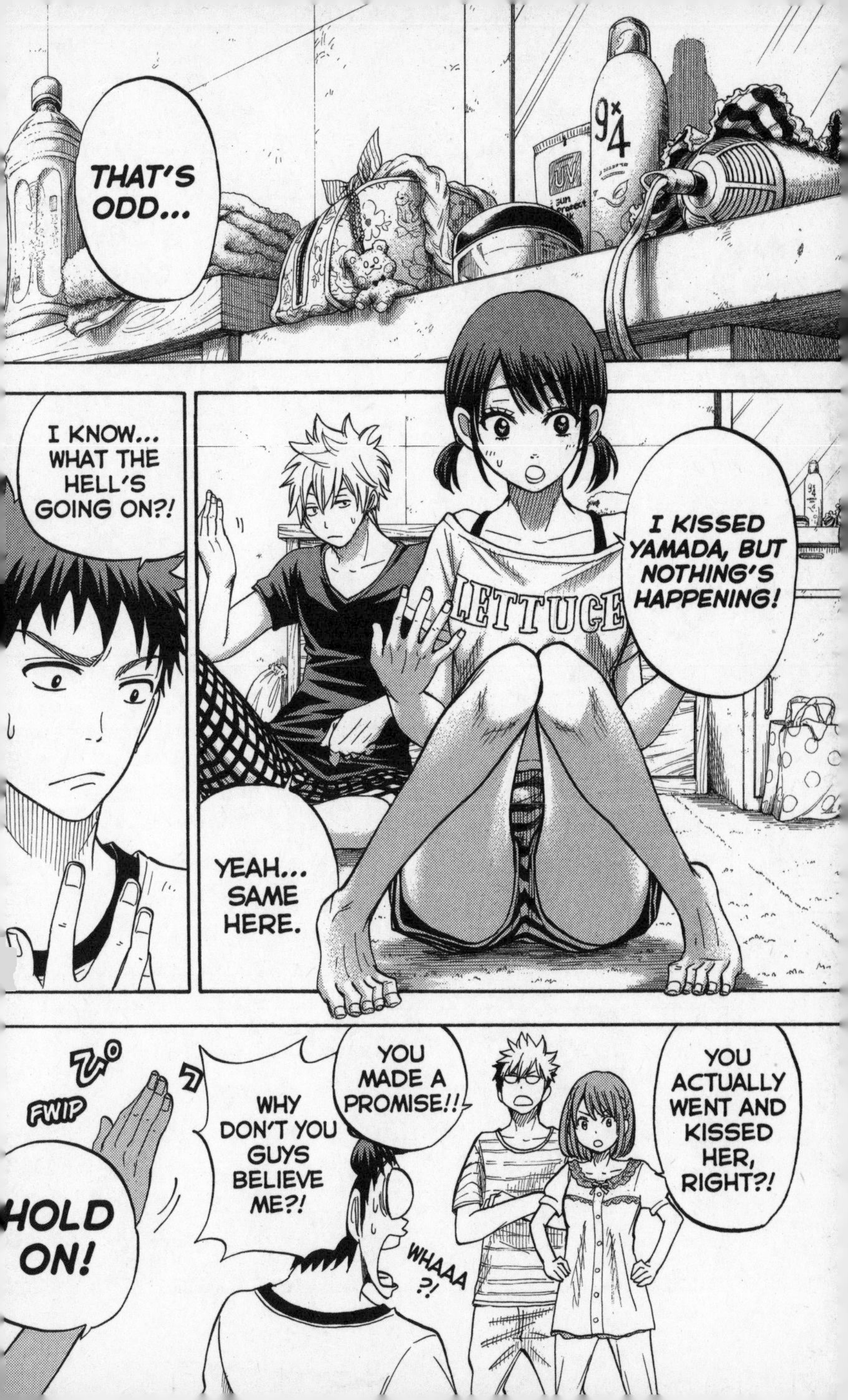
THAT'S ODD...
I KISSED YAMADA, BUT NOTHING'S HAPPENING!
YEAH... SAME HERE.
I KNOW... WHAT THE HELL'S GOING ON?!
YOU ACTUALLY WENT AND KISSED HER, RIGHT?!
YOU MADE A PROMISE!!
WHAAA ?!
WHY DON'T YOU GUYS BELIEVE ME?!
FWIP
HOLD ON!

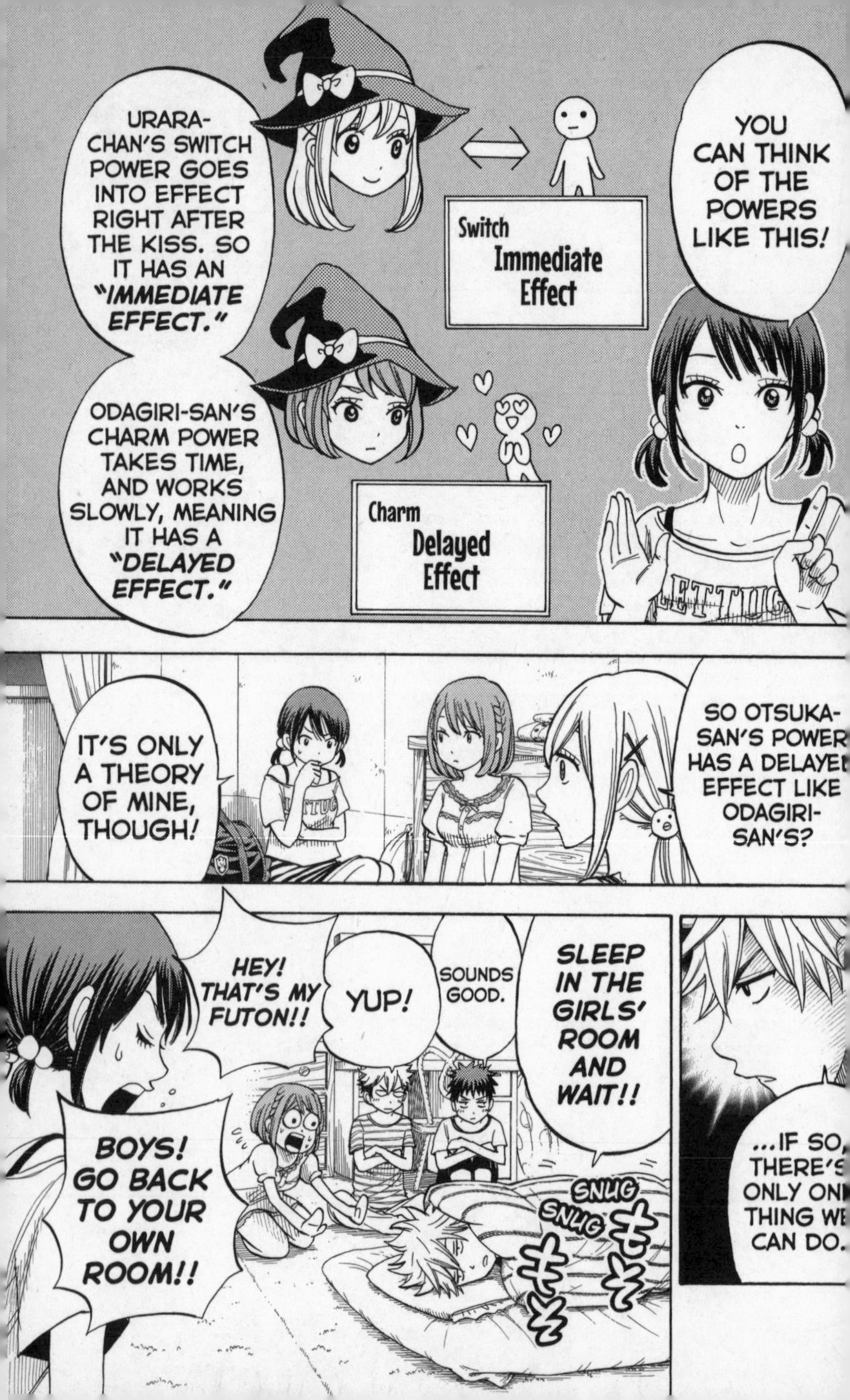
YOU CAN THINK OF THE POWERS LIKE THIS!
URARA-CHAN'S SWITCH POWER GOES INTO EFFECT RIGHT AFTER THE KISS. SO IT HAS AN "IMMEDIATE EFFECT."
Switch
Immediate Effect
ODAGIRI-SAN'S CHARM POWER TAKES TIME, AND WORKS SLOWLY, MEANING IT HAS A "DELAYED EFFECT."
Charm
Delayed Effect
SO OTSUKA-SAN'S POWER HAS A DELAYE EFFECT LIKE ODAGIRI-SAN'S?
IT'S ONLY A THEORY OF MINE, THOUGH!
...IF SO, THERE'S ONLY ON THING WE CAN DO.
SLEEP IN THE GIRLS' ROOM AND WAIT!!
SOUNDS GOOD.
YUP!
HEY! THAT'S MY FUTON!!
SNUG SNUG
BOYS! GO BACK TO YOUR OWN ROOM!!

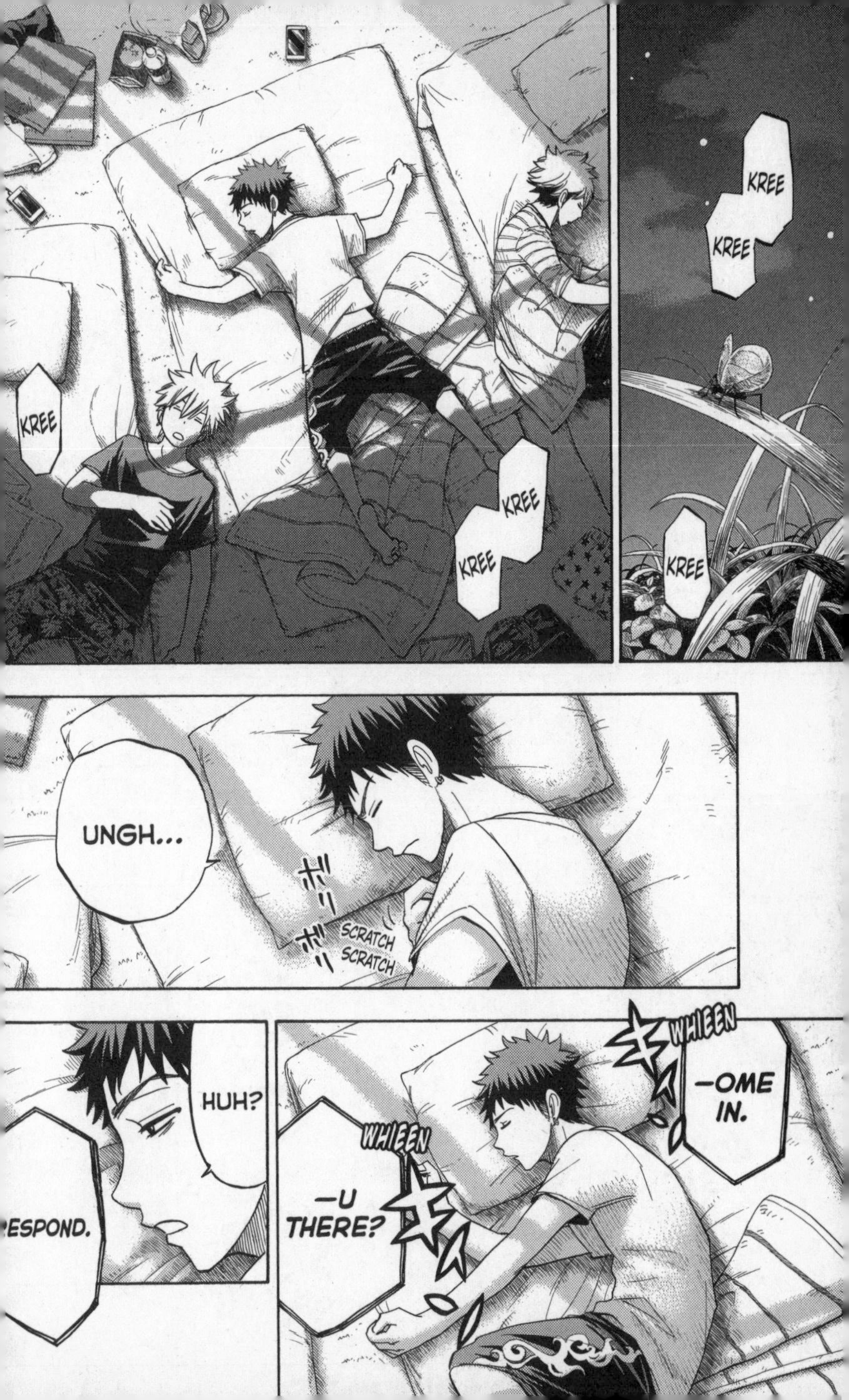

KREE
KREE
KREE
KREE
KREE
KREE
UNGH...
ボリボリ
SCRATCH SCRATCH
WHIEEN
—OME IN.
WHIEEN
—U THERE?
HUH?
ESPOND.

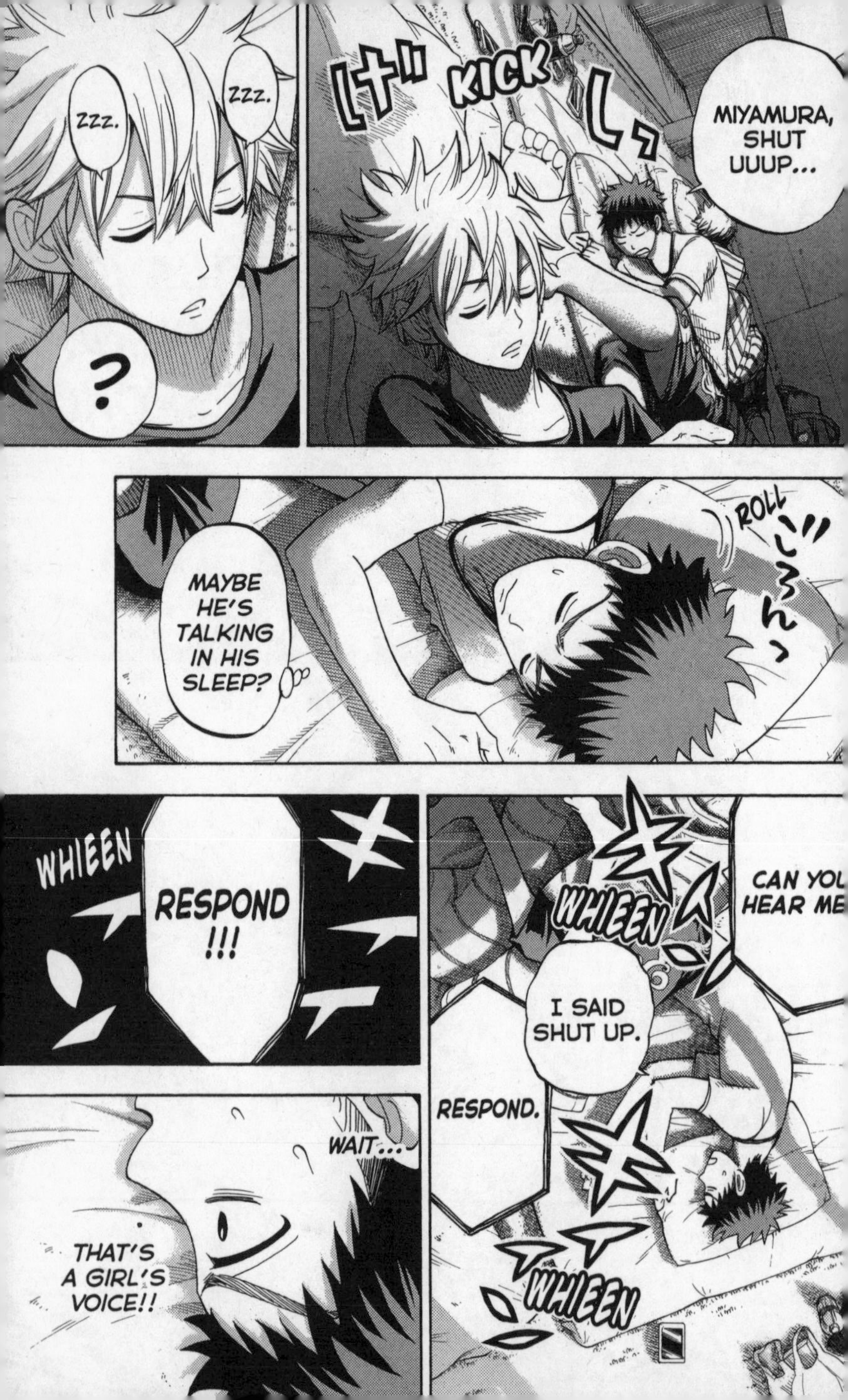

MIYAMURA, SHUT UUUP...
KICK
ZZZ.
ZZZ.
?
ROLL
MAYBE HE'S TALKING IN HIS SLEEP?
CAN YOU HEAR ME
WHIEEN
I SAID SHUT UP.
RESPOND.
WHIEEN
WHIEEN
RESPOND!!!
WAIT...
THAT'S A GIRL'S VOICE!!

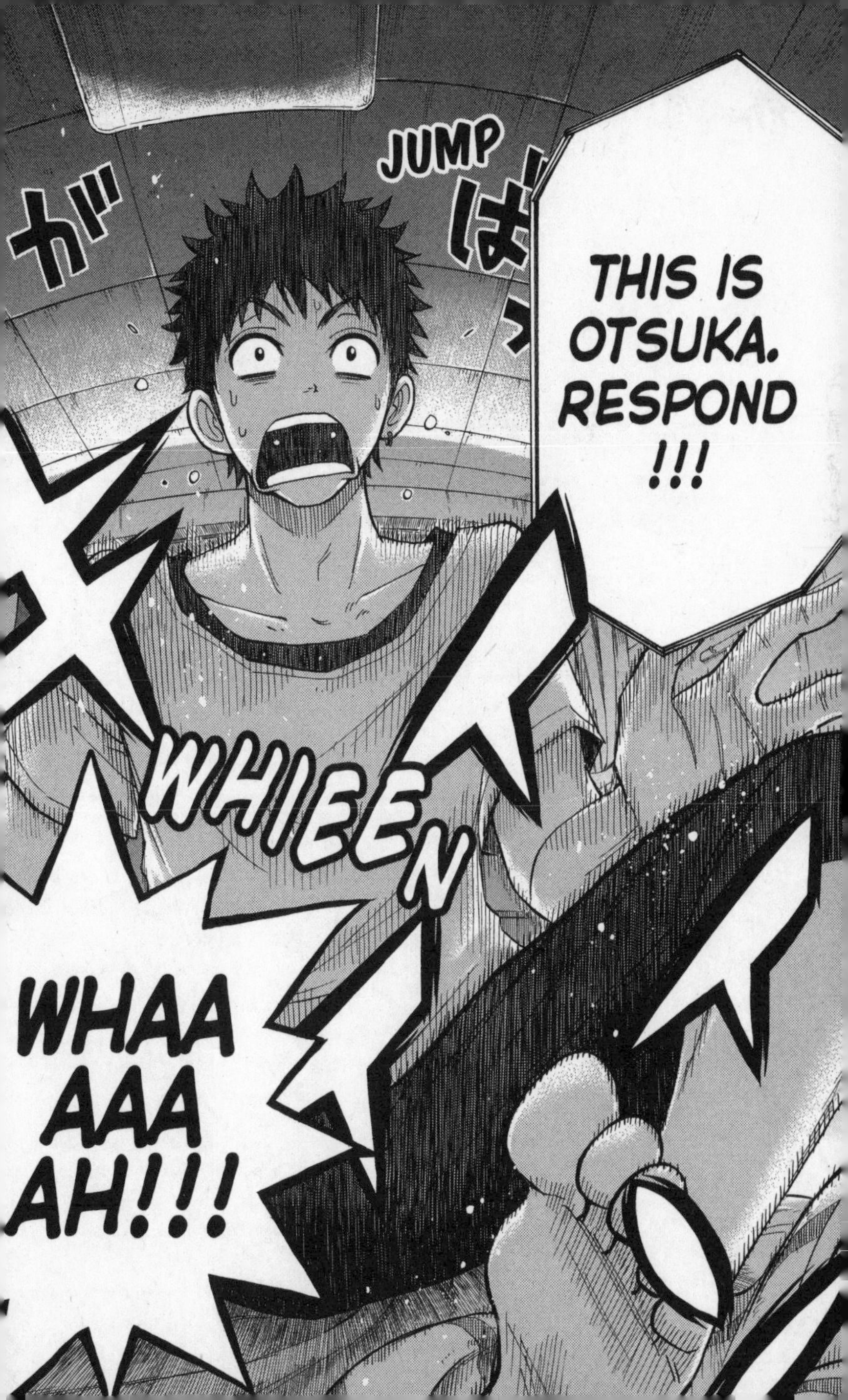
THIS IS OTSUKA. RESPOND !!!
JUMP
ば
ガ
WHIEEN
WHAAAAAAH!!!

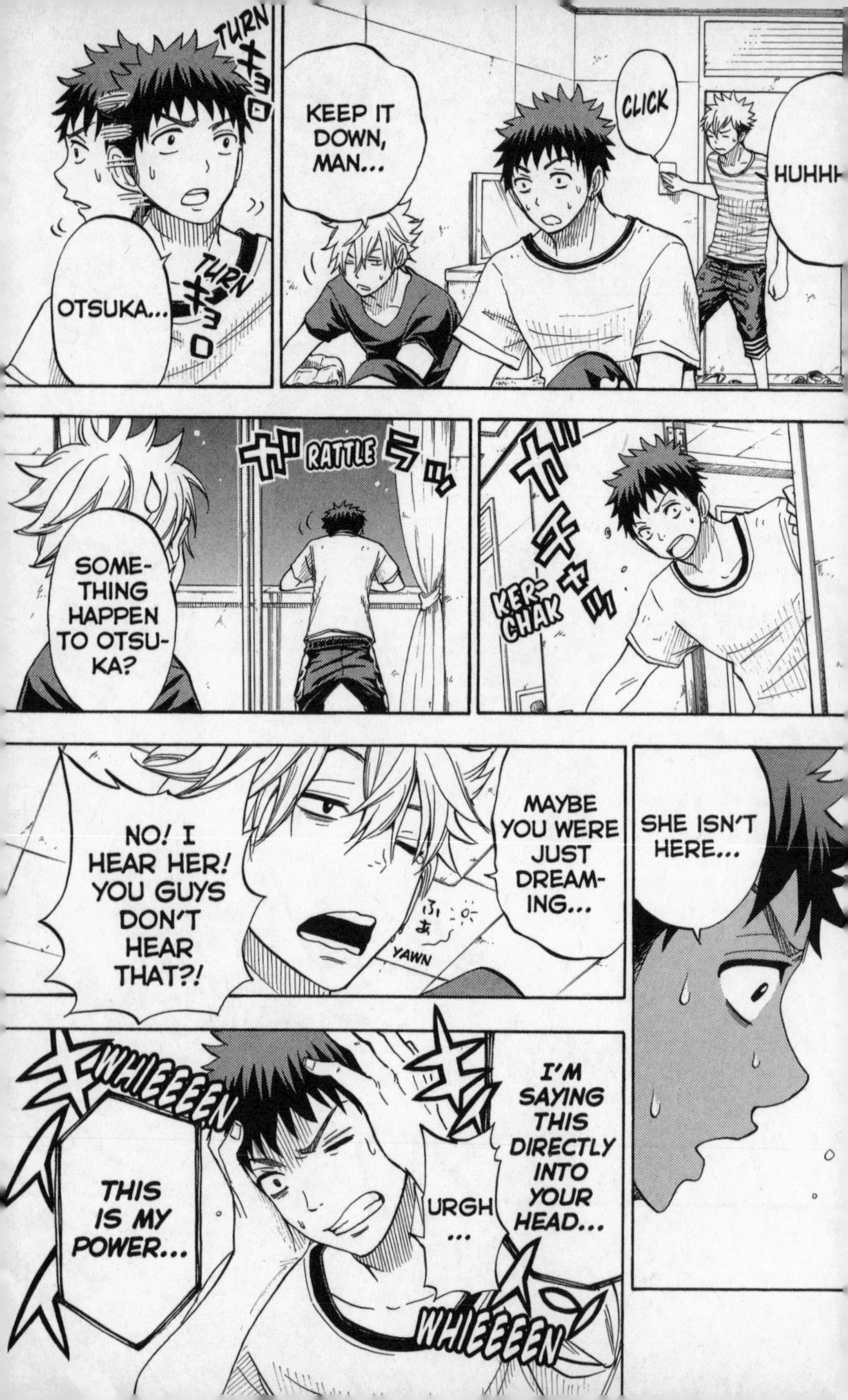
HUHHH
CLICK
KEEP IT DOWN, MAN...
TURN キョロ
OTSUKA...
TURN キョロ
KER-CHAK
RATTLE
SOME-THING HAPPEN TO OTSU-KA?
SHE ISN'T HERE...
MAYBE YOU WERE JUST DREAM-ING...
ふぁ YAWN
NO! I HEAR HER! YOU GUYS DON'T HEAR THAT?!
I'M SAYING THIS DIRECTLY INTO YOUR HEAD...
WHIEEEEN
URGH...
THIS IS MY POWER...
WHIEEEEN

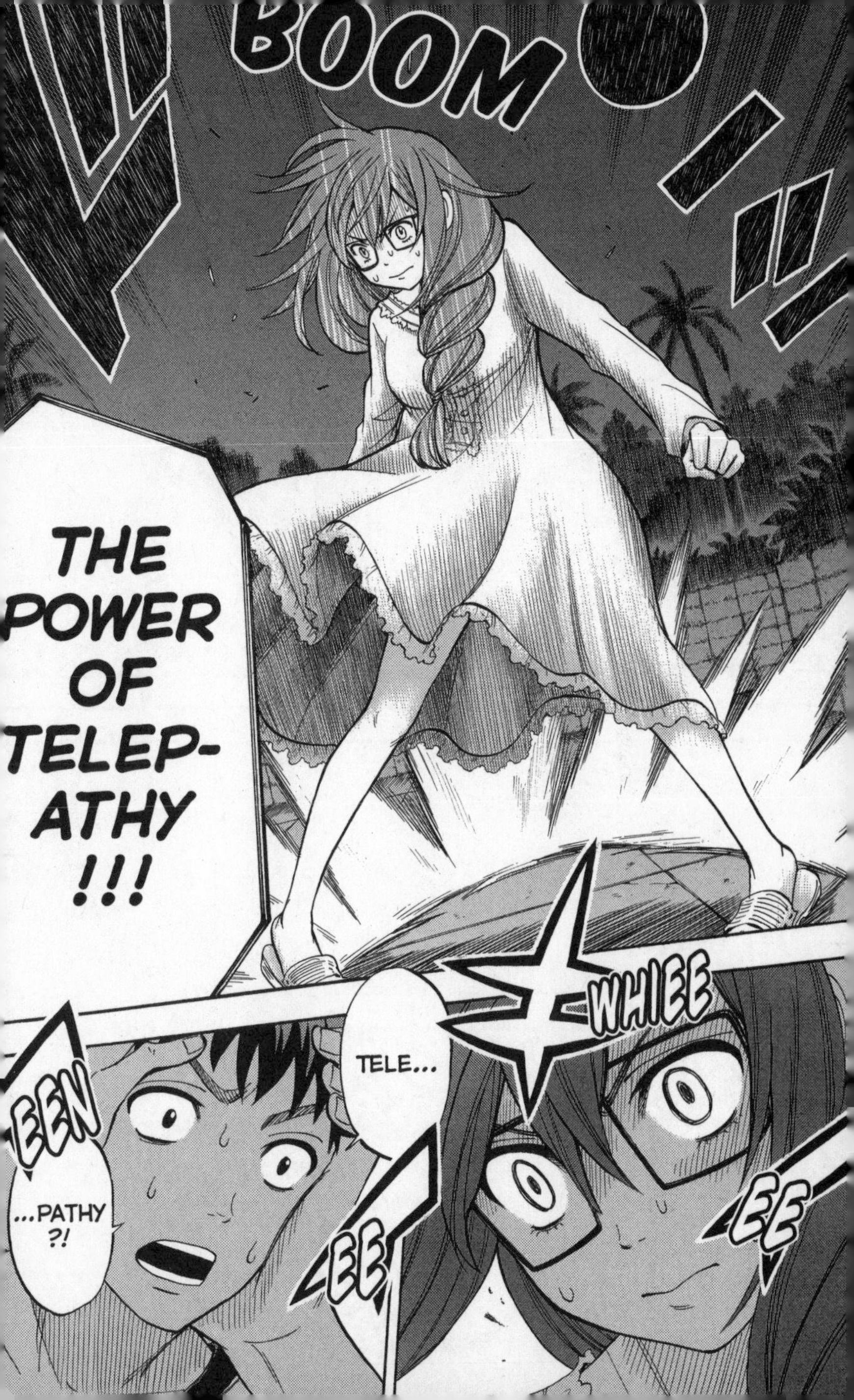
BOOM
THE POWER OF TELEPATHY!!!
WHIEE
TELE...
EE
EE
EEN
...PATHY?!

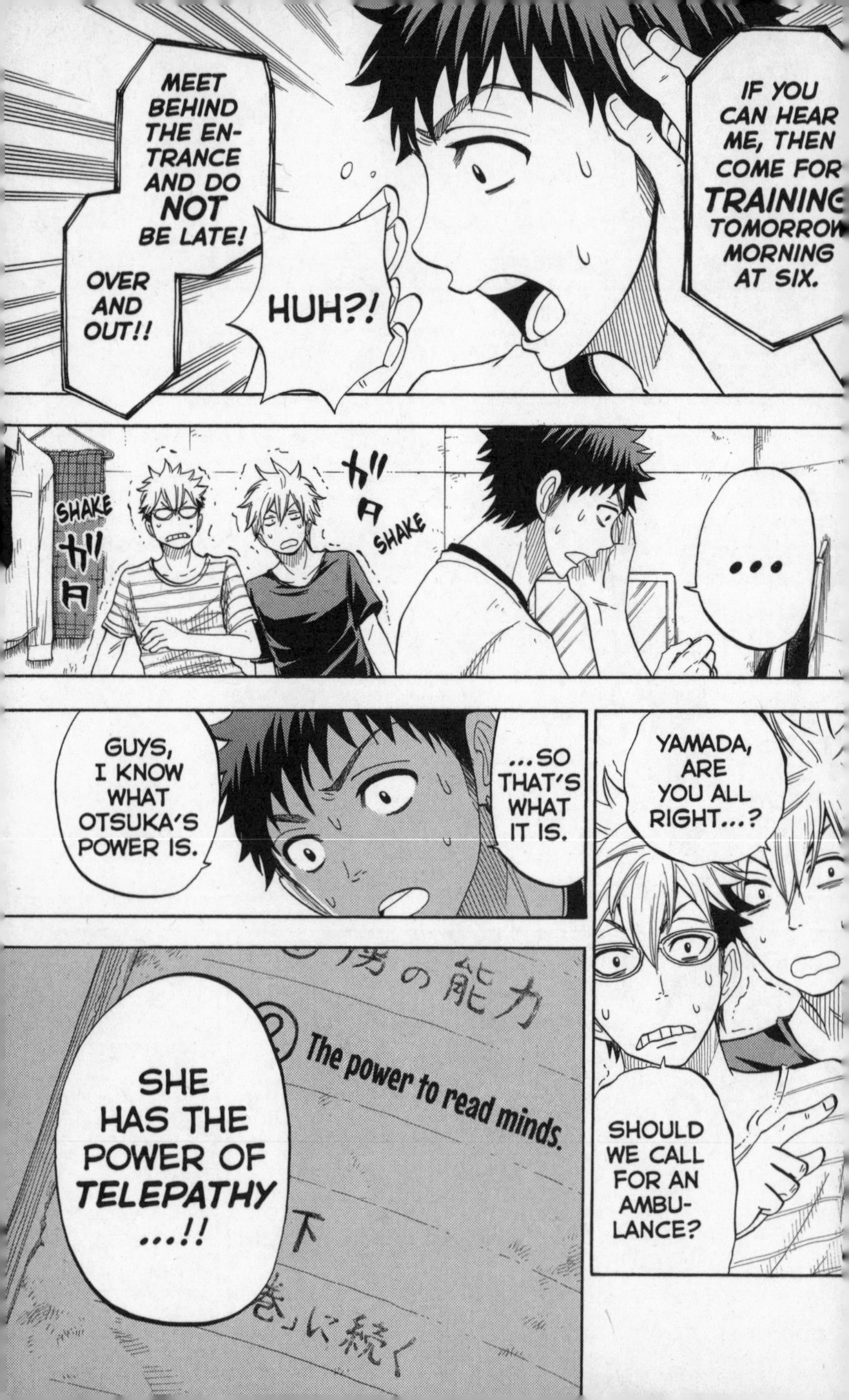
IF YOU CAN HEAR ME, THEN COME FOR TRAINING TOMORROW MORNING AT SIX.
MEET BEHIND THE EN-TRANCE AND DO NOT BE LATE!
OVER AND OUT!!
HUH?!
...
ガタ
SHAKE
SHAKE
ガタ
YAMADA, ARE YOU ALL RIGHT...?
SHOULD WE CALL FOR AN AMBU-LANCE?
...SO THAT'S WHAT IT IS.
GUYS, I KNOW WHAT OTSUKA'S POWER IS.
の能力
The power to read minds.
SHE HAS THE POWER OF TELEPATHY...!!
下
巻」に続く

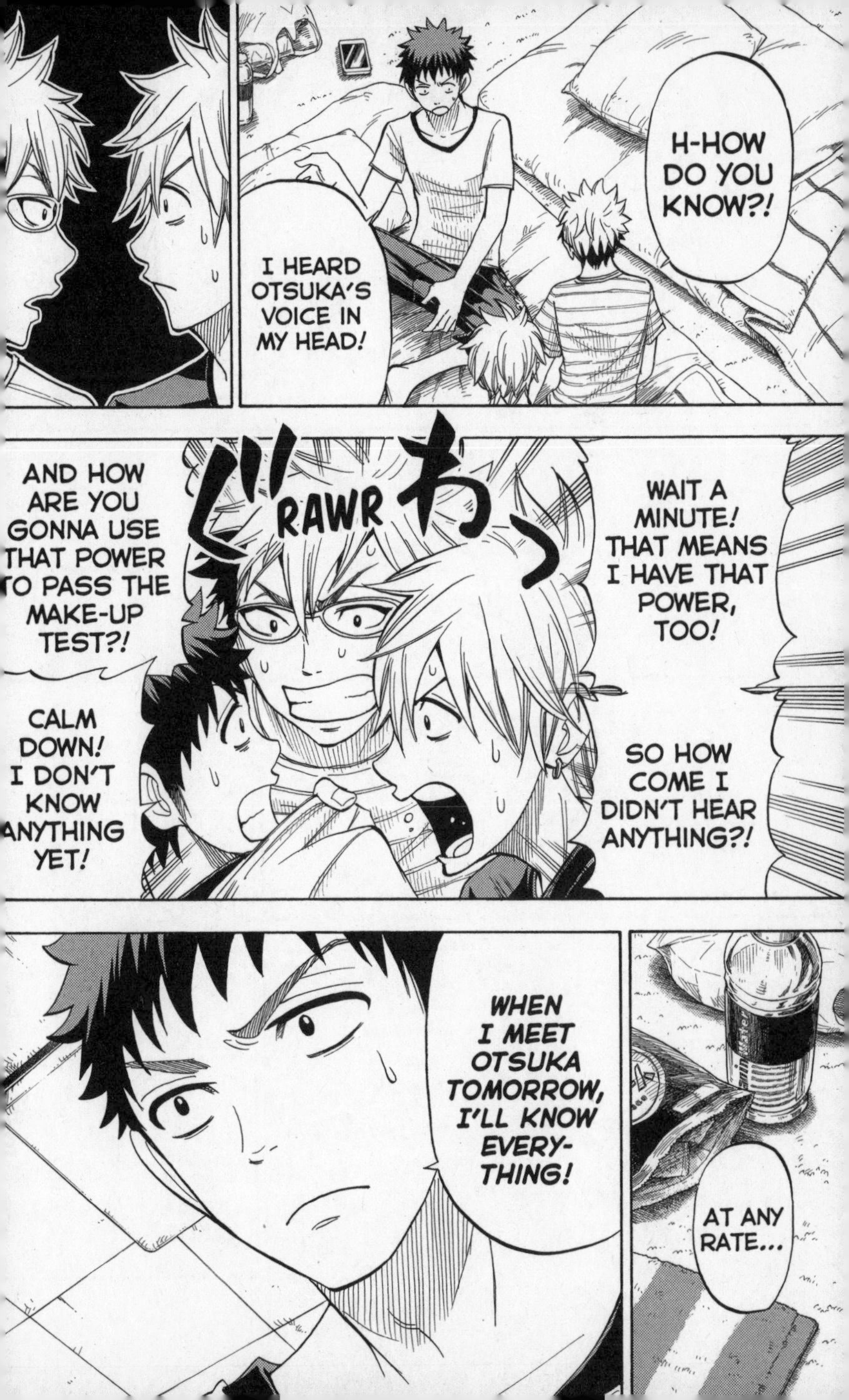
H-HOW DO YOU KNOW?!
I HEARD OTSUKA'S VOICE IN MY HEAD!
WAIT A MINUTE! THAT MEANS I HAVE THAT POWER, TOO!
RAWR
AND HOW ARE YOU GONNA USE THAT POWER TO PASS THE MAKE-UP TEST?!
SO HOW COME I DIDN'T HEAR ANYTHING?!
CALM DOWN! I DON'T KNOW ANYTHING YET!
AT ANY RATE...
WHEN I MEET OTSUKA TOMORROW, I'LL KNOW EVERY-THING!

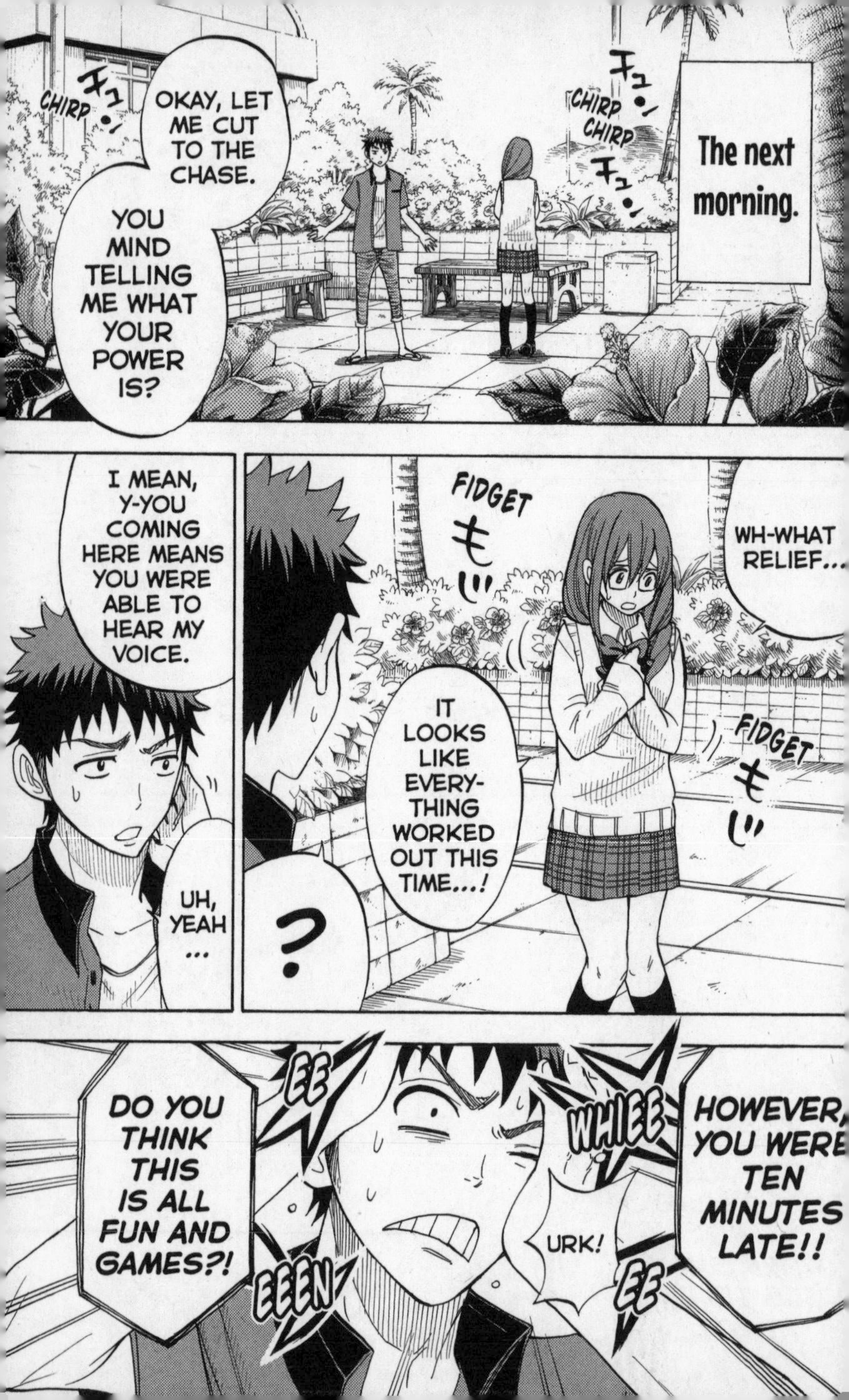

The next morning.
チュ
CHIRP CHIRP
チュ
OKAY, LET ME CUT TO THE CHASE.
YOU MIND TELLING ME WHAT YOUR POWER IS?
CHIRP
チュ
WH-WHAT RELIEF...
FIDGET
もじ
IT LOOKS LIKE EVERYTHING WORKED OUT THIS TIME...!
?
FIDGET
もじ
I MEAN, Y-YOU COMING HERE MEANS YOU WERE ABLE TO HEAR MY VOICE.
UH, YEAH...
HOWEVER, YOU WERE TEN MINUTES LATE!!
WHIEE
URK!
EE
EE
DO YOU THINK THIS IS ALL FUN AND GAMES?!
EEEN

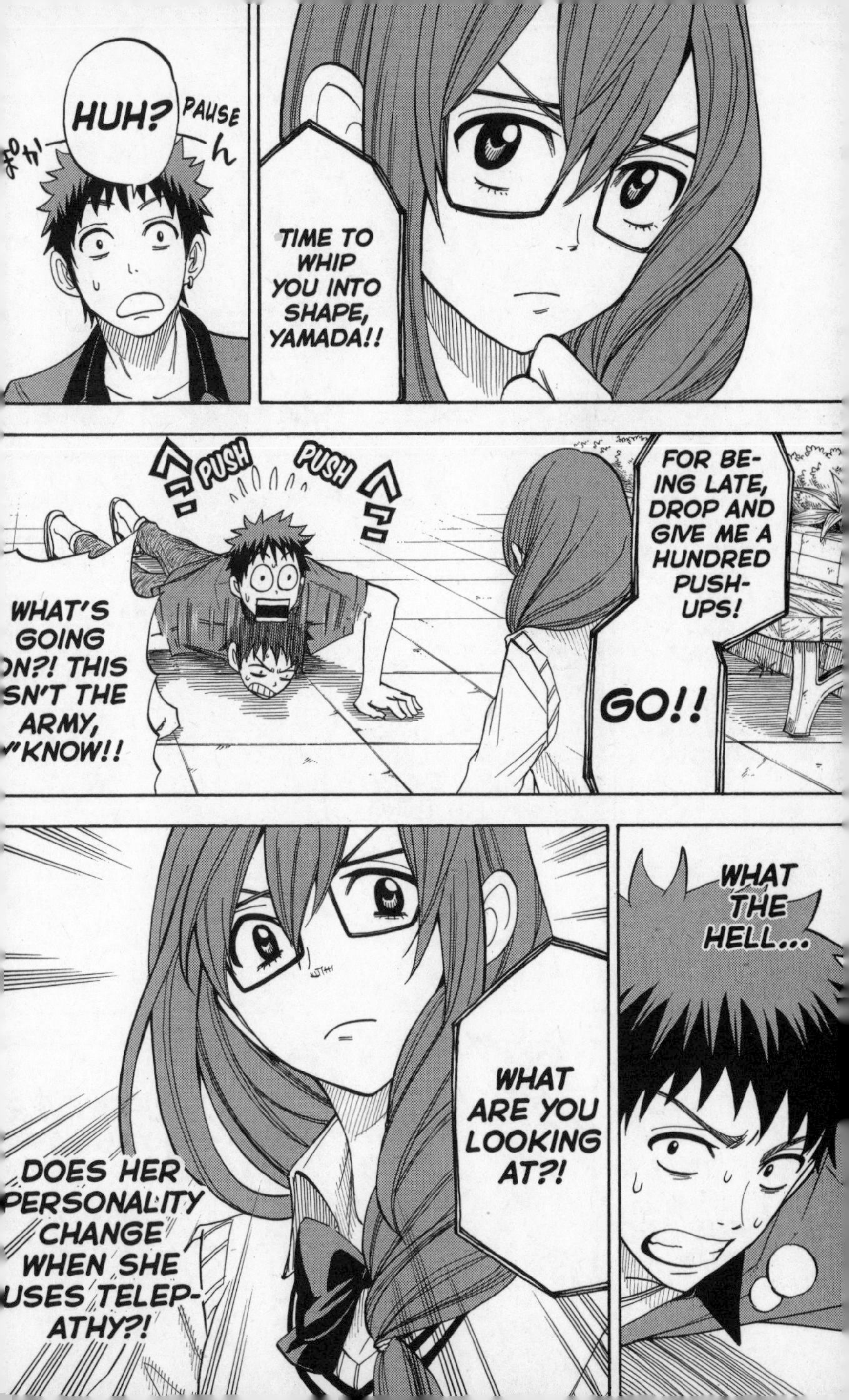

TIME TO WHIP YOU INTO SHAPE, YAMADA!!
HUH?
PAUSE
FOR BE-ING LATE, DROP AND GIVE ME A HUNDRED PUSH-UPS!
GO!!
PUSH
PUSH
WHAT'S GOING ON?! THIS SN'T THE ARMY, "KNOW!!
WHAT THE HELL...
WHAT ARE YOU LOOKING AT?!
DOES HER PERSONALITY CHANGE WHEN SHE USES TELEP-ATHY?!

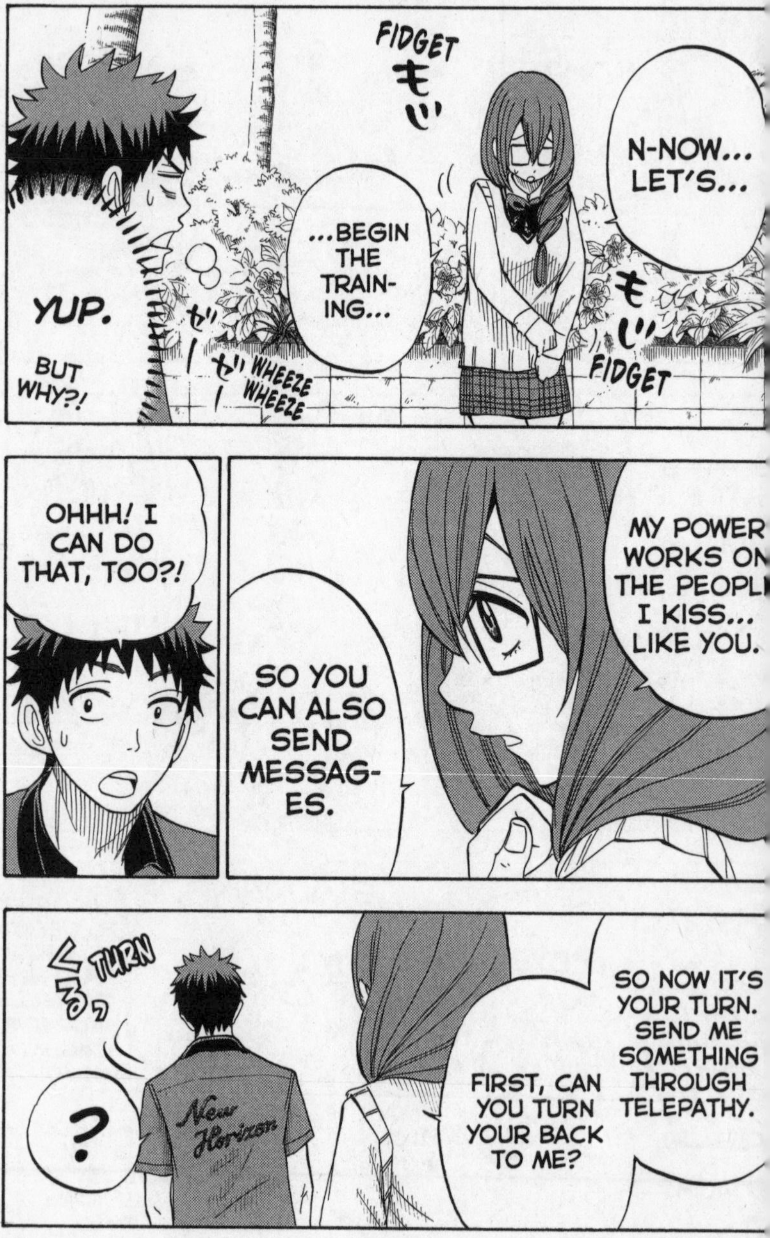
N-NOW... LET'S...
FIDGET
もじ
もじ
FIDGET
...BEGIN THE TRAINING...
ぜー ぜー
WHEEZE WHEEZE
YUP.
BUT WHY?!
MY POWER WORKS ON THE PEOPL I KISS... LIKE YOU.
SO YOU CAN ALSO SEND MESSAGES.
OHHH! I CAN DO THAT, TOO?!
SO NOW IT'S YOUR TURN. SEND ME SOMETHING THROUGH TELEPATHY.
FIRST, CAN YOU TURN YOUR BACK TO ME?
?
くるっ
TURN

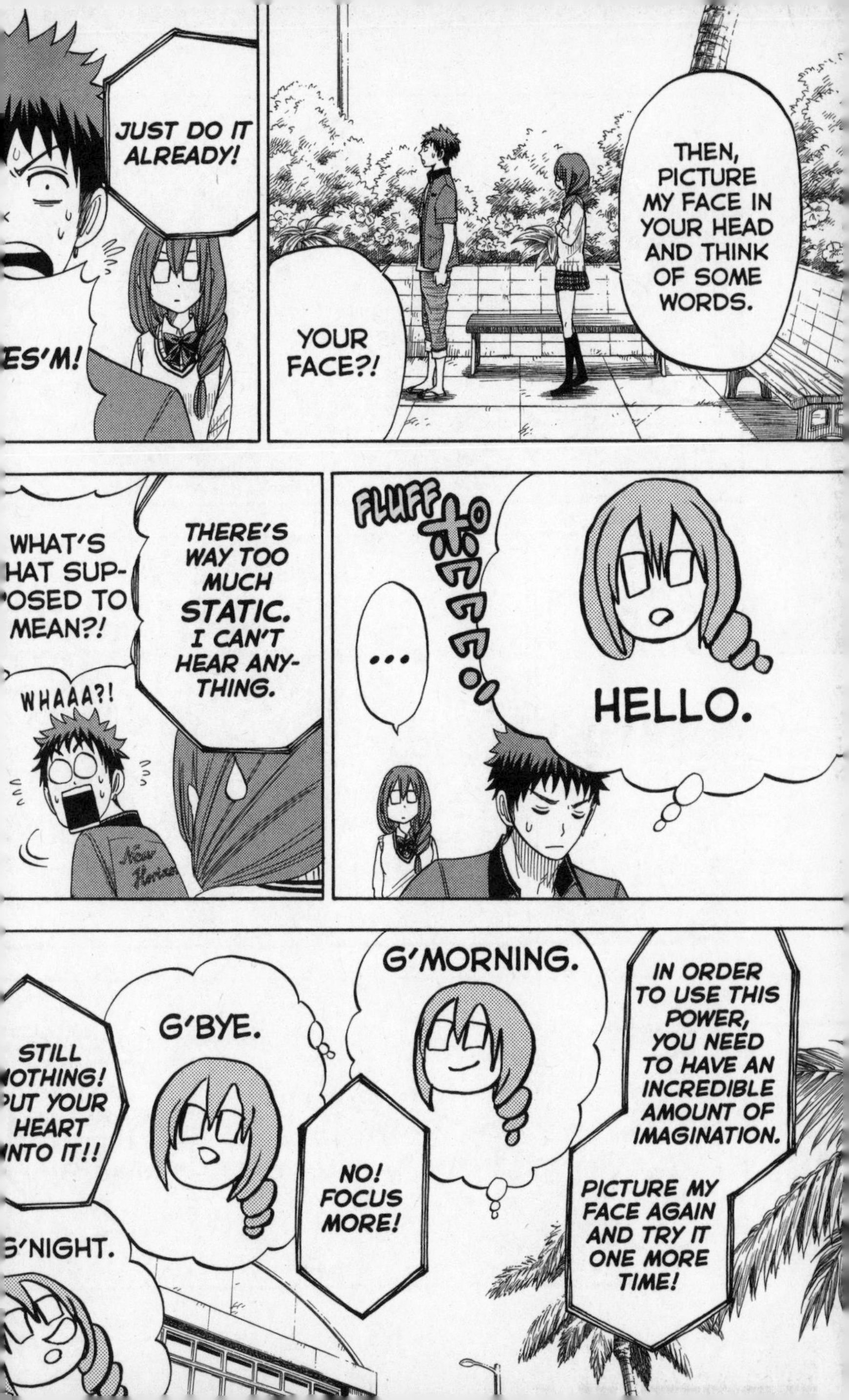

THEN, PICTURE MY FACE IN YOUR HEAD AND THINK OF SOME WORDS.
YOUR FACE?!
JUST DO IT ALREADY!
ES'M!
FLUFF
HELLO.
...
THERE'S WAY TOO MUCH STATIC. I CAN'T HEAR ANY-THING.
WHAT'S HAT SUP-OSED TO MEAN?!
WHAAA?!
IN ORDER TO USE THIS POWER, YOU NEED TO HAVE AN INCREDIBLE AMOUNT OF IMAGINATION.
PICTURE MY FACE AGAIN AND TRY IT ONE MORE TIME!
G'MORNING.
NO! FOCUS MORE!
G'BYE.
STILL OTHING! UT YOUR HEART NTO IT!!
'NIGHT.

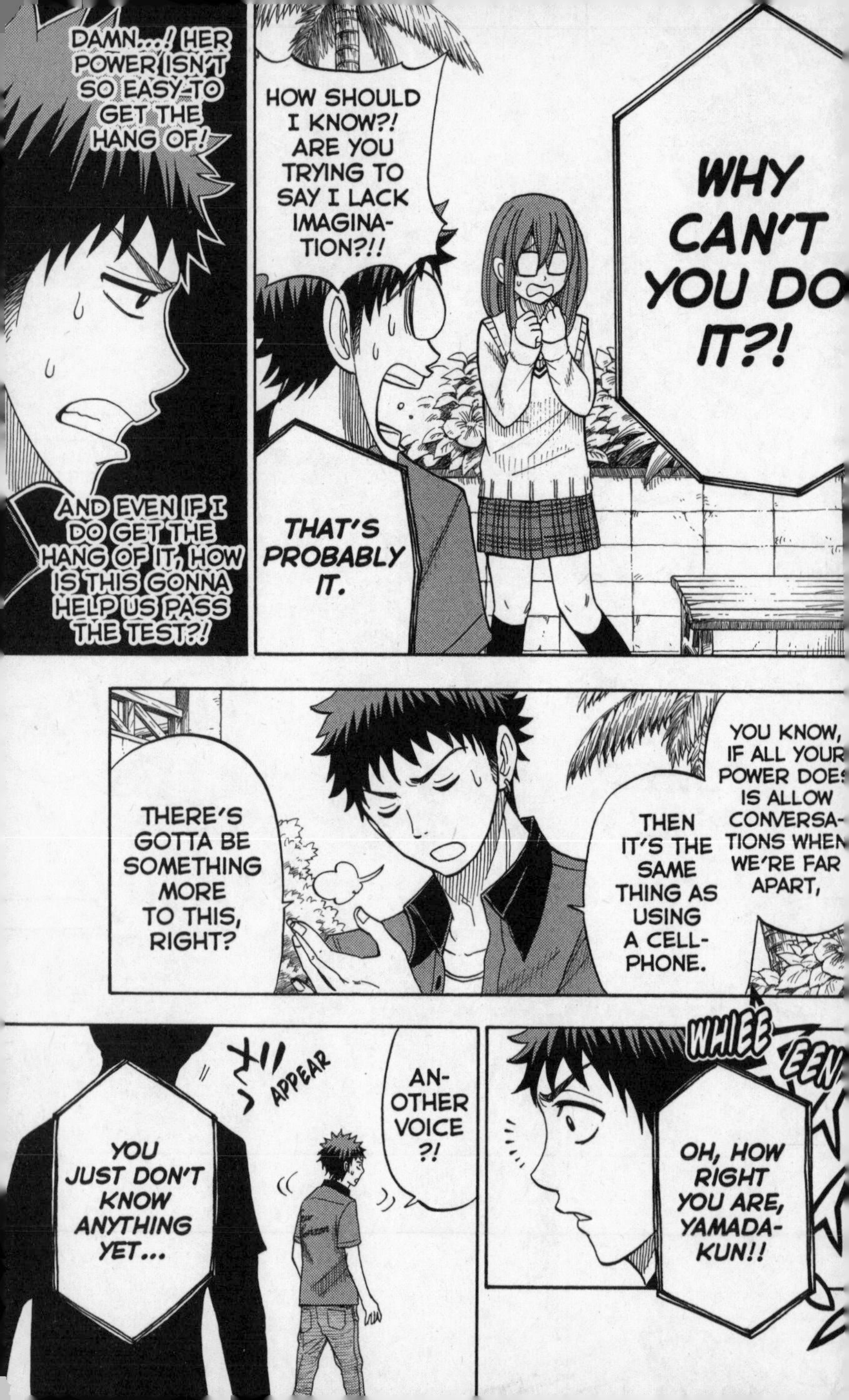
WHY CAN'T YOU DO IT?!
HOW SHOULD I KNOW?! ARE YOU TRYING TO SAY I LACK IMAGINA-TION?!!
THAT'S PROBABLY IT.
DAMN...! HER POWER ISN'T SO EASY TO GET THE HANG OF!
AND EVEN IF I DO GET THE HANG OF IT, HOW IS THIS GONNA HELP US PASS THE TEST?!
YOU KNOW, IF ALL YOUR POWER DOES IS ALLOW CONVERSA-TIONS WHEN WE'RE FAR APART,
THEN IT'S THE SAME THING AS USING A CELL-PHONE.
THERE'S GOTTA BE SOMETHING MORE TO THIS, RIGHT?
WHIEE EEN
OH, HOW RIGHT YOU ARE, YAMADA-KUN!!
AN-OTHER VOICE?!
APPEAR
YOU JUST DON'T KNOW ANYTHING YET...

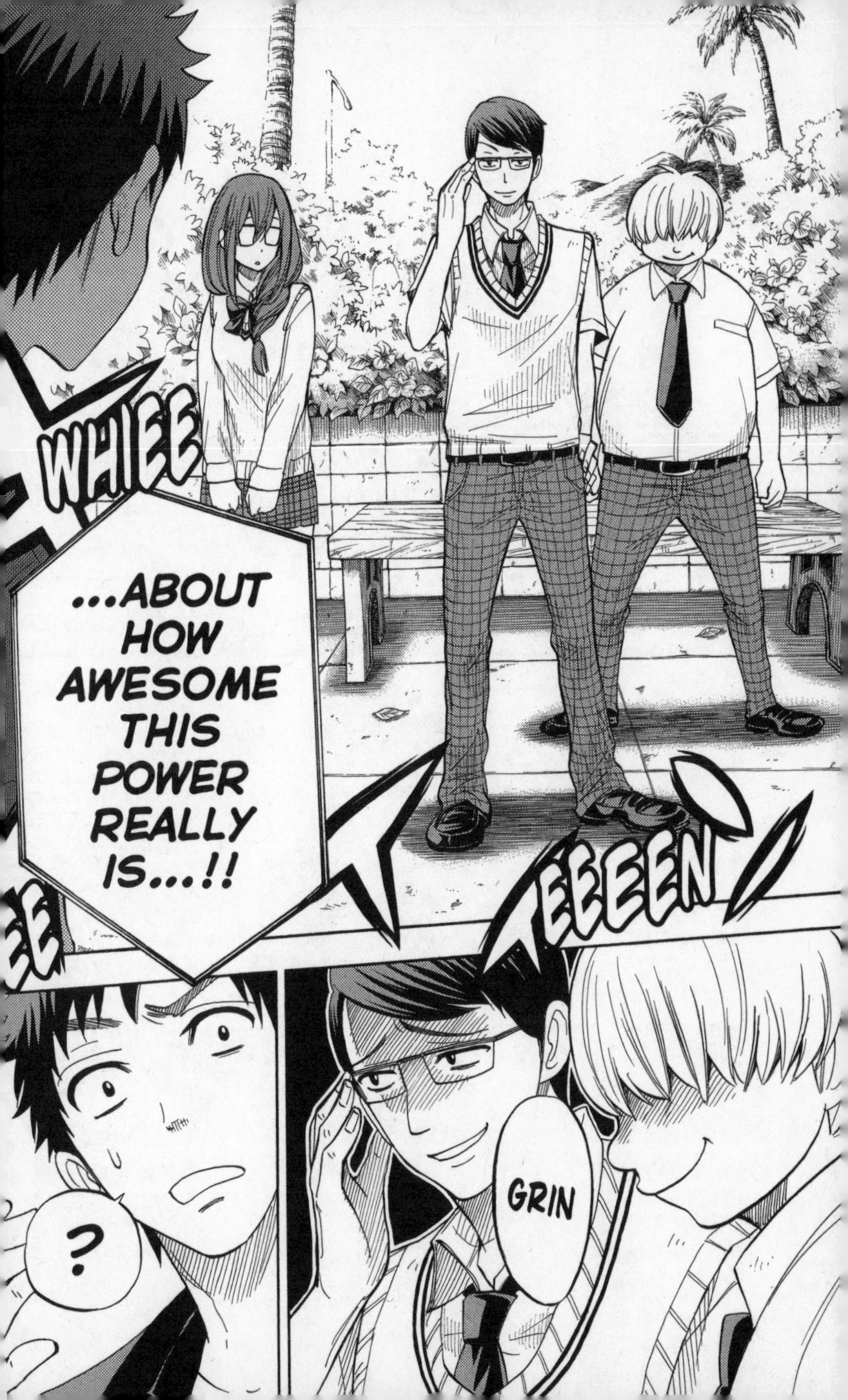
...ABOUT HOW AWESOME THIS POWER REALLY IS...!!
WHIEE
EEEEN
GRIN
?

Chapter 30: Boobs.

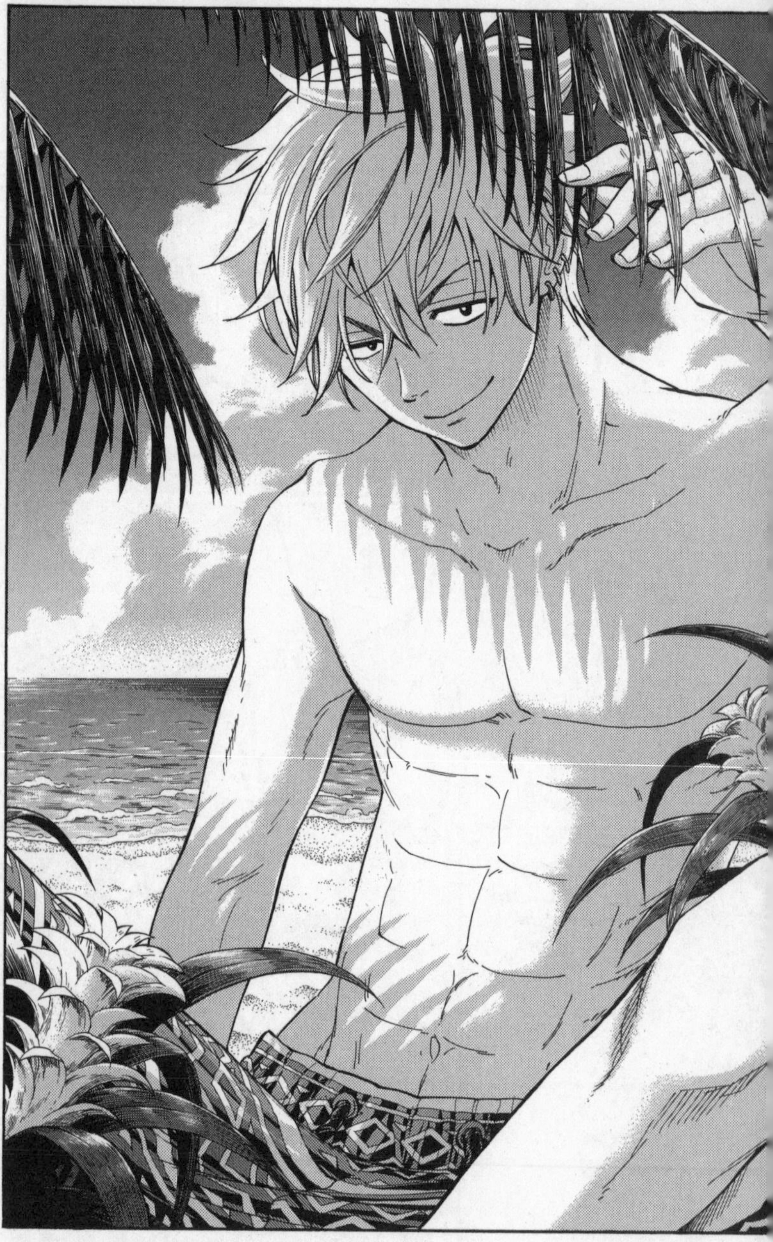

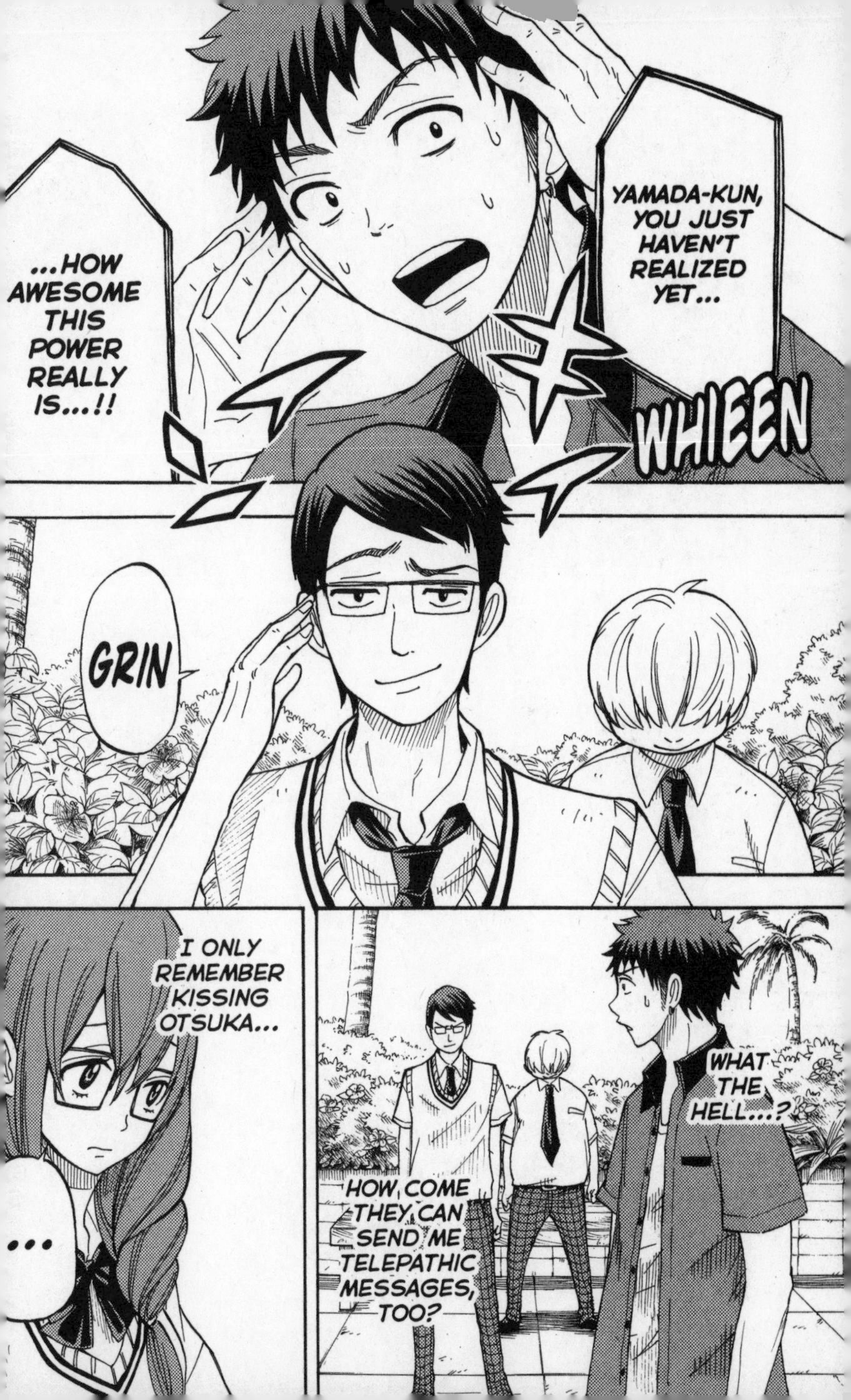
YAMADA-KUN, YOU JUST HAVEN'T REALIZED YET...
...HOW AWESOME THIS POWER REALLY IS...!!
WHIEEN
GRIN
WHAT THE HELL...?
HOW COME THEY CAN SEND ME TELEPATHIC MESSAGES, TOO?
I ONLY REMEMBER KISSING OTSUKA...
...

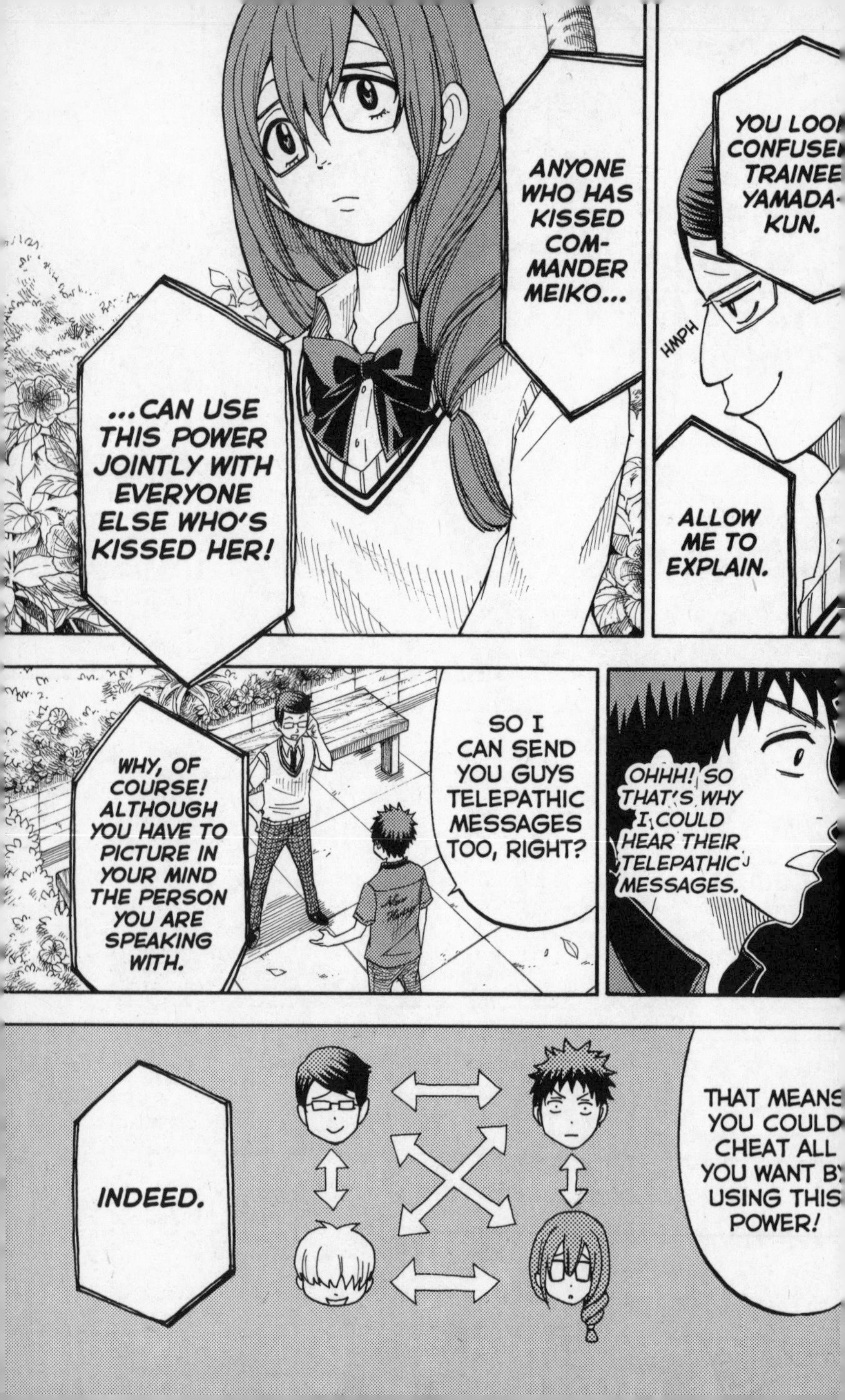
YOU LOO CONFUSE TRAINEE YAMADA-KUN.
HMPH
ALLOW ME TO EXPLAIN.
ANYONE WHO HAS KISSED COM-MANDER MEIKO...
...CAN USE THIS POWER JOINTLY WITH EVERYONE ELSE WHO'S KISSED HER!
OHHH! SO THAT'S WHY I COULD HEAR THEIR TELEPATHIC MESSAGES.
SO I CAN SEND YOU GUYS TELEPATHIC MESSAGES TOO, RIGHT?
WHY, OF COURSE! ALTHOUGH YOU HAVE TO PICTURE IN YOUR MIND THE PERSON YOU ARE SPEAKING WITH.
THAT MEANS YOU COULD CHEAT ALL YOU WANT B USING THIS POWER!
INDEED.

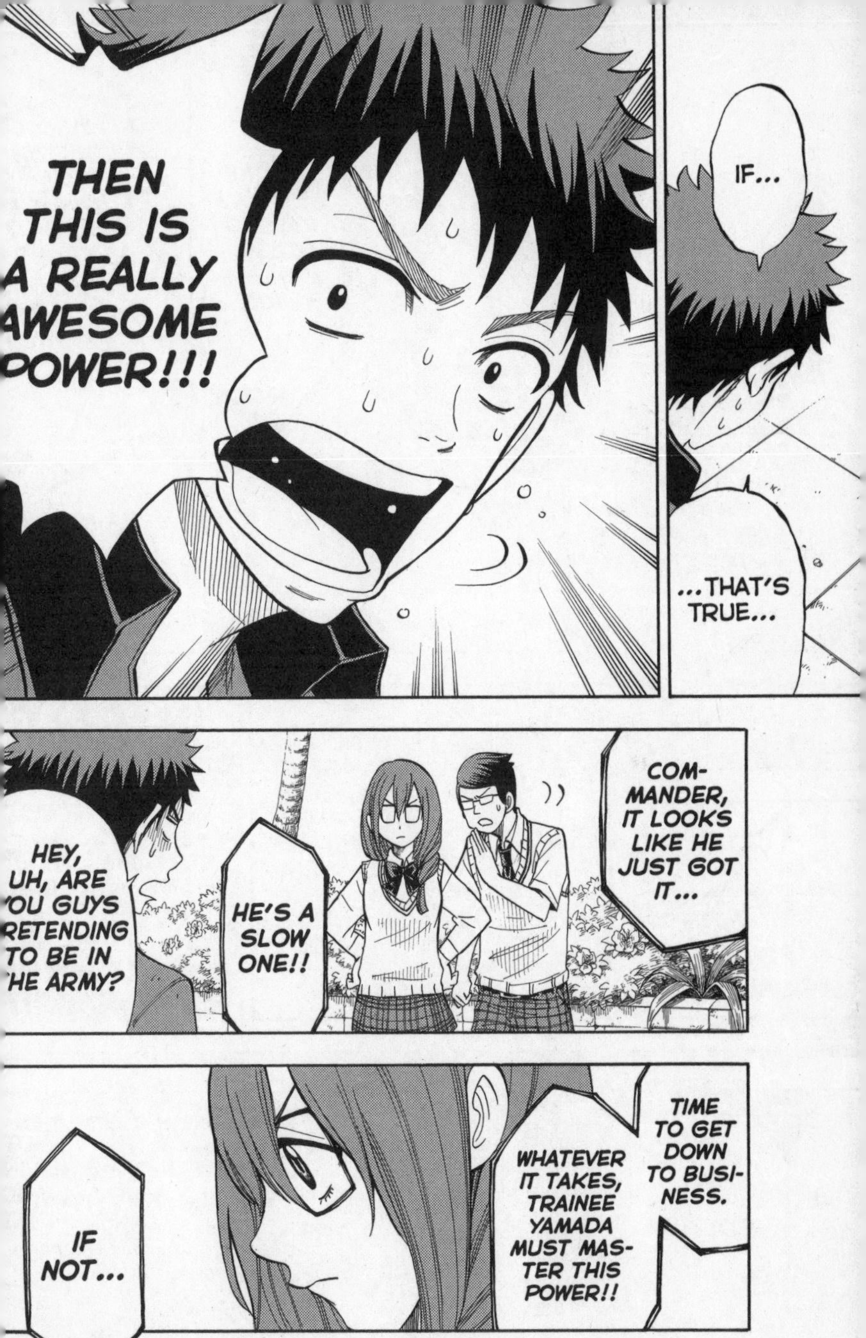
IF...
...THAT'S TRUE...
THEN THIS IS A REALLY AWESOME POWER!!!
COM-MANDER, IT LOOKS LIKE HE JUST GOT IT...
HE'S A SLOW ONE!!
HEY, UH, ARE 'OU GUYS RETENDING TO BE IN 'HE ARMY?
TIME TO GET DOWN TO BUSI-NESS.
WHATEVER IT TAKES, TRAINEE YAMADA MUST MAS-TER THIS POWER!!
IF NOT...

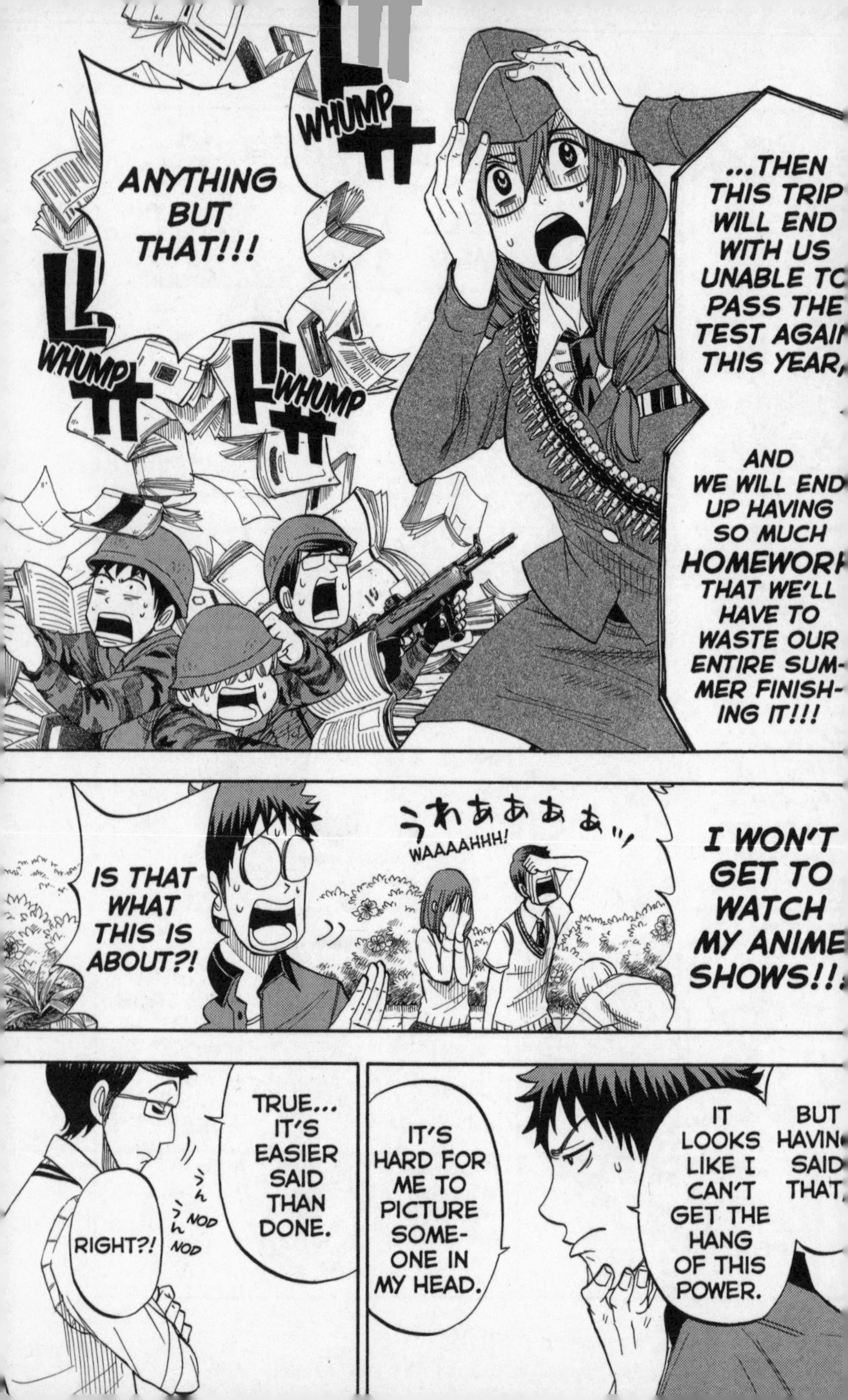
...THEN THIS TRIP WILL END WITH US UNABLE TO PASS THE TEST AGAIN THIS YEAR,
AND WE WILL END UP HAVING SO MUCH HOMEWORK THAT WE'LL HAVE TO WASTE OUR ENTIRE SUMMER FINISHING IT!!!
WHUMP
ANYTHING BUT THAT!!!
WHUMP
WHUMP
I WON'T GET TO WATCH MY ANIME SHOWS!!!
うわあああぁぁ
WAAAAHHH!
IS THAT WHAT THIS IS ABOUT?!
BUT HAVING SAID THAT,
IT LOOKS LIKE I CAN'T GET THE HANG OF THIS POWER.
IT'S HARD FOR ME TO PICTURE SOMEONE IN MY HEAD.
TRUE... IT'S EASIER SAID THAN DONE.
うん NOD
うん NOD
RIGHT?!

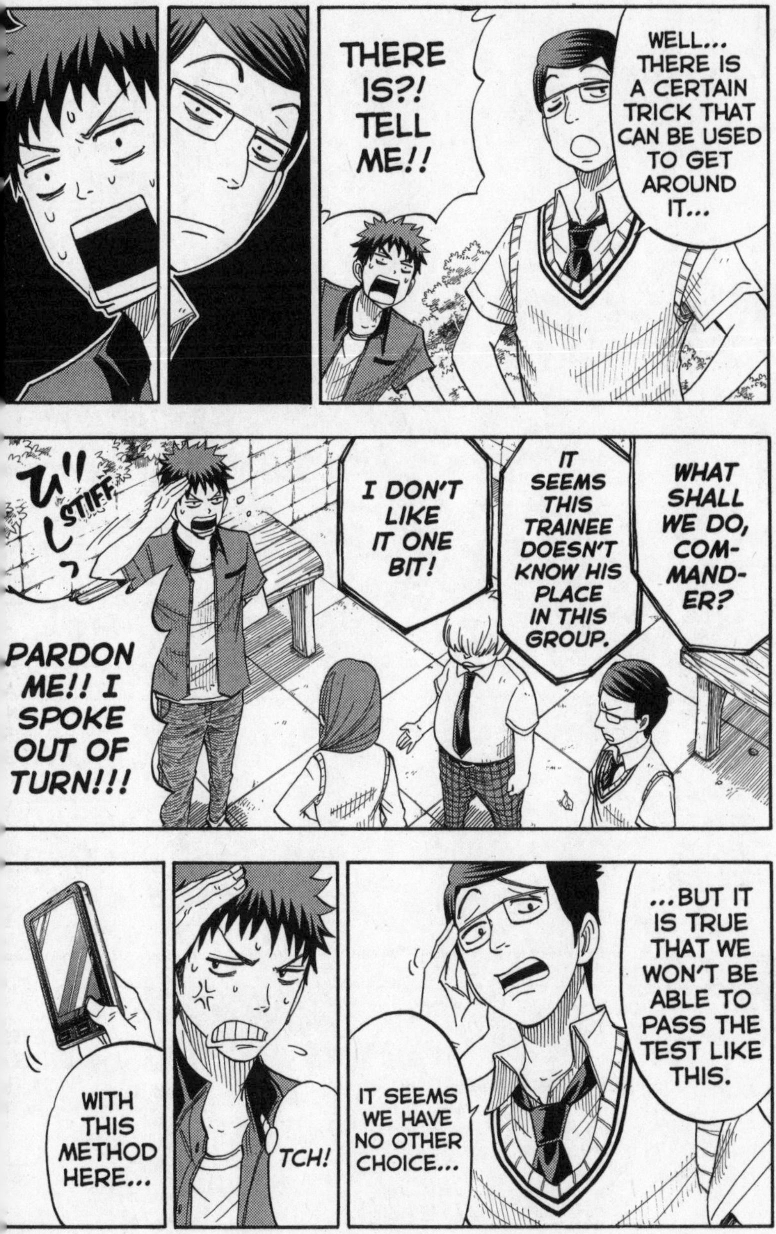

WELL... THERE IS A CERTAIN TRICK THAT CAN BE USED TO GET AROUND IT...
THERE IS?! TELL ME!!
WHAT SHALL WE DO, COM-MAND-ER?
IT SEEMS THIS TRAINEE DOESN'T KNOW HIS PLACE IN THIS GROUP.
I DON'T LIKE IT ONE BIT!
びしっ
STIFF
PARDON ME!! I SPOKE OUT OF TURN!!!
...BUT IT IS TRUE THAT WE WON'T BE ABLE TO PASS THE TEST LIKE THIS.
IT SEEMS WE HAVE NO OTHER CHOICE...
TCH!
WITH THIS METHOD HERE...

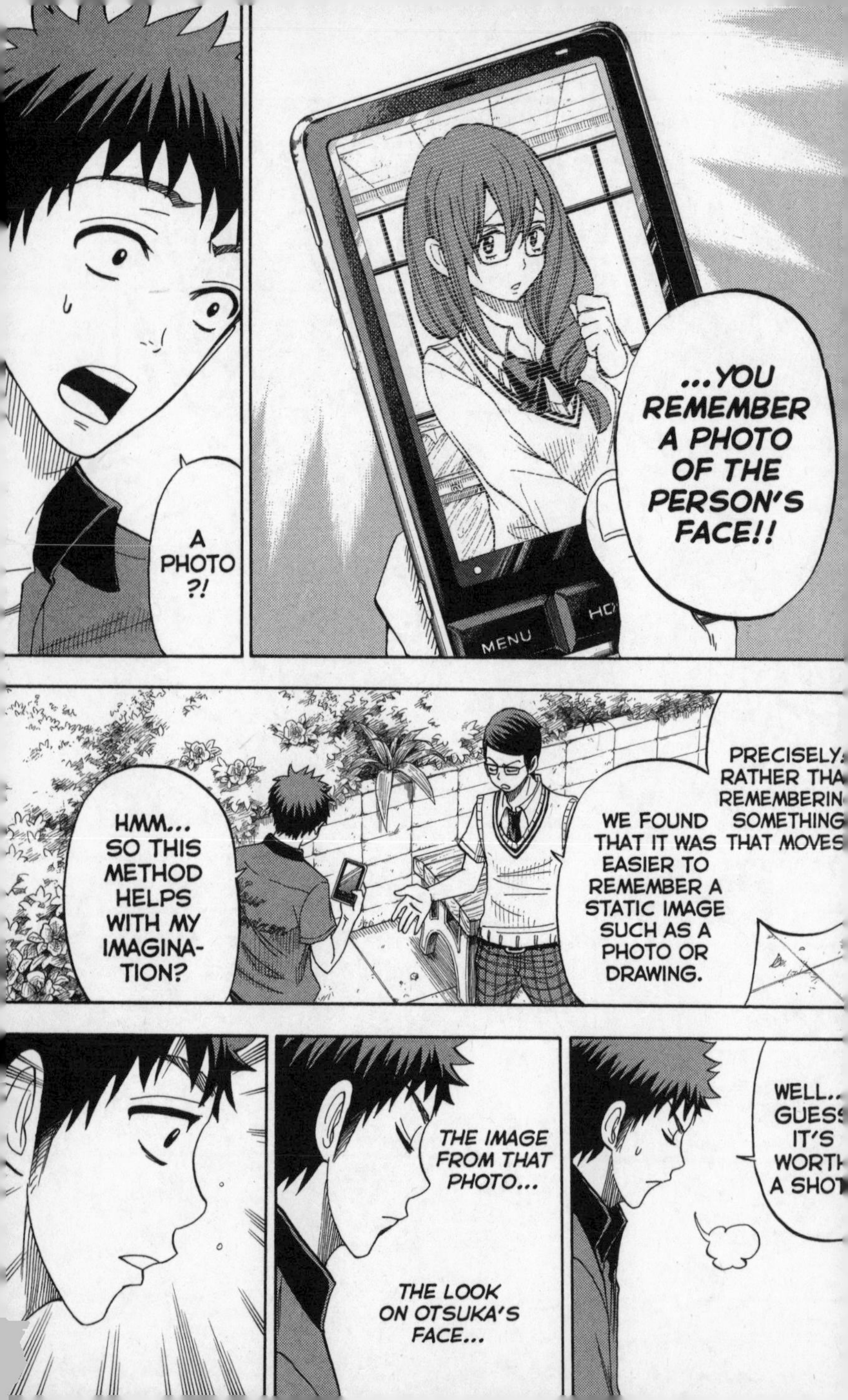
...YOU REMEMBER A PHOTO OF THE PERSON'S FACE!!
MENU
A PHOTO ?!
PRECISELY. RATHER THA REMEMBERIN SOMETHING THAT MOVES
WE FOUND THAT IT WAS EASIER TO REMEMBER A STATIC IMAGE SUCH AS A PHOTO OR DRAWING.
HMM... SO THIS METHOD HELPS WITH MY IMAGINATION?
WELL.. GUES IT'S WORT A SHO
THE IMAGE FROM THAT PHOTO...
THE LOOK ON OTSUKA'S FACE...

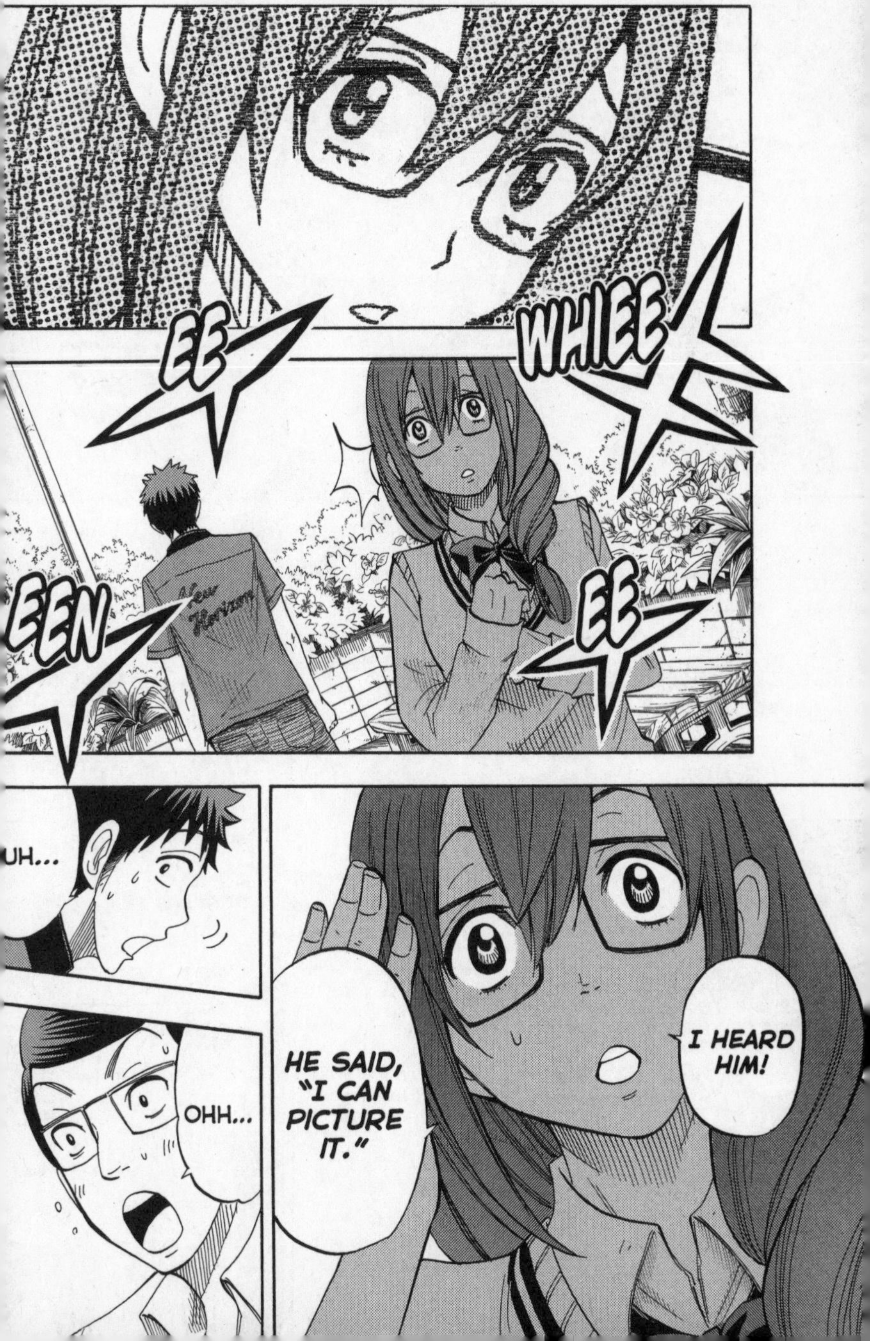
WHIEE
EE
EE
EEN
I HEARD HIM!
HE SAID, "I CAN PICTURE IT."
UH...
OHH...

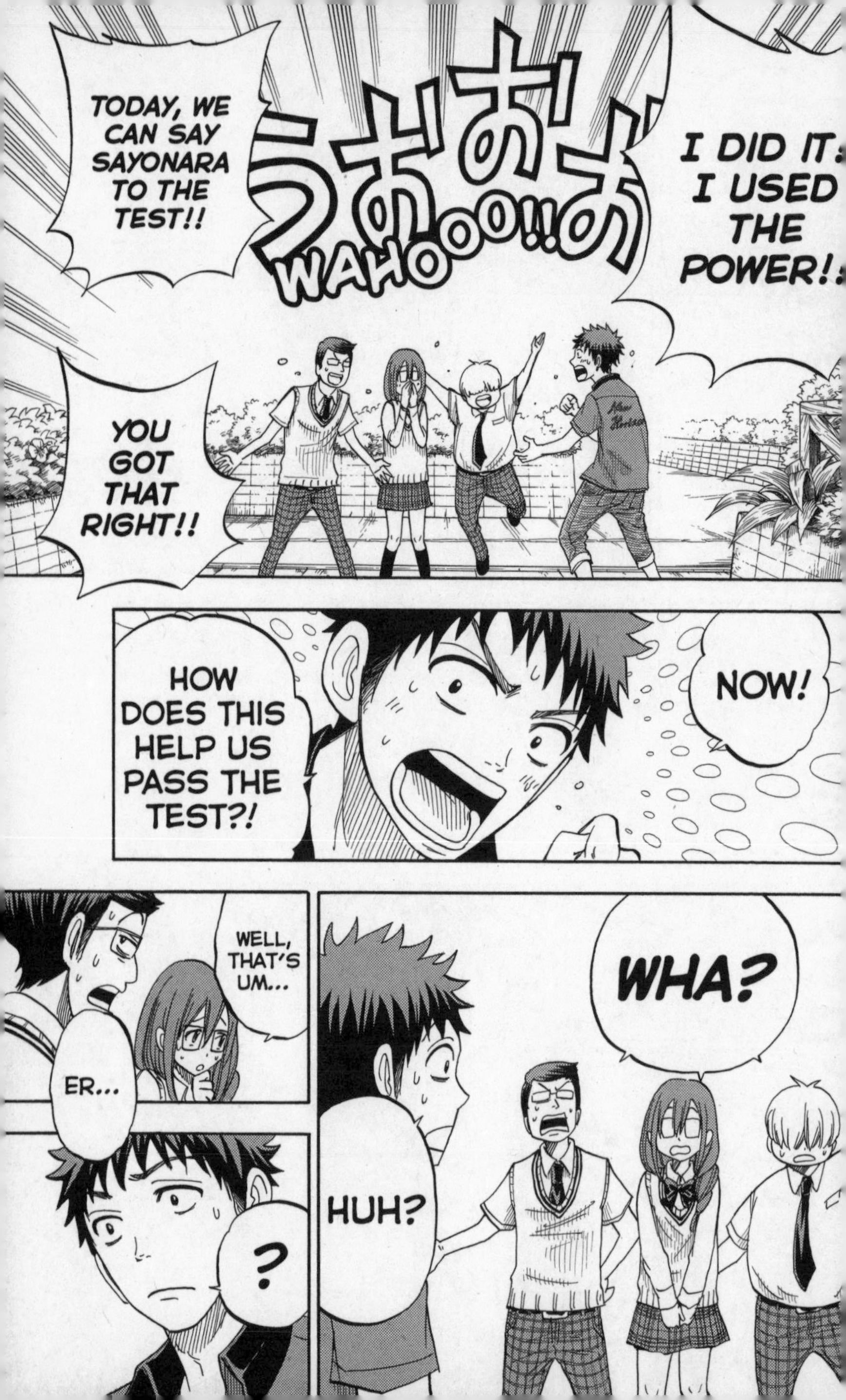

I DID IT! I USED THE POWER!!
うおおお
WAHOOO!!
TODAY, WE CAN SAY SAYONARA TO THE TEST!!
YOU GOT THAT RIGHT!!
NOW!
HOW DOES THIS HELP US PASS THE TEST?!
WHA?
HUH?
WELL, THAT'S UM...
ER...
?

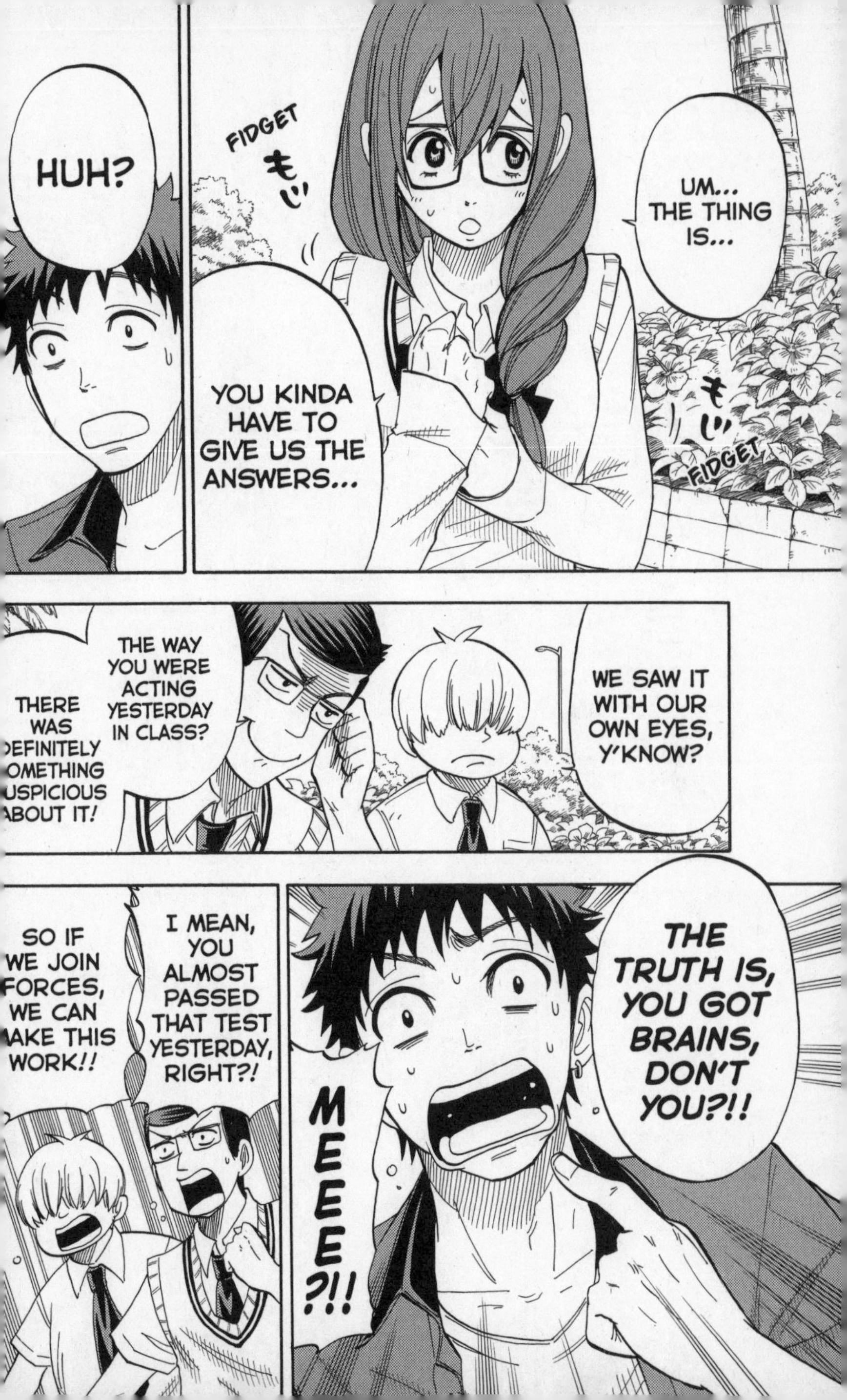
UM... THE THING IS...
FIDGET
もじ
YOU KINDA HAVE TO GIVE US THE ANSWERS...
もじ
FIDGET
HUH?
WE SAW IT WITH OUR OWN EYES, Y'KNOW?
THE WAY YOU WERE ACTING YESTERDAY IN CLASS?
THERE WAS EFINITELY OMETHING USPICIOUS BOUT IT!
THE TRUTH IS, YOU GOT BRAINS, DON'T YOU?!!
MEEEE?!!
I MEAN, YOU ALMOST PASSED THAT TEST YESTERDAY, RIGHT?!
SO IF WE JOIN ORCES, WE CAN AKE THIS WORK!!

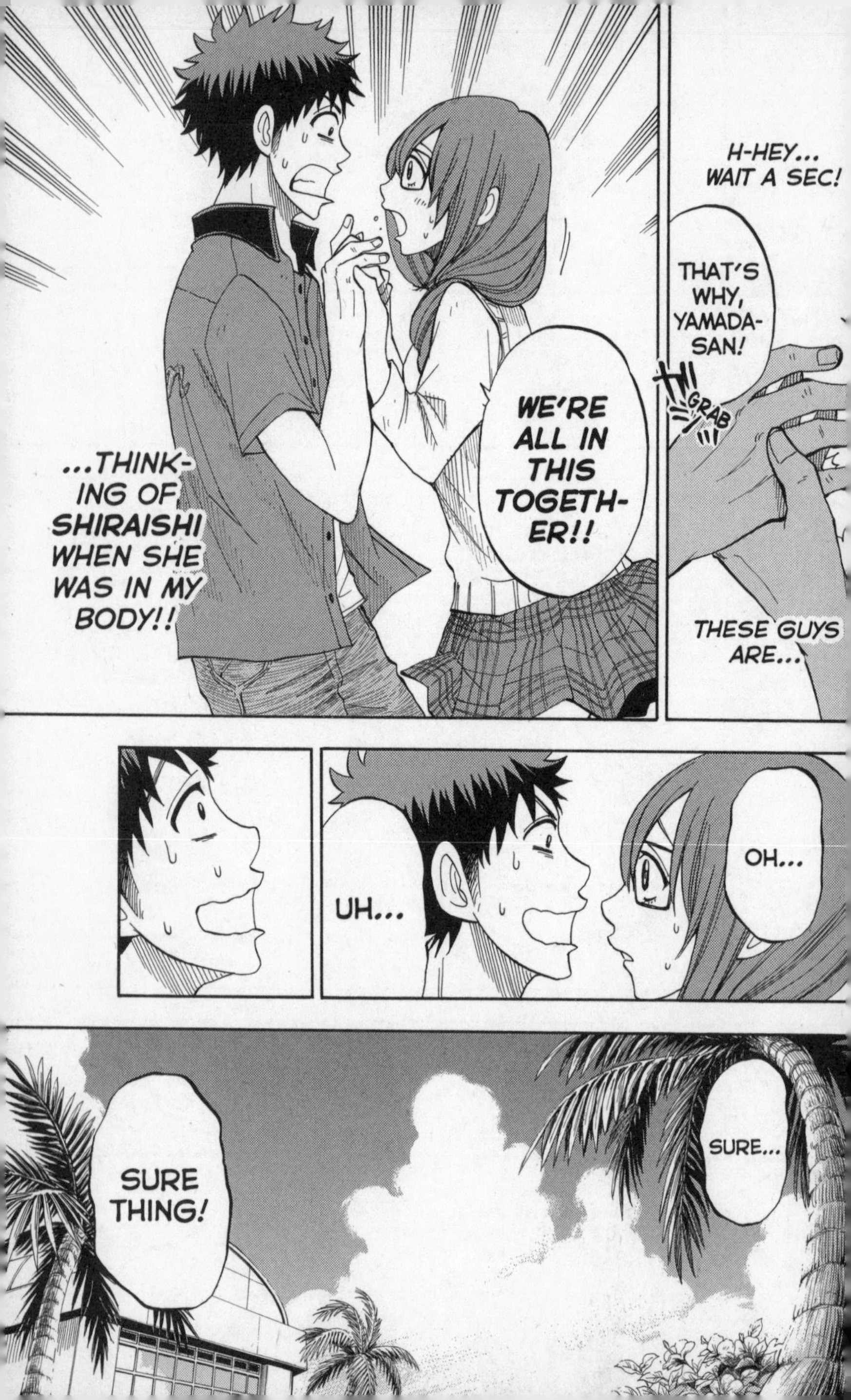
H-HEY... WAIT A SEC!
THAT'S WHY, YAMADA-SAN!
GRAB
THESE GUYS ARE...
WE'RE ALL IN THIS TOGETH-ER!!
...THINK-ING OF SHIRAISHI WHEN SHE WAS IN MY BODY!!
OH...
UH...
SURE...
SURE THING!

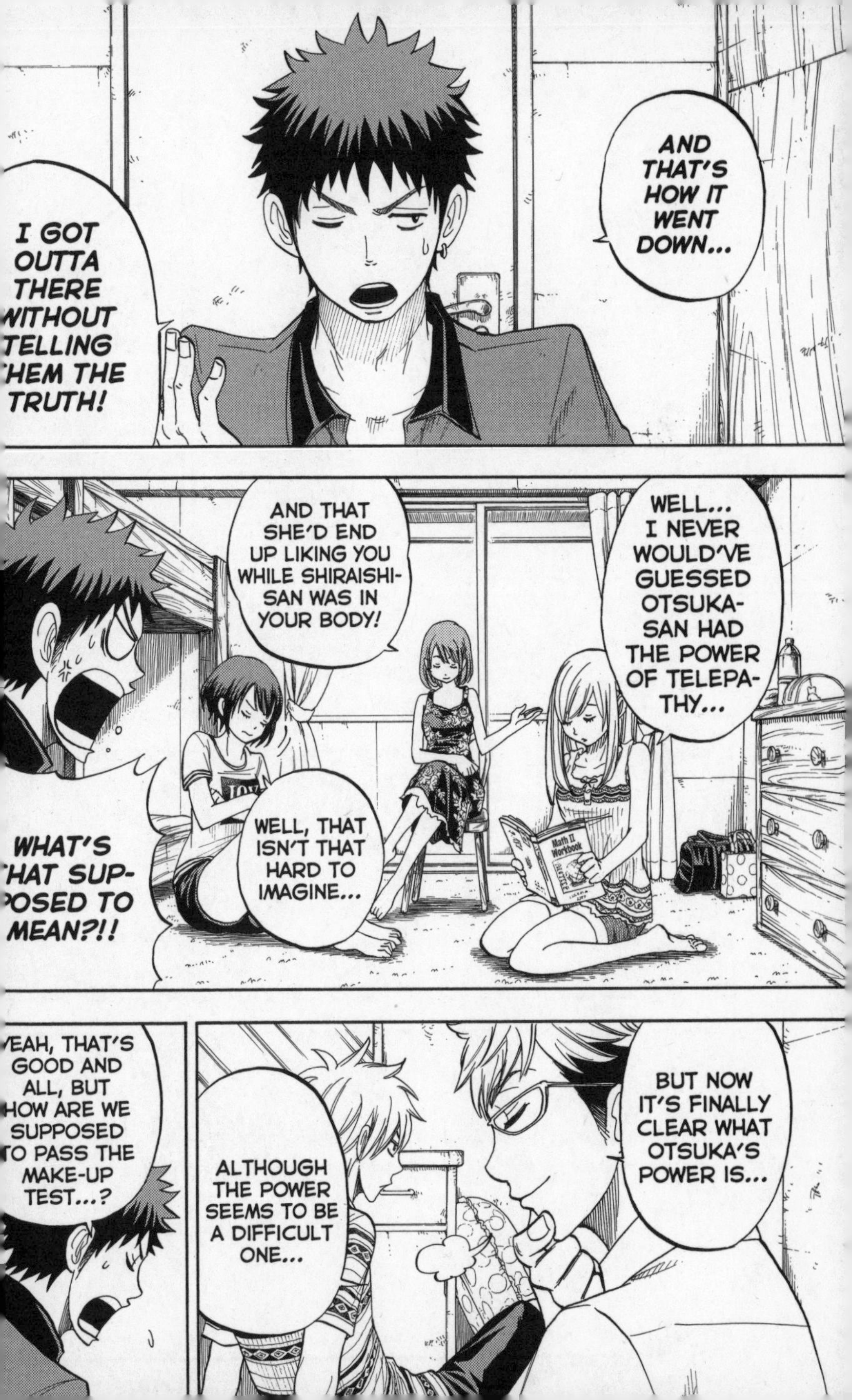
AND THAT'S HOW IT WENT DOWN...
I GOT OUTTA THERE WITHOUT TELLING THEM THE TRUTH!
WELL... I NEVER WOULD'VE GUESSED OTSUKA-SAN HAD THE POWER OF TELEPATHY...
AND THAT SHE'D END UP LIKING YOU WHILE SHIRAISHI-SAN WAS IN YOUR BODY!
Math II Workbook
WELL, THAT ISN'T THAT HARD TO IMAGINE...
WHAT'S THAT SUPPOSED TO MEAN?!!
BUT NOW IT'S FINALLY CLEAR WHAT OTSUKA'S POWER IS...
ALTHOUGH THE POWER SEEMS TO BE A DIFFICULT ONE...
YEAH, THAT'S GOOD AND ALL, BUT HOW ARE WE SUPPOSED TO PASS THE MAKE-UP TEST...?

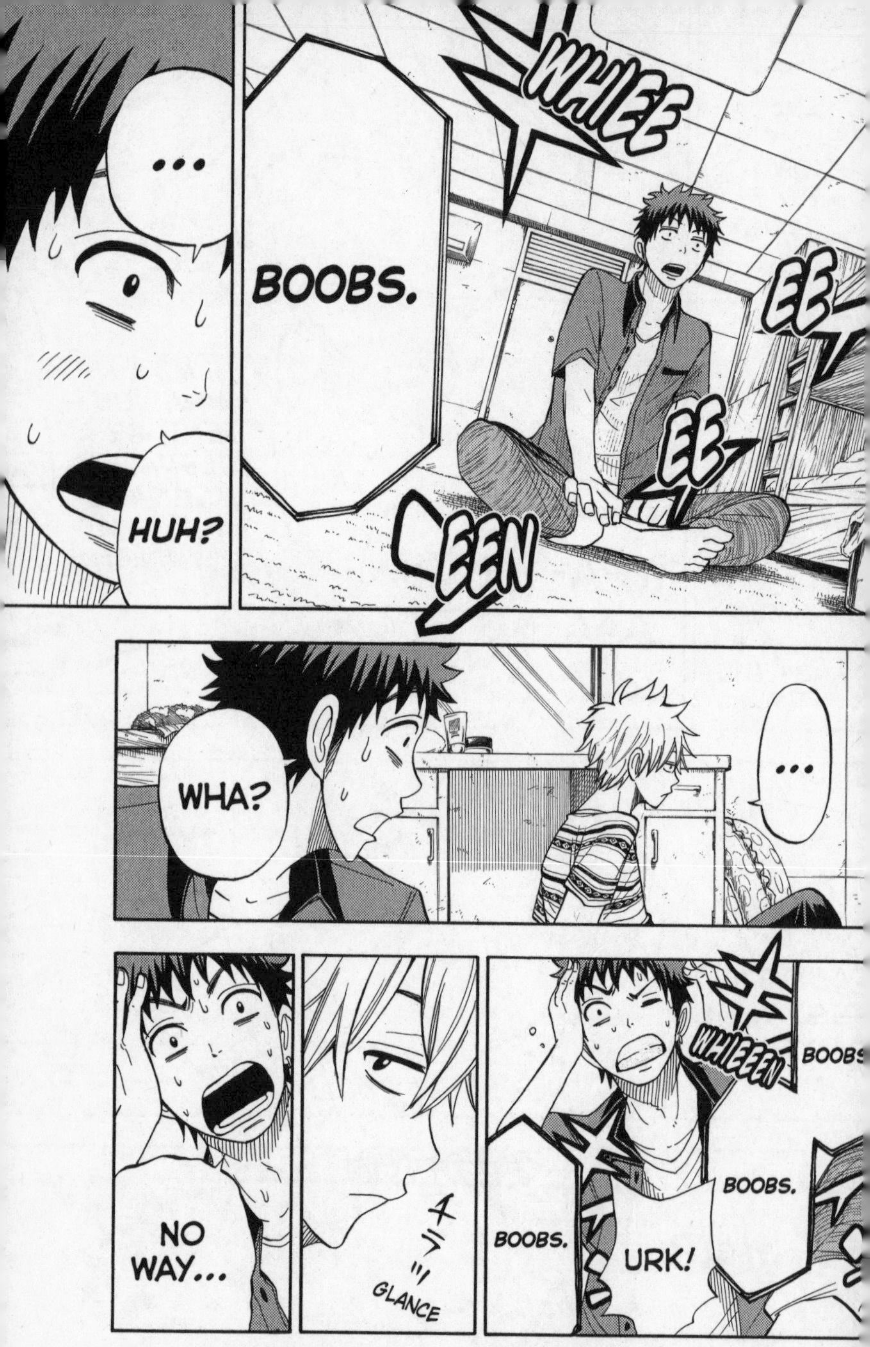
WHIEE
EE
EE
BOOBS.
EEN
...
HUH?
...
WHA?
WHIEEEN
BOOBS
BOOBS.
URK!
BOOBS.
イラッ
GLANCE
NO WAY...

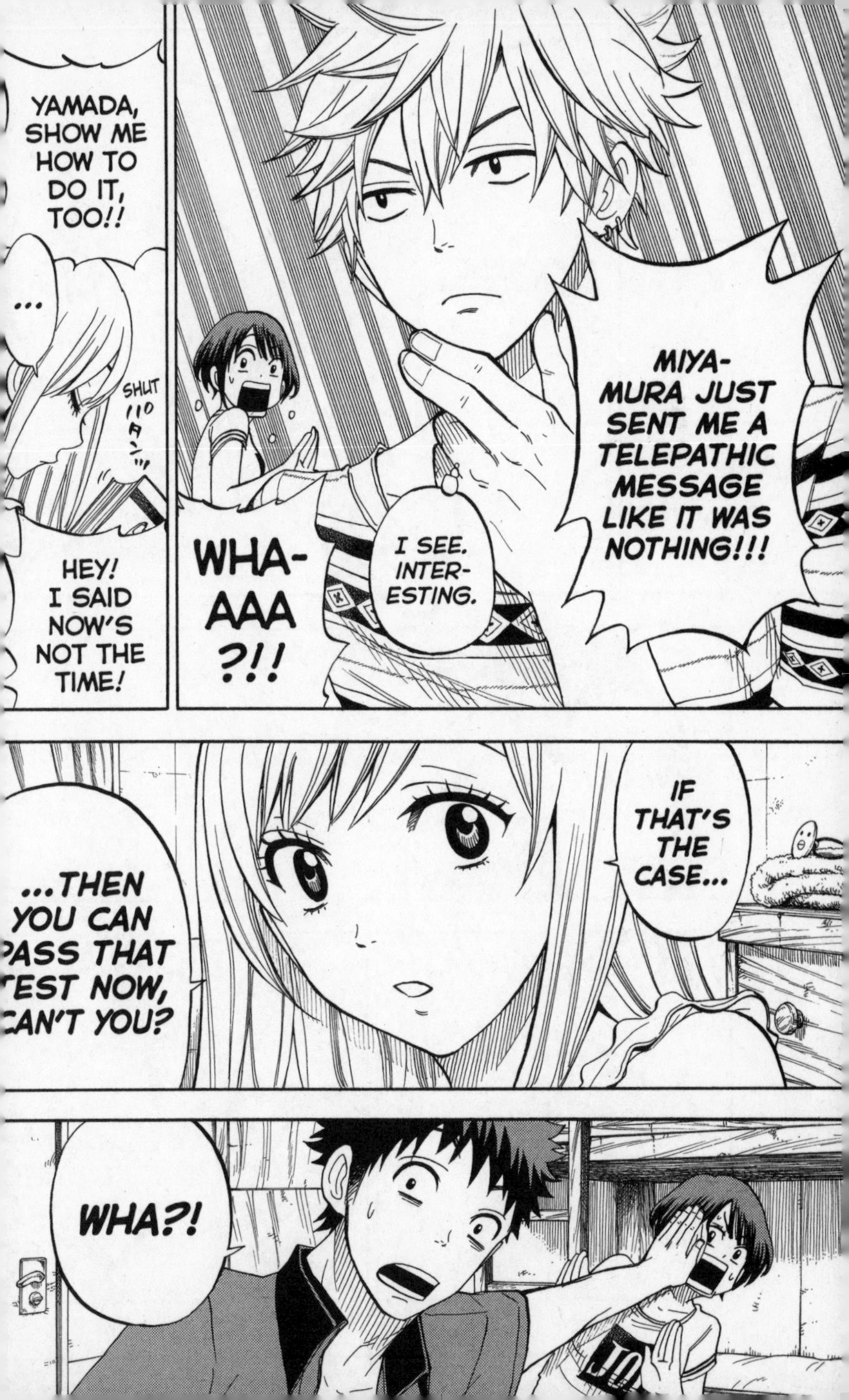
MIYA-MURA JUST SENT ME A TELEPATHIC MESSAGE LIKE IT WAS NOTHING!!!
I SEE. INTER-ESTING.
WHA-AAA?!!
YAMADA, SHOW ME HOW TO DO IT, TOO!!
...
SHUT
HEY! I SAID NOW'S NOT THE TIME!
IF THAT'S THE CASE...
...THEN YOU CAN ASS THAT EST NOW, AN'T YOU?
WHA?!

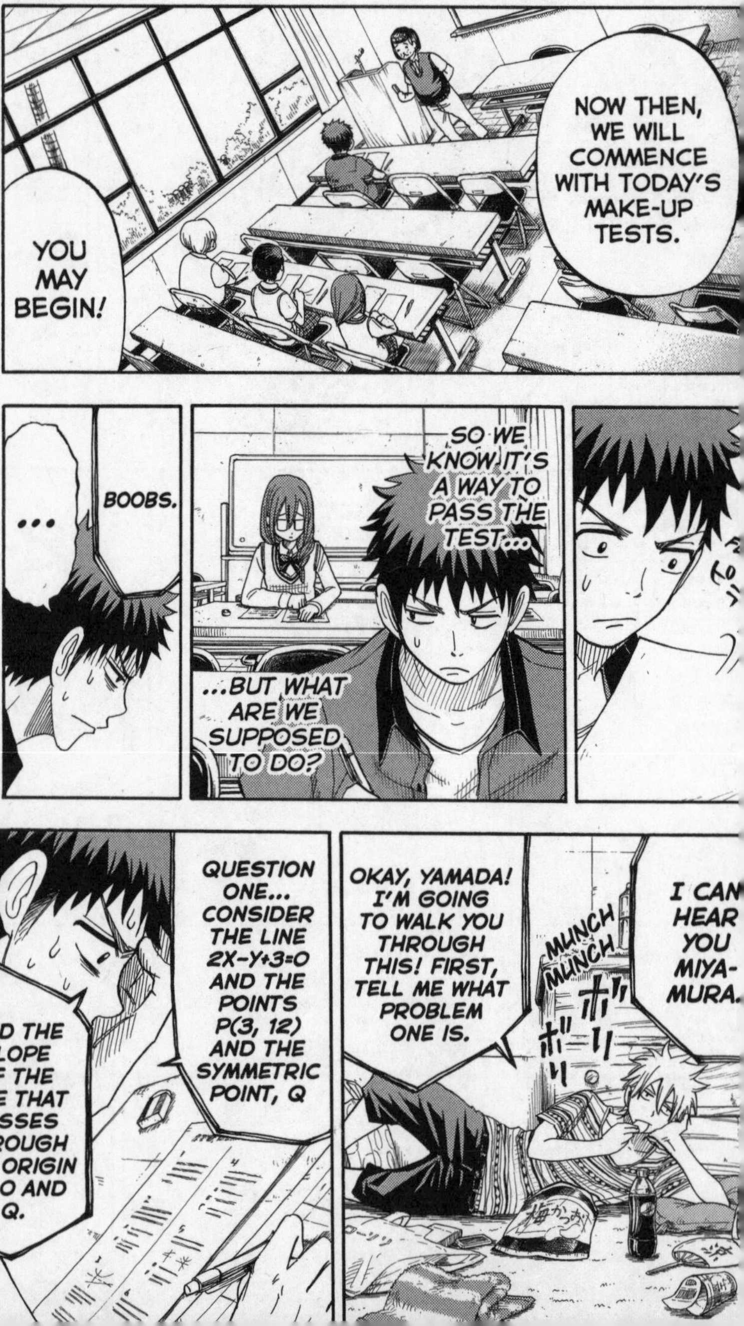
NOW THEN, WE WILL COMMENCE WITH TODAY'S MAKE-UP TESTS.
YOU MAY BEGIN!
SO WE KNOW IT'S A WAY TO PASS THE TEST...
...BUT WHAT ARE WE SUPPOSED TO DO?
BOOBS.
...
I CAN HEAR YOU MIYA-MURA.
MUNCH MUNCH
OKAY, YAMADA! I'M GOING TO WALK YOU THROUGH THIS! FIRST, TELL ME WHAT PROBLEM ONE IS.
QUESTION ONE... CONSIDER THE LINE 2X-Y+3=0 AND THE POINTS P(3, 12) AND THE SYMMETRIC POINT, Q
FIND THE SLOPE OF THE LINE THAT PASSES THROUGH THE ORIGIN OF O AND Q.

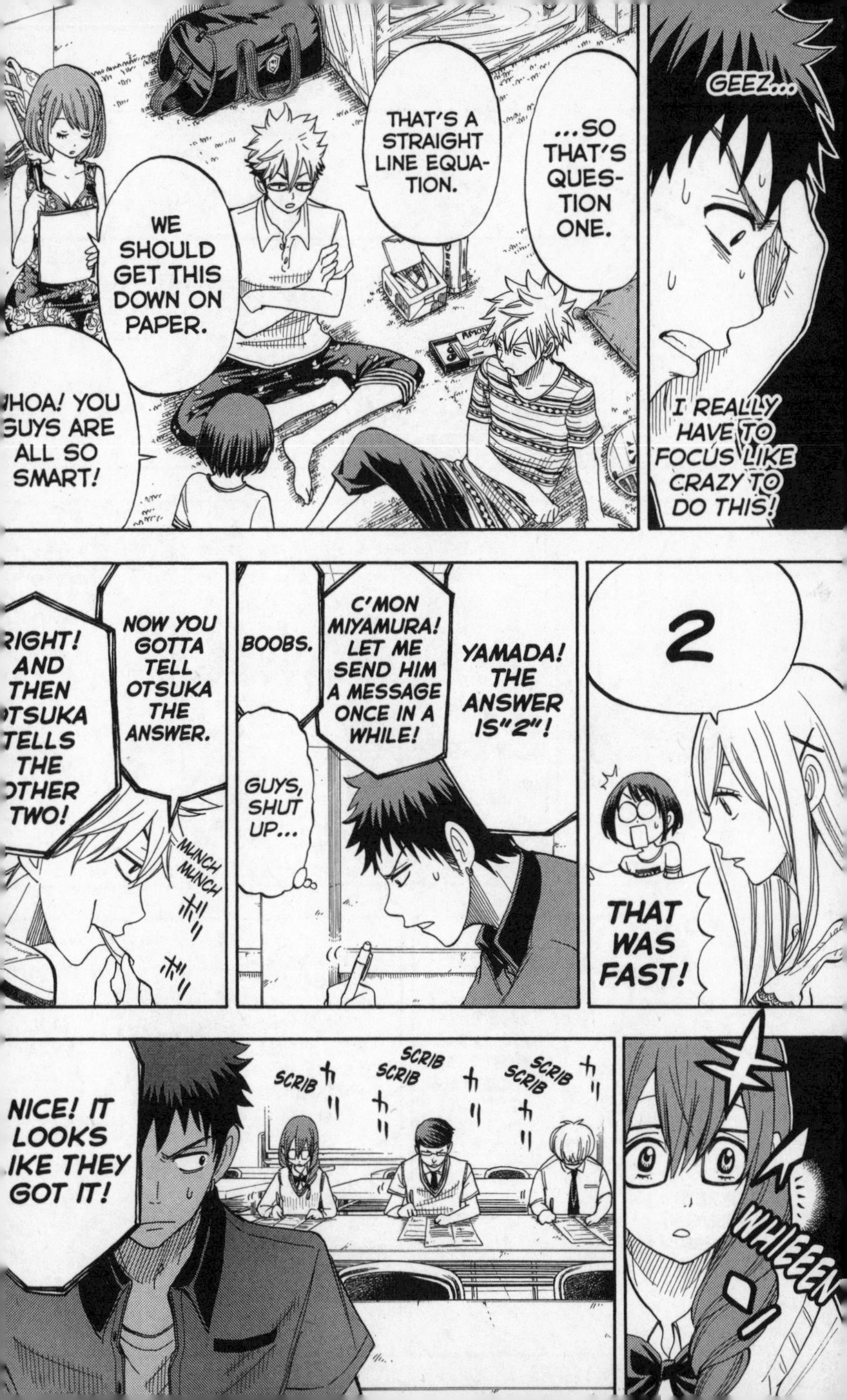
GEEZ...
I REALLY HAVE TO FOCUS LIKE CRAZY TO DO THIS!
...SO THAT'S QUES-TION ONE.
THAT'S A STRAIGHT LINE EQUA-TION.
WE SHOULD GET THIS DOWN ON PAPER.
HOA! YOU UYS ARE ALL SO SMART!
2
THAT WAS FAST!
YAMADA! THE ANSWER IS "2"!
C'MON MIYAMURA! LET ME SEND HIM A MESSAGE ONCE IN A WHILE!
BOOBS.
GUYS, SHUT UP...
NOW YOU GOTTA TELL OTSUKA THE ANSWER.
IGHT! AND THEN TSUKA TELLS THE THER TWO!
MUNCH MUNCH
WHIEEEN
SCRIB SCRIB
SCRIB SCRIB
SCRIB
NICE! IT LOOKS IKE THEY GOT IT!

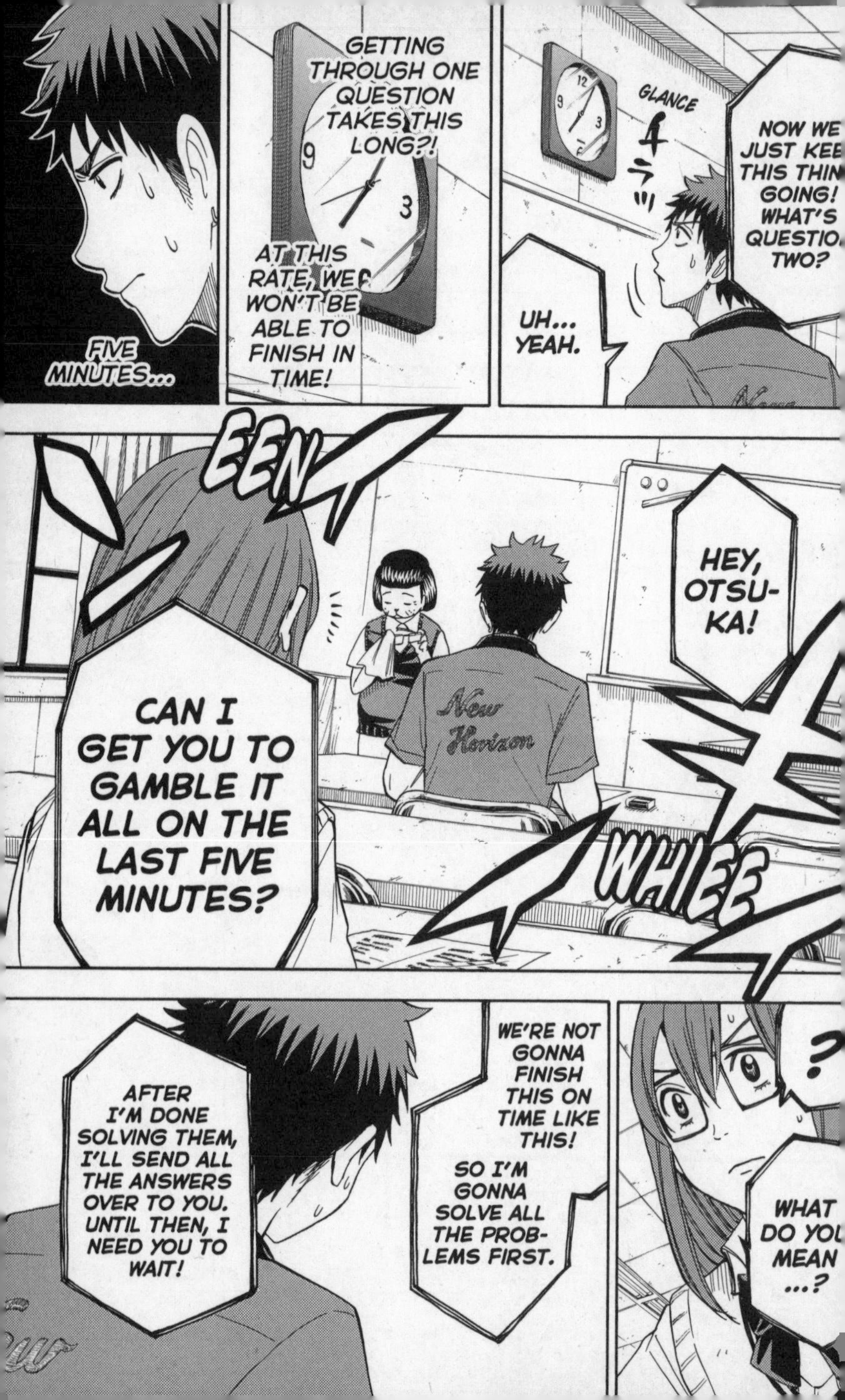
NOW WE JUST KEE THIS THIN GOING! WHAT'S QUESTIO TWO?
GLANCE
UH... YEAH.
GETTING THROUGH ONE QUESTION TAKES THIS LONG?!
AT THIS RATE, WE WON'T BE ABLE TO FINISH IN TIME!
FIVE MINUTES...
HEY, OTSU-KA!
WHIEE
EEN
CAN I GET YOU TO GAMBLE IT ALL ON THE LAST FIVE MINUTES?
?
WHAT DO YOU MEAN ...?
WE'RE NOT GONNA FINISH THIS ON TIME LIKE THIS!
SO I'M GONNA SOLVE ALL THE PROB-LEMS FIRST.
AFTER I'M DONE SOLVING THEM, I'LL SEND ALL THE ANSWERS OVER TO YOU. UNTIL THEN, I NEED YOU TO WAIT!

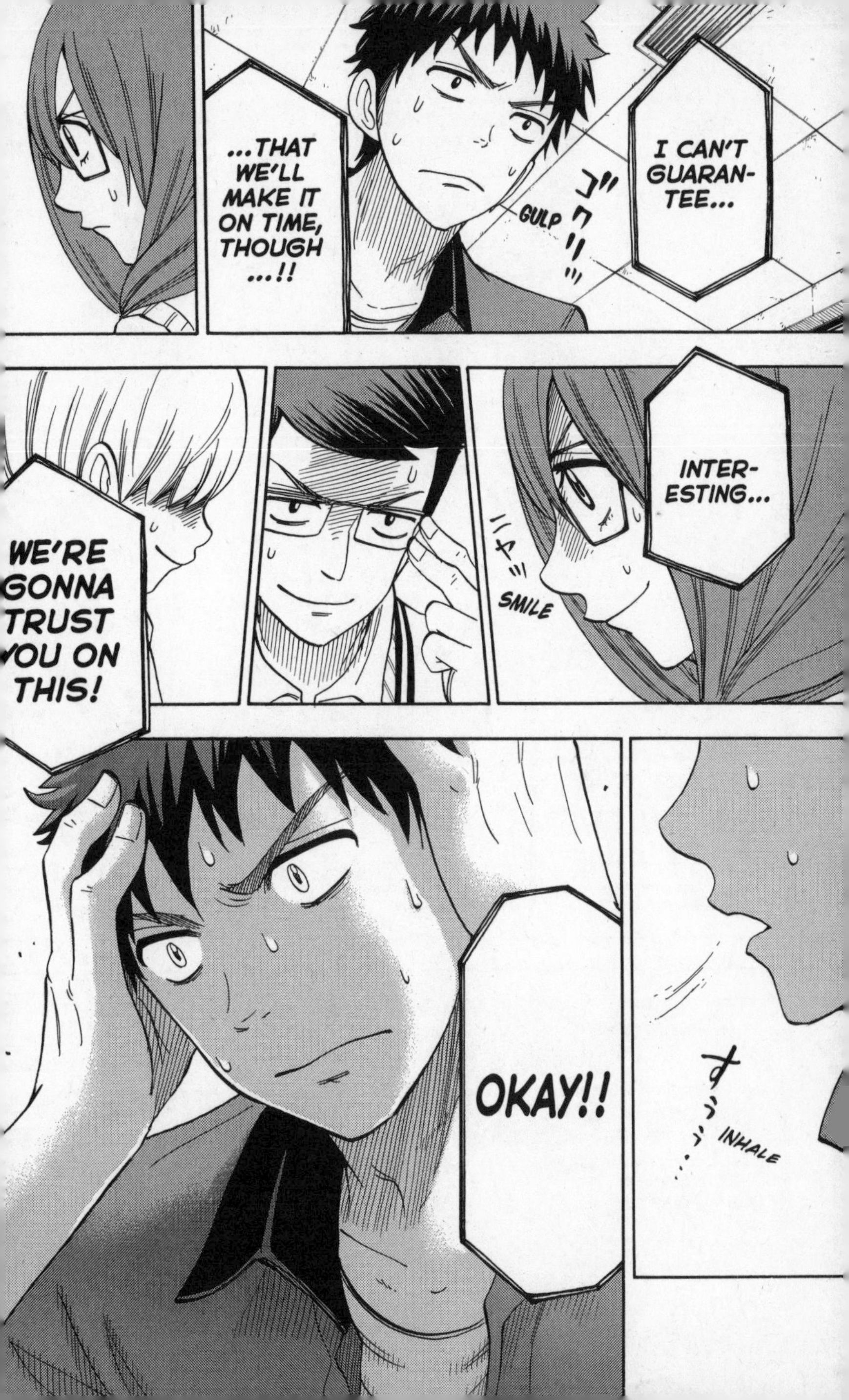
I CAN'T GUARAN-TEE...
GULP
...THAT WE'LL MAKE IT ON TIME, THOUGH ...!!
INTER-ESTING...
SMILE
WE'RE GONNA TRUST YOU ON THIS!
INHALE
OKAY!!

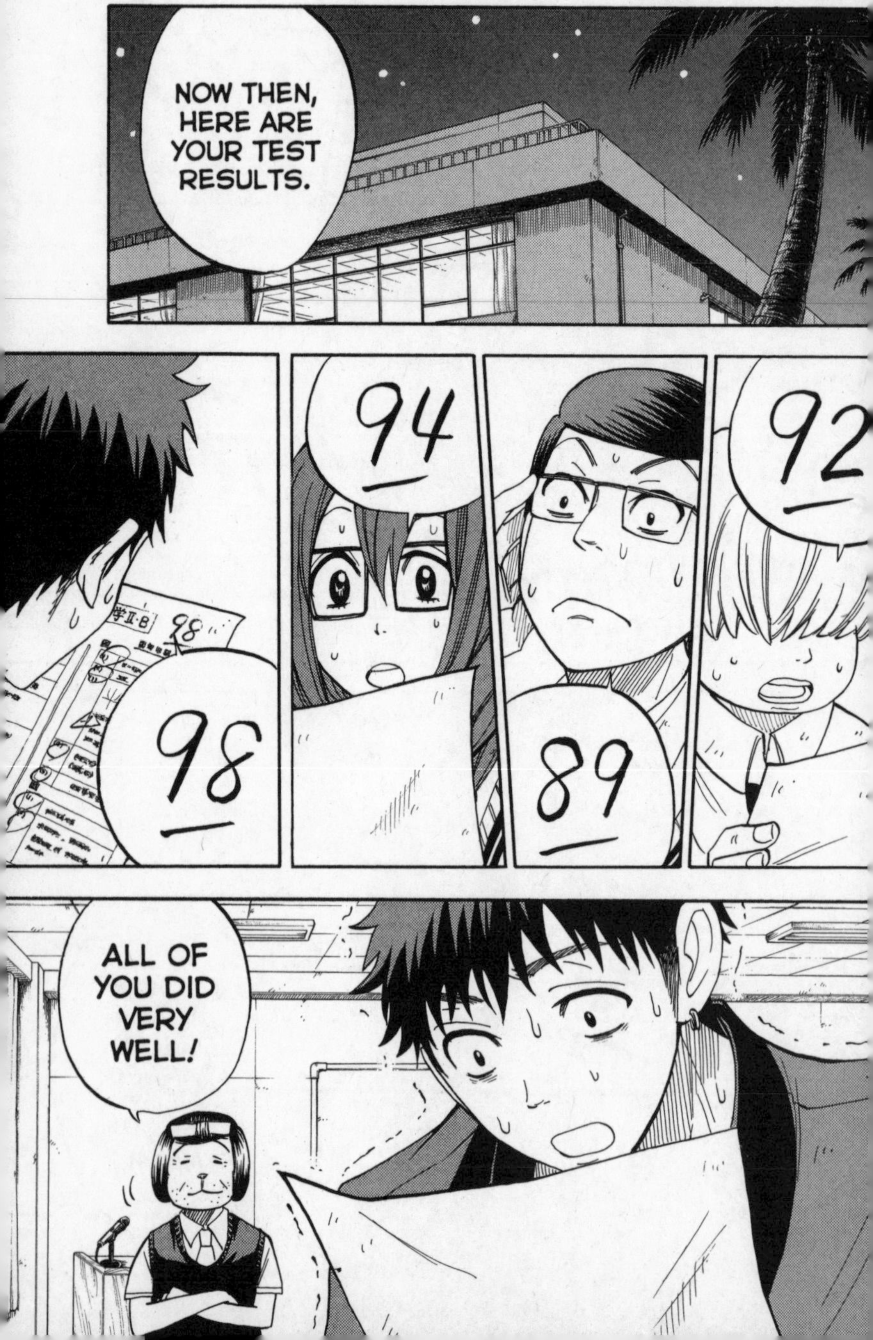
NOW THEN, HERE ARE YOUR TEST RESULTS.
92
89
94
98
ALL OF YOU DID VERY WELL!

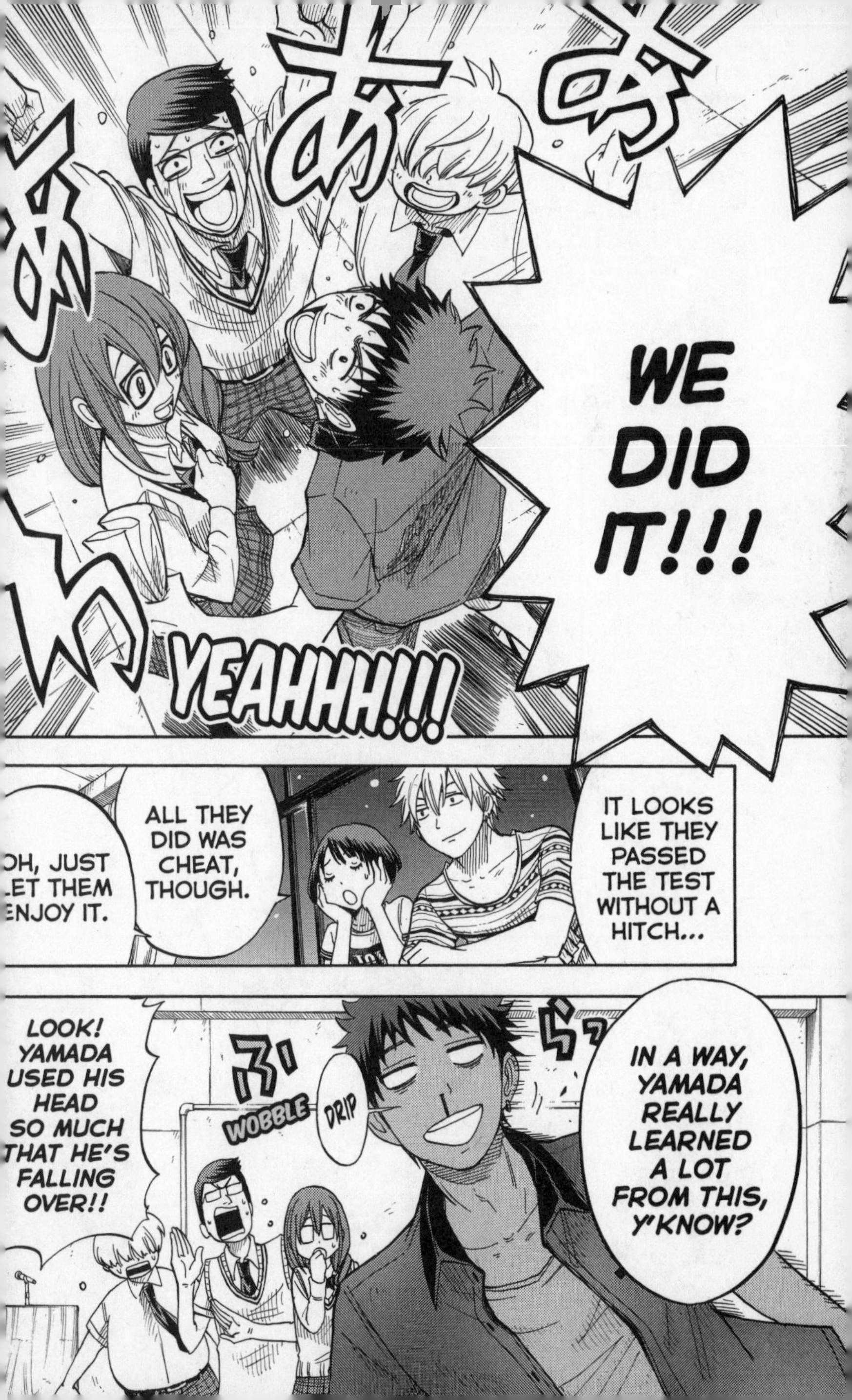
WE DID IT!!!
YEAHHH!!!!
IT LOOKS LIKE THEY PASSED THE TEST WITHOUT A HITCH...
ALL THEY DID WAS CHEAT, THOUGH.
OH, JUST LET THEM ENJOY IT.
IN A WAY, YAMADA REALLY LEARNED A LOT FROM THIS, Y'KNOW?
DRIP
WOBBLE
LOOK! YAMADA USED HIS HEAD SO MUCH THAT HE'S FALLING OVER!!

CHAPTER 31: Odagiri's Breasts.

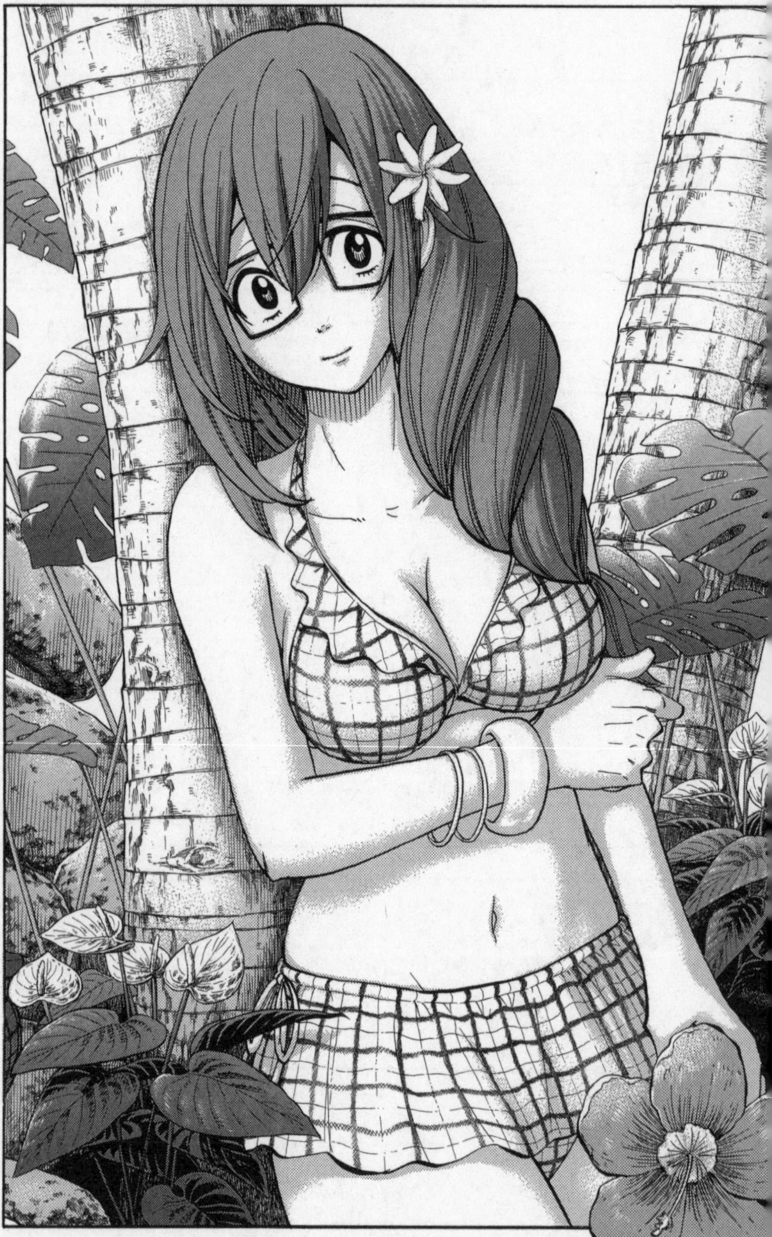

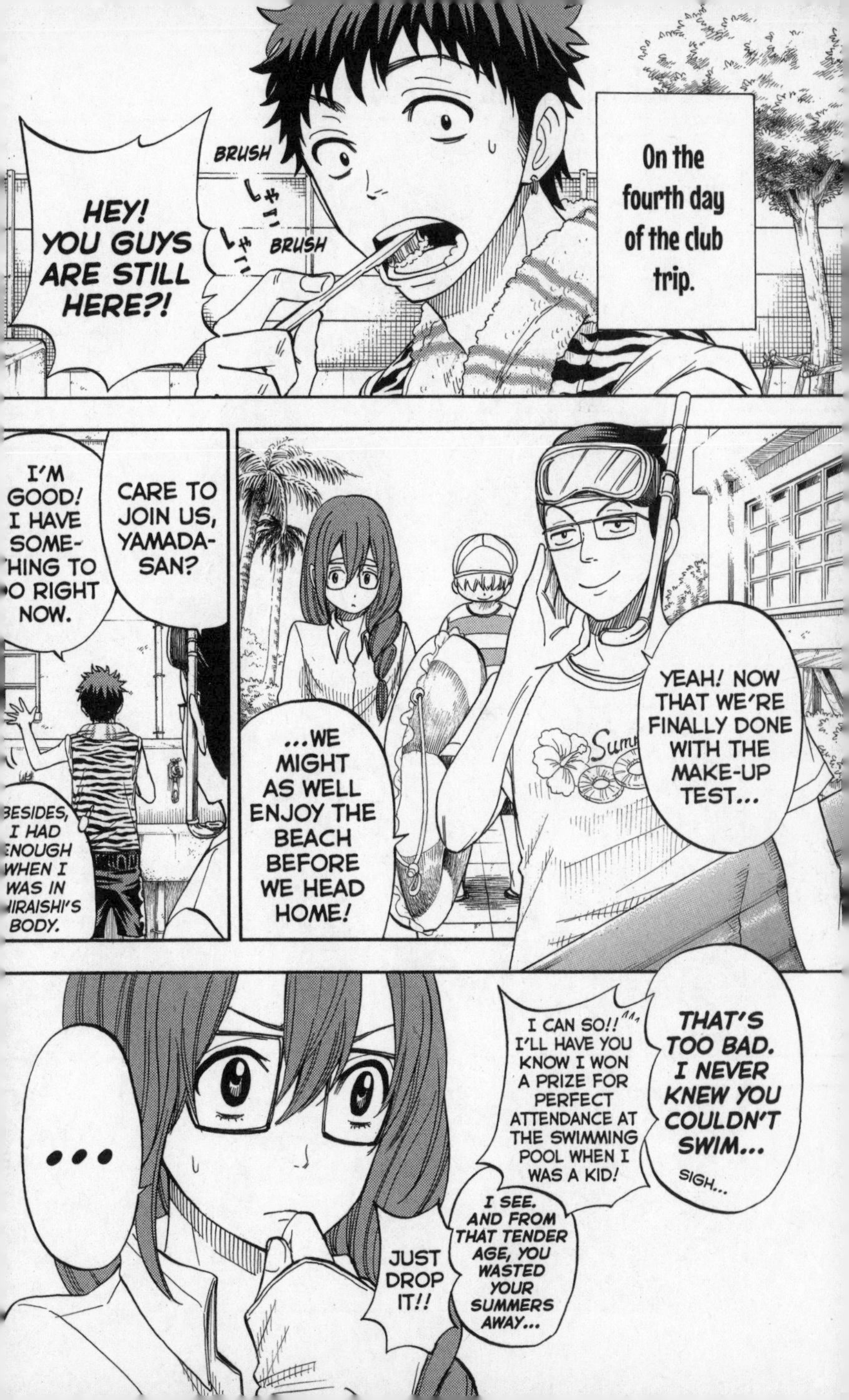
On the fourth day of the club trip.
BRUSH
BRUSH
HEY! YOU GUYS ARE STILL HERE?!
YEAH! NOW THAT WE'RE FINALLY DONE WITH THE MAKE-UP TEST...
...WE MIGHT AS WELL ENJOY THE BEACH BEFORE WE HEAD HOME!
CARE TO JOIN US, YAMADA-SAN?
I'M GOOD! I HAVE SOME- HING TO O RIGHT NOW.
ESIDES, I HAD NOUGH WHEN I WAS IN IRAISHI'S BODY.
THAT'S TOO BAD. I NEVER KNEW YOU COULDN'T SWIM...
SIGH...
I CAN SO!! I'LL HAVE YOU KNOW I WON A PRIZE FOR PERFECT ATTENDANCE AT THE SWIMMING POOL WHEN I WAS A KID!
I SEE. AND FROM THAT TENDER AGE, YOU WASTED YOUR SUMMERS AWAY...
JUST DROP IT!!
...

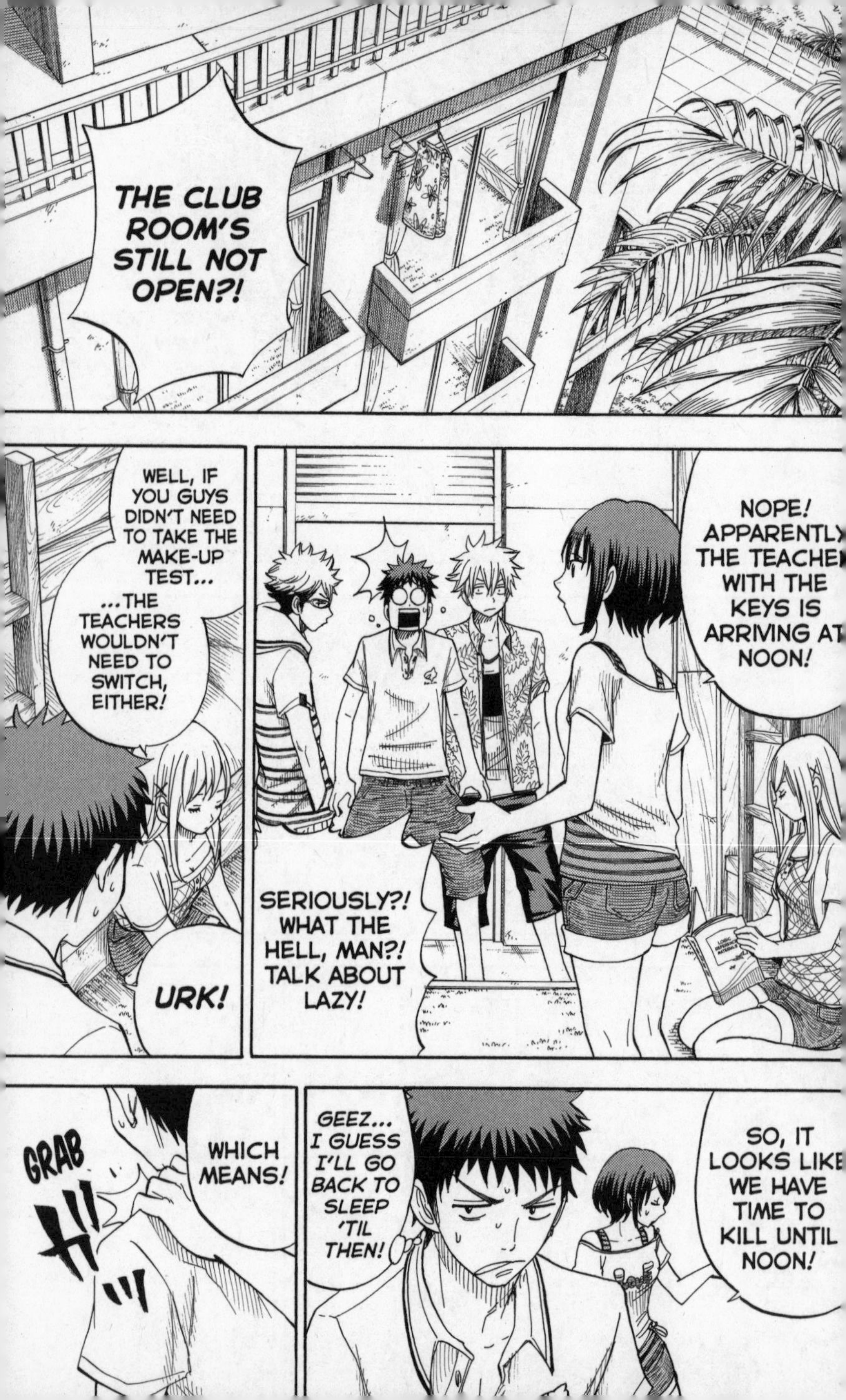
THE CLUB ROOM'S STILL NOT OPEN?!
NOPE! APPARENTLY THE TEACHER WITH THE KEYS IS ARRIVING AT NOON!
SERIOUSLY?! WHAT THE HELL, MAN?! TALK ABOUT LAZY!
WELL, IF YOU GUYS DIDN'T NEED TO TAKE THE MAKE-UP TEST...
...THE TEACHERS WOULDN'T NEED TO SWITCH, EITHER!
URK!
SO, IT LOOKS LIKE WE HAVE TIME TO KILL UNTIL NOON!
GEEZ... I GUESS I'LL GO BACK TO SLEEP 'TIL THEN!
WHICH MEANS!
GRAB

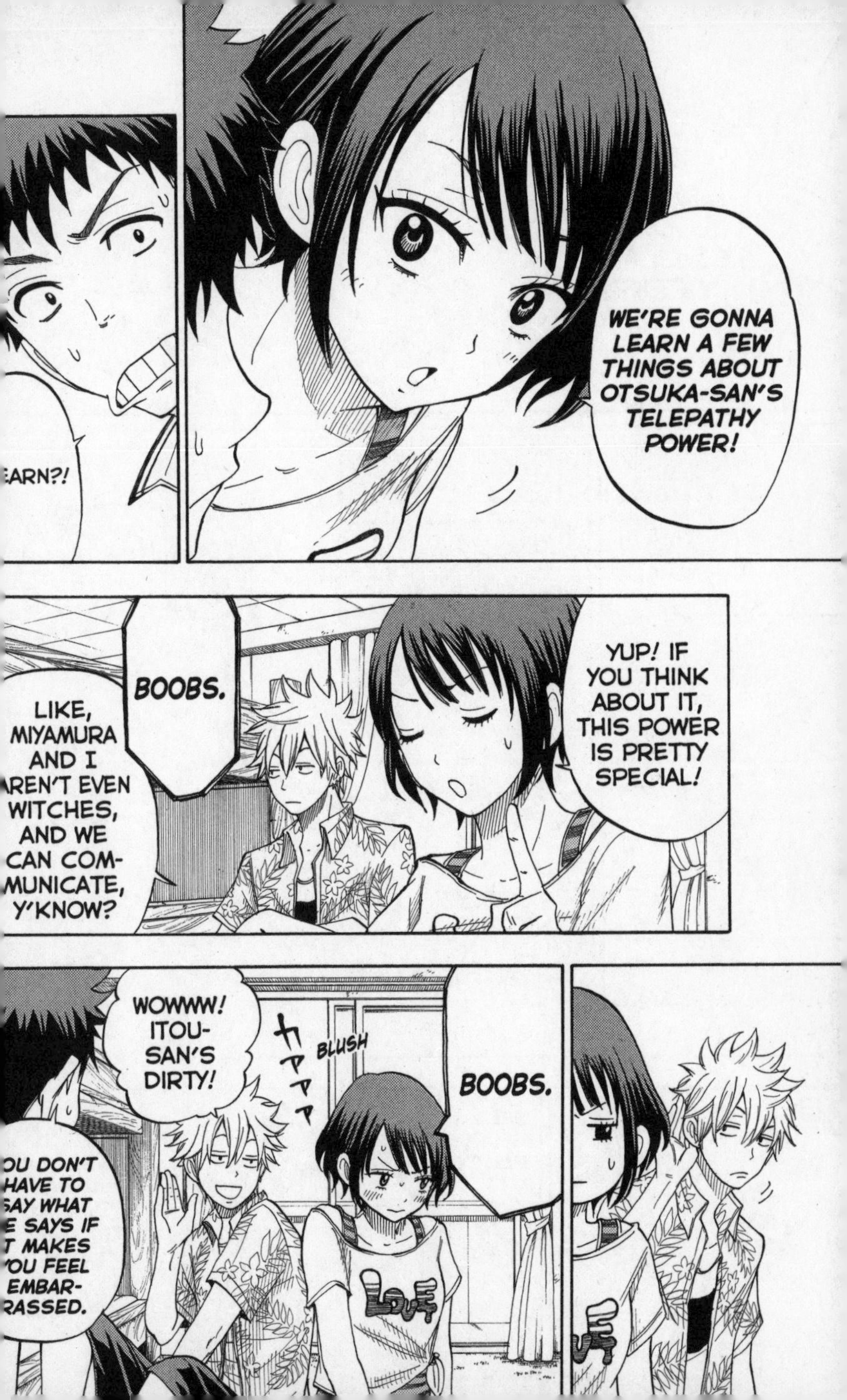
WE'RE GONNA LEARN A FEW THINGS ABOUT OTSUKA-SAN'S TELEPATHY POWER!
EARN?!
YUP! IF YOU THINK ABOUT IT, THIS POWER IS PRETTY SPECIAL!
BOOBS.
LIKE, MIYAMURA AND I AREN'T EVEN WITCHES, AND WE CAN COM-MUNICATE, Y'KNOW?
BOOBS.
BLUSH
WOWWW! ITOU-SAN'S DIRTY!
OU DON'T HAVE TO SAY WHAT E SAYS IF T MAKES OU FEEL EMBAR-RASSED.

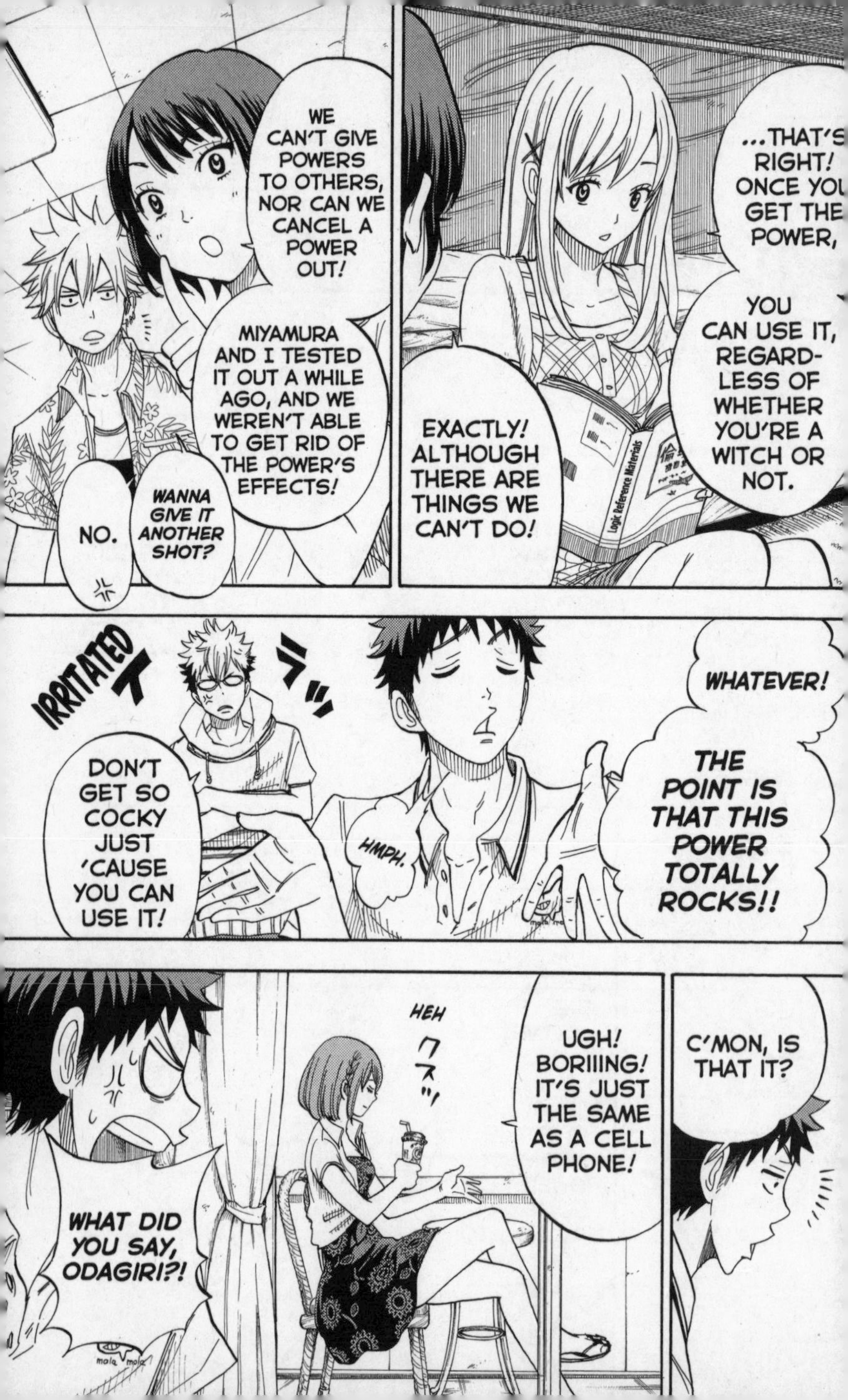
...THAT'S RIGHT! ONCE YOU GET THE POWER,
YOU CAN USE IT, REGARDLESS OF WHETHER YOU'RE A WITCH OR NOT.
EXACTLY! ALTHOUGH THERE ARE THINGS WE CAN'T DO!
Logic Reference Materials
WE CAN'T GIVE POWERS TO OTHERS, NOR CAN WE CANCEL A POWER OUT!
MIYAMURA AND I TESTED IT OUT A WHILE AGO, AND WE WEREN'T ABLE TO GET RID OF THE POWER'S EFFECTS!
WANNA GIVE IT ANOTHER SHOT?
NO.
WHATEVER!
THE POINT IS THAT THIS POWER TOTALLY ROCKS!!
HMPH.
IRRITATED
DON'T GET SO COCKY JUST 'CAUSE YOU CAN USE IT!
C'MON, IS THAT IT?
UGH! BORIIING! IT'S JUST THE SAME AS A CELL PHONE!
HEH
WHAT DID YOU SAY, ODAGIRI?!

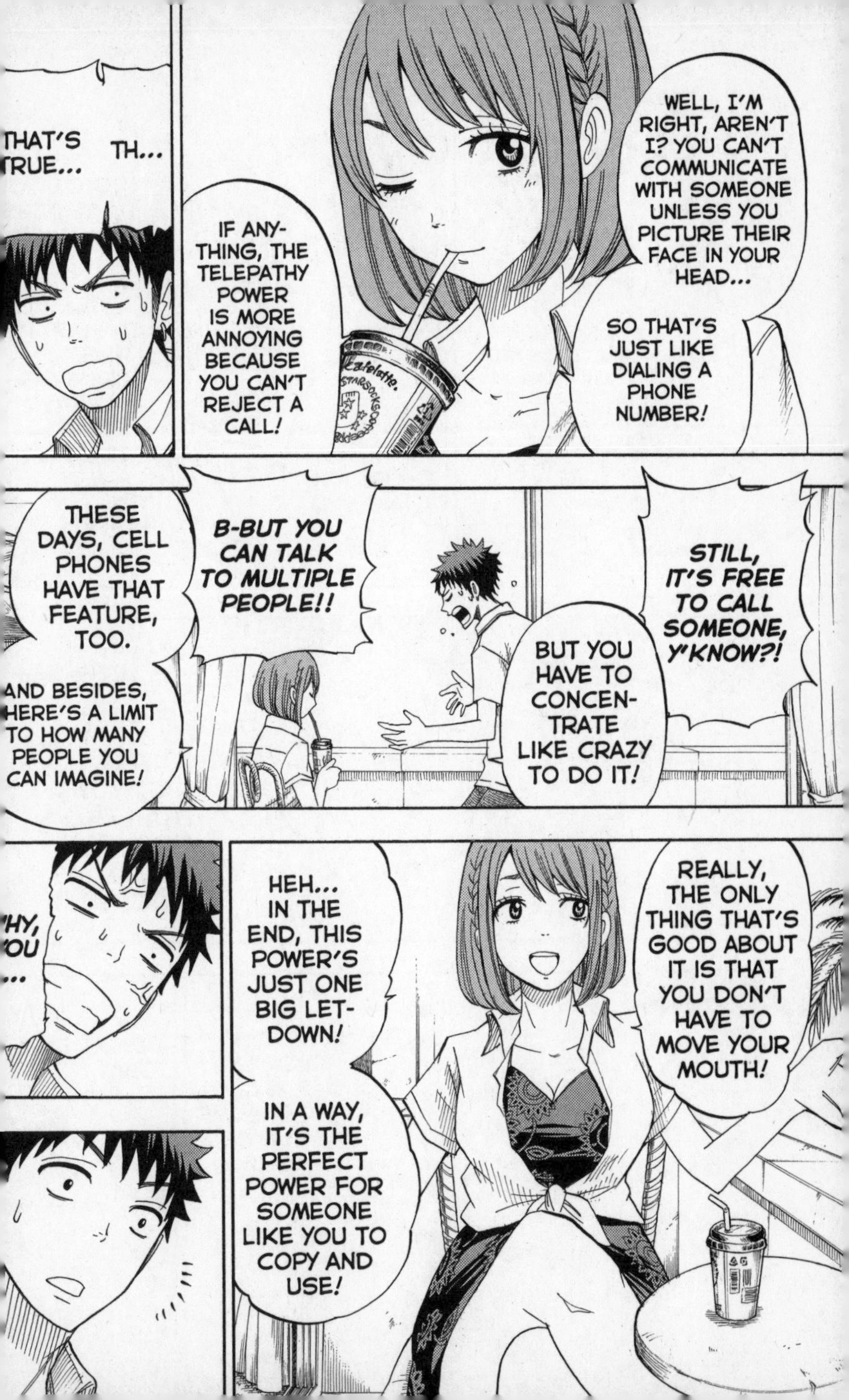
WELL, I'M RIGHT, AREN'T I? YOU CAN'T COMMUNICATE WITH SOMEONE UNLESS YOU PICTURE THEIR FACE IN YOUR HEAD...
SO THAT'S JUST LIKE DIALING A PHONE NUMBER!
IF ANY-THING, THE TELEPATHY POWER IS MORE ANNOYING BECAUSE YOU CAN'T REJECT A CALL!
TH...
THAT'S TRUE...
STILL, IT'S FREE TO CALL SOMEONE, Y'KNOW?!
BUT YOU HAVE TO CONCEN-TRATE LIKE CRAZY TO DO IT!
B-BUT YOU CAN TALK TO MULTIPLE PEOPLE!!
THESE DAYS, CELL PHONES HAVE THAT FEATURE, TOO.
AND BESIDES, HERE'S A LIMIT TO HOW MANY PEOPLE YOU CAN IMAGINE!
REALLY, THE ONLY THING THAT'S GOOD ABOUT IT IS THAT YOU DON'T HAVE TO MOVE YOUR MOUTH!
HEH... IN THE END, THIS POWER'S JUST ONE BIG LET-DOWN!
IN A WAY, IT'S THE PERFECT POWER FOR SOMEONE LIKE YOU TO COPY AND USE!
HY, OU ...

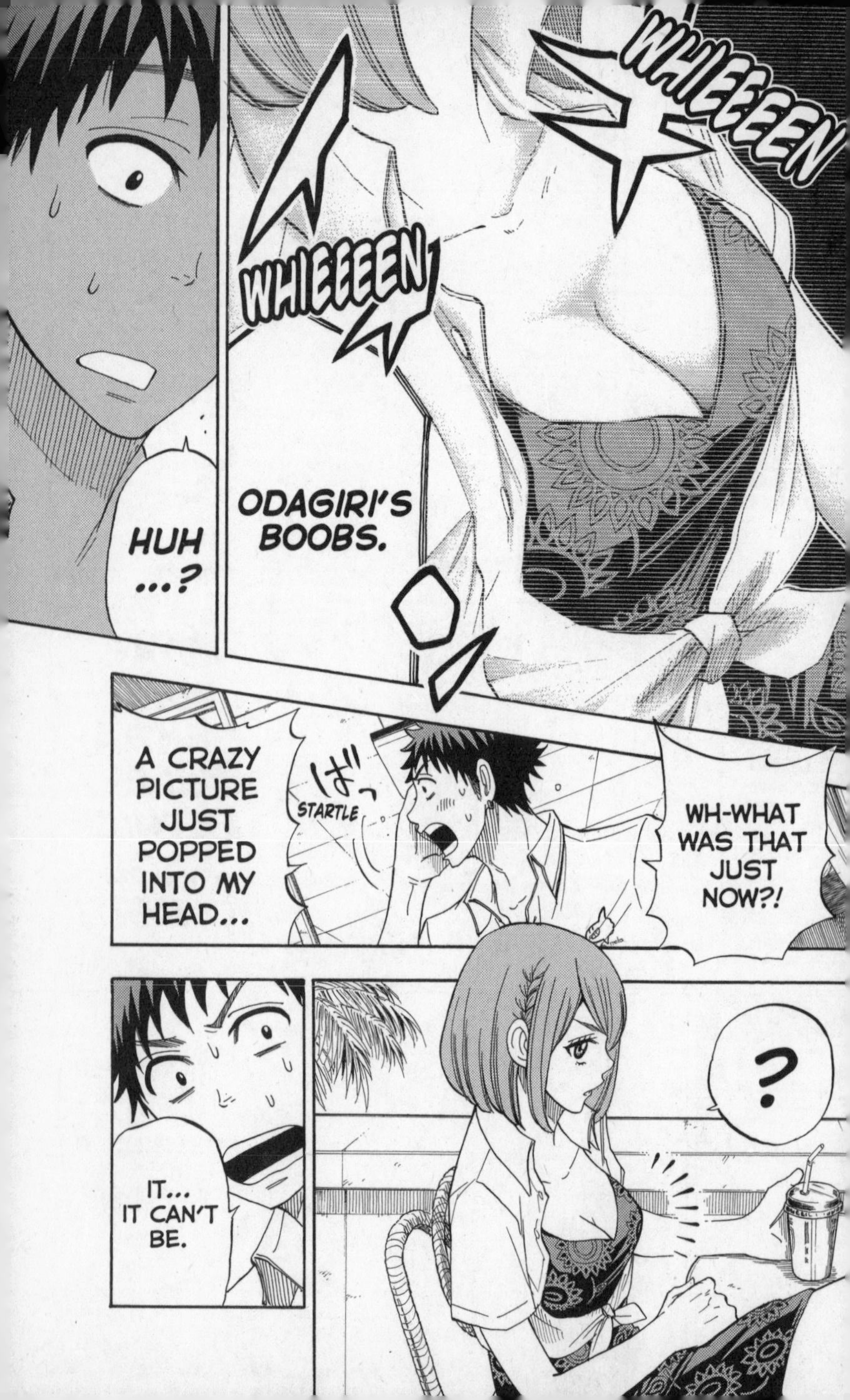
WHIEEEEN
WHIEEEEN
ODAGIRI'S BOOBS.
HUH ...?
WH-WHAT WAS THAT JUST NOW?!
ばっ
STARTLE
A CRAZY PICTURE JUST POPPED INTO MY HEAD...
?
IT... IT CAN'T BE.

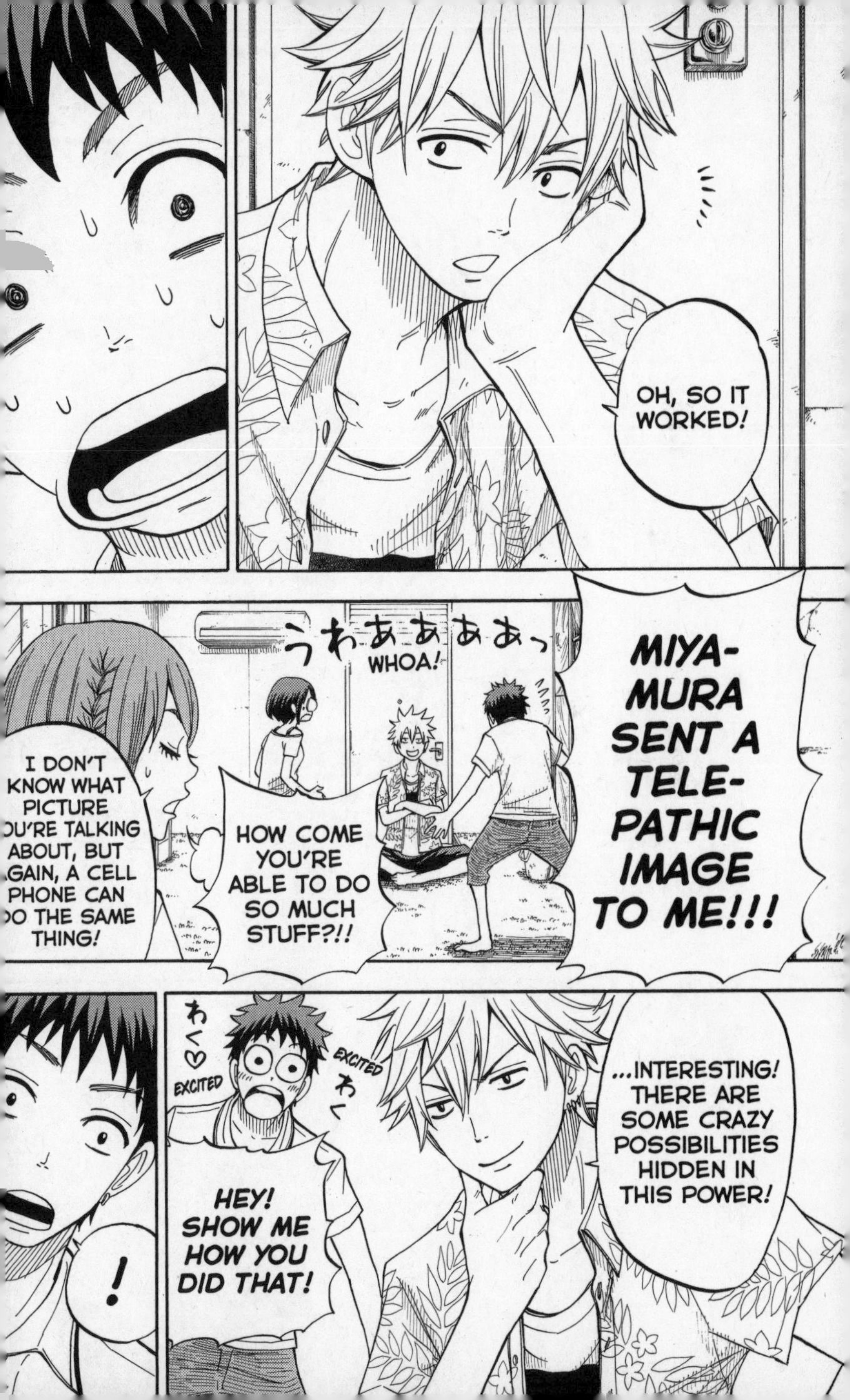
OH, SO IT WORKED!
MIYAMURA SENT A TELEPATHIC IMAGE TO ME!!!
うわあああああっ
WHOA!
HOW COME YOU'RE ABLE TO DO SO MUCH STUFF?!!
I DON'T KNOW WHAT PICTURE OU'RE TALKING ABOUT, BUT GAIN, A CELL PHONE CAN O THE SAME THING!
...INTERESTING! THERE ARE SOME CRAZY POSSIBILITIES HIDDEN IN THIS POWER!
わく
EXCITED
わく♡
EXCITED
HEY! SHOW ME HOW YOU DID THAT!
!

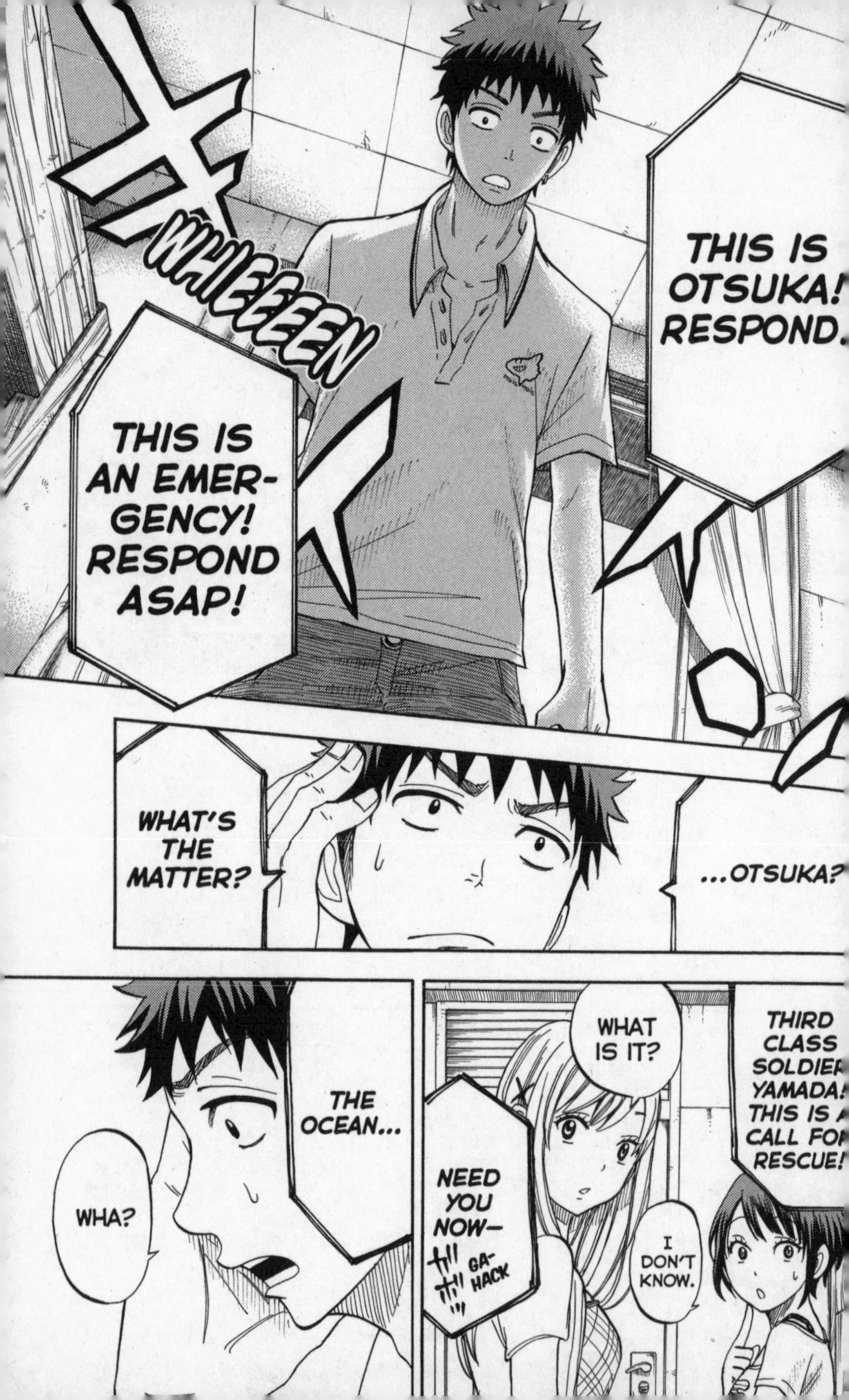
THIS IS OTSUKA! RESPOND.
WHIEEEEN
THIS IS AN EMERGENCY! RESPOND ASAP!
...OTSUKA?
WHAT'S THE MATTER?
THIRD CLASS SOLDIER YAMADA! THIS IS A CALL FOR RESCUE!
WHAT IS IT?
NEED YOU NOW—
GA-HACK
I DON'T KNOW.
THE OCEAN...
WHA?

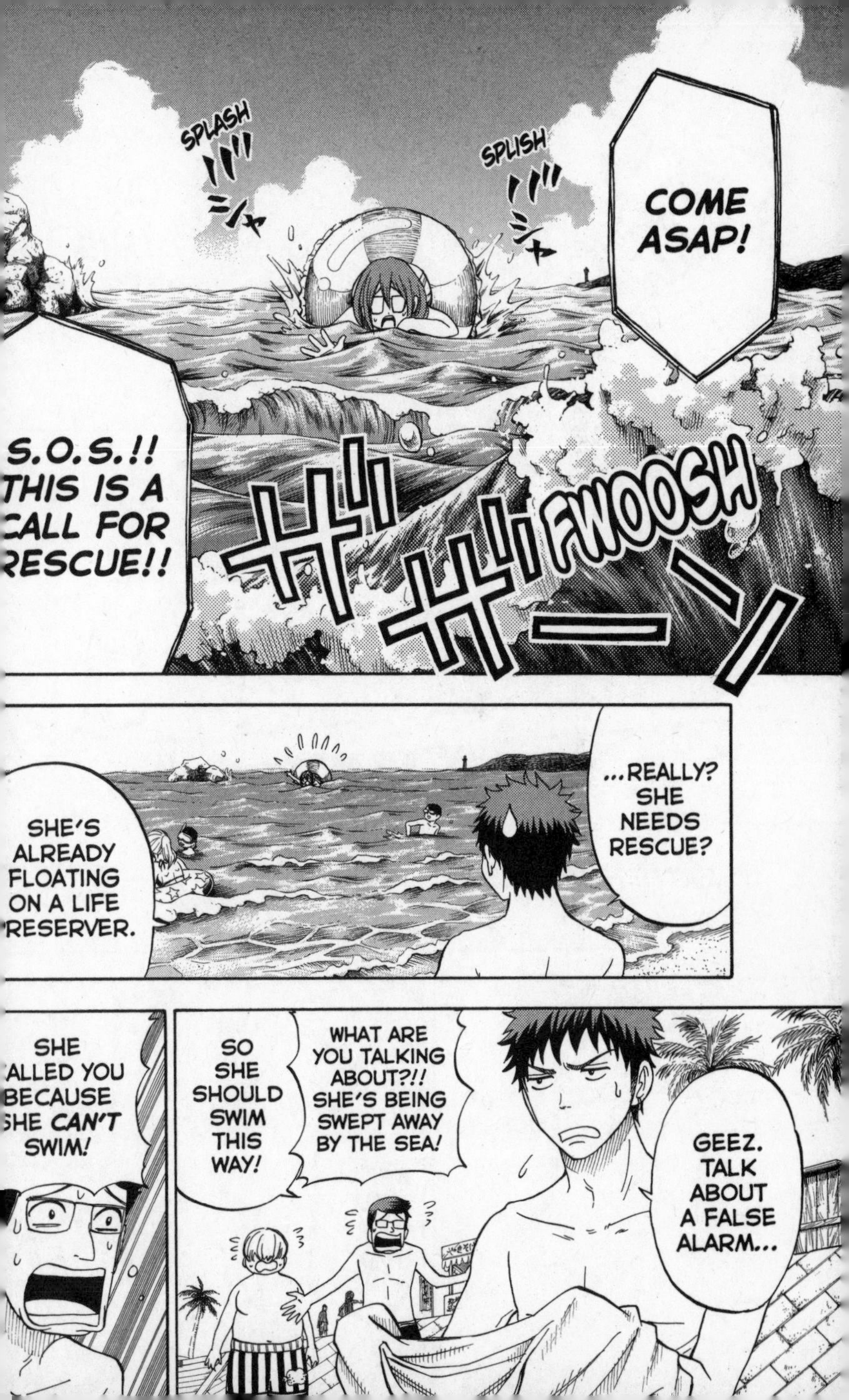
COME ASAP!
SPLISH
SPLASH
S.O.S.!! THIS IS A CALL FOR RESCUE!!
FWOOSH
...REALLY? SHE NEEDS RESCUE?
SHE'S ALREADY FLOATING ON A LIFE PRESERVER.
GEEZ. TALK ABOUT A FALSE ALARM...
WHAT ARE YOU TALKING ABOUT?!! SHE'S BEING SWEPT AWAY BY THE SEA!
SO SHE SHOULD SWIM THIS WAY!
SHE CALLED YOU BECAUSE SHE *CAN'T* SWIM!

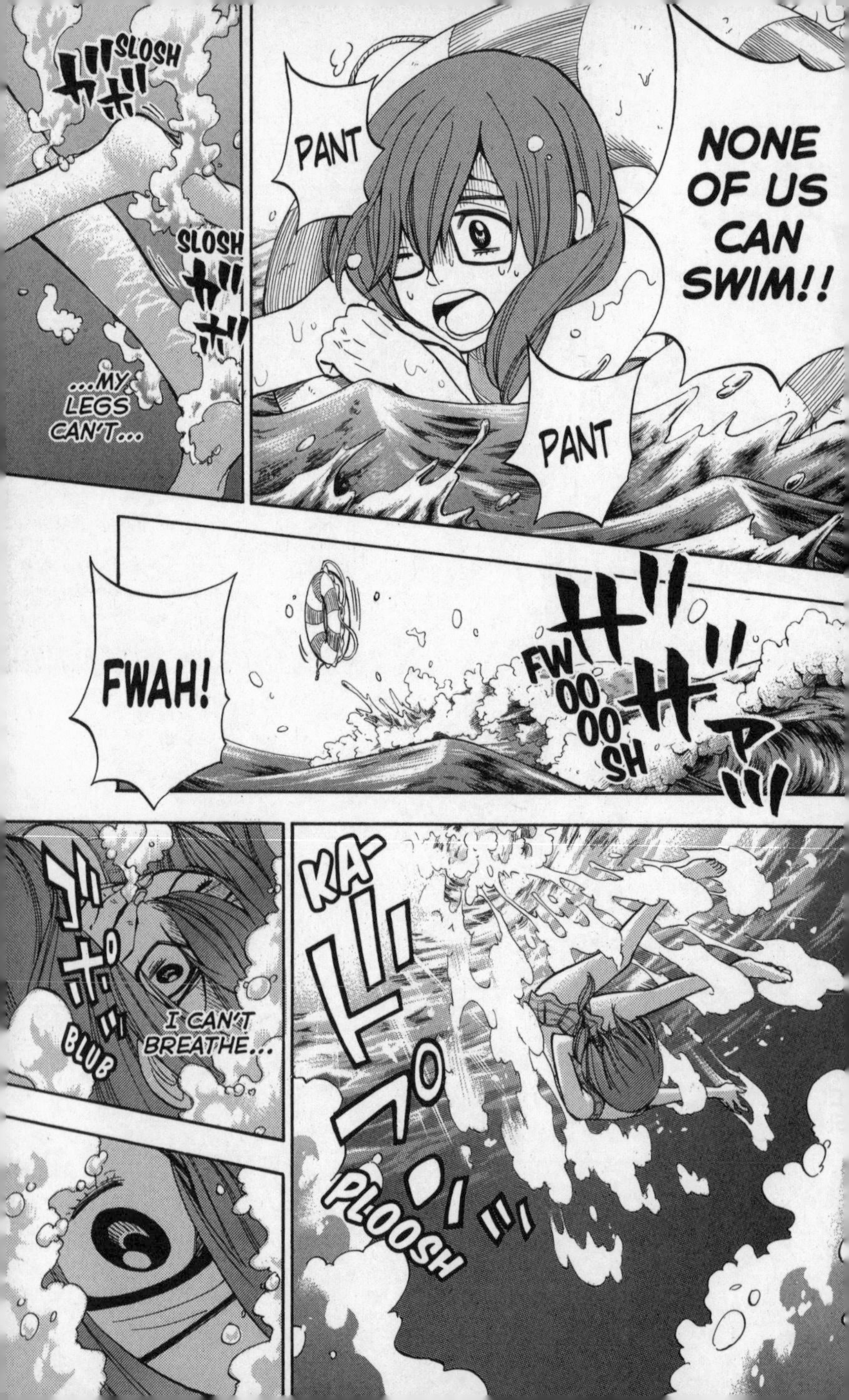
NONE OF US CAN SWIM!!
PANT
PANT
SLOSH
SLOSH
...MY LEGS CAN'T...
FWOOOOSH
FWAH!
KA-PLOOSH
BLUB
I CAN'T BREATHE...

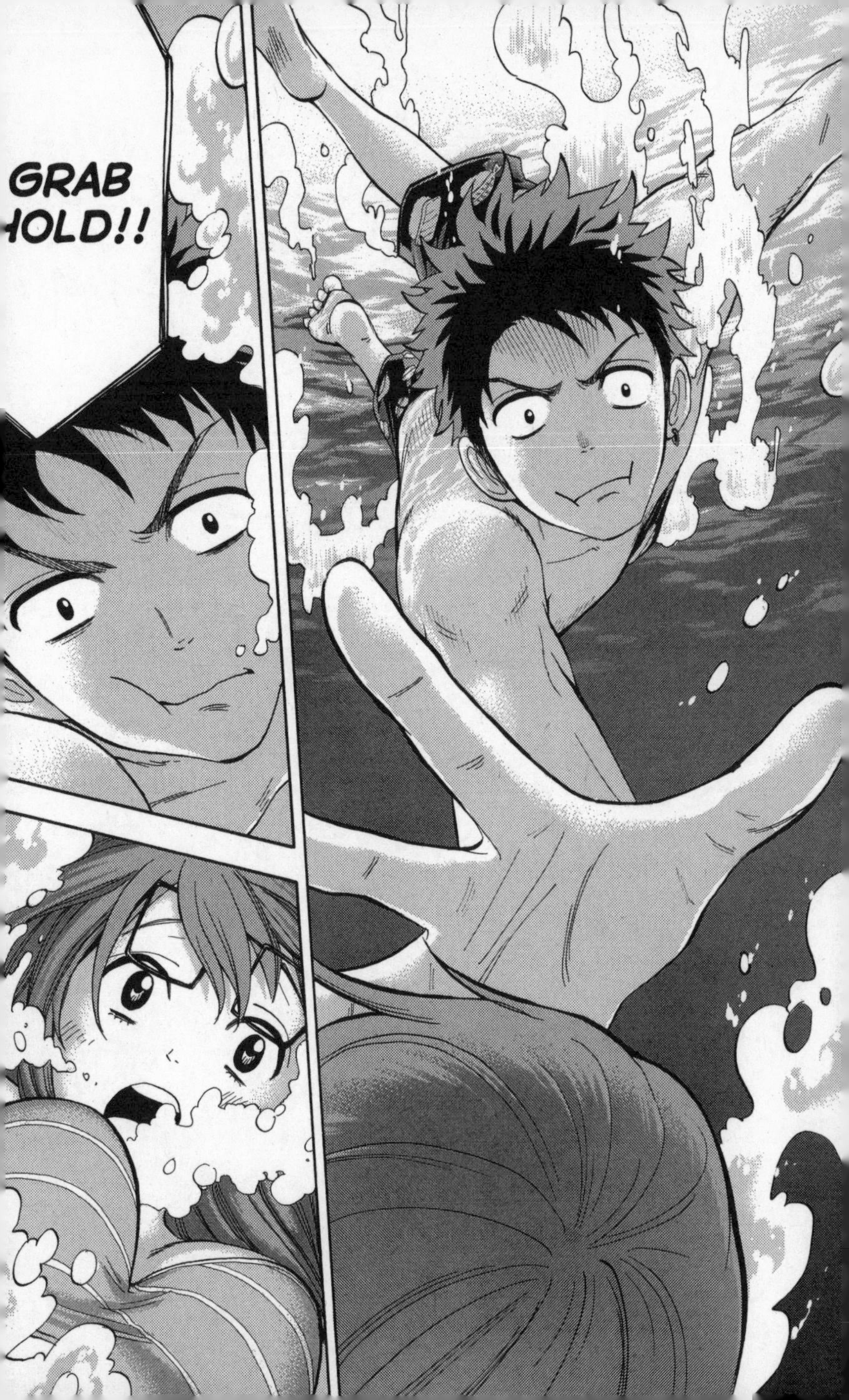
GRAB HOLD!!

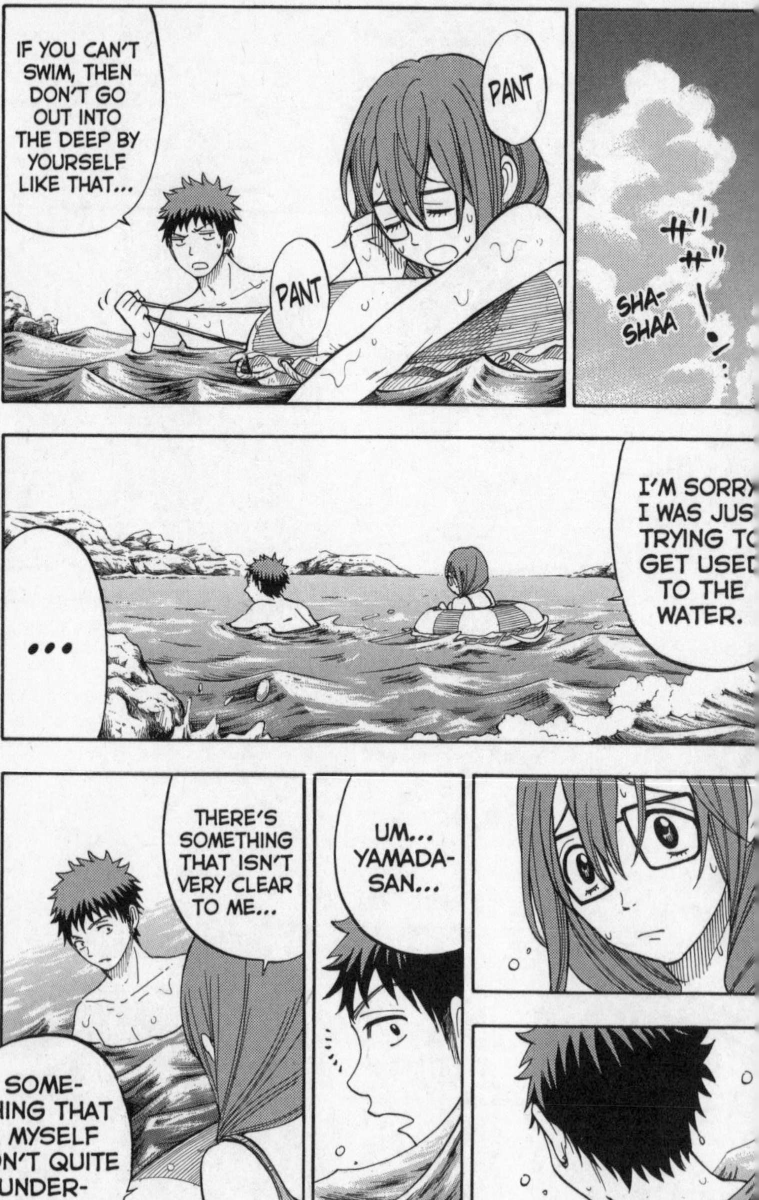
SHA-SHAA
PANT
IF YOU CAN'T SWIM, THEN DON'T GO OUT INTO THE DEEP BY YOURSELF LIKE THAT...
PANT
I'M SORRY I WAS JUS TRYING TO GET USED TO THE WATER.
...
UM... YAMADA-SAN...
THERE'S SOMETHING THAT ISN'T VERY CLEAR TO ME...
SOME-THING THAT I MYSELF DON'T QUITE UNDER-STAND...

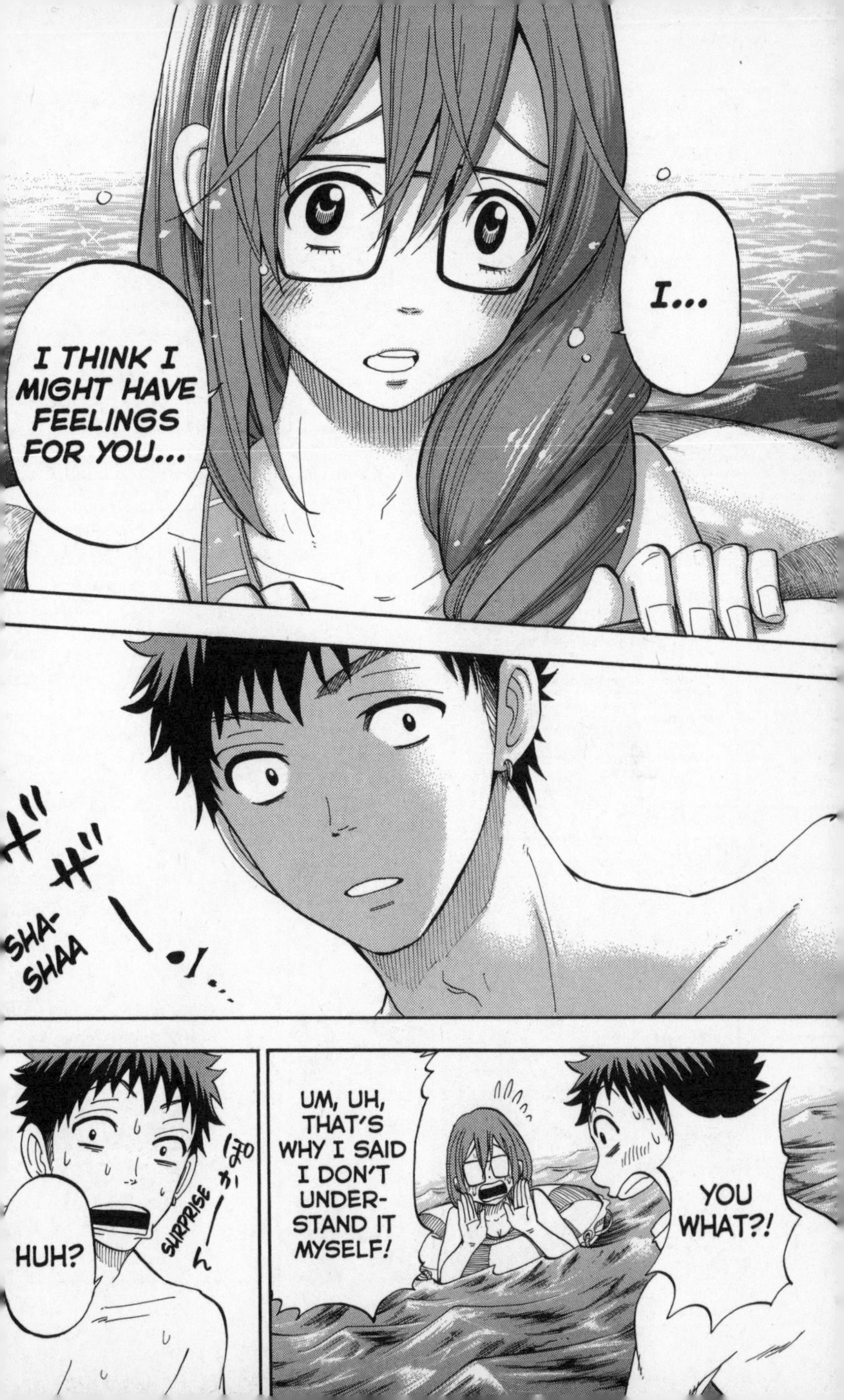
I...
I THINK I MIGHT HAVE FEELINGS FOR YOU...
SHA-SHAA
YOU WHAT?!
UM, UH, THAT'S WHY I SAID I DON'T UNDER-STAND IT MYSELF!
SURPRISE
HUH?

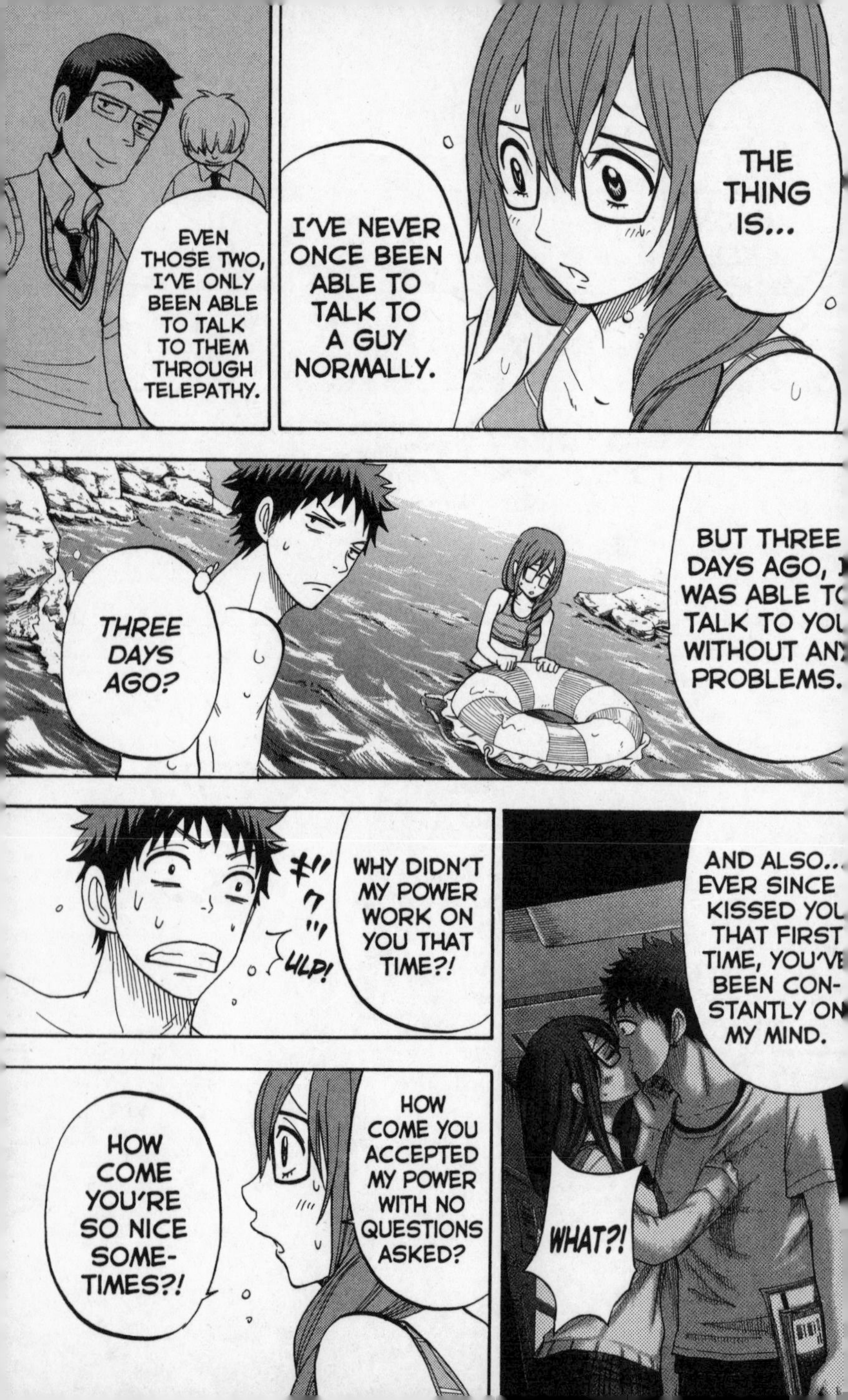
THE THING IS...
I'VE NEVER ONCE BEEN ABLE TO TALK TO A GUY NORMALLY.
EVEN THOSE TWO, I'VE ONLY BEEN ABLE TO TALK TO THEM THROUGH TELEPATHY.
BUT THREE DAYS AGO, I WAS ABLE TO TALK TO YOU WITHOUT ANY PROBLEMS.
THREE DAYS AGO?
AND ALSO... EVER SINCE KISSED YOU THAT FIRST TIME, YOU'VE BEEN CON-STANTLY ON MY MIND.
WHAT?!
WHY DIDN'T MY POWER WORK ON YOU THAT TIME?!
ギクッ
ULP!
HOW COME YOU ACCEPTED MY POWER WITH NO QUESTIONS ASKED?
HOW COME YOU'RE SO NICE SOME-TIMES?!

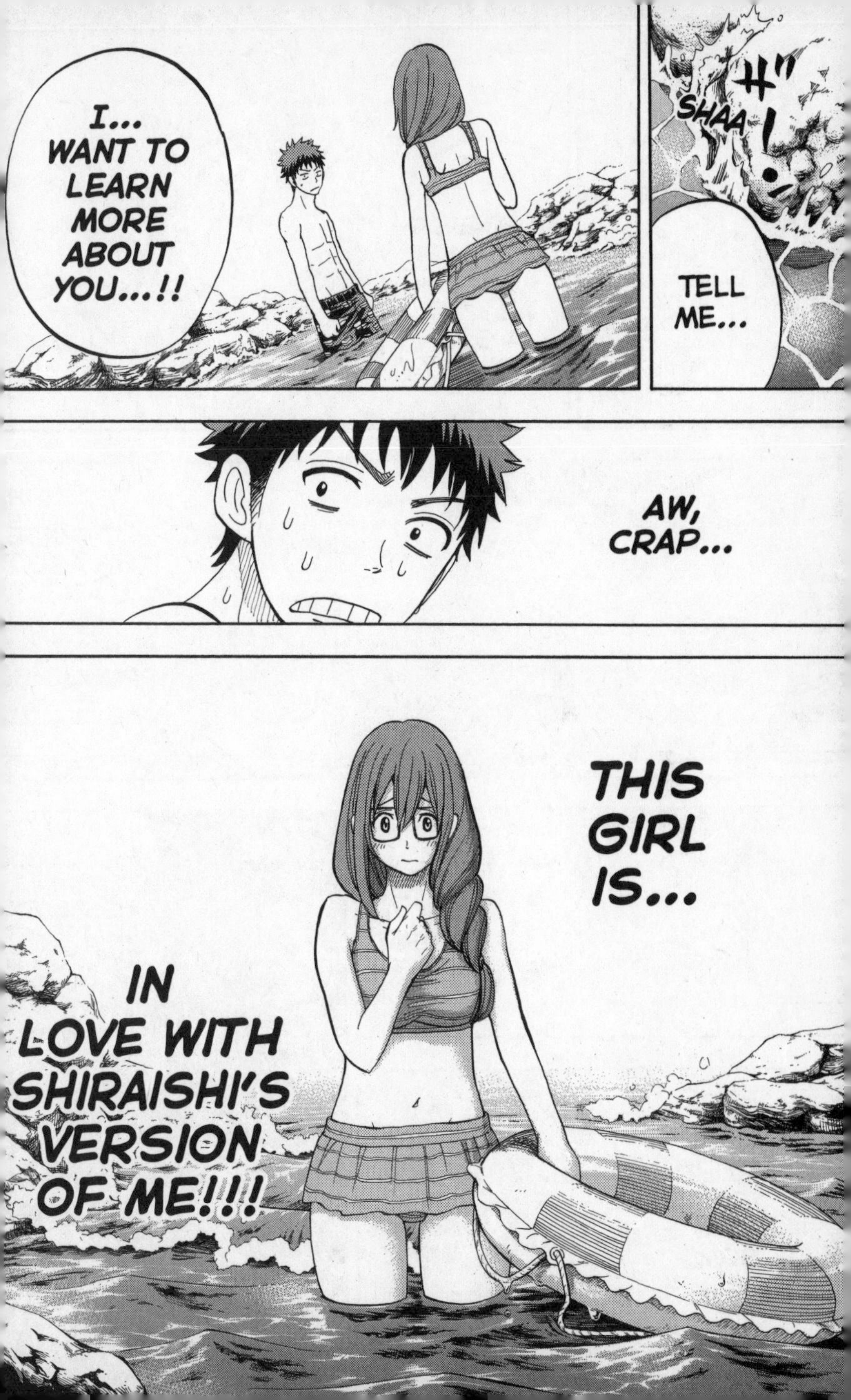
SHAA
TELL ME...
I... WANT TO LEARN MORE ABOUT YOU...!!
AW, CRAP...
THIS GIRL IS...
IN LOVE WITH SHIRAISHI'S VERSION OF ME!!!

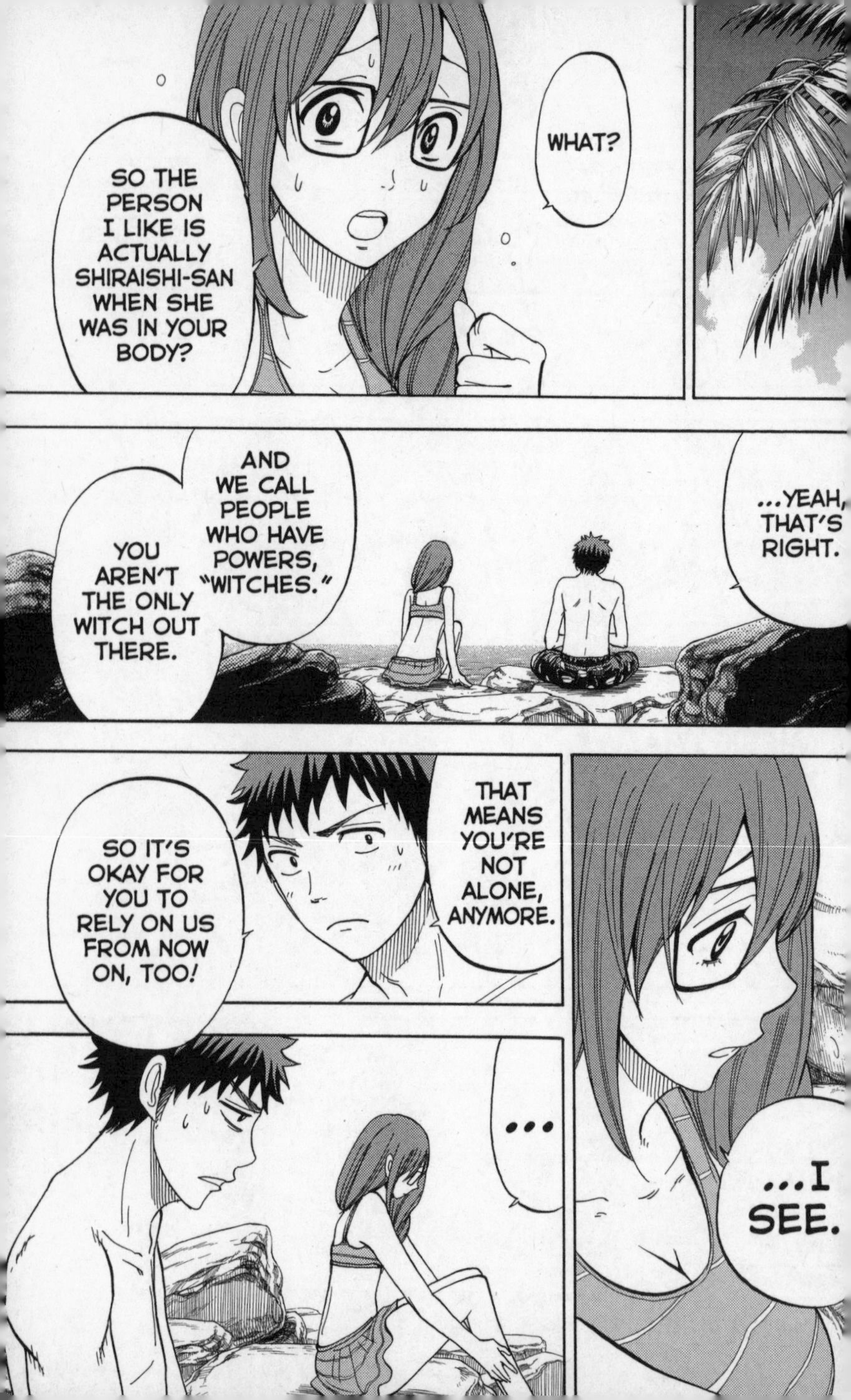
WHAT?
SO THE PERSON I LIKE IS ACTUALLY SHIRAISHI-SAN WHEN SHE WAS IN YOUR BODY?
...YEAH, THAT'S RIGHT.
AND WE CALL PEOPLE WHO HAVE POWERS, "WITCHES."
YOU AREN'T THE ONLY WITCH OUT THERE.
...I SEE.
THAT MEANS YOU'RE NOT ALONE, ANYMORE.
SO IT'S OKAY FOR YOU TO RELY ON US FROM NOW ON, TOO!
...

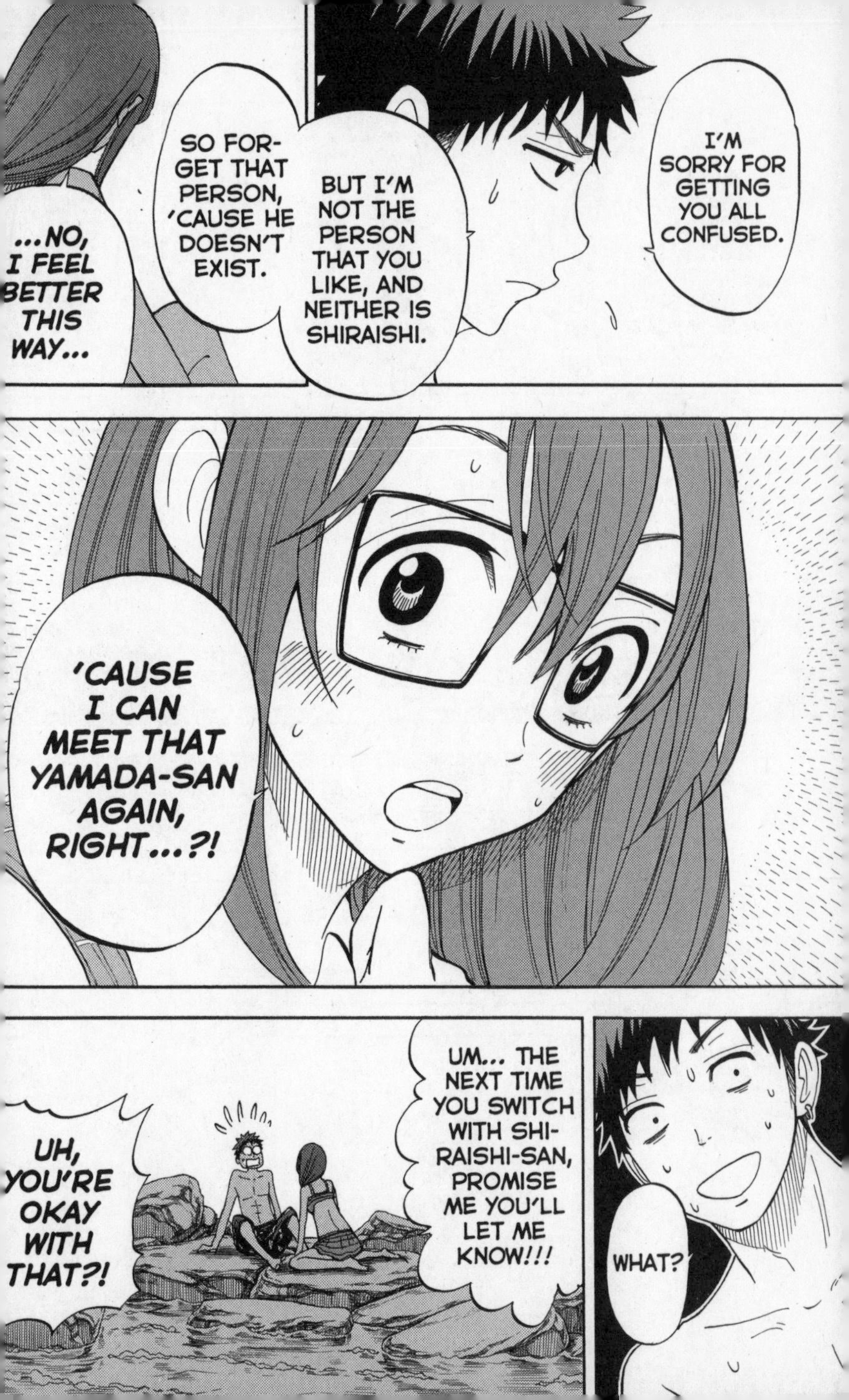
I'M SORRY FOR GETTING YOU ALL CONFUSED.
BUT I'M NOT THE PERSON THAT YOU LIKE, AND NEITHER IS SHIRAISHI.
SO FOR-GET THAT PERSON, 'CAUSE HE DOESN'T EXIST.
...NO, I FEEL BETTER THIS WAY...
'CAUSE I CAN MEET THAT YAMADA-SAN AGAIN, RIGHT...?!
WHAT?
UM... THE NEXT TIME YOU SWITCH WITH SHI-RAISHI-SAN, PROMISE ME YOU'LL LET ME KNOW!!!
UH, YOU'RE OKAY WITH THAT?!

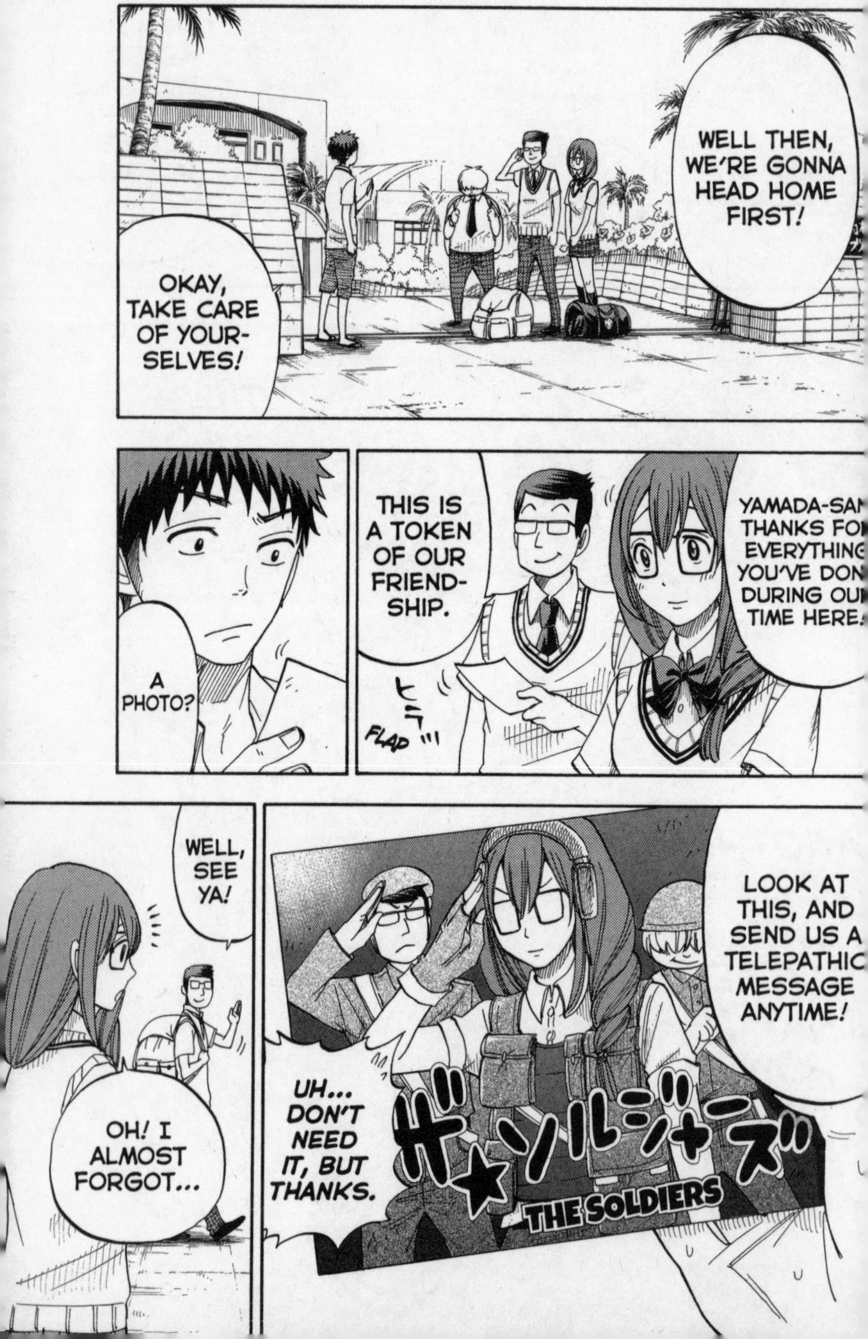
WELL THEN, WE'RE GONNA HEAD HOME FIRST!
OKAY, TAKE CARE OF YOUR-SELVES!
YAMADA-SAN THANKS FOR EVERYTHING YOU'VE DONE DURING OUR TIME HERE.
THIS IS A TOKEN OF OUR FRIEND-SHIP.
FLAP
A PHOTO?
LOOK AT THIS, AND SEND US A TELEPATHIC MESSAGE ANYTIME!
ザ★ソルジャーズ
THE SOLDIERS
UH... DON'T NEED IT, BUT THANKS.
WELL, SEE YA!
OH! I ALMOST FORGOT...

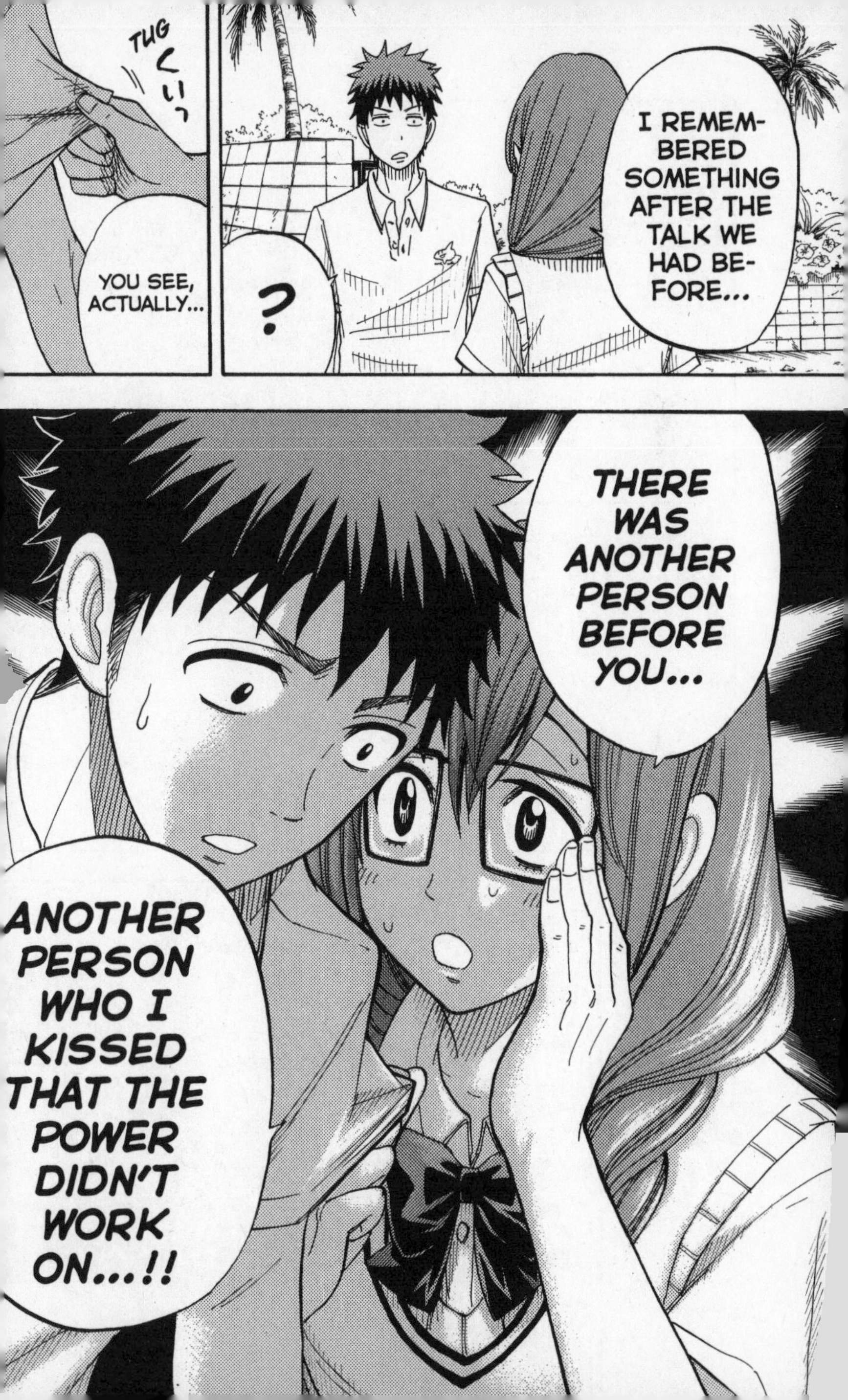
I REMEMBERED SOMETHING AFTER THE TALK WE HAD BEFORE...
?
TUG
くいっ
YOU SEE, ACTUALLY...
THERE WAS ANOTHER PERSON BEFORE YOU...
ANOTHER PERSON WHO I KISSED THAT THE POWER DIDN'T WORK ON...!!

CHAPTER 32: Fsshhh! Pop! Pop!

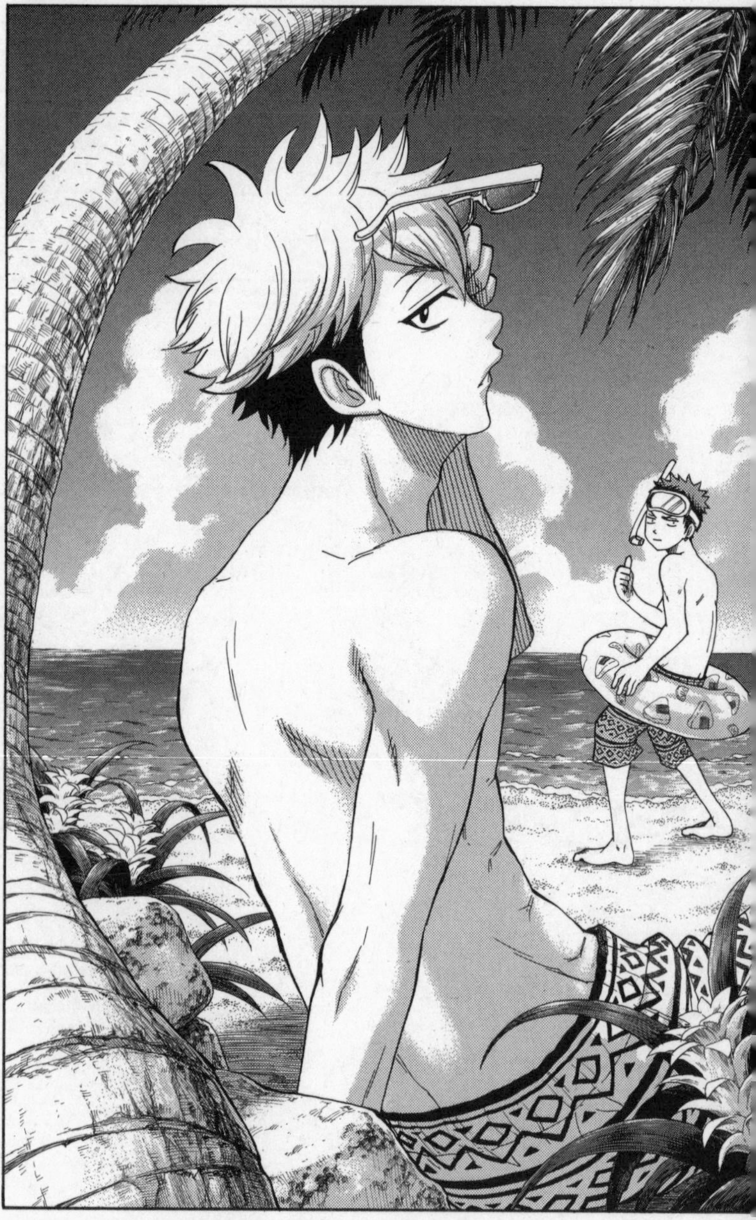

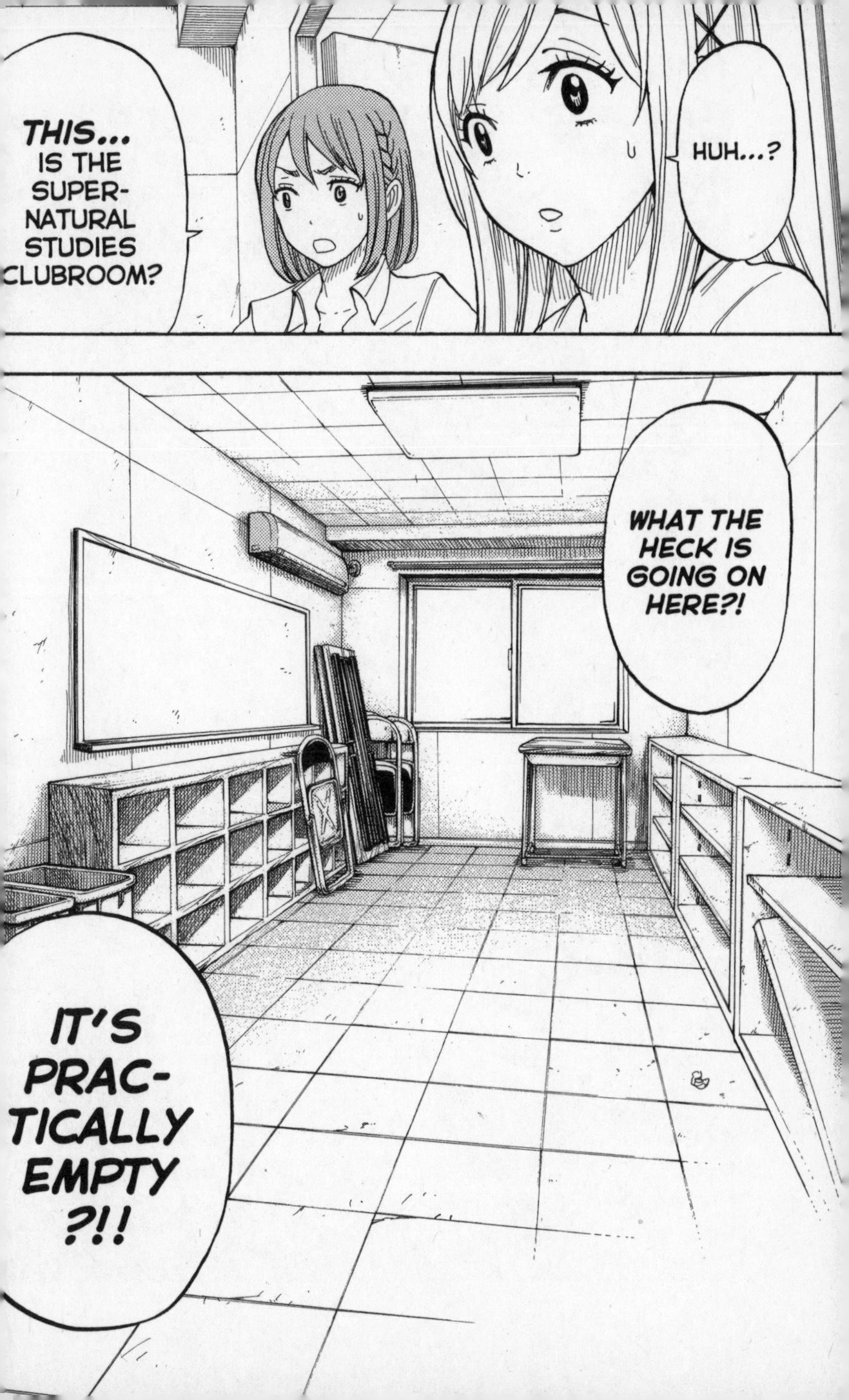
HUH...?
THIS... IS THE SUPER-NATURAL STUDIES CLUBROOM?
WHAT THE HECK IS GOING ON HERE?!
IT'S PRAC-TICALLY EMPTY ?!!

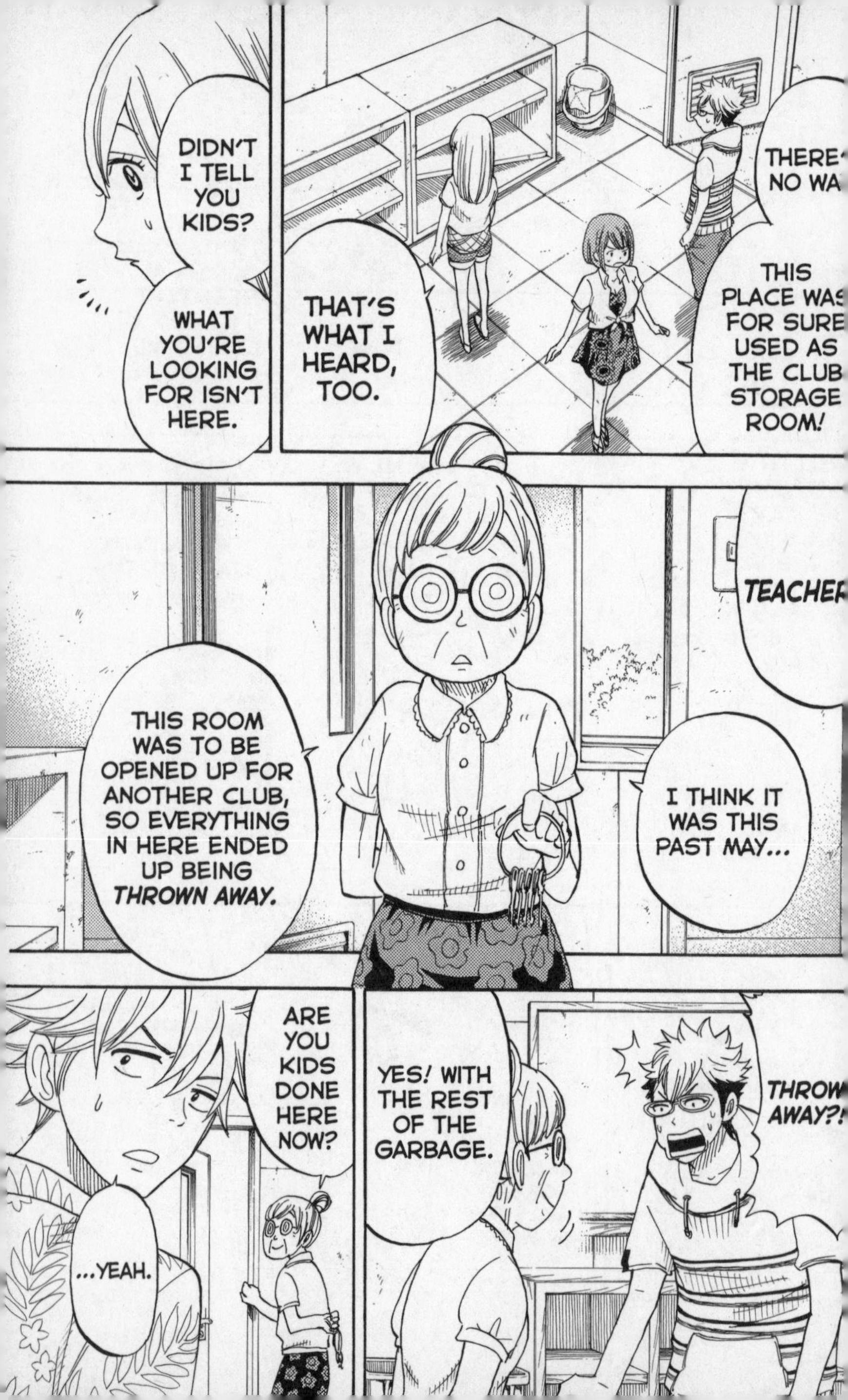
THERE' NO WA
THIS PLACE WAS FOR SURE USED AS THE CLUB STORAGE ROOM!
THAT'S WHAT I HEARD, TOO.
DIDN'T I TELL YOU KIDS?
WHAT YOU'RE LOOKING FOR ISN'T HERE.
TEACHER
I THINK IT WAS THIS PAST MAY...
THIS ROOM WAS TO BE OPENED UP FOR ANOTHER CLUB, SO EVERYTHING IN HERE ENDED UP BEING *THROWN AWAY.*
THROW AWAY?!
YES! WITH THE REST OF THE GARBAGE.
ARE YOU KIDS DONE HERE NOW?
...YEAH.

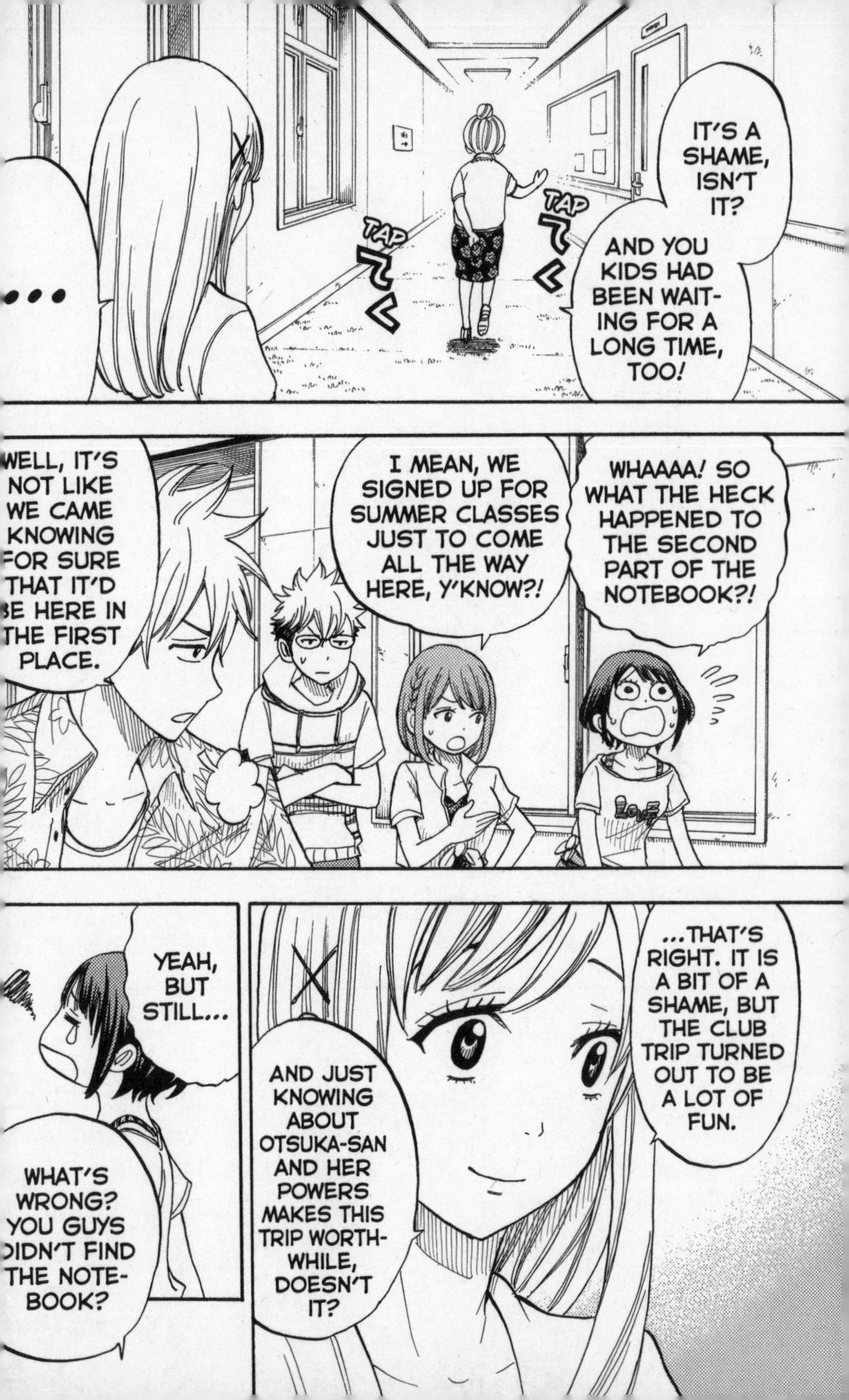
IT'S A SHAME, ISN'T IT?
AND YOU KIDS HAD BEEN WAIT-ING FOR A LONG TIME, TOO!
TAP
TAP
...
WHAAAA! SO WHAT THE HECK HAPPENED TO THE SECOND PART OF THE NOTEBOOK?!
I MEAN, WE SIGNED UP FOR SUMMER CLASSES JUST TO COME ALL THE WAY HERE, Y'KNOW?!
WELL, IT'S NOT LIKE WE CAME KNOWING FOR SURE THAT IT'D BE HERE IN THE FIRST PLACE.
...THAT'S RIGHT. IT IS A BIT OF A SHAME, BUT THE CLUB TRIP TURNED OUT TO BE A LOT OF FUN.
AND JUST KNOWING ABOUT OTSUKA-SAN AND HER POWERS MAKES THIS TRIP WORTH-WHILE, DOESN'T IT?
YEAH, BUT STILL...
WHAT'S WRONG? YOU GUYS DIDN'T FIND THE NOTE-BOOK?

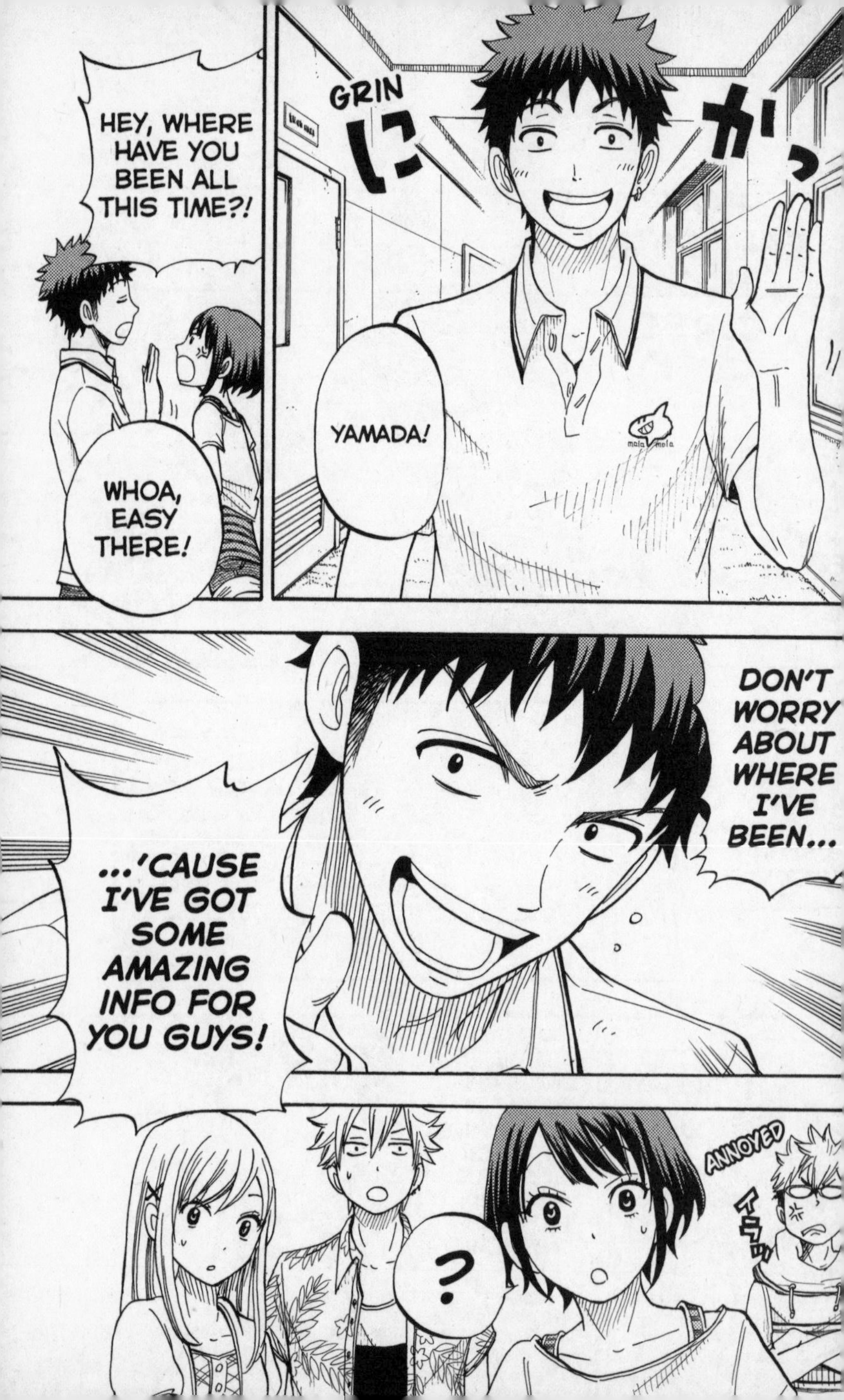
かっ
GRIN
に
YAMADA!
HEY, WHERE HAVE YOU BEEN ALL THIS TIME?!
WHOA, EASY THERE!
DON'T WORRY ABOUT WHERE I'VE BEEN...
...'CAUSE I'VE GOT SOME AMAZING INFO FOR YOU GUYS!
ANNOYED
イラッ
?

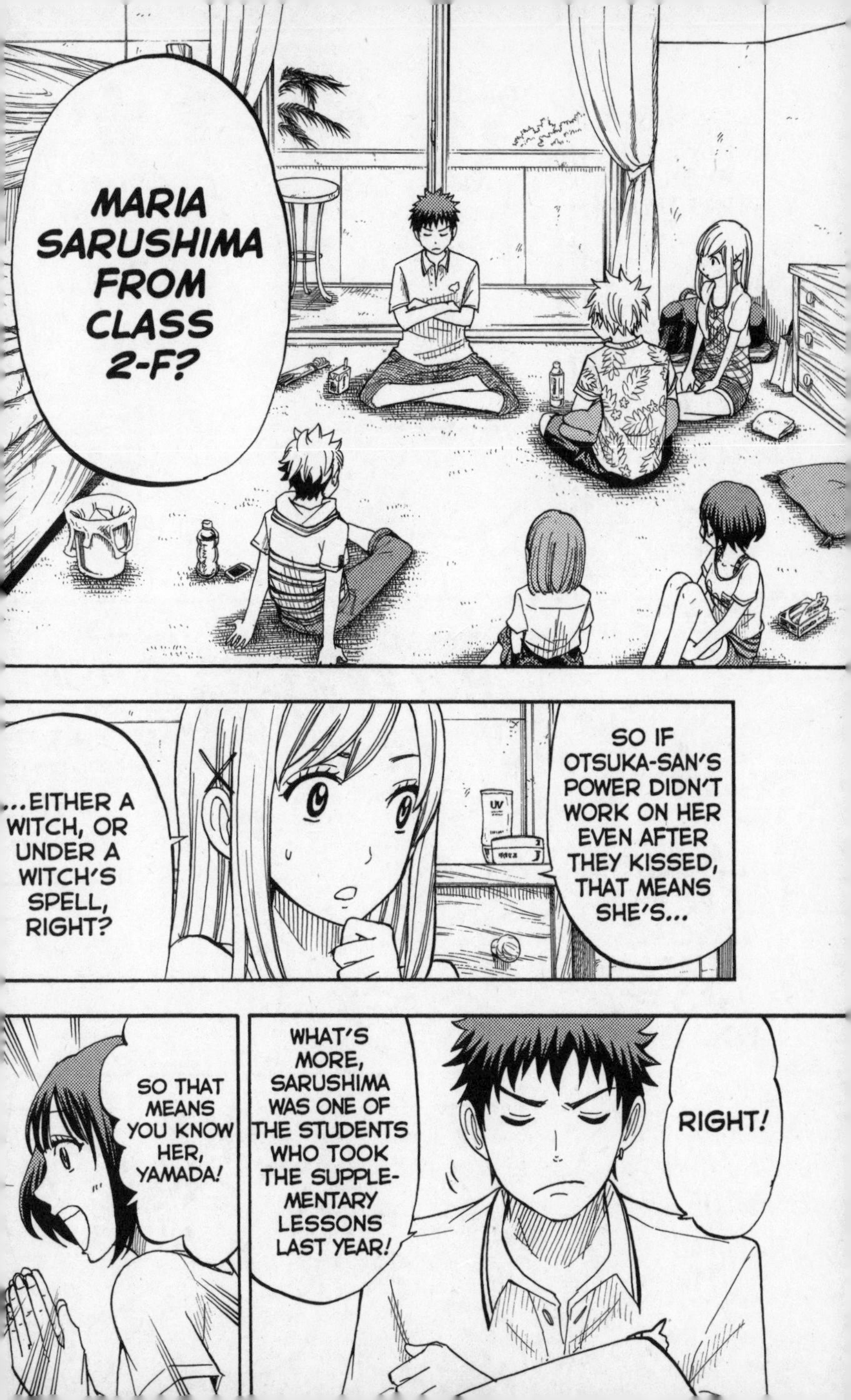
MARIA SARUSHIMA FROM CLASS 2-F?
SO IF OTSUKA-SAN'S POWER DIDN'T WORK ON HER EVEN AFTER THEY KISSED, THAT MEANS SHE'S...
...EITHER A WITCH, OR UNDER A WITCH'S SPELL, RIGHT?
RIGHT!
WHAT'S MORE, SARUSHIMA WAS ONE OF THE STUDENTS WHO TOOK THE SUPPLE-MENTARY LESSONS LAST YEAR!
SO THAT MEANS YOU KNOW HER, YAMADA!

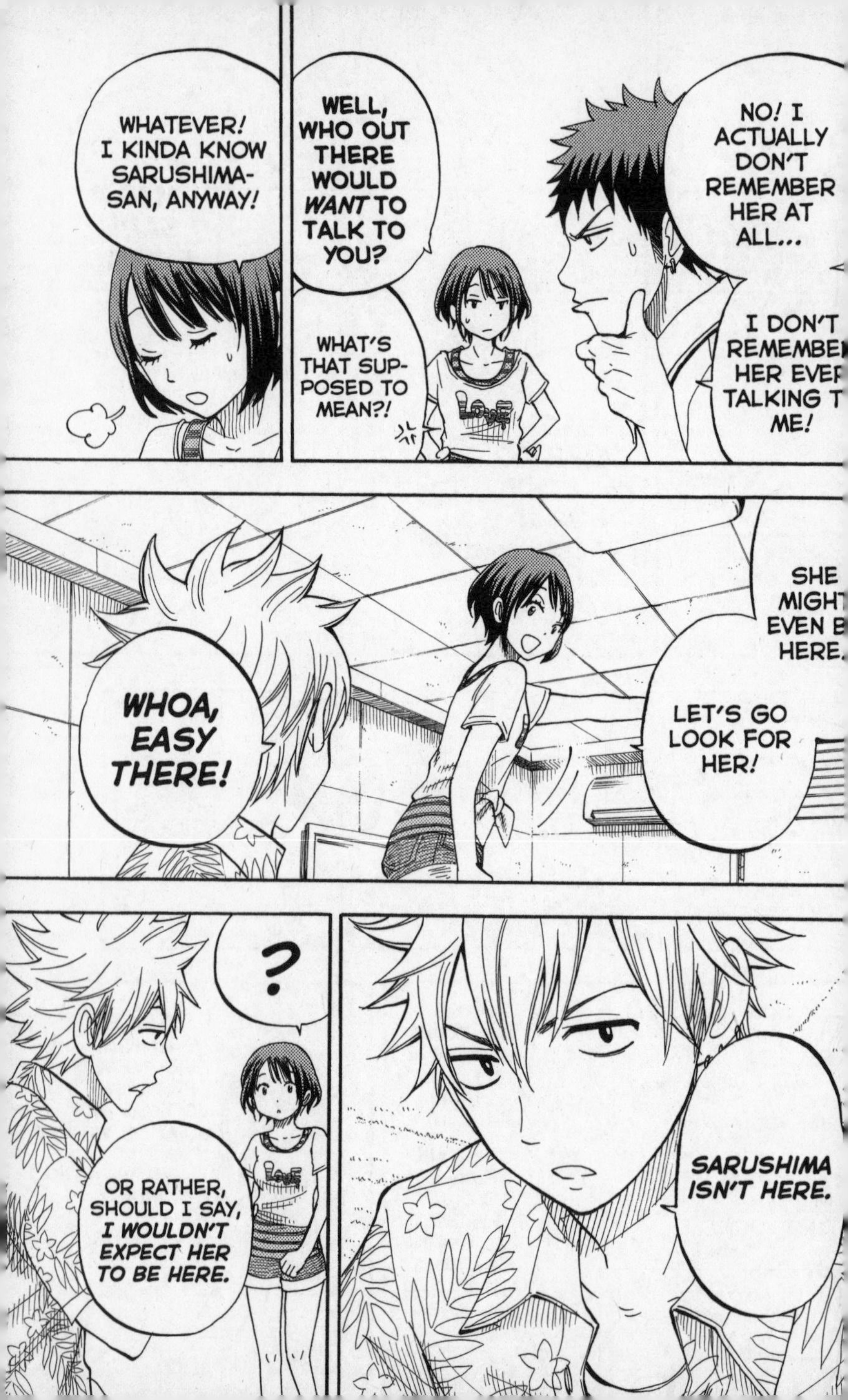
NO! I ACTUALLY DON'T REMEMBER HER AT ALL...
I DON'T REMEMBE HER EVE TALKING T ME!
WELL, WHO OUT THERE WOULD *WANT* TO TALK TO YOU?
WHAT'S THAT SUP-POSED TO MEAN?!
WHATEVER! I KINDA KNOW SARUSHIMA-SAN, ANYWAY!
SHE MIGHT EVEN B HERE.
LET'S GO LOOK FOR HER!
WHOA, EASY THERE!
SARUSHIMA ISN'T HERE.
?
OR RATHER, SHOULD I SAY, I WOULDN'T EXPECT HER TO BE HERE.

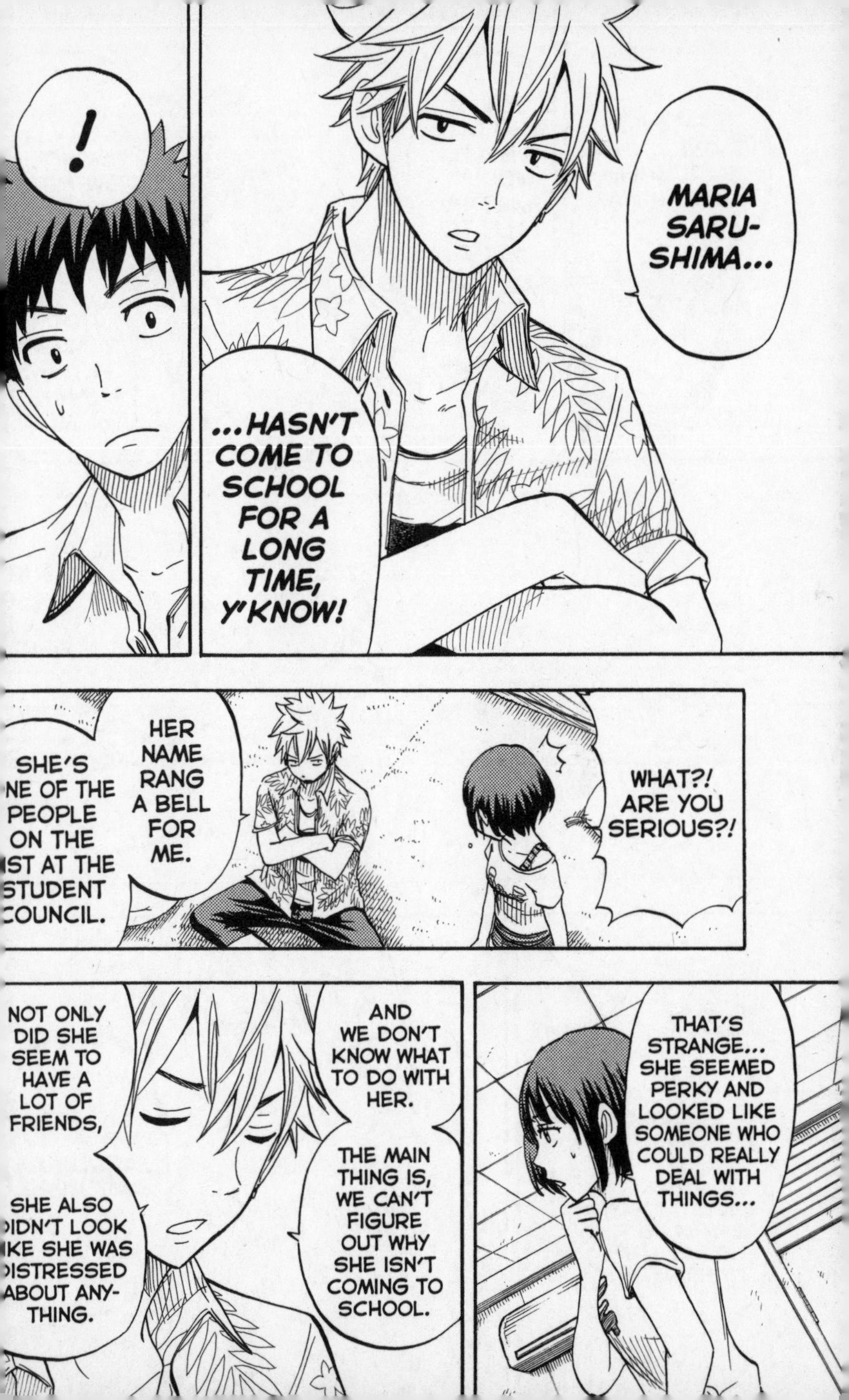
MARIA SARU-SHIMA...
...HASN'T COME TO SCHOOL FOR A LONG TIME, Y'KNOW!
!
WHAT?! ARE YOU SERIOUS?!
HER NAME RANG A BELL FOR ME.
SHE'S NE OF THE PEOPLE ON THE IST AT THE STUDENT COUNCIL.
THAT'S STRANGE... SHE SEEMED PERKY AND LOOKED LIKE SOMEONE WHO COULD REALLY DEAL WITH THINGS...
AND WE DON'T KNOW WHAT TO DO WITH HER.
NOT ONLY DID SHE SEEM TO HAVE A LOT OF FRIENDS,
THE MAIN THING IS, WE CAN'T FIGURE OUT WHY SHE ISN'T COMING TO SCHOOL.
SHE ALSO IDN'T LOOK IKE SHE WAS ISTRESSED ABOUT ANY-THING.

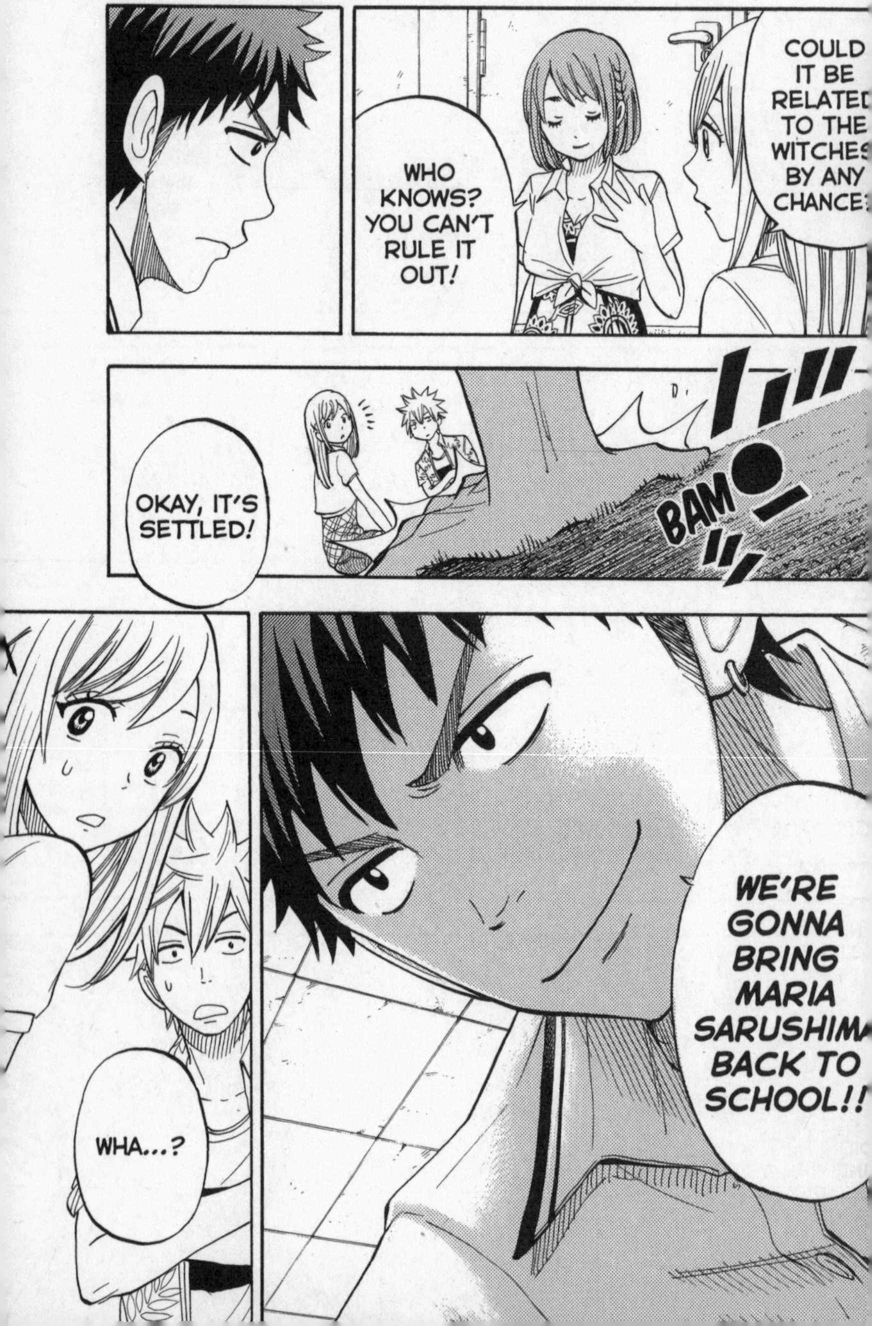
COULD IT BE RELATED TO THE WITCHES BY ANY CHANCE?
WHO KNOWS? YOU CAN'T RULE IT OUT!
BAM
OKAY, IT'S SETTLED!
WE'RE GONNA BRING MARIA SARUSHIMA BACK TO SCHOOL!!
WHA...?

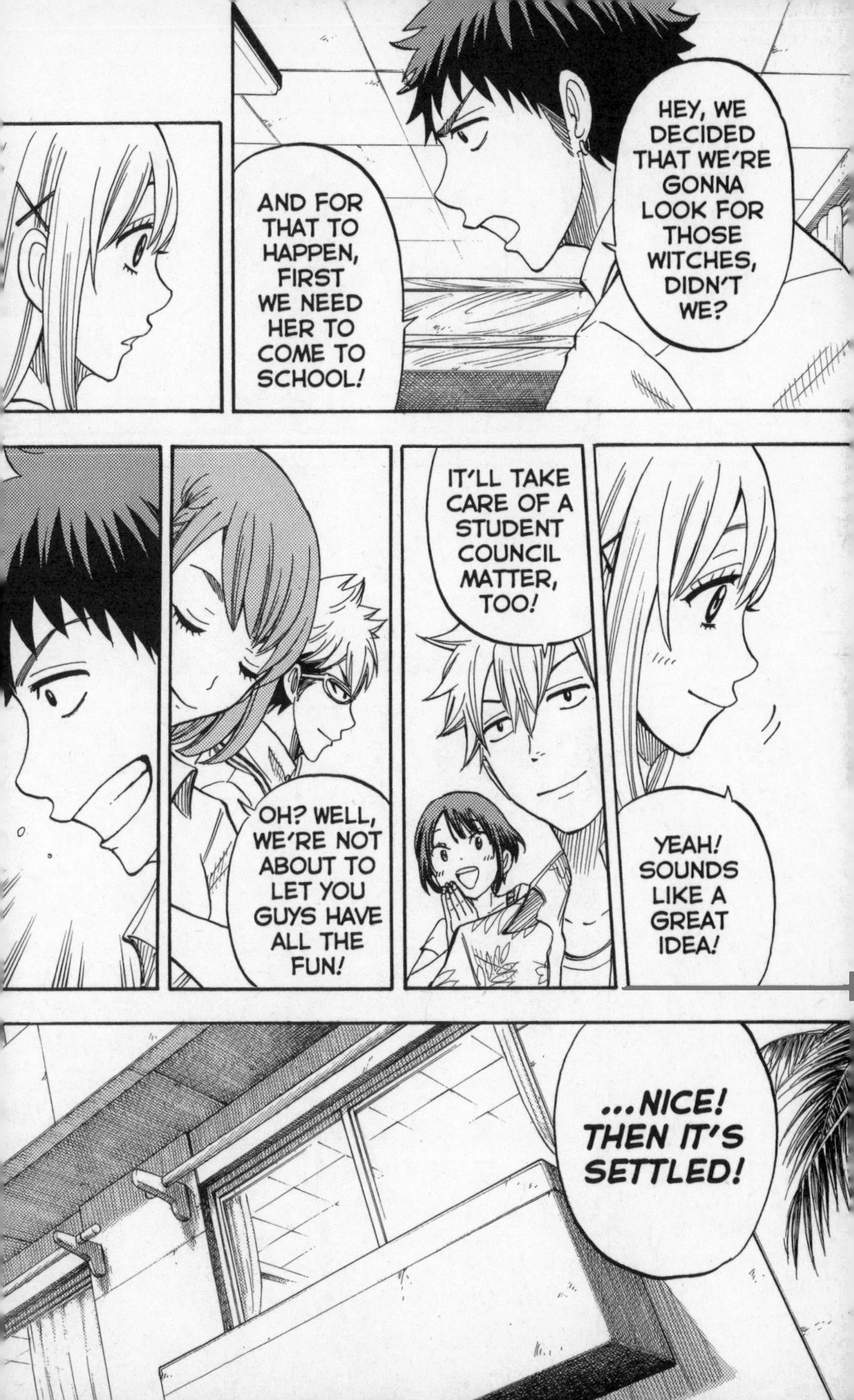
HEY, WE DECIDED THAT WE'RE GONNA LOOK FOR THOSE WITCHES, DIDN'T WE?
AND FOR THAT TO HAPPEN, FIRST WE NEED HER TO COME TO SCHOOL!
YEAH! SOUNDS LIKE A GREAT IDEA!
IT'LL TAKE CARE OF A STUDENT COUNCIL MATTER, TOO!
OH? WELL, WE'RE NOT ABOUT TO LET YOU GUYS HAVE ALL THE FUN!
...NICE! THEN IT'S SETTLED!

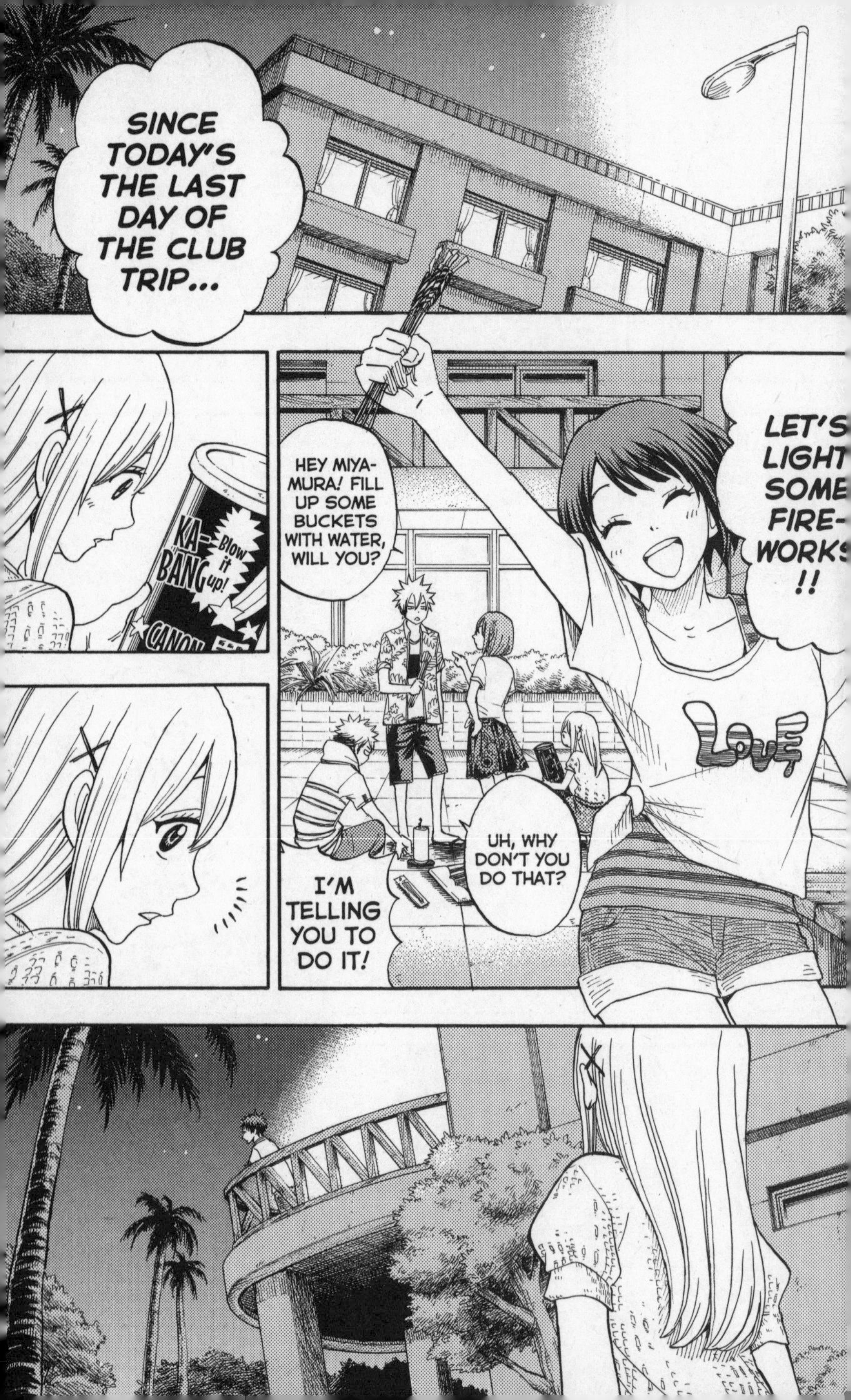
SINCE TODAY'S THE LAST DAY OF THE CLUB TRIP...
LET'S LIGHT SOME FIRE-WORKS!!
HEY MIYA-MURA! FILL UP SOME BUCKETS WITH WATER, WILL YOU?
UH, WHY DON'T YOU DO THAT?
I'M TELLING YOU TO DO IT!
KA-BANG
Blow it up!

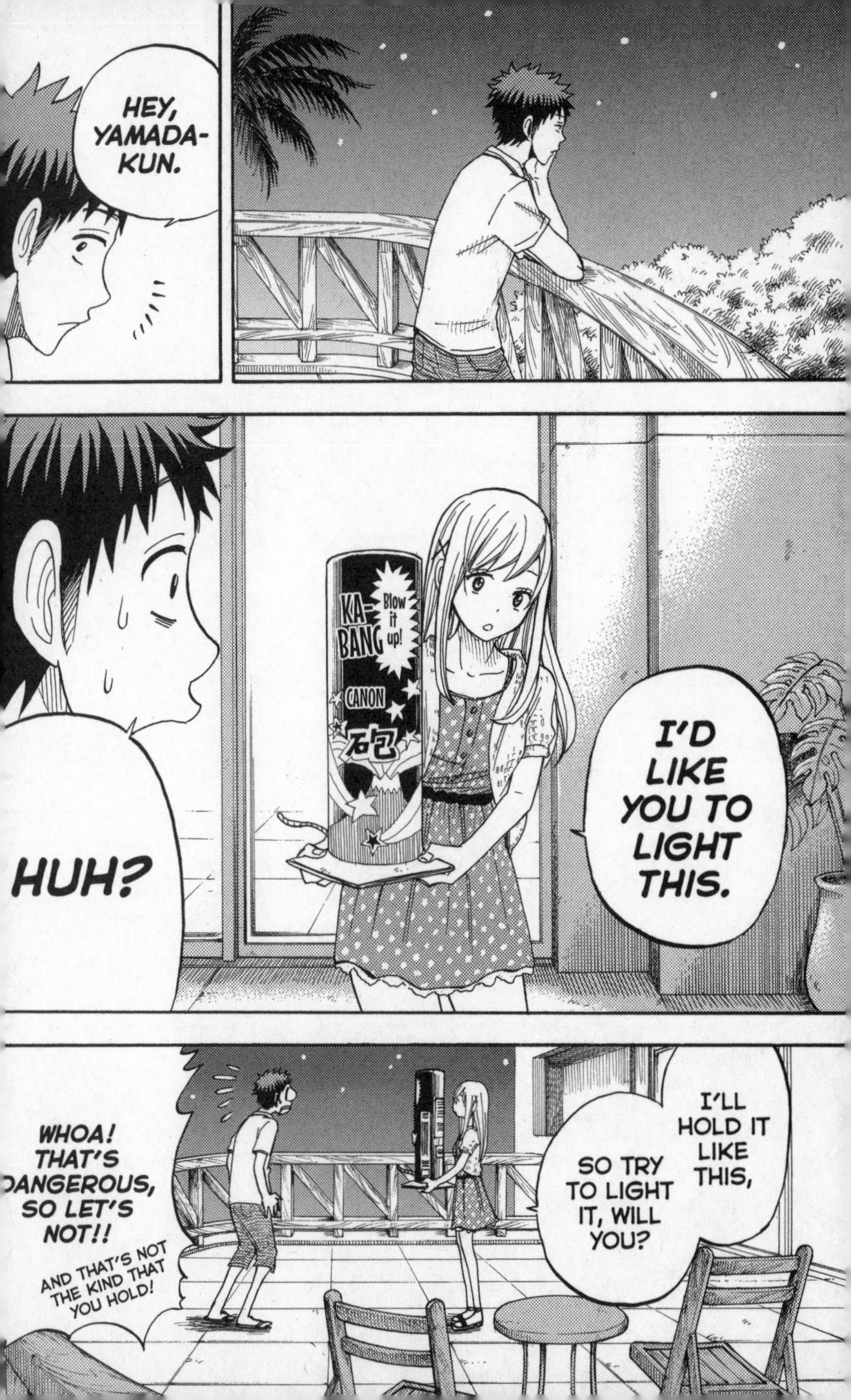
HEY, YAMADA-KUN.
I'D LIKE YOU TO LIGHT THIS.
KA-BANG
Blow it up!
CANON
砲
HUH?
I'LL HOLD IT LIKE THIS,
SO TRY TO LIGHT IT, WILL YOU?
WHOA! THAT'S DANGEROUS, SO LET'S NOT!!
AND THAT'S NOT THE KIND THAT YOU HOLD!

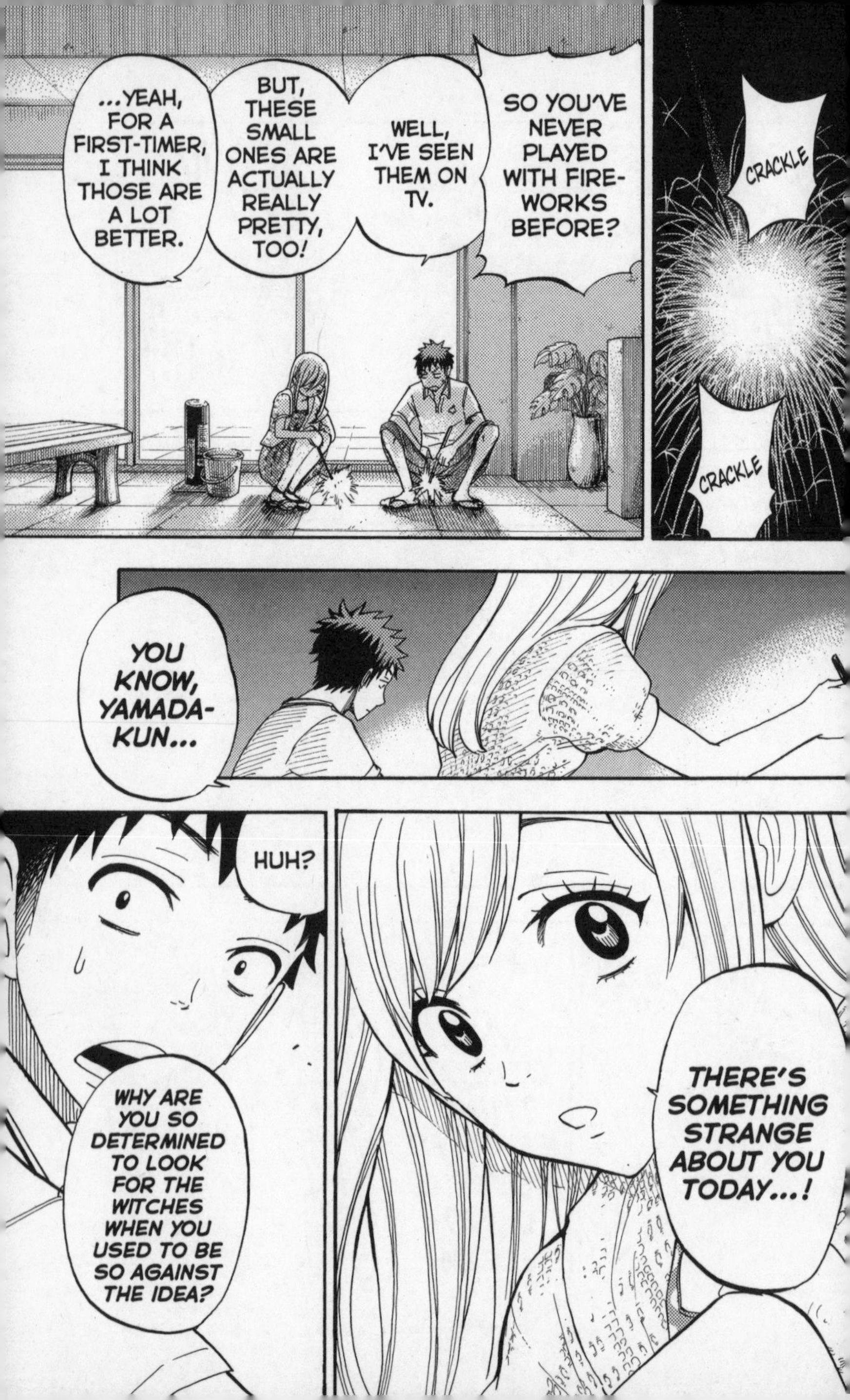
CRACKLE
CRACKLE
SO YOU'VE NEVER PLAYED WITH FIRE-WORKS BEFORE?
WELL, I'VE SEEN THEM ON TV.
BUT, THESE SMALL ONES ARE ACTUALLY REALLY PRETTY, TOO!
...YEAH, FOR A FIRST-TIMER, I THINK THOSE ARE A LOT BETTER.
YOU KNOW, YAMADA-KUN...
THERE'S SOMETHING STRANGE ABOUT YOU TODAY...!
HUH?
WHY ARE YOU SO DETERMINED TO LOOK FOR THE WITCHES WHEN YOU USED TO BE SO AGAINST THE IDEA?

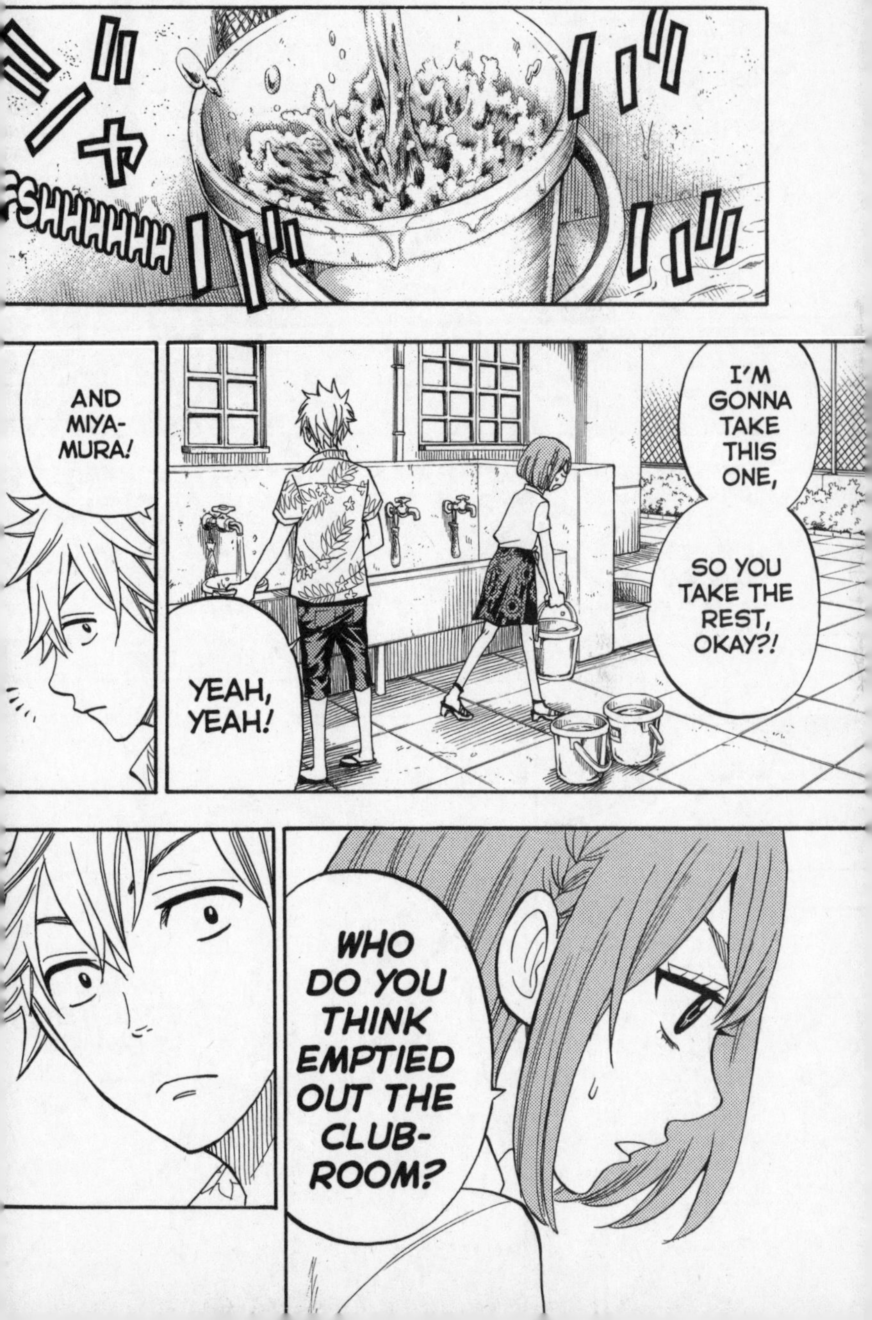
SHHHHHH
I'M GONNA TAKE THIS ONE,
SO YOU TAKE THE REST, OKAY?!
YEAH, YEAH!
AND MIYA-MURA!
WHO DO YOU THINK EMPTIED OUT THE CLUB-ROOM?

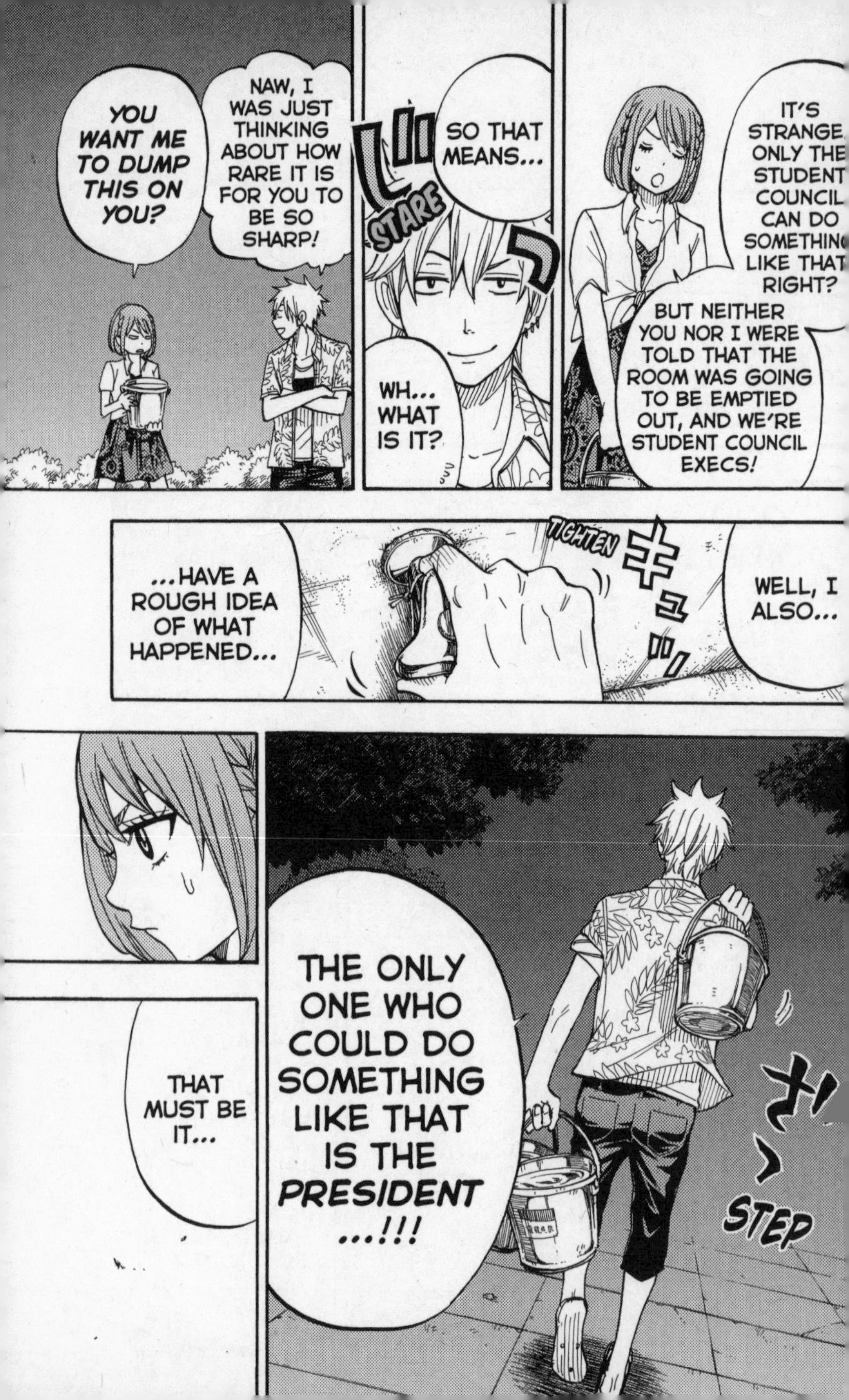
IT'S STRANGE ONLY THE STUDENT COUNCIL CAN DO SOMETHIN LIKE THAT RIGHT?
BUT NEITHER YOU NOR I WERE TOLD THAT THE ROOM WAS GOING TO BE EMPTIED OUT, AND WE'RE STUDENT COUNCIL EXECS!
SO THAT MEANS...
STARE
WH... WHAT IS IT?
NAW, I WAS JUST THINKING ABOUT HOW RARE IT IS FOR YOU TO BE SO SHARP!
YOU WANT ME TO DUMP THIS ON YOU?
WELL, I ALSO...
TIGHTEN
...HAVE A ROUGH IDEA OF WHAT HAPPENED...
THE ONLY ONE WHO COULD DO SOMETHING LIKE THAT IS THE PRESIDENT ...!!!
STEP
THAT MUST BE IT...

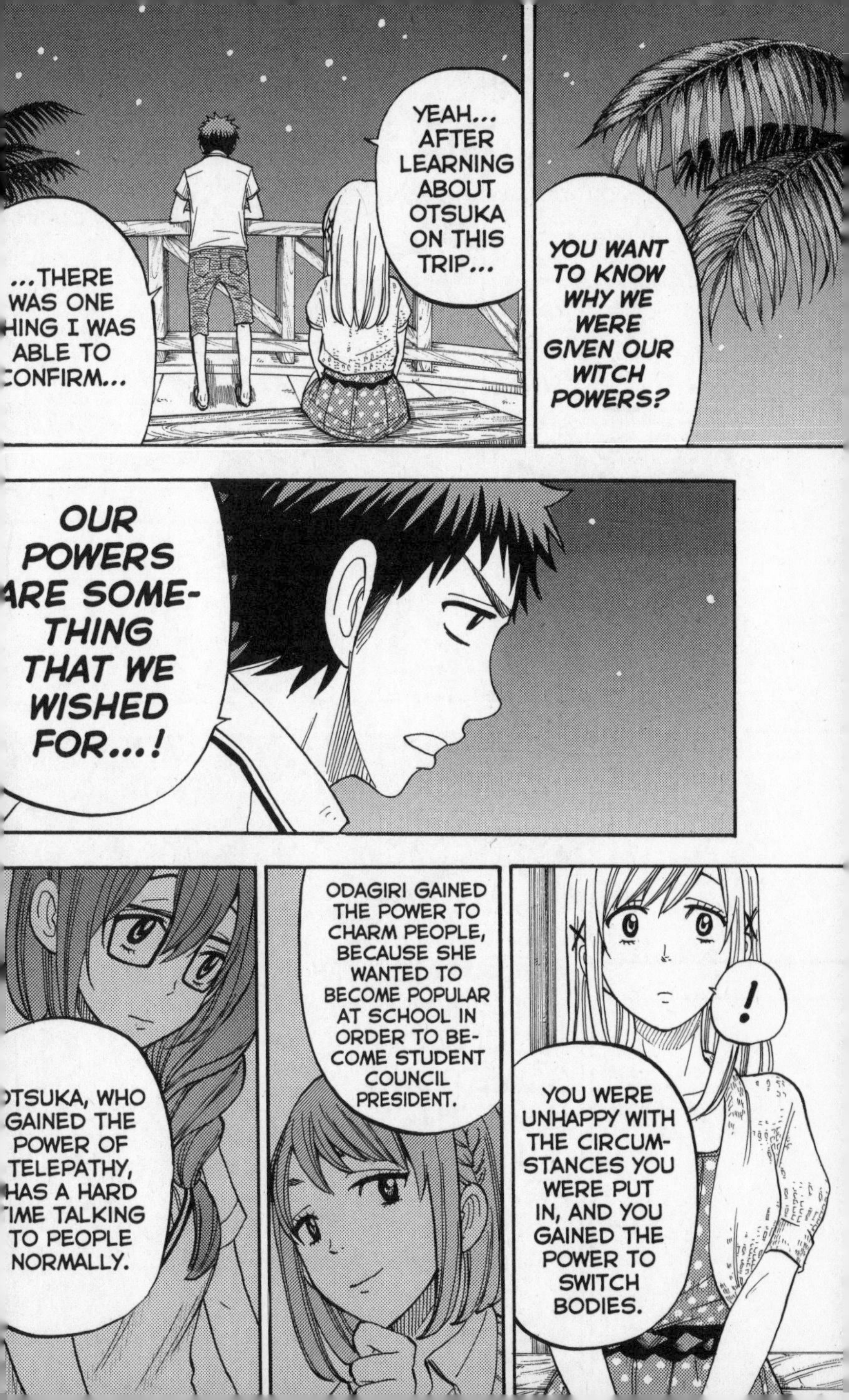
YOU WANT TO KNOW WHY WE WERE GIVEN OUR WITCH POWERS?
YEAH... AFTER LEARNING ABOUT OTSUKA ON THIS TRIP...
...THERE WAS ONE THING I WAS ABLE TO CONFIRM...
OUR POWERS ARE SOME-THING THAT WE WISHED FOR...!
!
YOU WERE UNHAPPY WITH THE CIRCUM-STANCES YOU WERE PUT IN, AND YOU GAINED THE POWER TO SWITCH BODIES.
ODAGIRI GAINED THE POWER TO CHARM PEOPLE, BECAUSE SHE WANTED TO BECOME POPULAR AT SCHOOL IN ORDER TO BE-COME STUDENT COUNCIL PRESIDENT.
OTSUKA, WHO GAINED THE POWER OF TELEPATHY, HAS A HARD TIME TALKING TO PEOPLE NORMALLY.

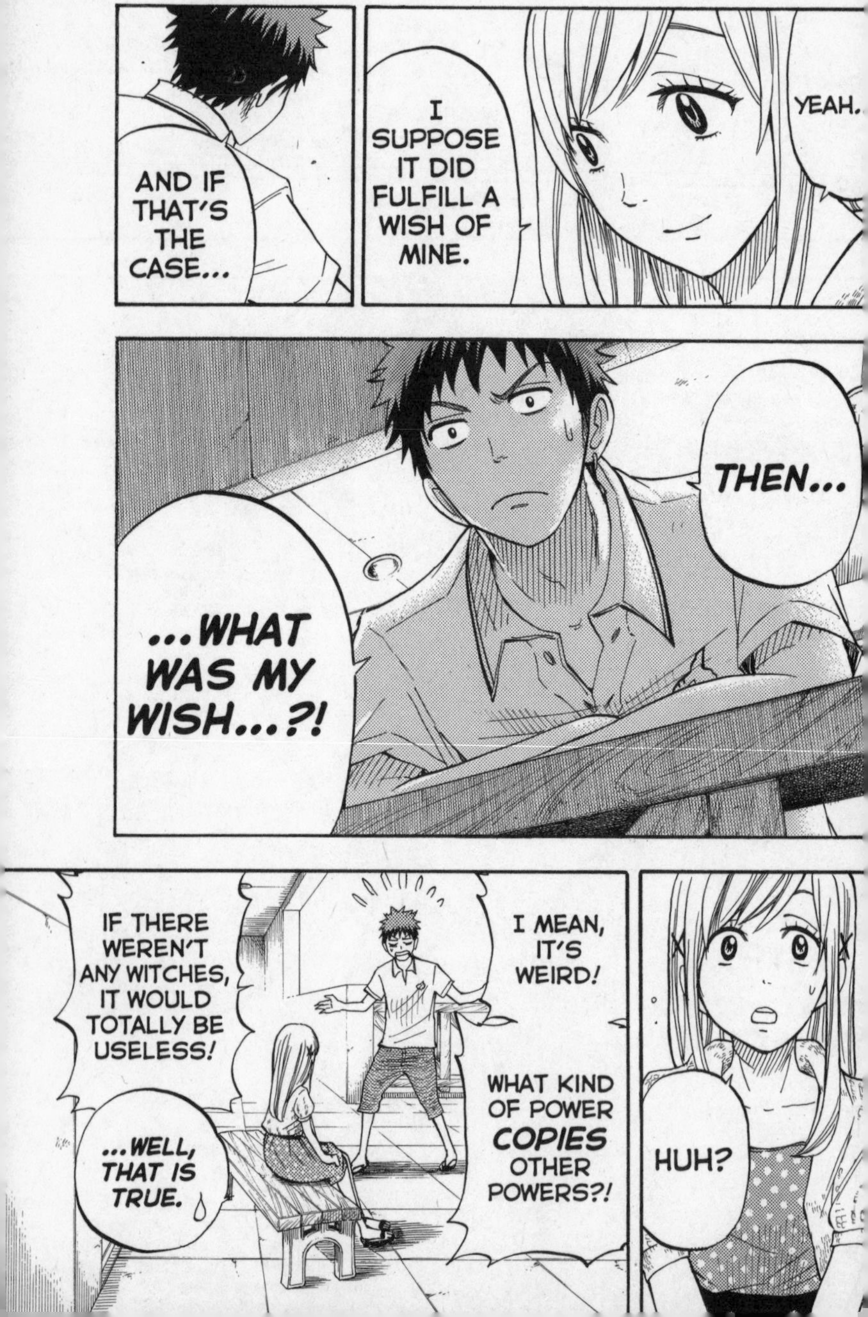
YEAH.
I SUPPOSE IT DID FULFILL A WISH OF MINE.
AND IF THAT'S THE CASE...
THEN...
...WHAT WAS MY WISH...?!
HUH?
I MEAN, IT'S WEIRD!
WHAT KIND OF POWER COPIES OTHER POWERS?!
IF THERE WEREN'T ANY WITCHES, IT WOULD TOTALLY BE USELESS!
...WELL, THAT IS TRUE.

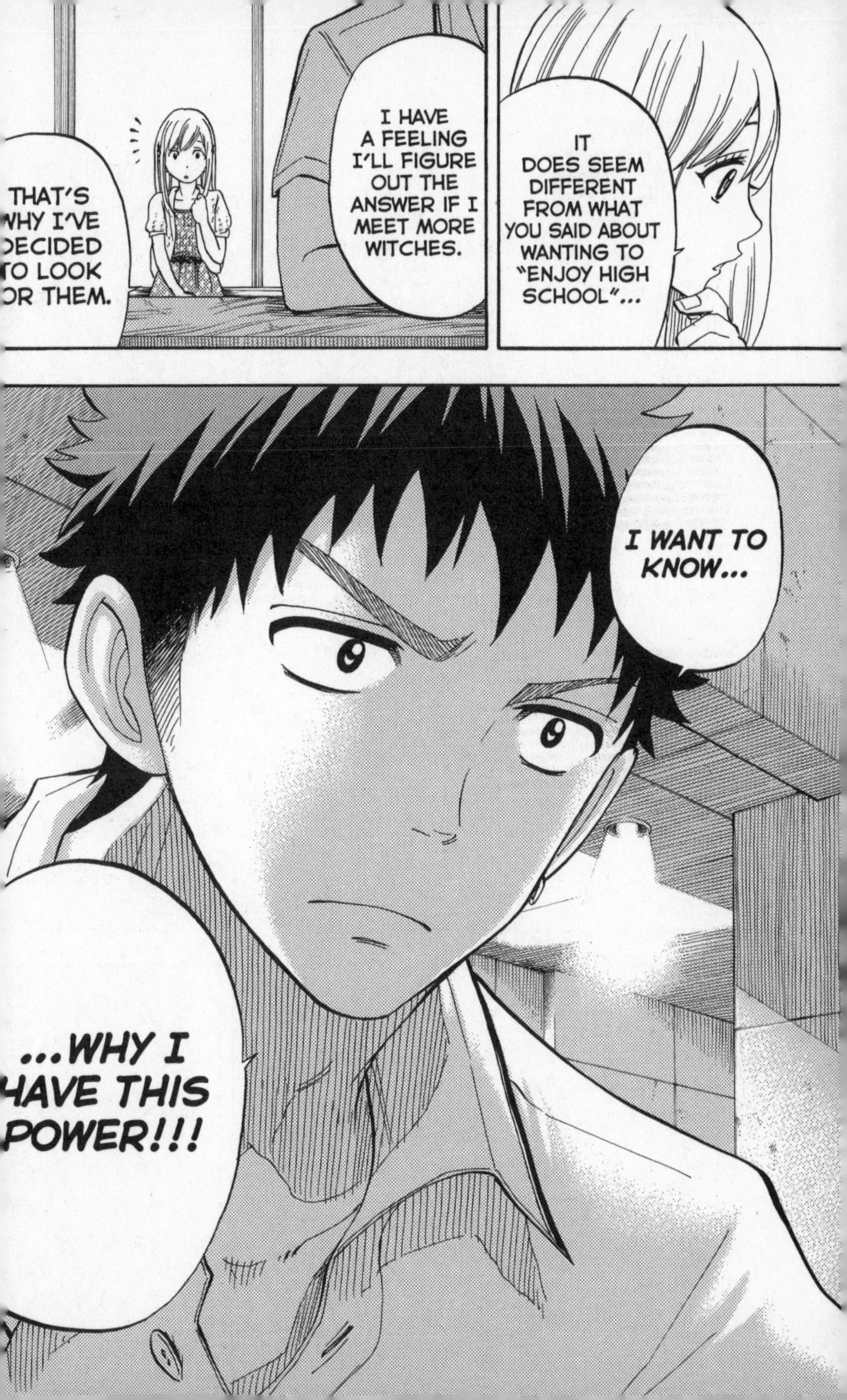

IT DOES SEEM DIFFERENT FROM WHAT YOU SAID ABOUT WANTING TO "ENJOY HIGH SCHOOL"...
I HAVE A FEELING I'LL FIGURE OUT THE ANSWER IF I MEET MORE WITCHES.
THAT'S WHY I'VE DECIDED TO LOOK FOR THEM.
I WANT TO KNOW...
...WHY I HAVE THIS POWER!!!

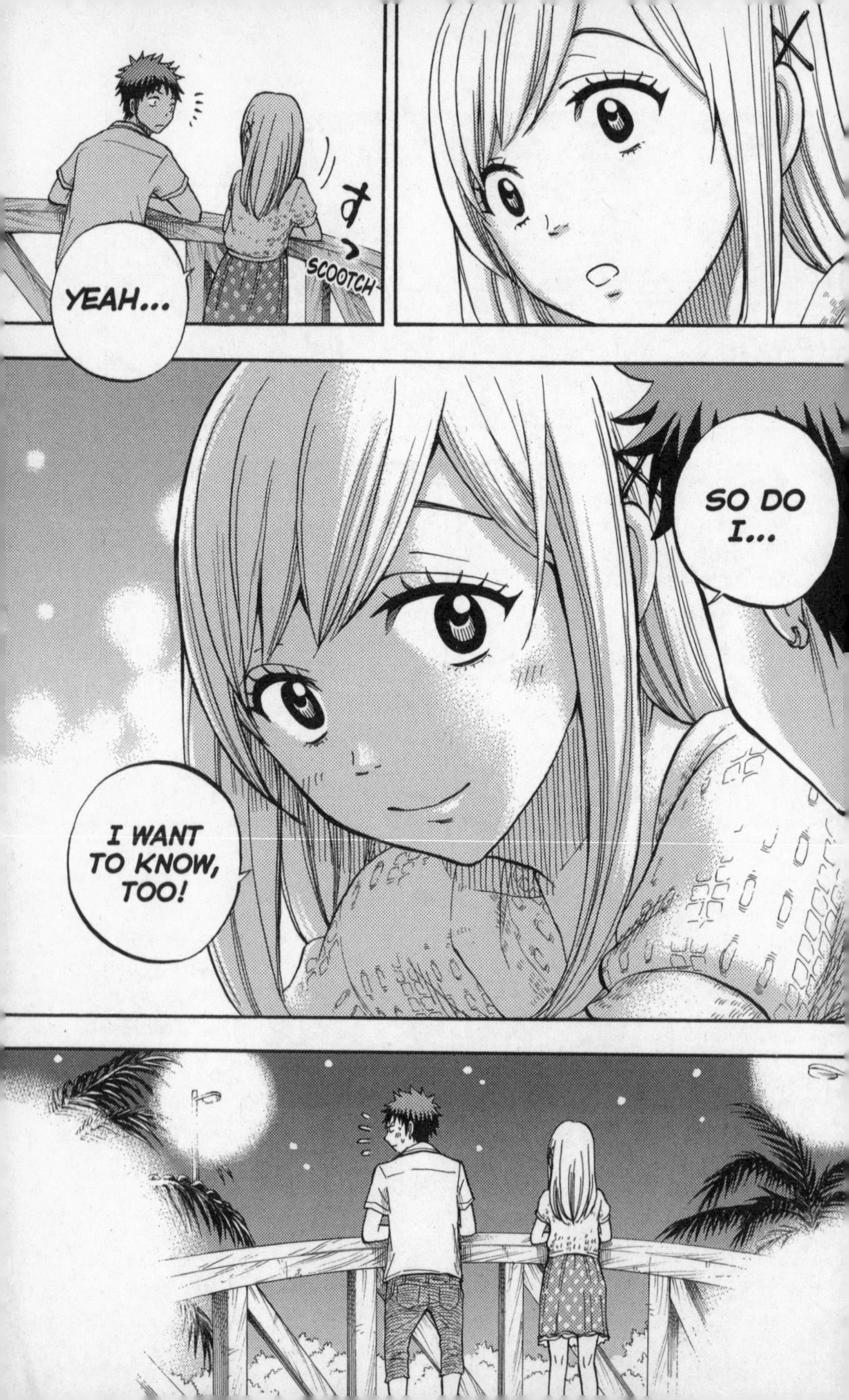
すっ
SCOOTCH
YEAH...
SO DO I...
I WANT TO KNOW, TOO!

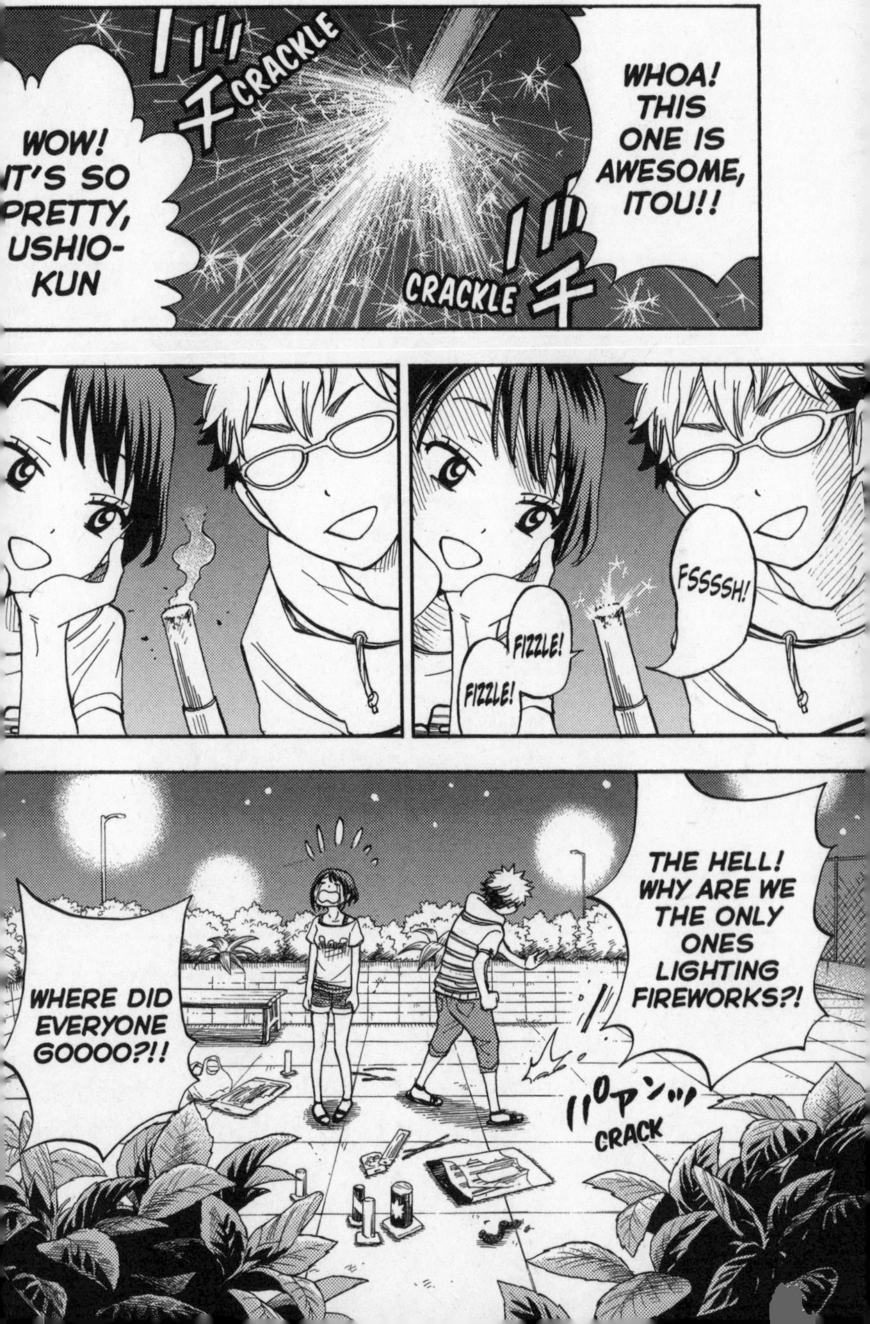
WHOA! THIS ONE IS AWESOME, ITOU!!
CRACKLE
CRACKLE
WOW! IT'S SO PRETTY, USHIO-KUN
FSSSSH!
FIZZLE!
FIZZLE!
THE HELL! WHY ARE WE THE ONLY ONES LIGHTING FIREWORKS?!
CRACK
WHERE DID EVERYONE GOOOO?!!

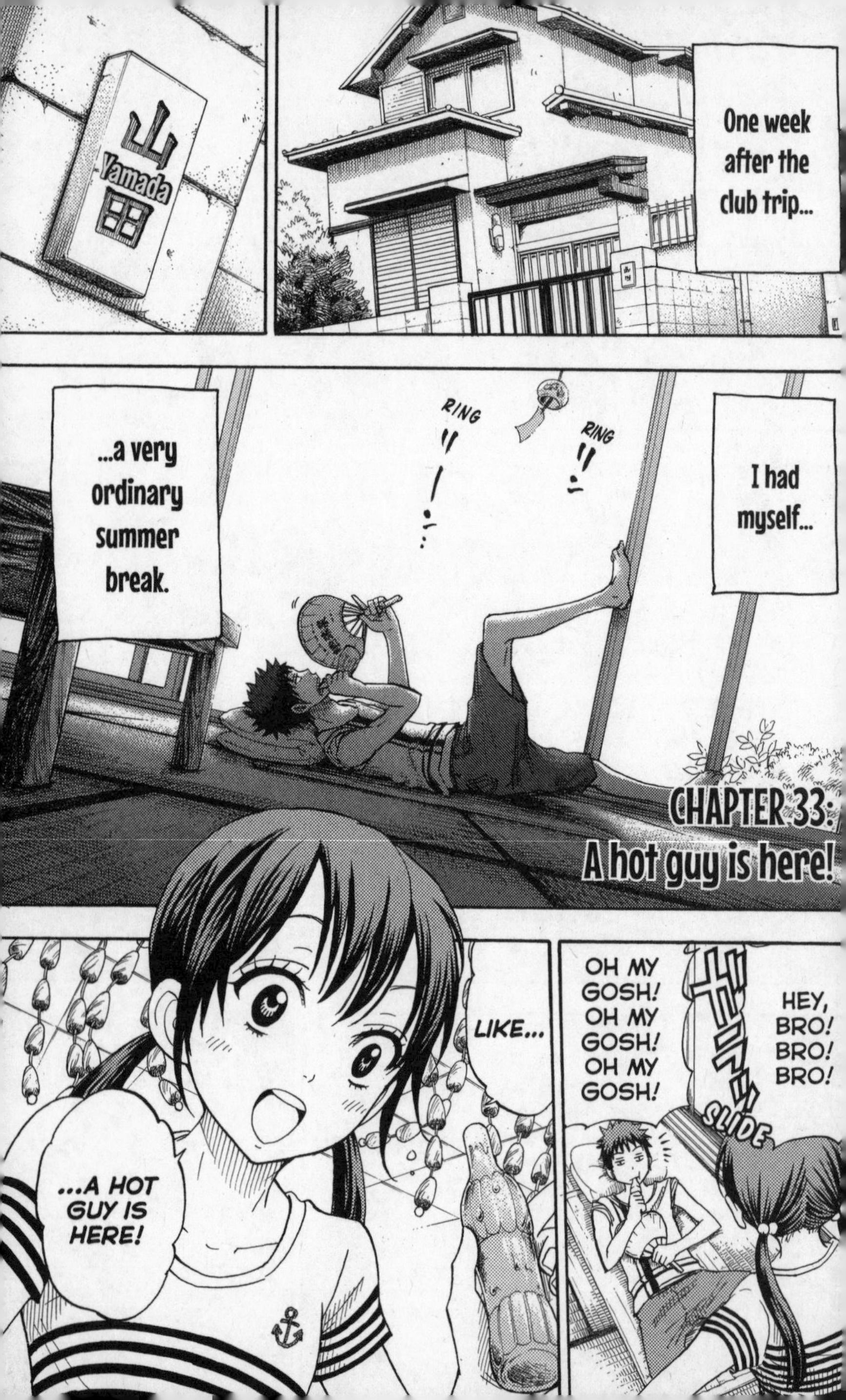
One week after the club trip...
Yamada
I had myself...
RING
RING
...a very ordinary summer break.
CHAPTER 33: A hot guy is here!
HEY, BRO! BRO! BRO!
SLIDE
OH MY GOSH! OH MY GOSH! OH MY GOSH!
LIKE...
...A HOT GUY IS HERE!

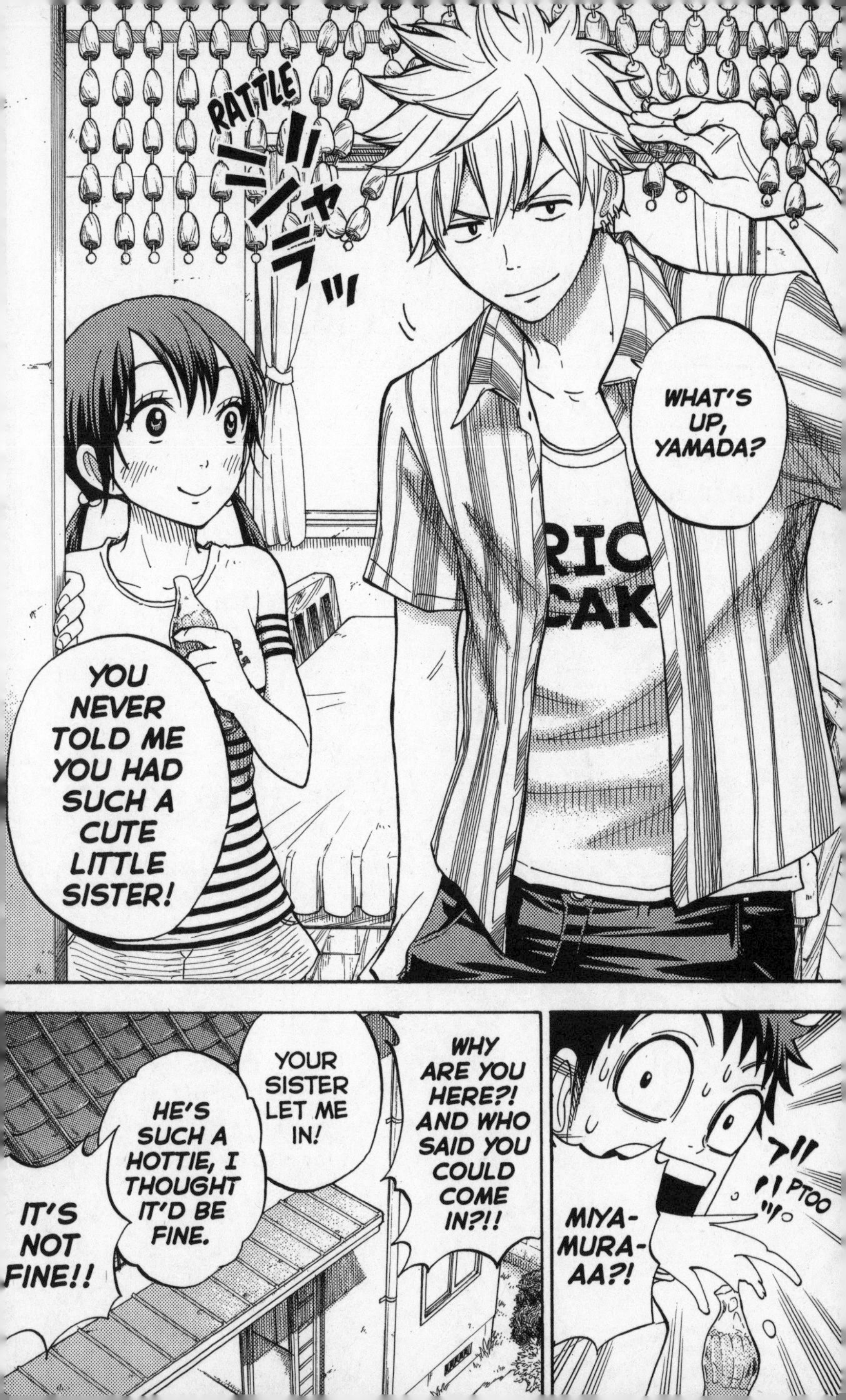
RATTLE
WHAT'S UP, YAMADA?
RIC
CAK
YOU NEVER TOLD ME YOU HAD SUCH A CUTE LITTLE SISTER!
PTOO
MIYA-MURA-AA?!
WHY ARE YOU HERE?! AND WHO SAID YOU COULD COME IN?!!
YOUR SISTER LET ME IN!
HE'S SUCH A HOTTIE, I THOUGHT IT'D BE FINE.
IT'S NOT FINE!!

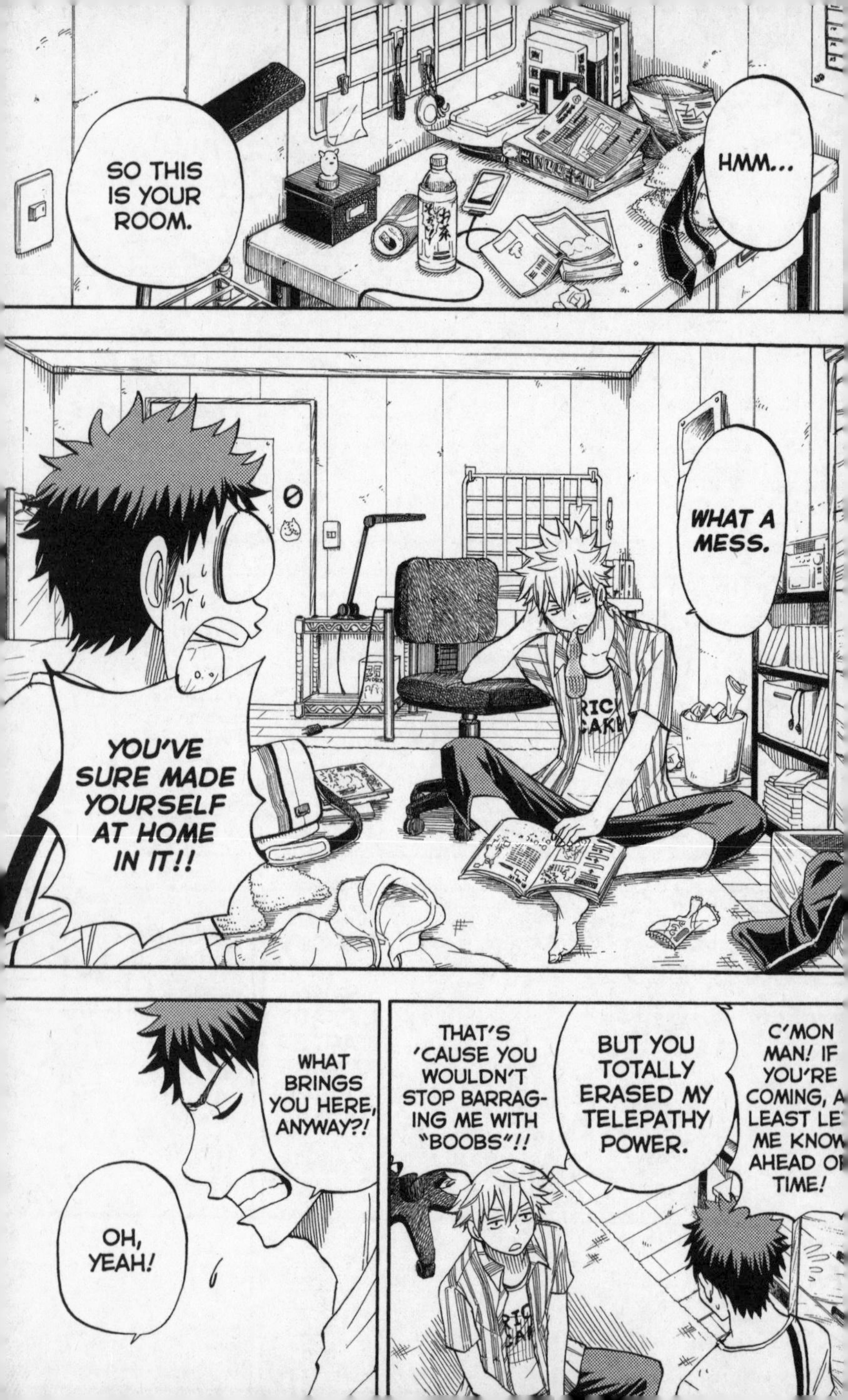
HMM...
SO THIS IS YOUR ROOM.
WHAT A MESS.
YOU'VE SURE MADE YOURSELF AT HOME IN IT!!
C'MON MAN! IF YOU'RE COMING, A LEAST LE ME KNOW AHEAD O TIME!
BUT YOU TOTALLY ERASED MY TELEPATHY POWER.
THAT'S 'CAUSE YOU WOULDN'T STOP BARRAG-ING ME WITH "BOOBS"!!
WHAT BRINGS YOU HERE, ANYWAY?!
OH, YEAH!

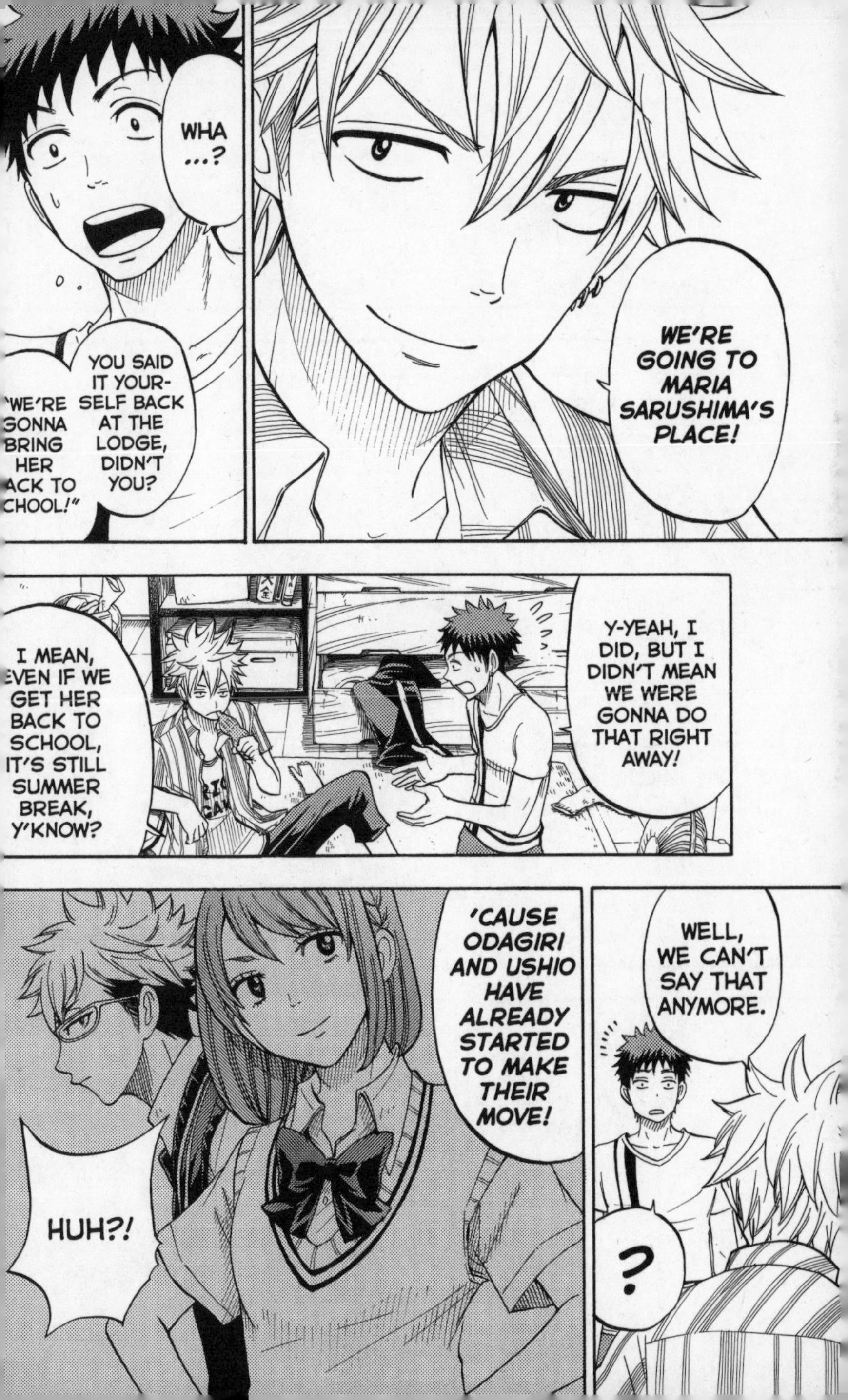
WE'RE GOING TO MARIA SARUSHIMA'S PLACE!
WHA ...?
YOU SAID IT YOURSELF BACK AT THE LODGE, DIDN'T YOU?
"WE'RE GONNA BRING HER BACK TO SCHOOL!"
Y-YEAH, I DID, BUT I DIDN'T MEAN WE WERE GONNA DO THAT RIGHT AWAY!
I MEAN, EVEN IF WE GET HER BACK TO SCHOOL, IT'S STILL SUMMER BREAK, Y'KNOW?
WELL, WE CAN'T SAY THAT ANYMORE.
?
'CAUSE ODAGIRI AND USHIO HAVE ALREADY STARTED TO MAKE THEIR MOVE!
HUH?!

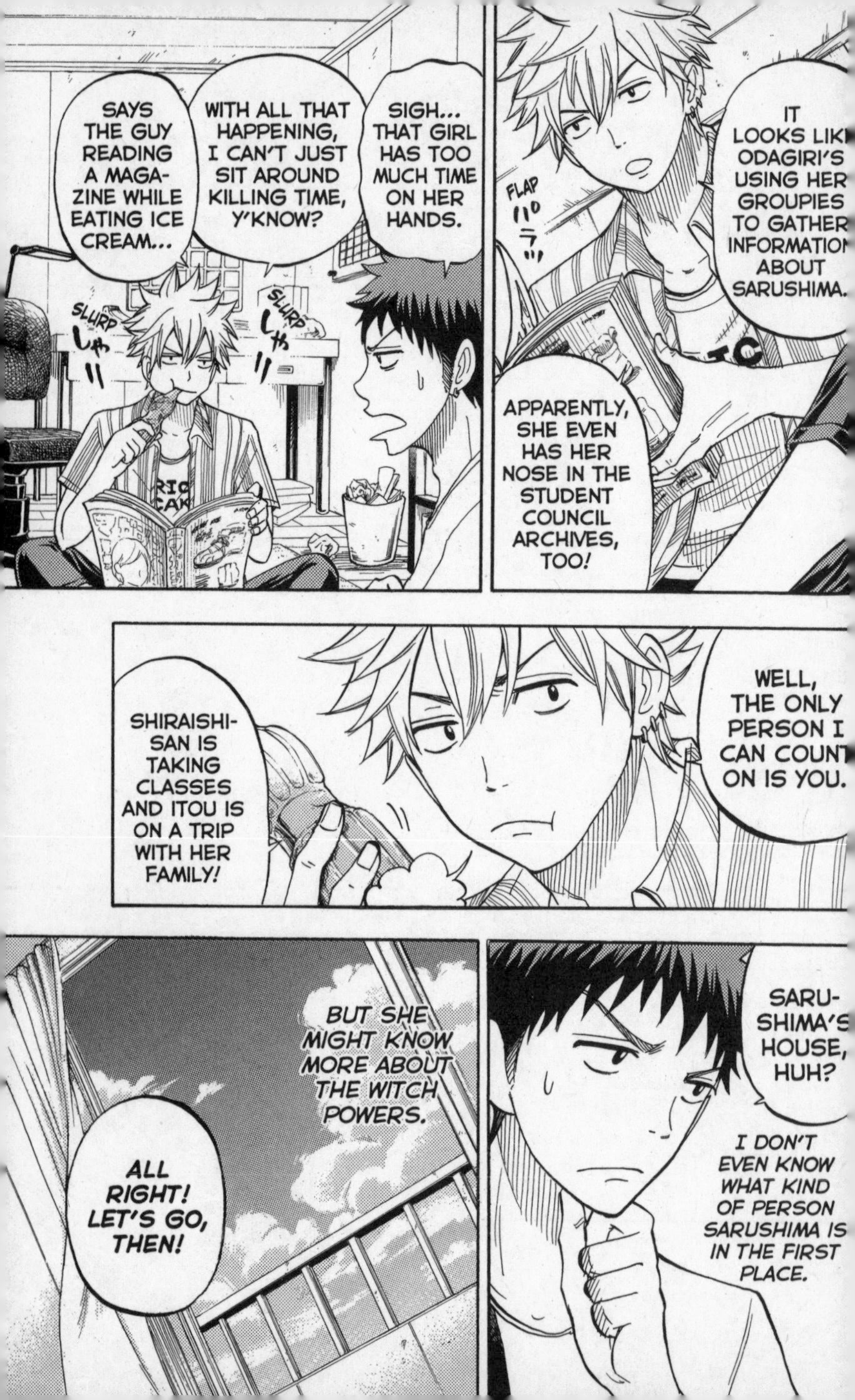
IT LOOKS LIK ODAGIRI'S USING HER GROUPIES TO GATHER INFORMATIO ABOUT SARUSHIMA.
FLAP
APPARENTLY, SHE EVEN HAS HER NOSE IN THE STUDENT COUNCIL ARCHIVES, TOO!
SIGH... THAT GIRL HAS TOO MUCH TIME ON HER HANDS.
WITH ALL THAT HAPPENING, I CAN'T JUST SIT AROUND KILLING TIME, Y'KNOW?
SAYS THE GUY READING A MAGA-ZINE WHILE EATING ICE CREAM...
SLURP
SLURP
WELL, THE ONLY PERSON I CAN COUNT ON IS YOU.
SHIRAISHI-SAN IS TAKING CLASSES AND ITOU IS ON A TRIP WITH HER FAMILY!
SARU-SHIMA'S HOUSE, HUH?
I DON'T EVEN KNOW WHAT KIND OF PERSON SARUSHIMA IS IN THE FIRST PLACE.
BUT SHE MIGHT KNOW MORE ABOUT THE WITCH POWERS.
ALL RIGHT! LET'S GO, THEN!

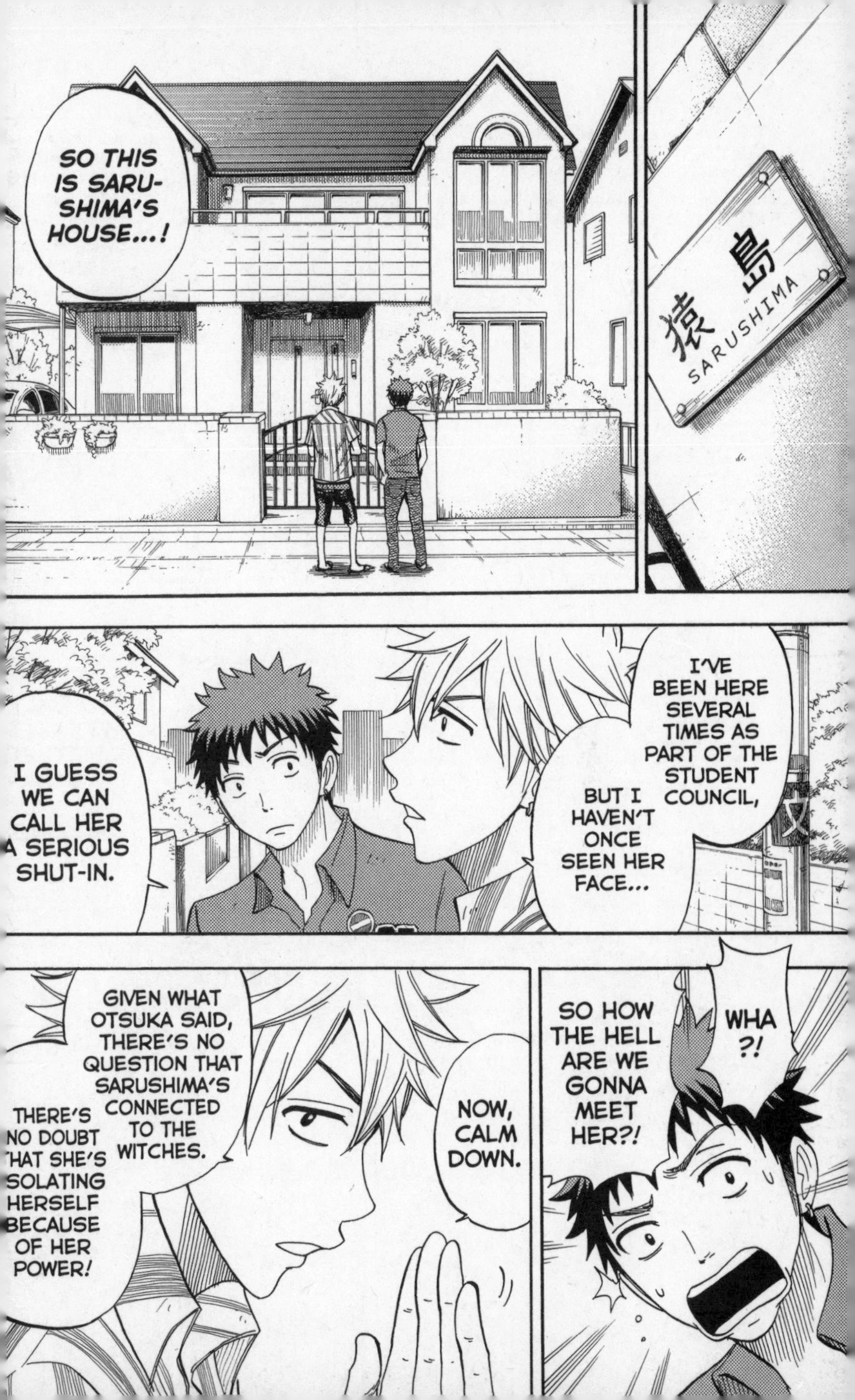
猿島
SARUSHIMA
SO THIS IS SARU-SHIMA'S HOUSE...!
I'VE BEEN HERE SEVERAL TIMES AS PART OF THE STUDENT COUNCIL,
BUT I HAVEN'T ONCE SEEN HER FACE...
I GUESS WE CAN CALL HER A SERIOUS SHUT-IN.
WHA?!
SO HOW THE HELL ARE WE GONNA MEET HER?!
NOW, CALM DOWN.
GIVEN WHAT OTSUKA SAID, THERE'S NO QUESTION THAT SARUSHIMA'S CONNECTED TO THE WITCHES.
THERE'S NO DOUBT HAT SHE'S SOLATING HERSELF BECAUSE OF HER POWER!

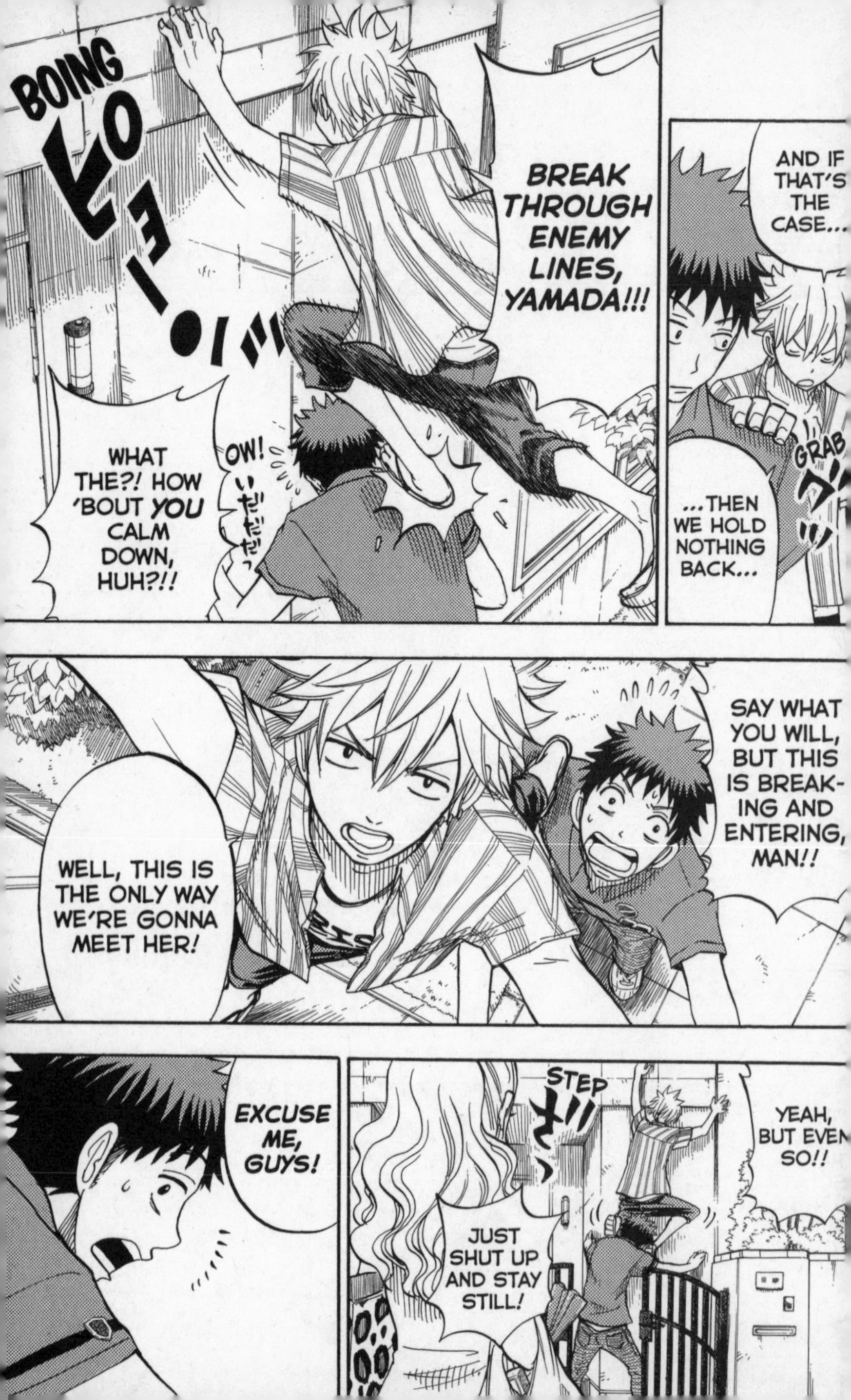

AND IF THAT'S THE CASE...
GRAB
...THEN WE HOLD NOTHING BACK...
BREAK THROUGH ENEMY LINES, YAMADA!!!
BOING
OW!
WHAT THE?! HOW 'BOUT YOU CALM DOWN, HUH?!!
SAY WHAT YOU WILL, BUT THIS IS BREAK-ING AND ENTERING, MAN!!
WELL, THIS IS THE ONLY WAY WE'RE GONNA MEET HER!
YEAH, BUT EVEN SO!!
STEP
JUST SHUT UP AND STAY STILL!
EXCUSE ME, GUYS!

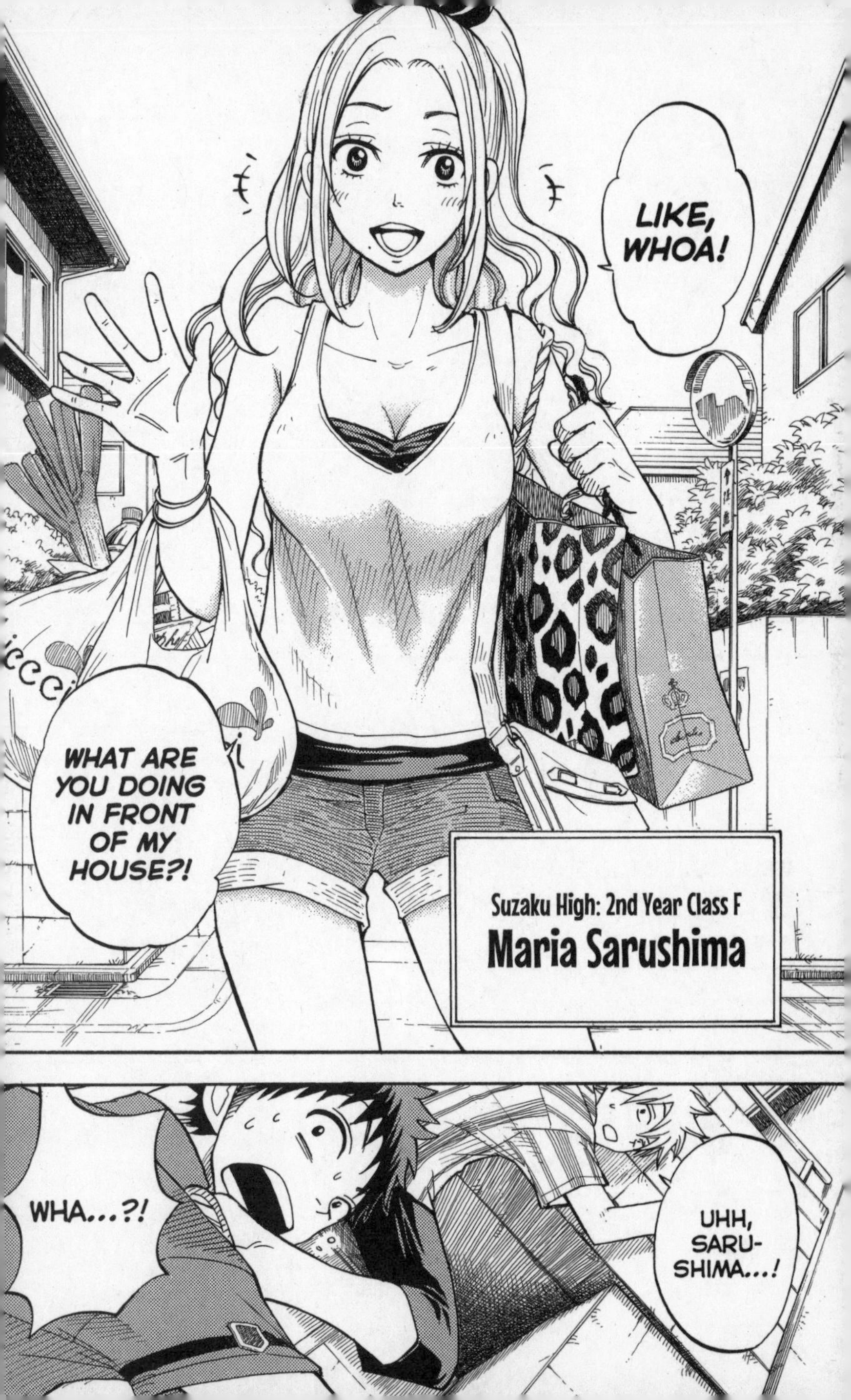
LIKE, WHOA!
WHAT ARE YOU DOING IN FRONT OF MY HOUSE?!
Suzaku High: 2nd Year Class F
Maria Sarushima
UHH, SARU-SHIMA...!
WHA...?!

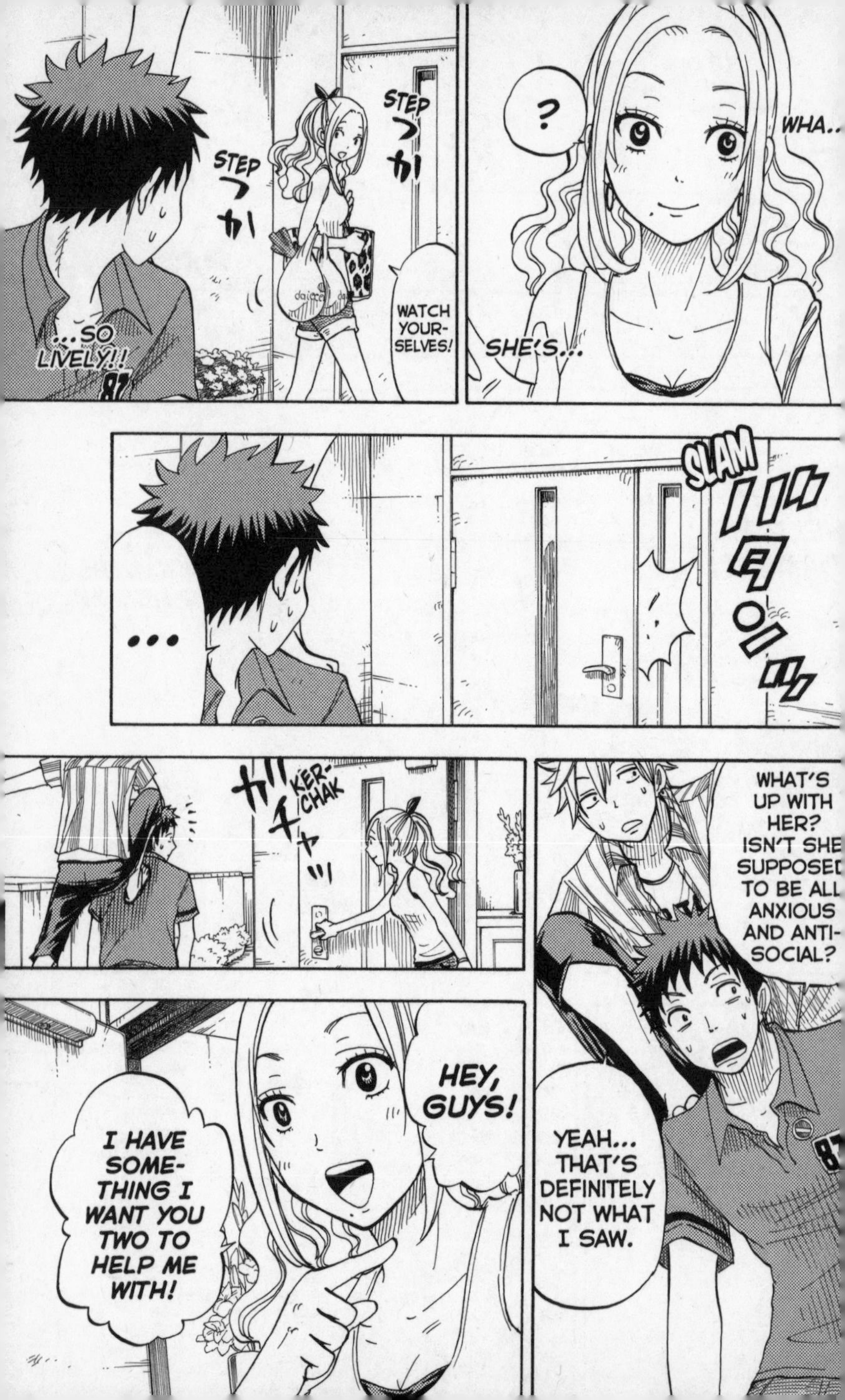
?
WHA..
SHE'S...
WATCH YOURSELVES!
STEP
STEP
...SO LIVELY!!
SLAM
...
WHAT'S UP WITH HER? ISN'T SHE SUPPOSED TO BE ALL ANXIOUS AND ANTI-SOCIAL?
YEAH... THAT'S DEFINITELY NOT WHAT I SAW.
KER-CHAK
HEY, GUYS!
I HAVE SOMETHING I WANT YOU TWO TO HELP ME WITH!

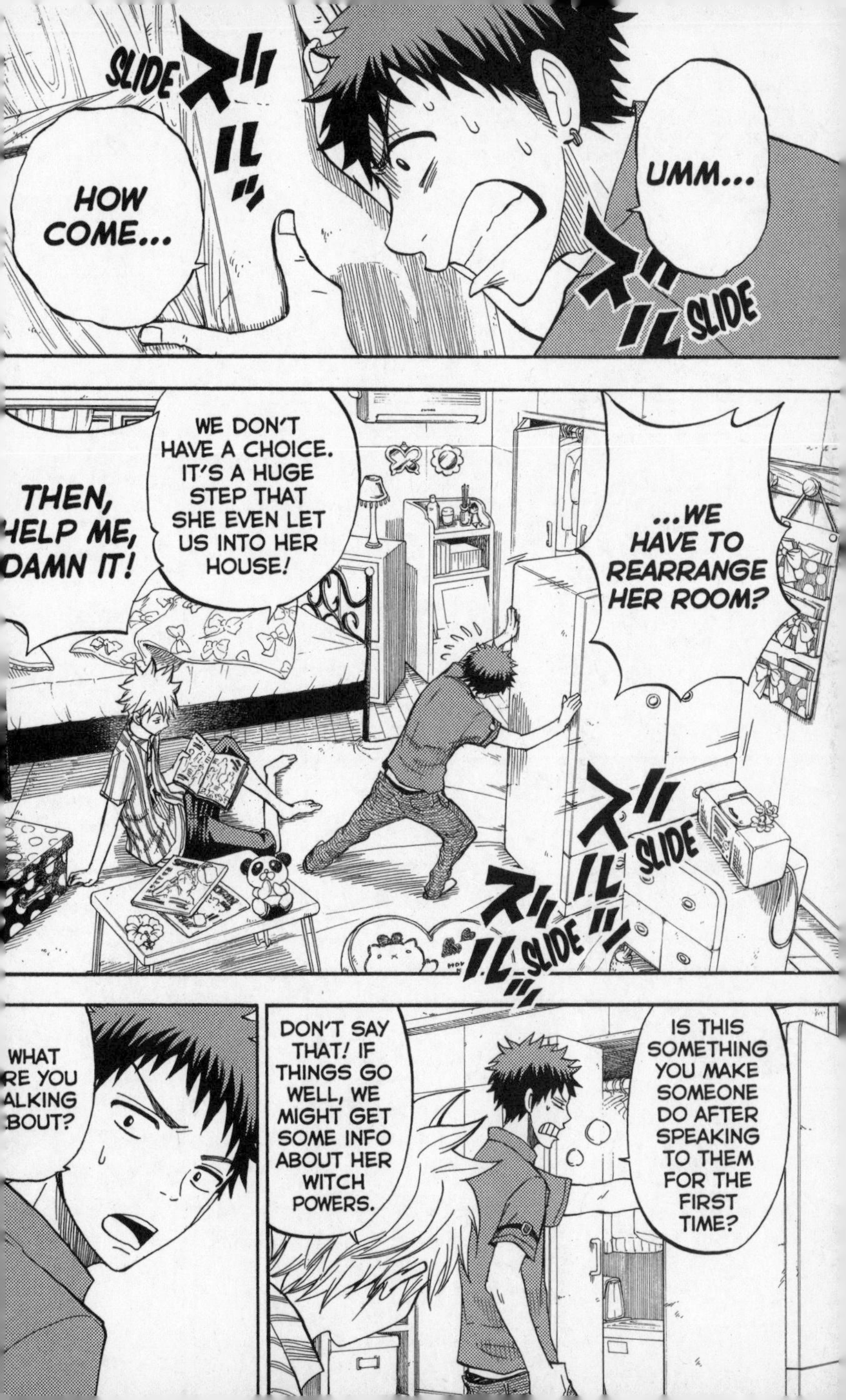
UMM...
SLIDE
SLIDE
HOW COME...
...WE HAVE TO REARRANGE HER ROOM?
WE DON'T HAVE A CHOICE. IT'S A HUGE STEP THAT SHE EVEN LET US INTO HER HOUSE!
THEN, HELP ME, DAMN IT!
SLIDE
SLIDE
SLIDE
IS THIS SOMETHING YOU MAKE SOMEONE DO AFTER SPEAKING TO THEM FOR THE FIRST TIME?
DON'T SAY THAT! IF THINGS GO WELL, WE MIGHT GET SOME INFO ABOUT HER WITCH POWERS.
WHAT RE YOU ALKING BOUT?

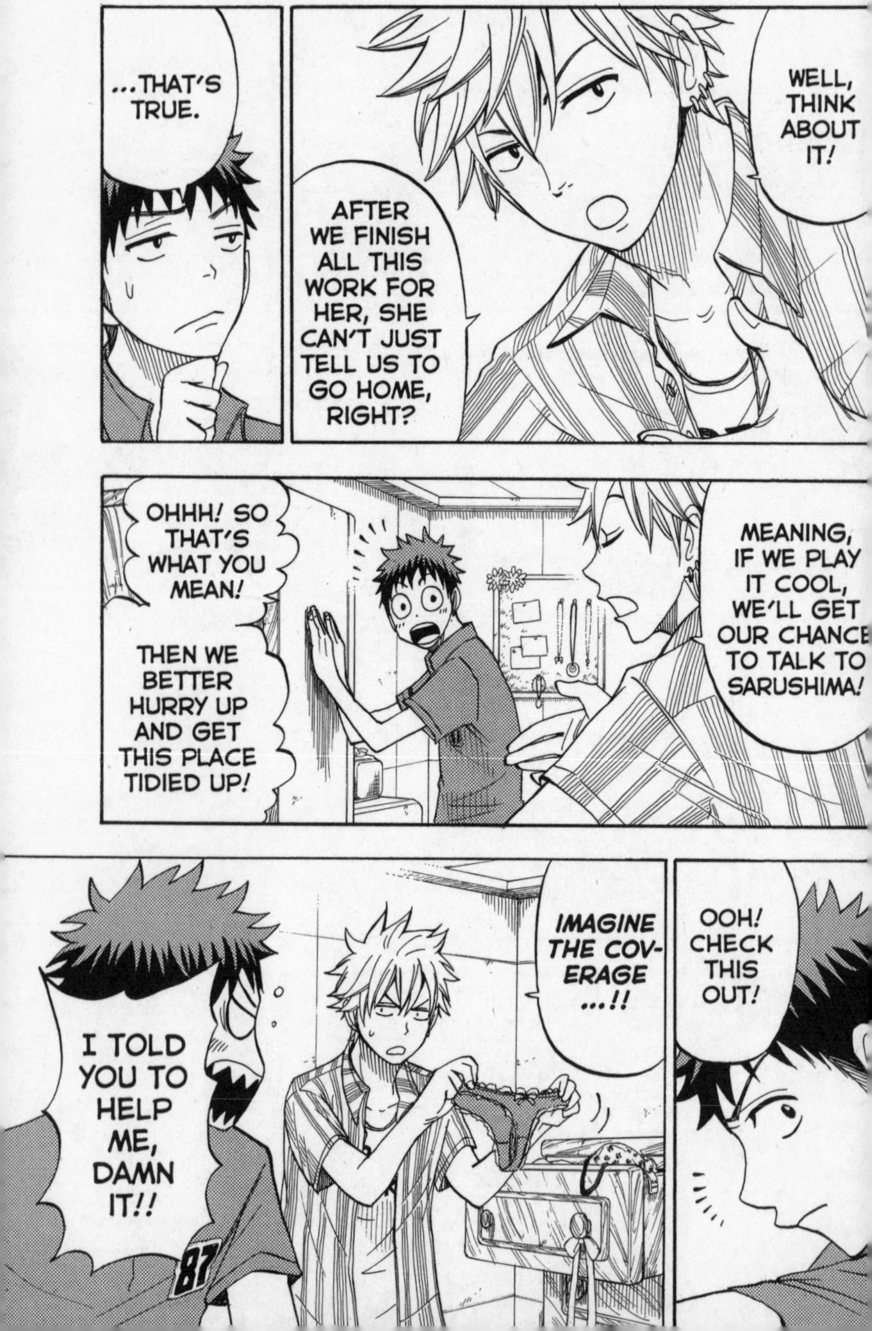
WELL, THINK ABOUT IT!
AFTER WE FINISH ALL THIS WORK FOR HER, SHE CAN'T JUST TELL US TO GO HOME, RIGHT?
...THAT'S TRUE.
MEANING, IF WE PLAY IT COOL, WE'LL GET OUR CHANCE TO TALK TO SARUSHIMA!
OHHH! SO THAT'S WHAT YOU MEAN!
THEN WE BETTER HURRY UP AND GET THIS PLACE TIDIED UP!
OOH! CHECK THIS OUT!
IMAGINE THE COV-ERAGE ...!!
I TOLD YOU TO HELP ME, DAMN IT!!

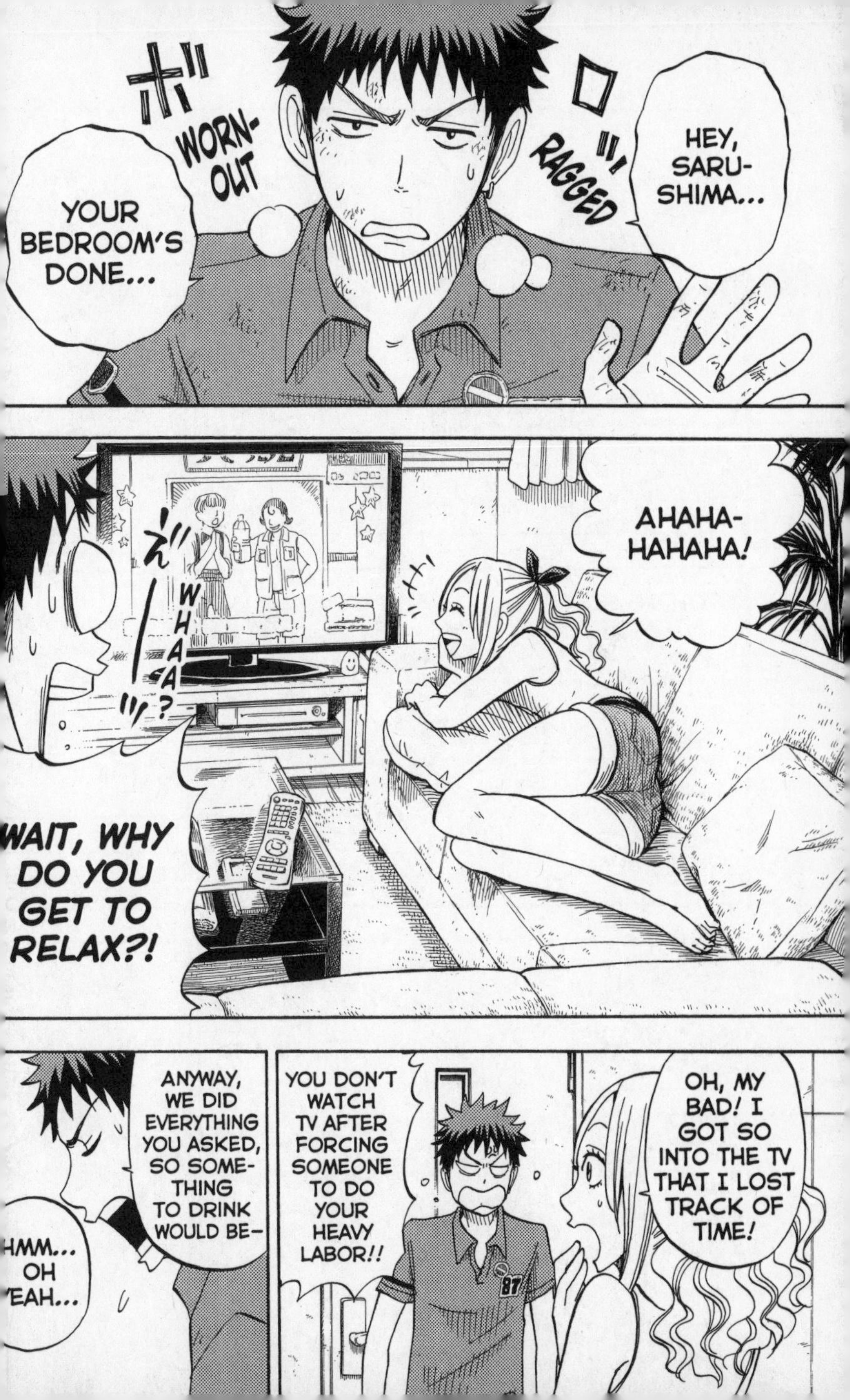
HEY, SARU-SHIMA...
ロ
RAGGED
ボ
WORN-OUT
YOUR BEDROOM'S DONE...
AHAHA-HAHAHA!
ん
WHAAA?
WAIT, WHY DO YOU GET TO RELAX?!
OH, MY BAD! I GOT SO INTO THE TV THAT I LOST TRACK OF TIME!
YOU DON'T WATCH TV AFTER FORCING SOMEONE TO DO YOUR HEAVY LABOR!!
ANYWAY, WE DID EVERYTHING YOU ASKED, SO SOME-THING TO DRINK WOULD BE-
HMM... OH YEAH...

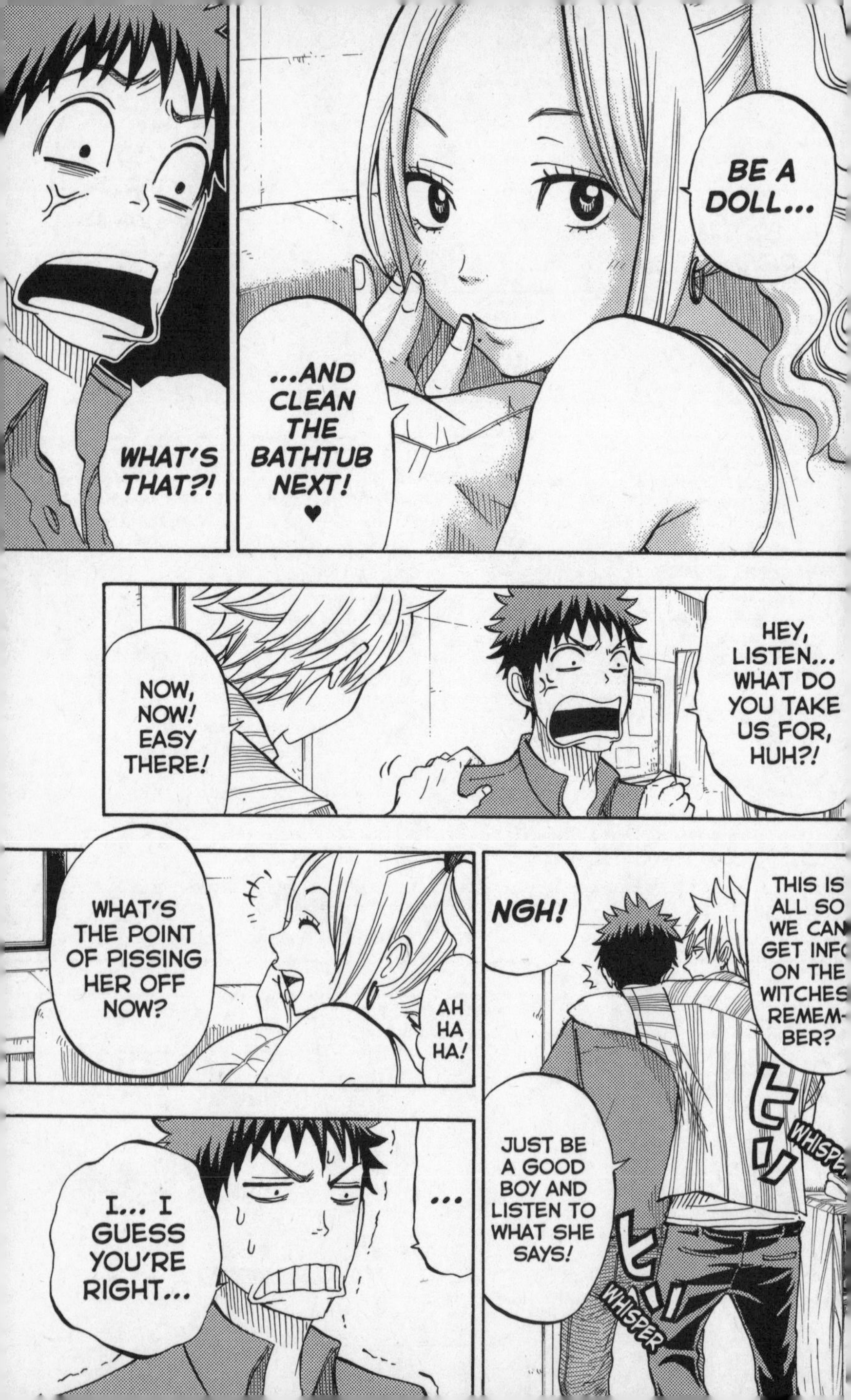
BE A DOLL...
...AND CLEAN THE BATHTUB NEXT! ♥
WHAT'S THAT?!
HEY, LISTEN... WHAT DO YOU TAKE US FOR, HUH?!
NOW, NOW! EASY THERE!
THIS IS ALL SO WE CAN GET INFO ON THE WITCHES REMEMBER?
NGH!
WHISPER
WHISPER
JUST BE A GOOD BOY AND LISTEN TO WHAT SHE SAYS!
AH HA HA!
WHAT'S THE POINT OF PISSING HER OFF NOW?
...
I... I GUESS YOU'RE RIGHT...

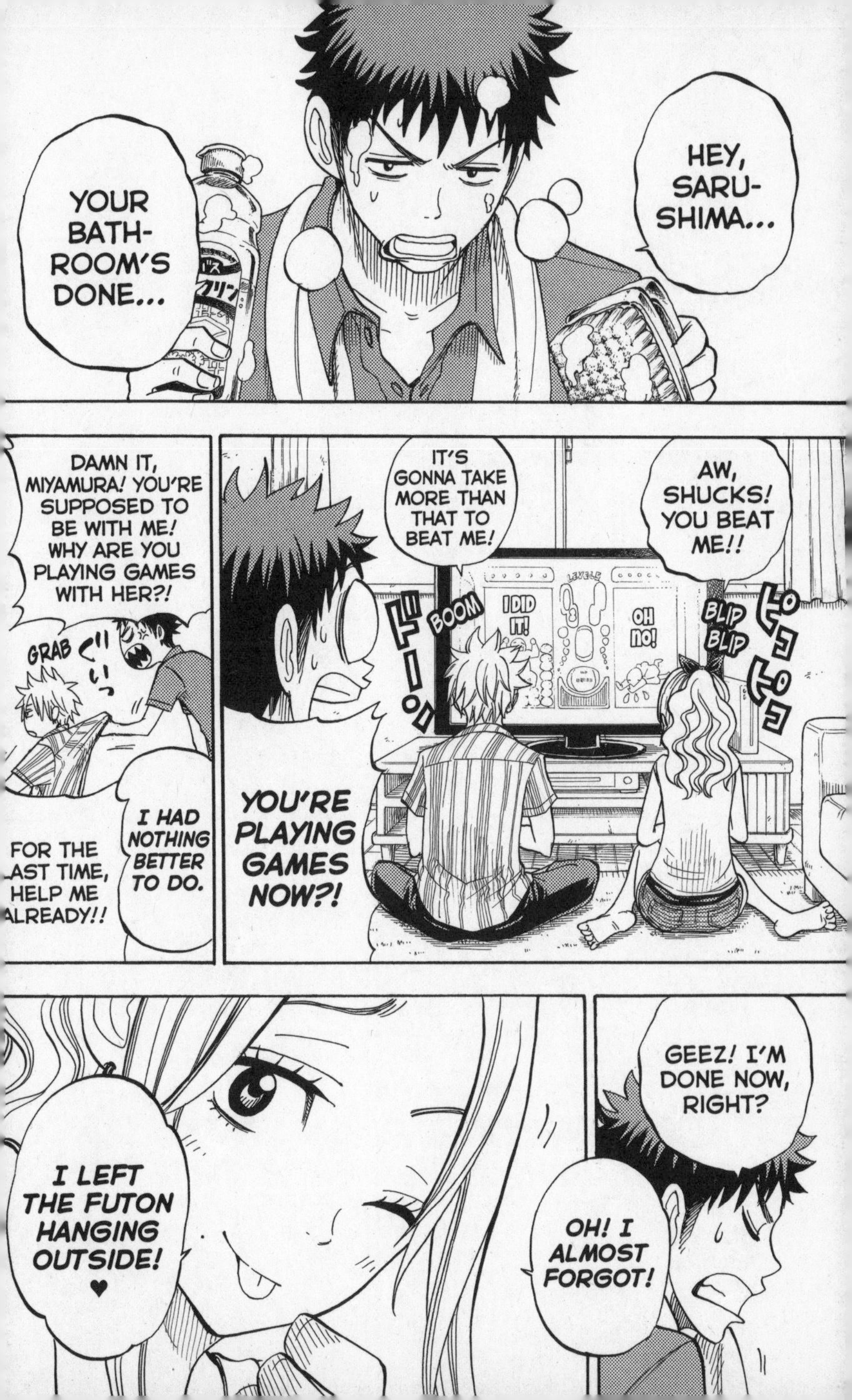
HEY, SARU-SHIMA...
YOUR BATH-ROOM'S DONE...
AW, SHUCKS! YOU BEAT ME!!
BLIP BLIP
IT'S GONNA TAKE MORE THAN THAT TO BEAT ME!
OH NO!
I DID IT!
BOOM
YOU'RE PLAYING GAMES NOW?!
DAMN IT, MIYAMURA! YOU'RE SUPPOSED TO BE WITH ME! WHY ARE YOU PLAYING GAMES WITH HER?!
GRAB
I HAD NOTHING BETTER TO DO.
FOR THE LAST TIME, HELP ME ALREADY!!
GEEZ! I'M DONE NOW, RIGHT?
OH! I ALMOST FORGOT!
I LEFT THE FUTON HANGING OUTSIDE! ♥

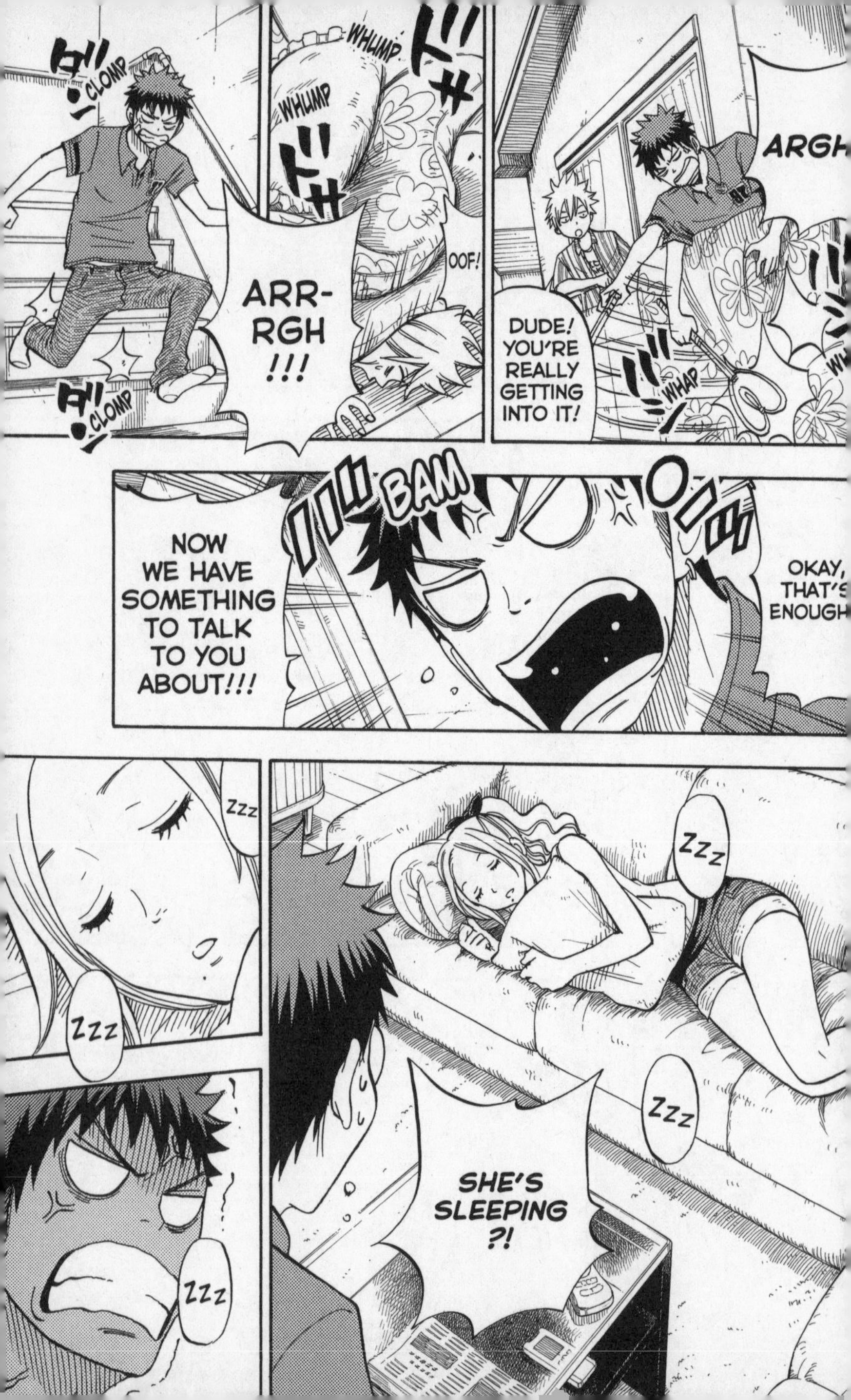

ARGH
DUDE! YOU'RE REALLY GETTING INTO IT!
WHAP
WHUMP
WHUMP
OOF!
ARR-RGH!!!
CLOMP
CLOMP
OKAY, THAT'S ENOUGH
BAM
NOW WE HAVE SOMETHING TO TALK TO YOU ABOUT!!!
Zzz
Zzz
SHE'S SLEEPING?!
Zzz
Zzz
Zzz

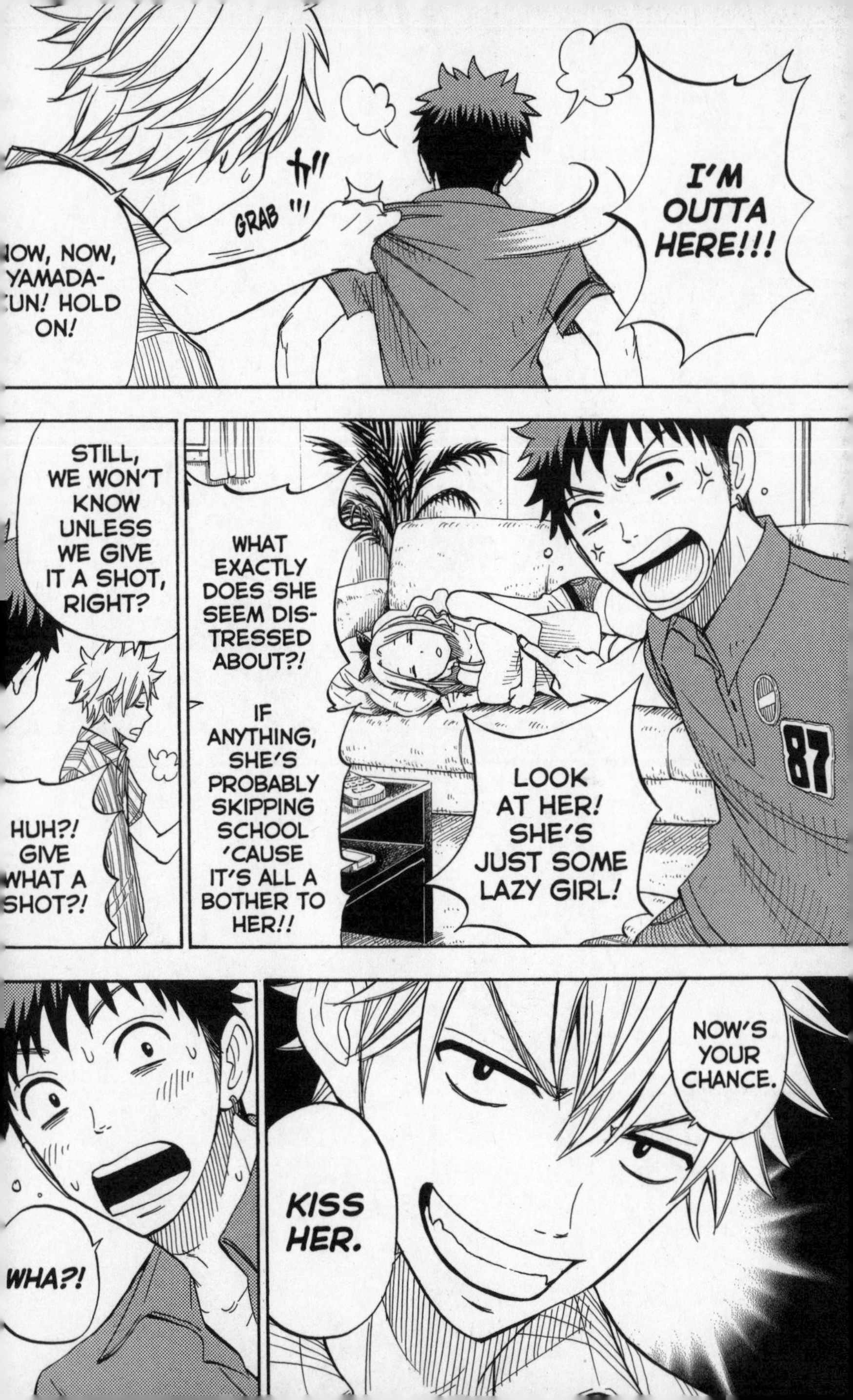
I'M OUTTA HERE!!!
GRAB
NOW, NOW, YAMADA-KUN! HOLD ON!
WHAT EXACTLY DOES SHE SEEM DIS-TRESSED ABOUT?!
LOOK AT HER! SHE'S JUST SOME LAZY GIRL!
IF ANYTHING, SHE'S PROBABLY SKIPPING SCHOOL 'CAUSE IT'S ALL A BOTHER TO HER!!
STILL, WE WON'T KNOW UNLESS WE GIVE IT A SHOT, RIGHT?
HUH?! GIVE WHAT A SHOT?!
NOW'S YOUR CHANCE.
KISS HER.
WHA?!

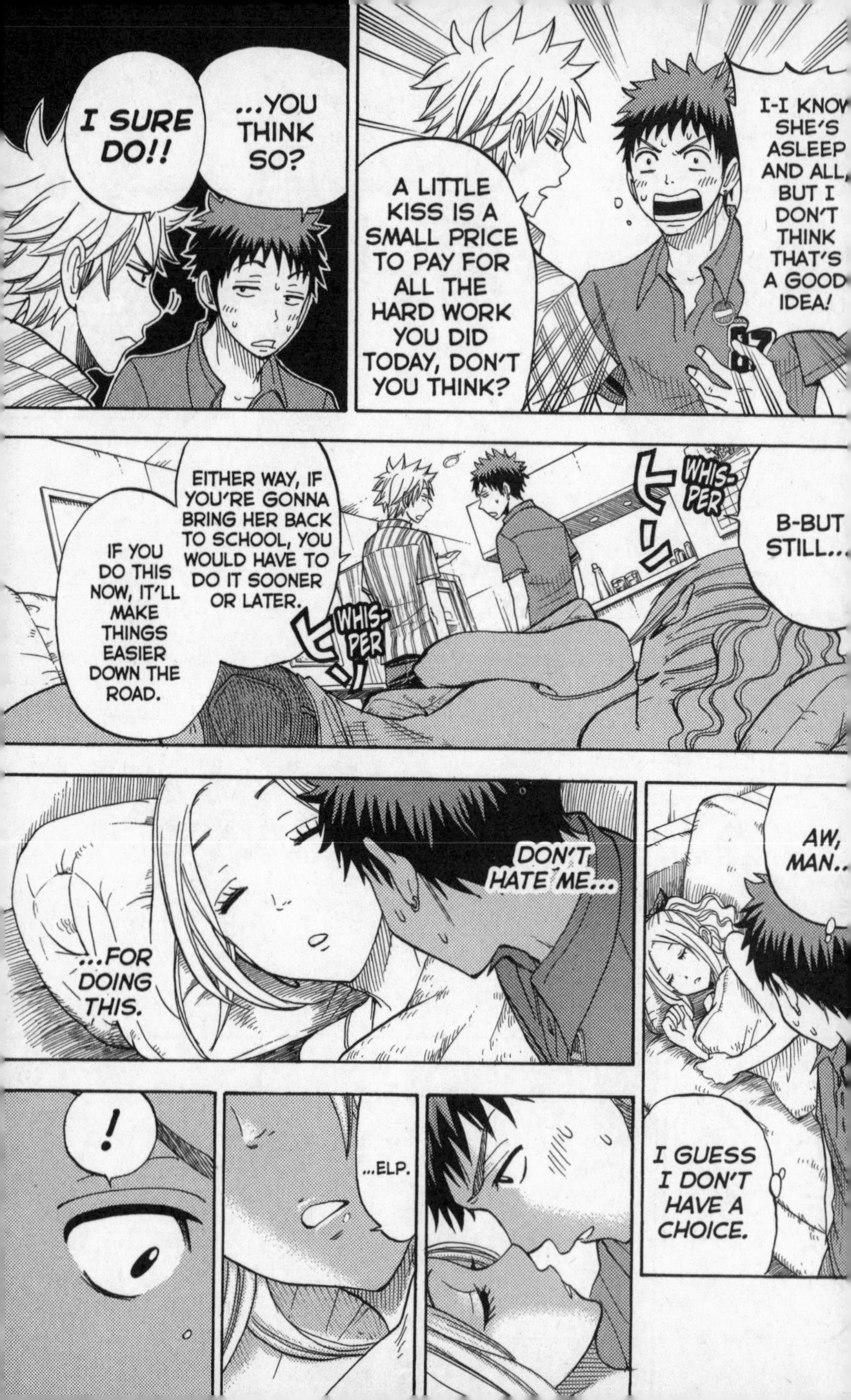
I-I KNOW SHE'S ASLEEP AND ALL, BUT I DON'T THINK THAT'S A GOOD IDEA!
A LITTLE KISS IS A SMALL PRICE TO PAY FOR ALL THE HARD WORK YOU DID TODAY, DON'T YOU THINK?
...YOU THINK SO?
I SURE DO!!
B-BUT STILL...
WHIS-PER
EITHER WAY, IF YOU'RE GONNA BRING HER BACK TO SCHOOL, YOU WOULD HAVE TO DO IT SOONER OR LATER.
IF YOU DO THIS NOW, IT'LL MAKE THINGS EASIER DOWN THE ROAD.
WHIS-PER
AW, MAN...
I GUESS I DON'T HAVE A CHOICE.
DON'T HATE ME...
...FOR DOING THIS.
...ELP.
!

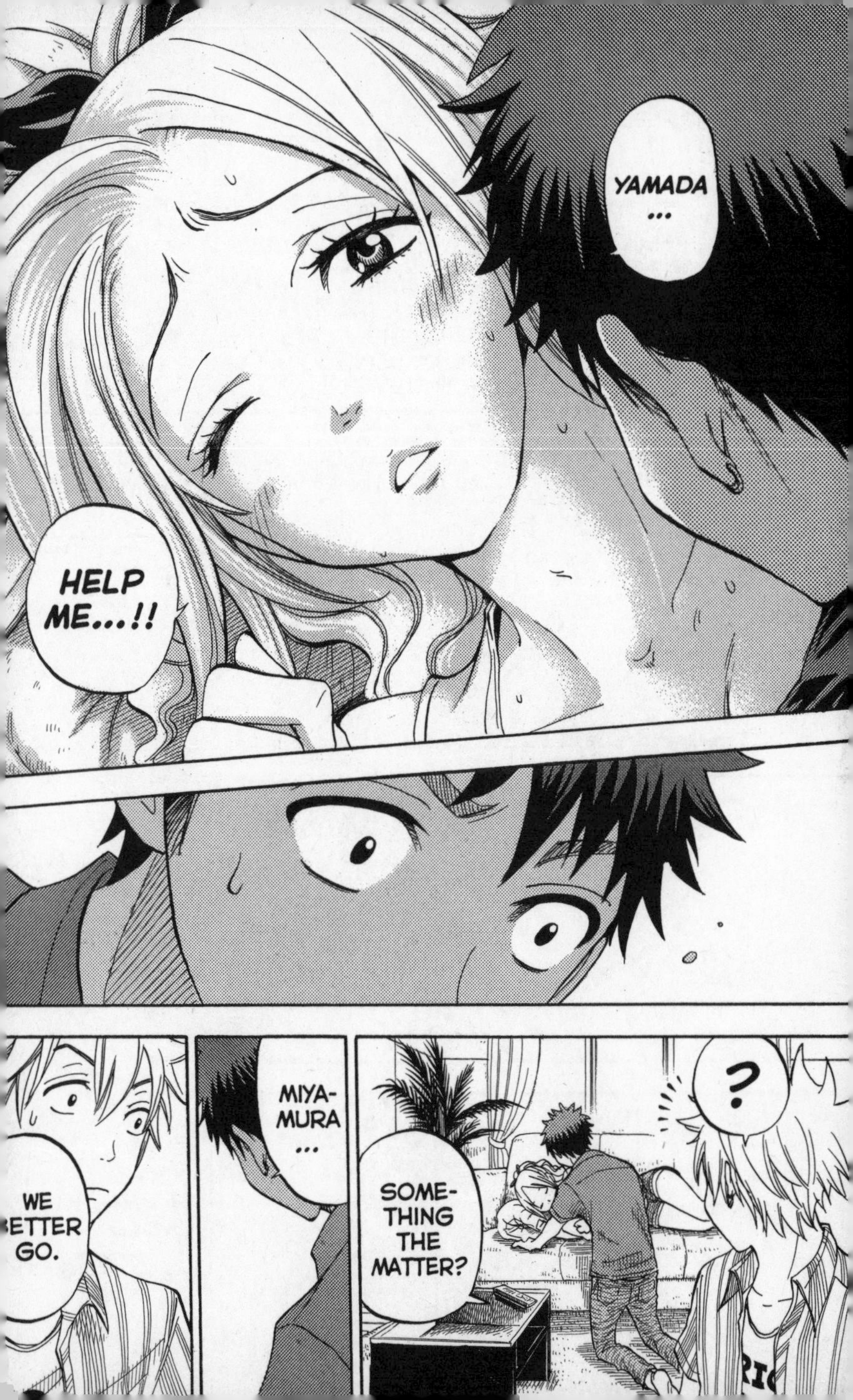
YAMADA...
HELP ME...!!
?
MIYA-MURA...
SOME-THING THE MATTER?
WE BETTER GO.

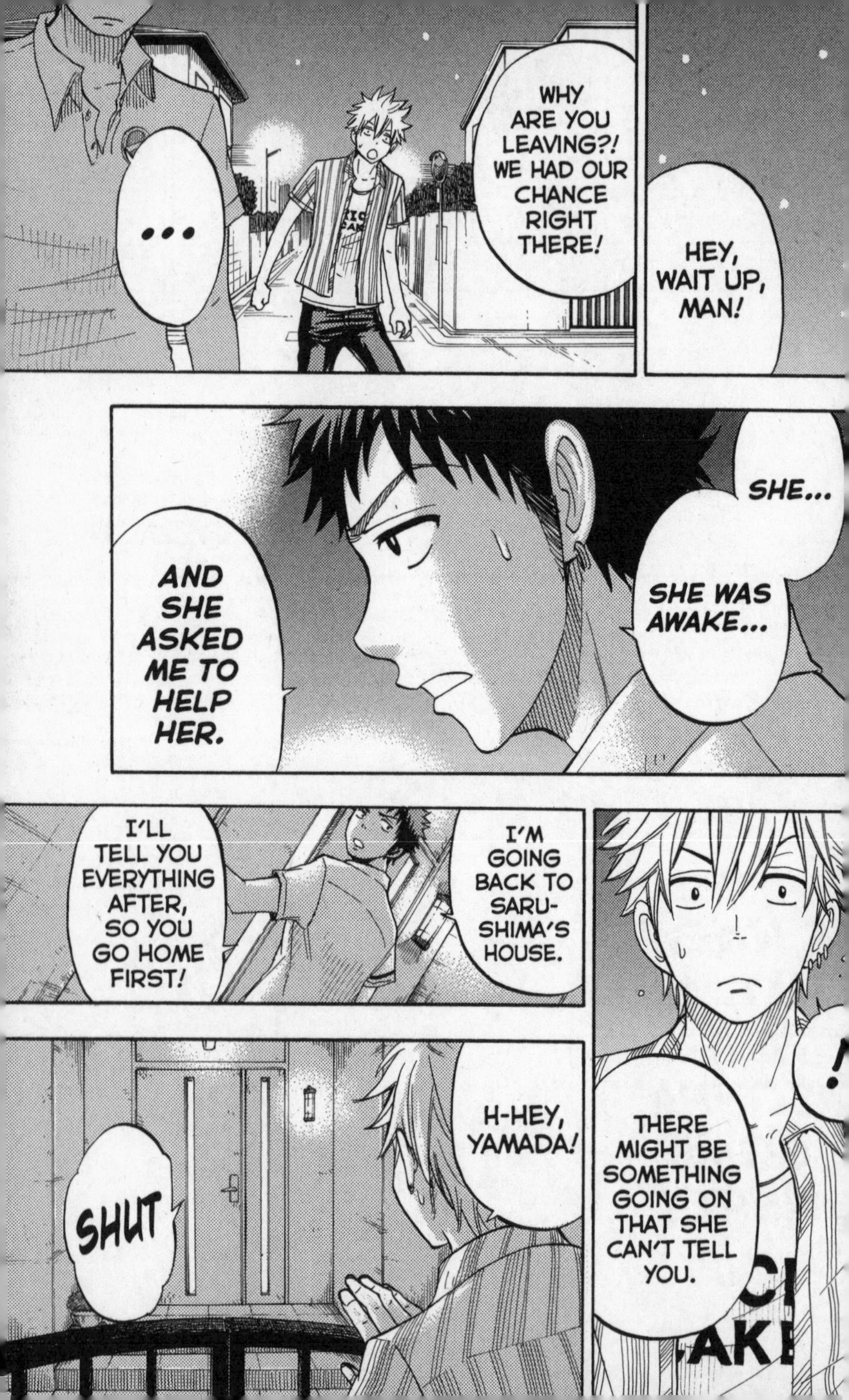
HEY, WAIT UP, MAN!
WHY ARE YOU LEAVING?! WE HAD OUR CHANCE RIGHT THERE!
...
SHE...
SHE WAS AWAKE...
AND SHE ASKED ME TO HELP HER.
!
THERE MIGHT BE SOMETHING GOING ON THAT SHE CAN'T TELL YOU.
I'M GOING BACK TO SARU-SHIMA'S HOUSE.
I'LL TELL YOU EVERYTHING AFTER, SO YOU GO HOME FIRST!
H-HEY, YAMADA!
SHUT

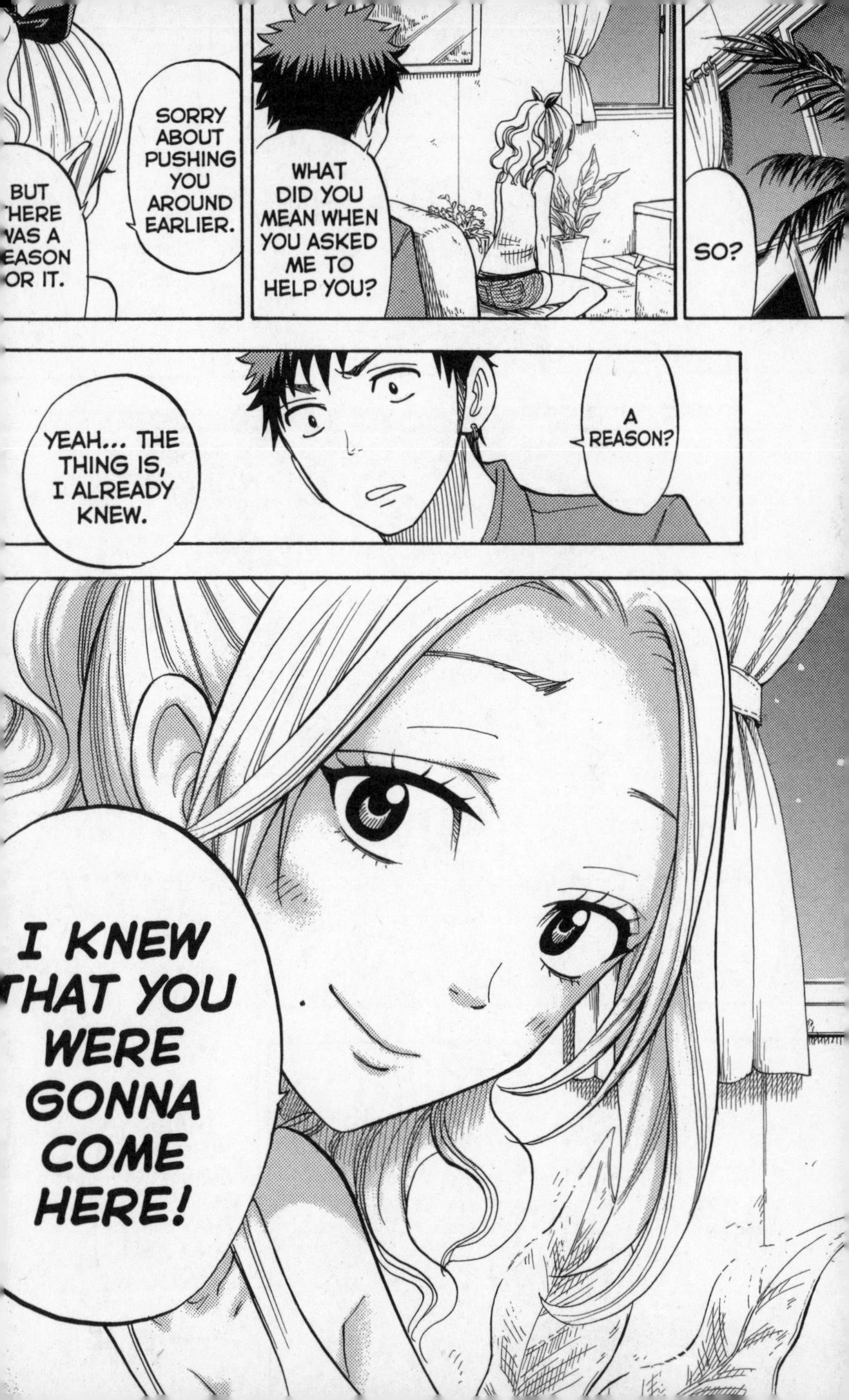
SO?
WHAT DID YOU MEAN WHEN YOU ASKED ME TO HELP YOU?
SORRY ABOUT PUSHING YOU AROUND EARLIER.
BUT HERE VAS A EASON OR IT.
A REASON?
YEAH... THE THING IS, I ALREADY KNEW.
I KNEW THAT YOU WERE GONNA COME HERE!

CHAPTER 34: Pay you with my body?

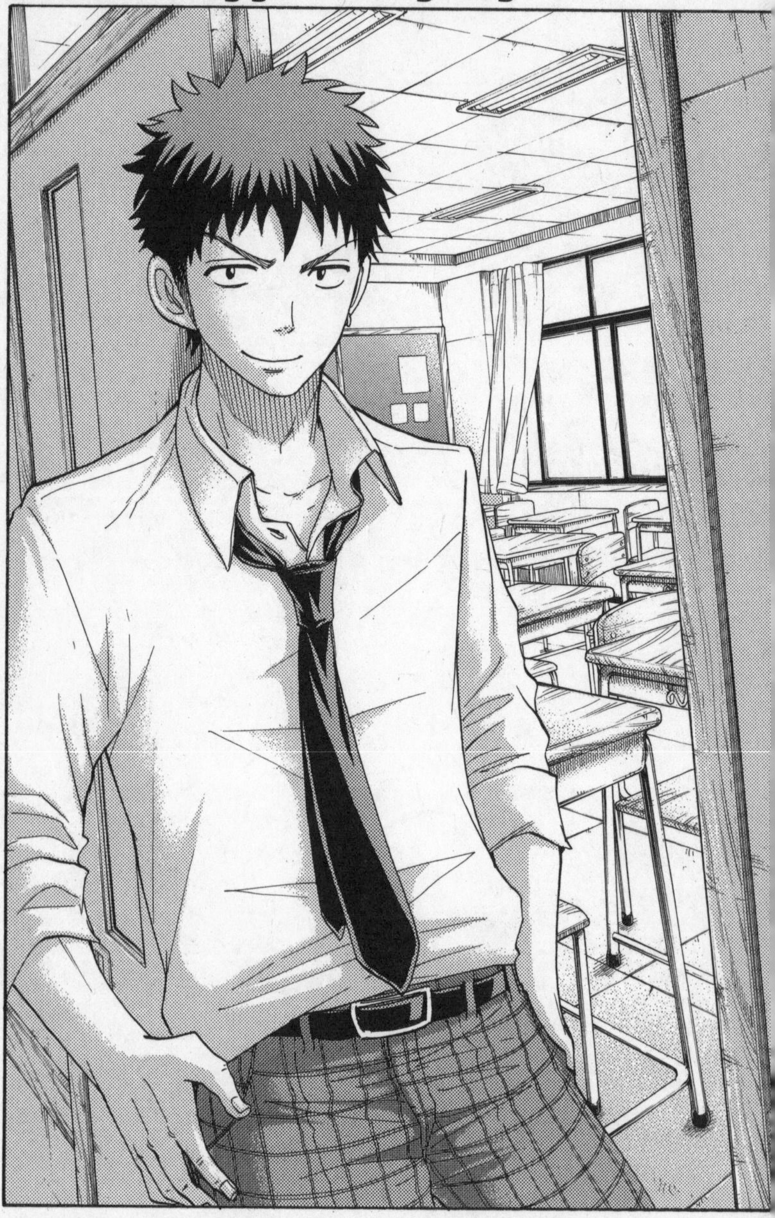

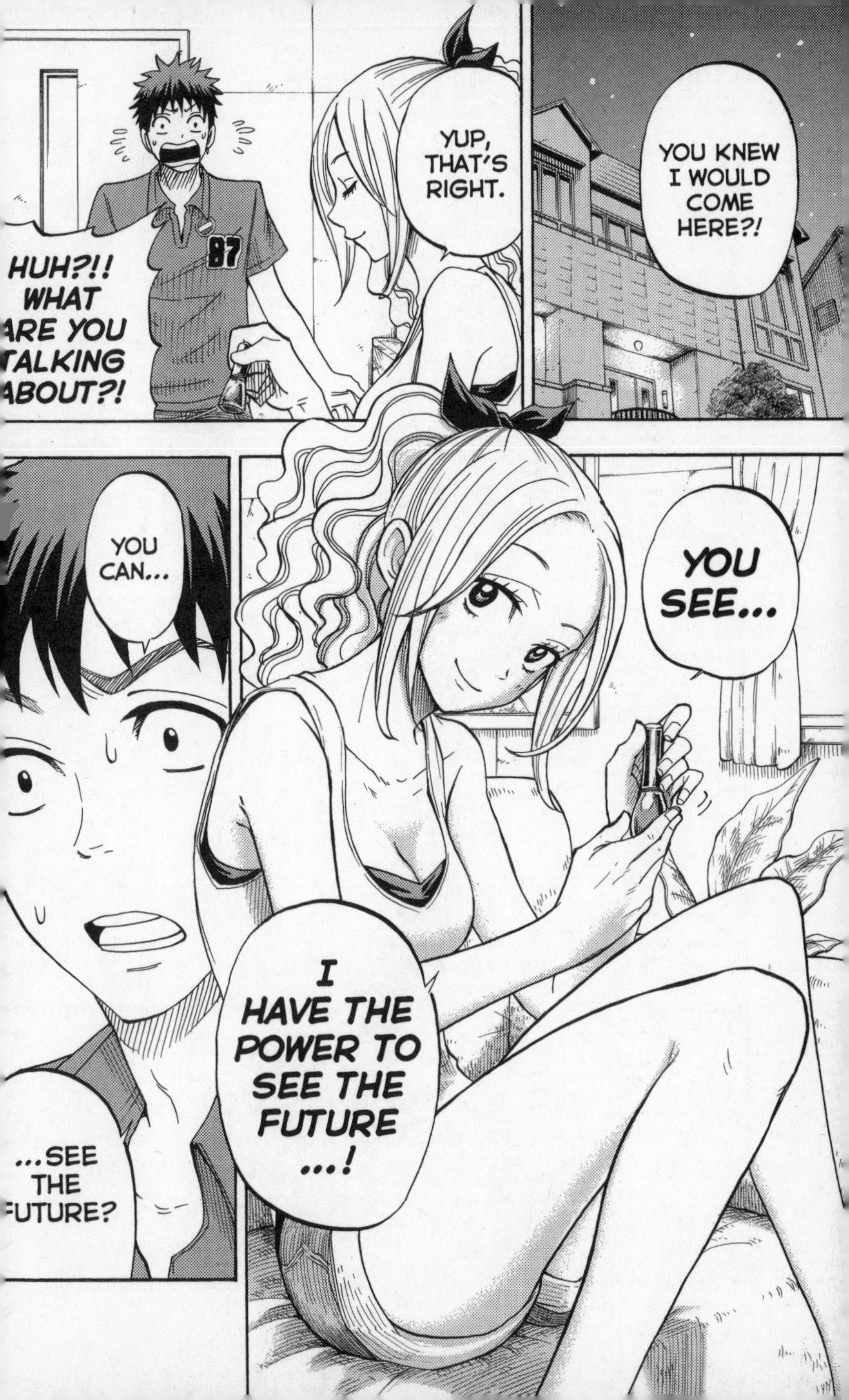
YOU KNEW I WOULD COME HERE?!
YUP, THAT'S RIGHT.
HUH?!! WHAT ARE YOU TALKING ABOUT?!
YOU SEE...
I HAVE THE POWER TO SEE THE FUTURE ...!
YOU CAN...
...SEE THE FUTURE?

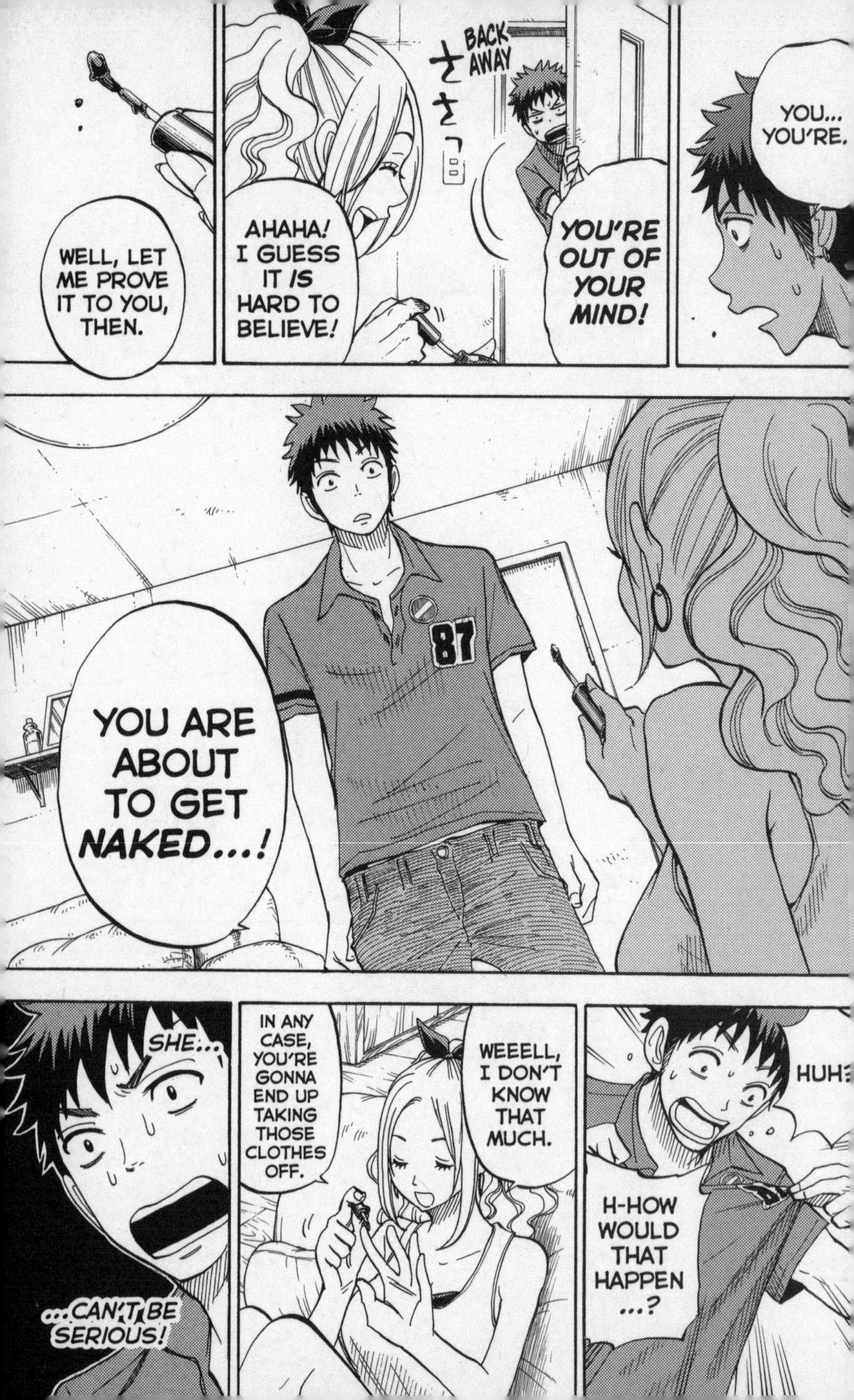
YOU... YOU'RE.
BACK AWAY
YOU'RE OUT OF YOUR MIND!
AHAHA! I GUESS IT *IS* HARD TO BELIEVE!
WELL, LET ME PROVE IT TO YOU, THEN.
YOU ARE ABOUT TO GET *NAKED...!*
HUH!?
H-HOW WOULD THAT HAPPEN ...?
WEEELL, I DON'T KNOW THAT MUCH.
IN ANY CASE, YOU'RE GONNA END UP TAKING THOSE CLOTHES OFF.
SHE...
...CAN'T BE SERIOUS!

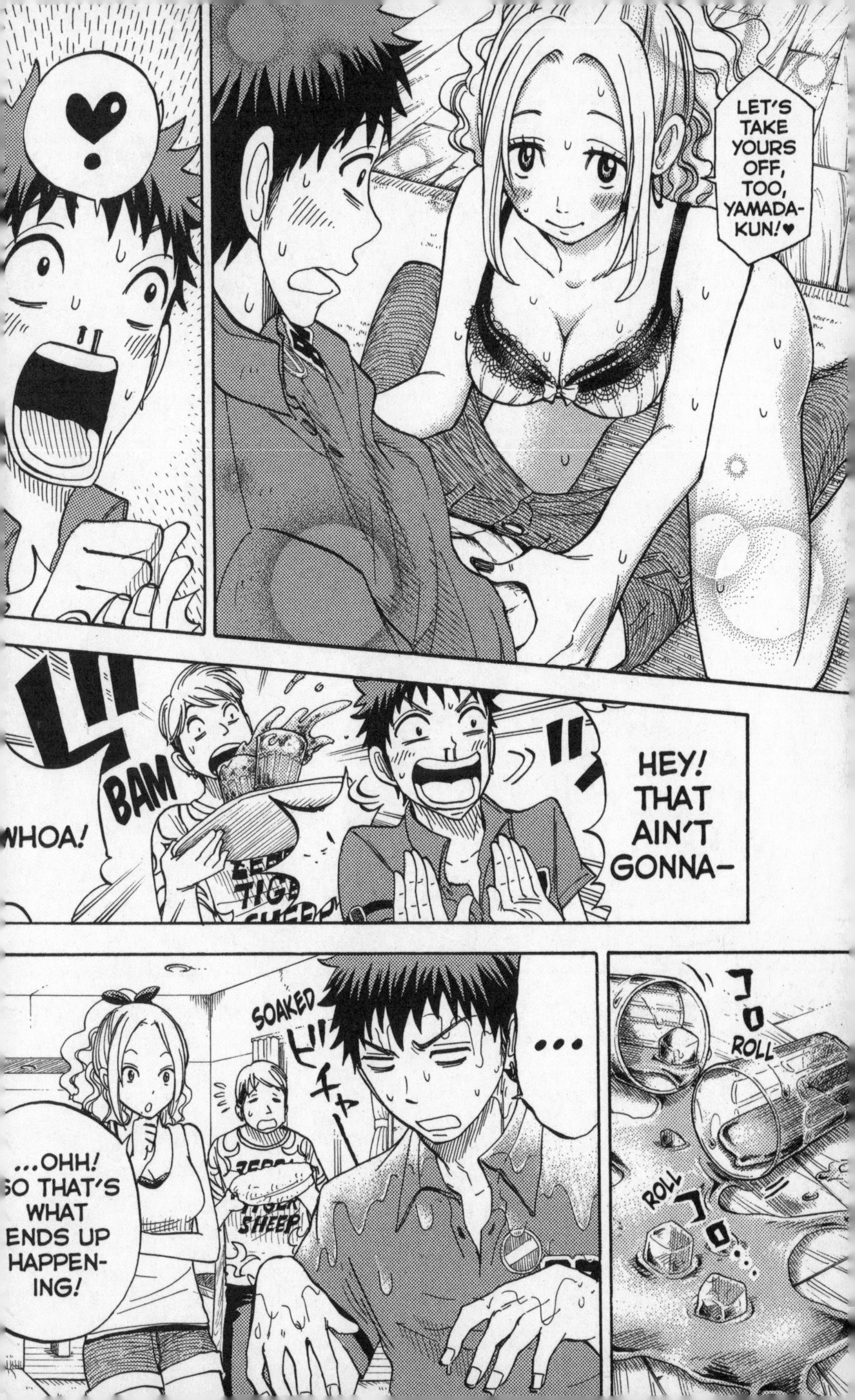

LET'S TAKE YOURS OFF, TOO, YAMADA-KUN!♥
HEY! THAT AIN'T GONNA-
BAM
WHOA!
コロ ROLL
ROLL コロ...
...
SOAKED ビチャ
...OHH! SO THAT'S WHAT ENDS UP HAPPEN-ING!

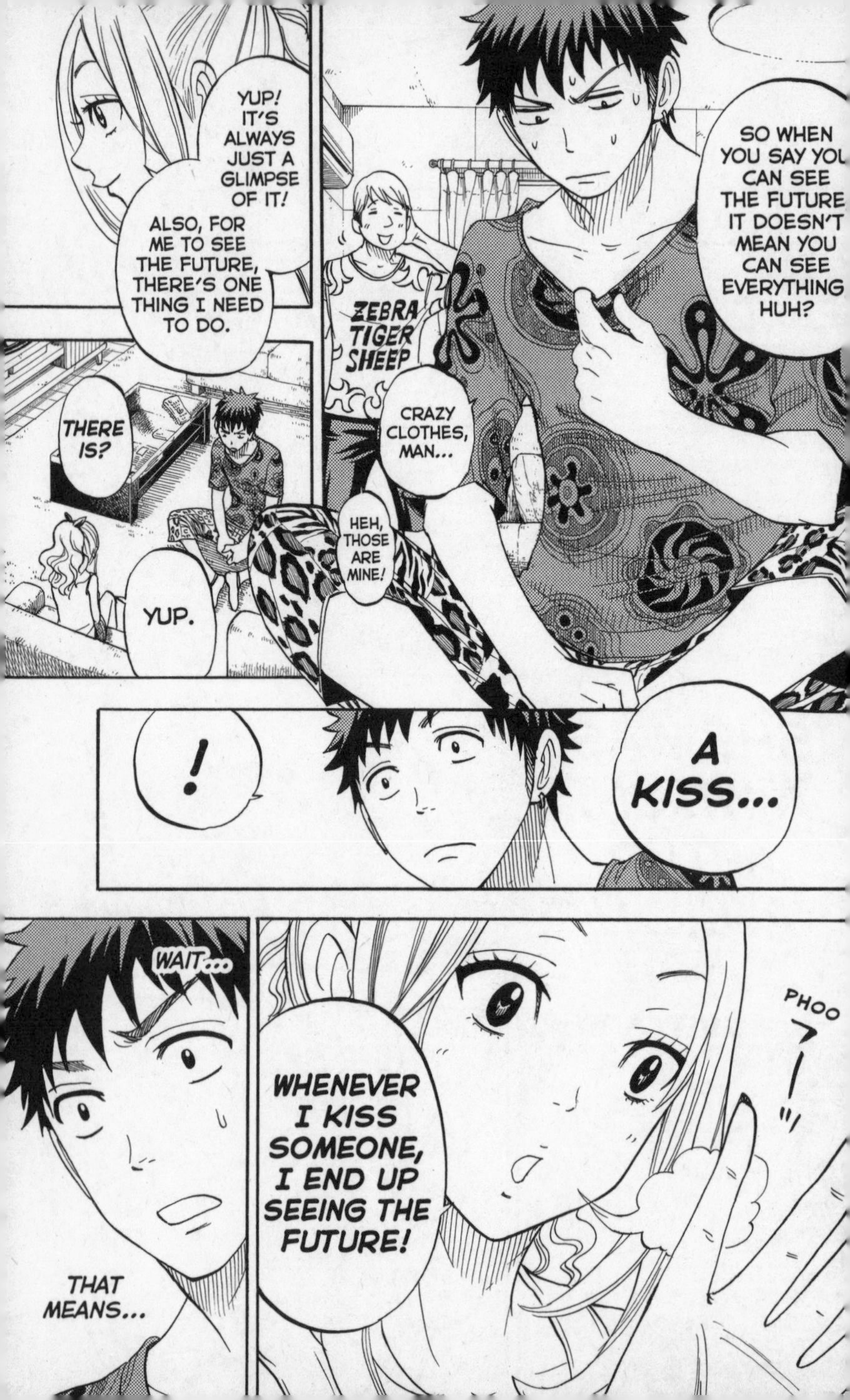
SO WHEN YOU SAY YOU CAN SEE THE FUTURE IT DOESN'T MEAN YOU CAN SEE EVERYTHING HUH?
ZEBRA TIGER SHEEP
CRAZY CLOTHES, MAN...
HEH, THOSE ARE MINE!
YUP! IT'S ALWAYS JUST A GLIMPSE OF IT!
ALSO, FOR ME TO SEE THE FUTURE, THERE'S ONE THING I NEED TO DO.
THERE IS?
YUP.
A KISS...
!
PHOO
WHENEVER I KISS SOMEONE, I END UP SEEING THE FUTURE!
WAIT...
THAT MEANS...

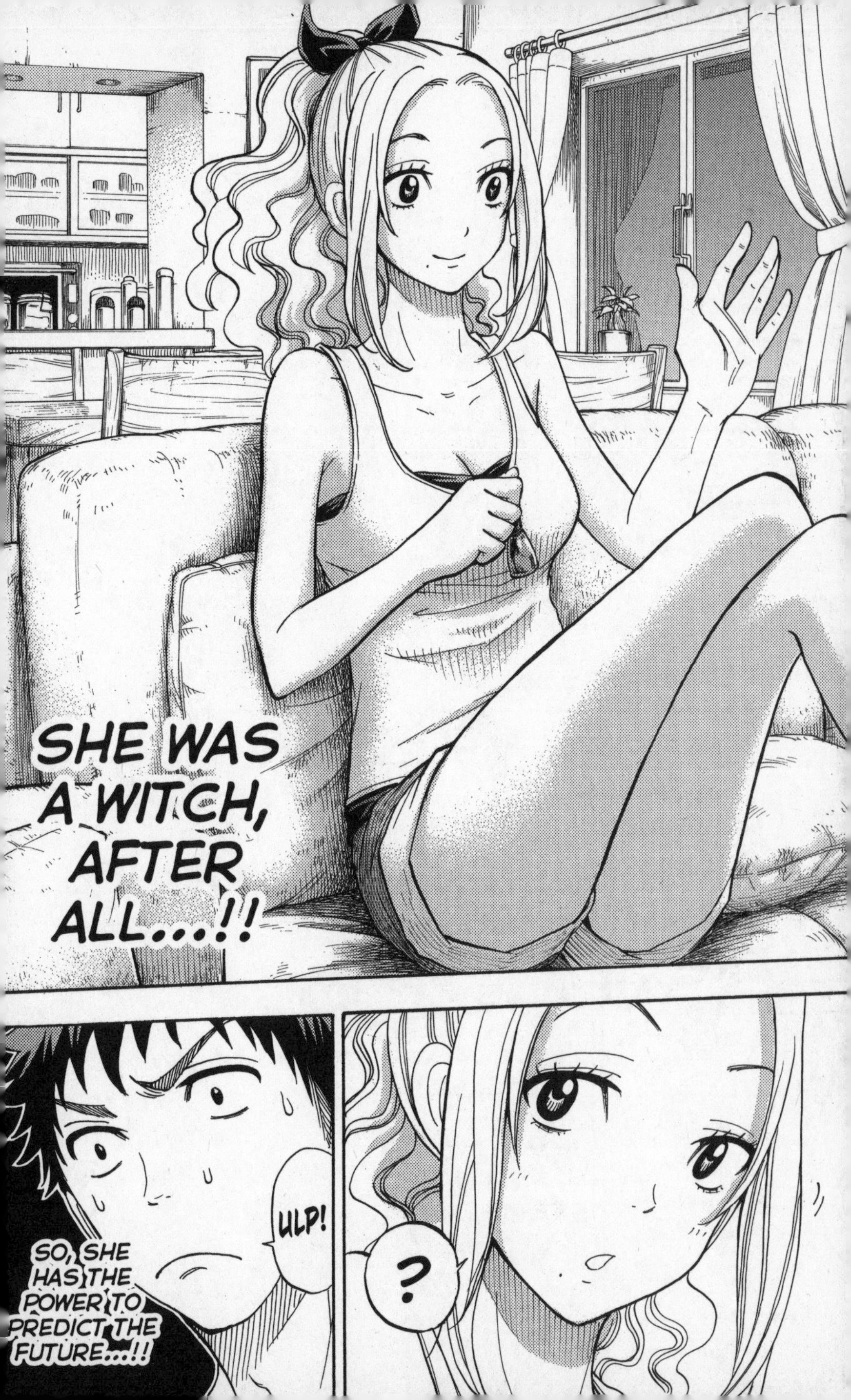
SHE WAS A WITCH, AFTER ALL...!!
?
ULP!
SO, SHE HAS THE POWER TO PREDICT THE FUTURE...!!

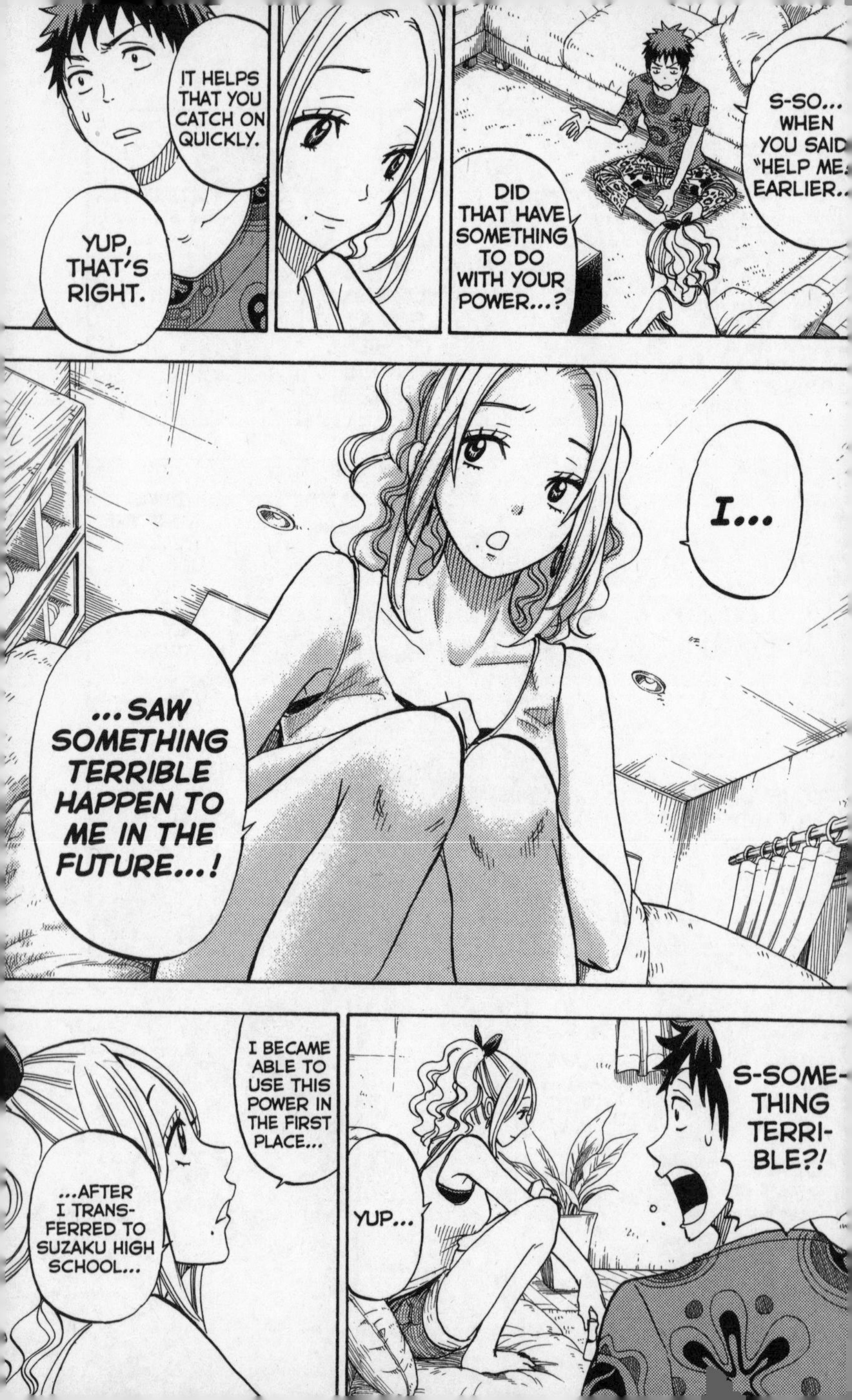
S-SO... WHEN YOU SAID "HELP ME" EARLIER...
DID THAT HAVE SOMETHING TO DO WITH YOUR POWER...?
IT HELPS THAT YOU CATCH ON QUICKLY.
YUP, THAT'S RIGHT.
I...
...SAW SOMETHING TERRIBLE HAPPEN TO ME IN THE FUTURE...!
S-SOME-THING TERRI-BLE?!
YUP...
I BECAME ABLE TO USE THIS POWER IN THE FIRST PLACE...
...AFTER I TRANS-FERRED TO SUZAKU HIGH SCHOOL...

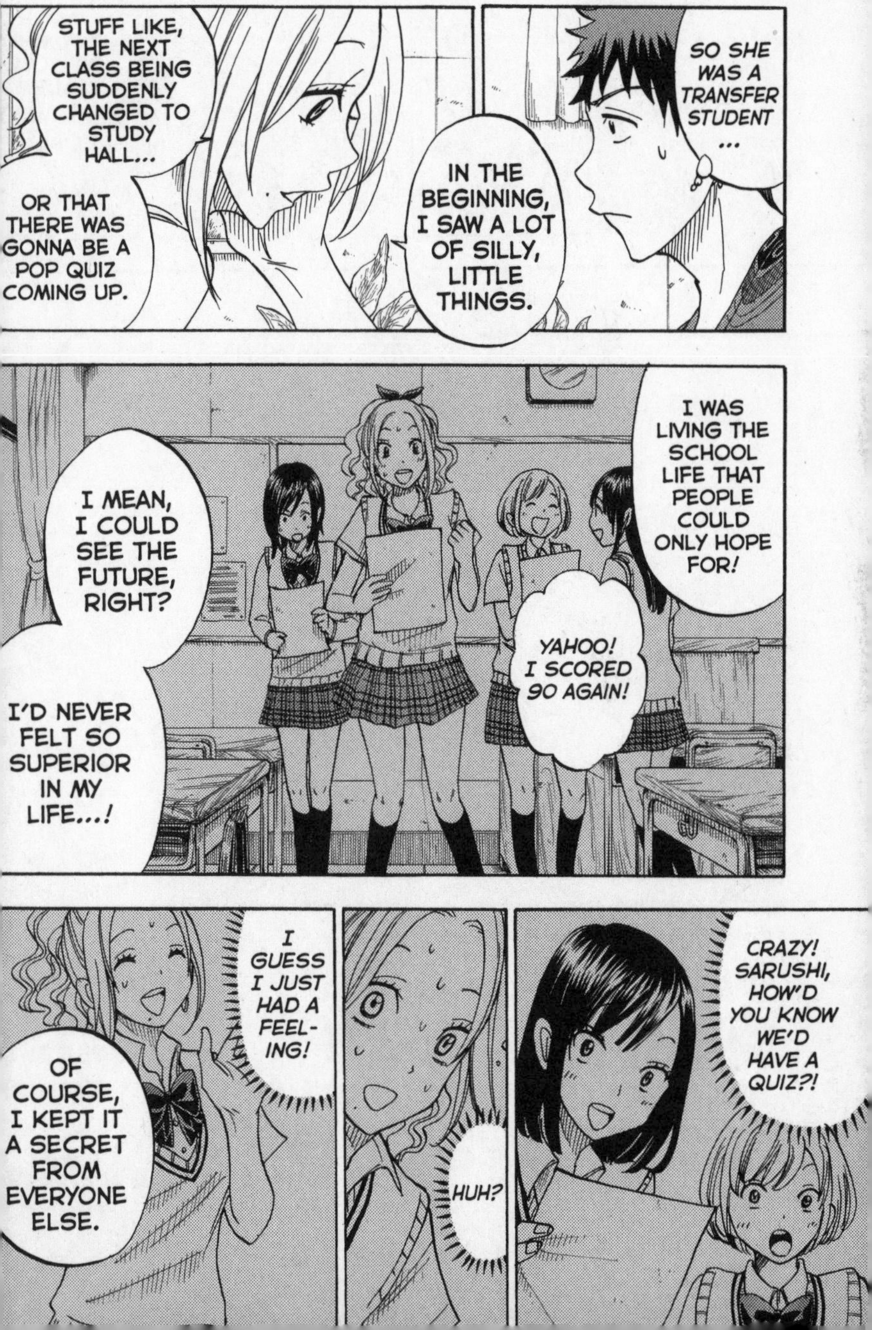
SO SHE WAS A TRANSFER STUDENT ...
IN THE BEGINNING, I SAW A LOT OF SILLY, LITTLE THINGS.
STUFF LIKE, THE NEXT CLASS BEING SUDDENLY CHANGED TO STUDY HALL...
OR THAT THERE WAS GONNA BE A POP QUIZ COMING UP.
I WAS LIVING THE SCHOOL LIFE THAT PEOPLE COULD ONLY HOPE FOR!
YAHOO! I SCORED 90 AGAIN!
I MEAN, I COULD SEE THE FUTURE, RIGHT?
I'D NEVER FELT SO SUPERIOR IN MY LIFE...!
CRAZY! SARUSHI, HOW'D YOU KNOW WE'D HAVE A QUIZ?!
HUH?
I GUESS I JUST HAD A FEEL-ING!
OF COURSE, I KEPT IT A SECRET FROM EVERYONE ELSE.

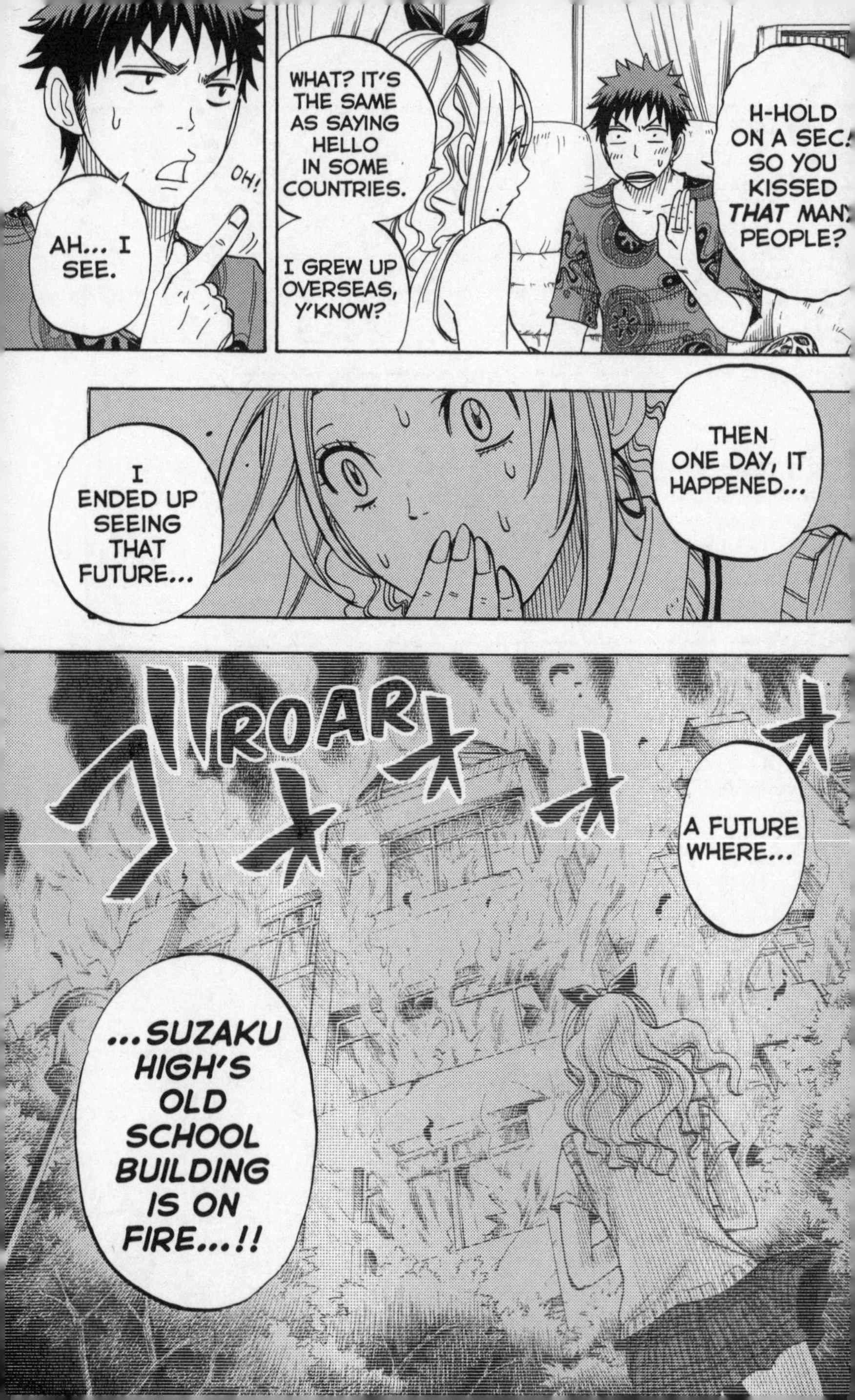
H-HOLD ON A SEC! SO YOU KISSED *THAT* MANY PEOPLE?
WHAT? IT'S THE SAME AS SAYING HELLO IN SOME COUNTRIES.
I GREW UP OVERSEAS, Y'KNOW?
OH!
AH... I SEE.
THEN ONE DAY, IT HAPPENED...
I ENDED UP SEEING THAT FUTURE...
ROAR
A FUTURE WHERE...
...SUZAKU HIGH'S OLD SCHOOL BUILDING IS ON FIRE...!!

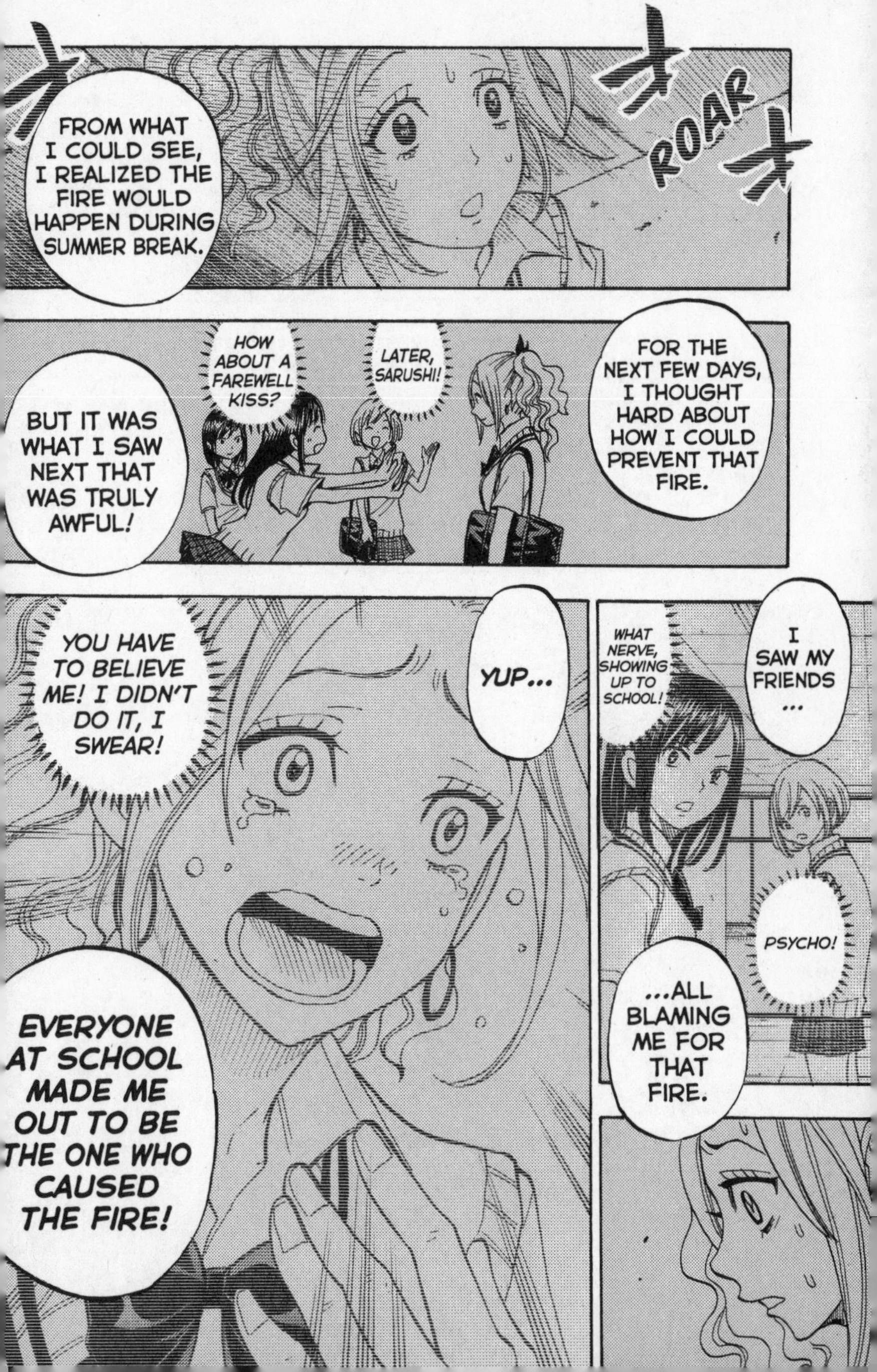
ROAR
FROM WHAT I COULD SEE, I REALIZED THE FIRE WOULD HAPPEN DURING SUMMER BREAK.
FOR THE NEXT FEW DAYS, I THOUGHT HARD ABOUT HOW I COULD PREVENT THAT FIRE.
LATER, SARUSHI!
HOW ABOUT A FAREWELL KISS?
BUT IT WAS WHAT I SAW NEXT THAT WAS TRULY AWFUL!
I SAW MY FRIENDS ...
WHAT NERVE, SHOWING UP TO SCHOOL!
PSYCHO!
...ALL BLAMING ME FOR THAT FIRE.
YUP...
YOU HAVE TO BELIEVE ME! I DIDN'T DO IT, I SWEAR!
EVERYONE AT SCHOOL MADE ME OUT TO BE THE ONE WHO CAUSED THE FIRE!

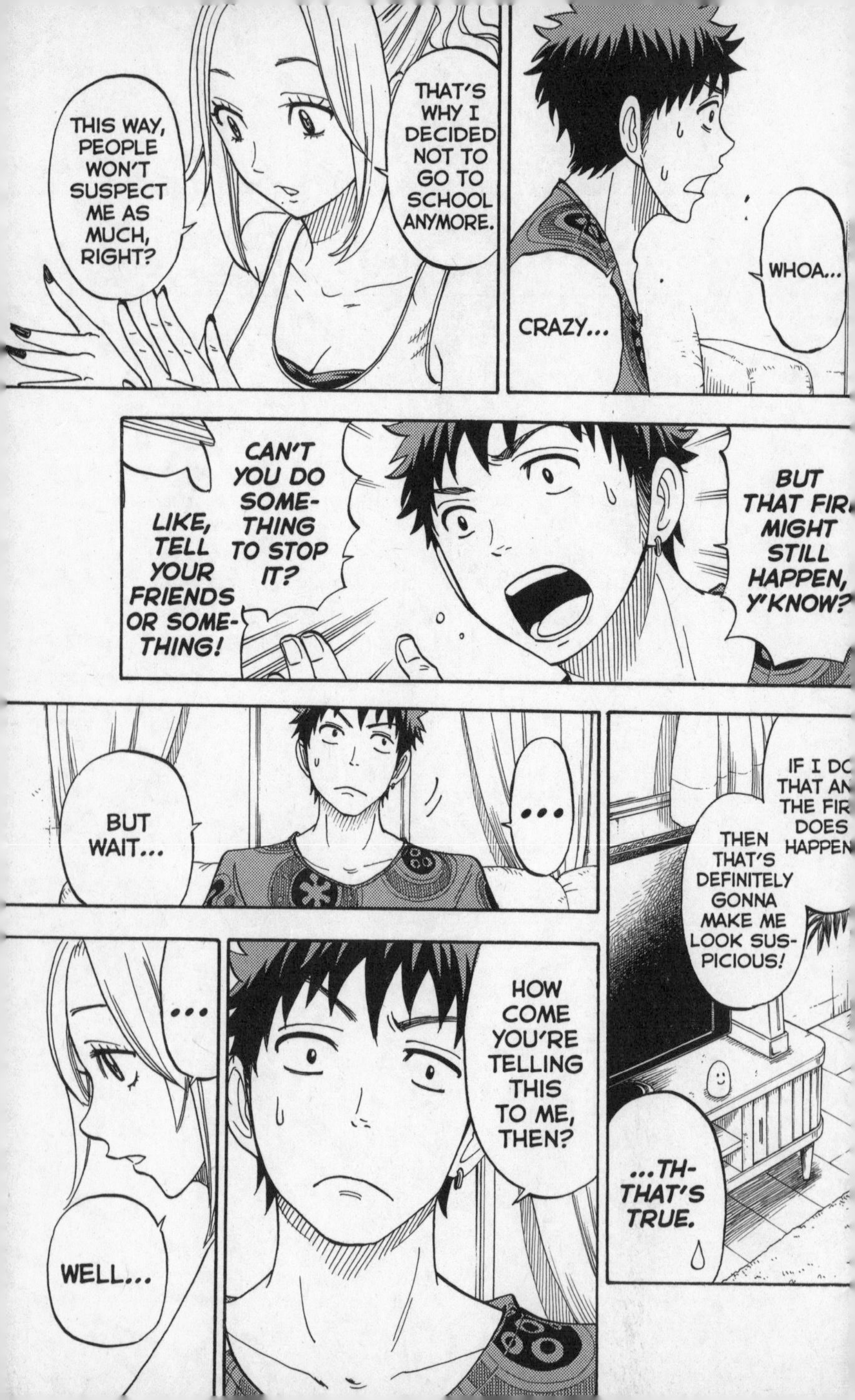
WHOA...
CRAZY...
THAT'S WHY I DECIDED NOT TO GO TO SCHOOL ANYMORE.
THIS WAY, PEOPLE WON'T SUSPECT ME AS MUCH, RIGHT?
BUT THAT FIR MIGHT STILL HAPPEN, Y'KNOW?
CAN'T YOU DO SOME-THING TO STOP IT?
LIKE, TELL YOUR FRIENDS OR SOME-THING!
IF I DO THAT AN THE FIR DOES HAPPEN
THEN THAT'S DEFINITELY GONNA MAKE ME LOOK SUS-PICIOUS!
...TH-THAT'S TRUE.
...
BUT WAIT...
HOW COME YOU'RE TELLING THIS TO ME, THEN?
...
WELL...

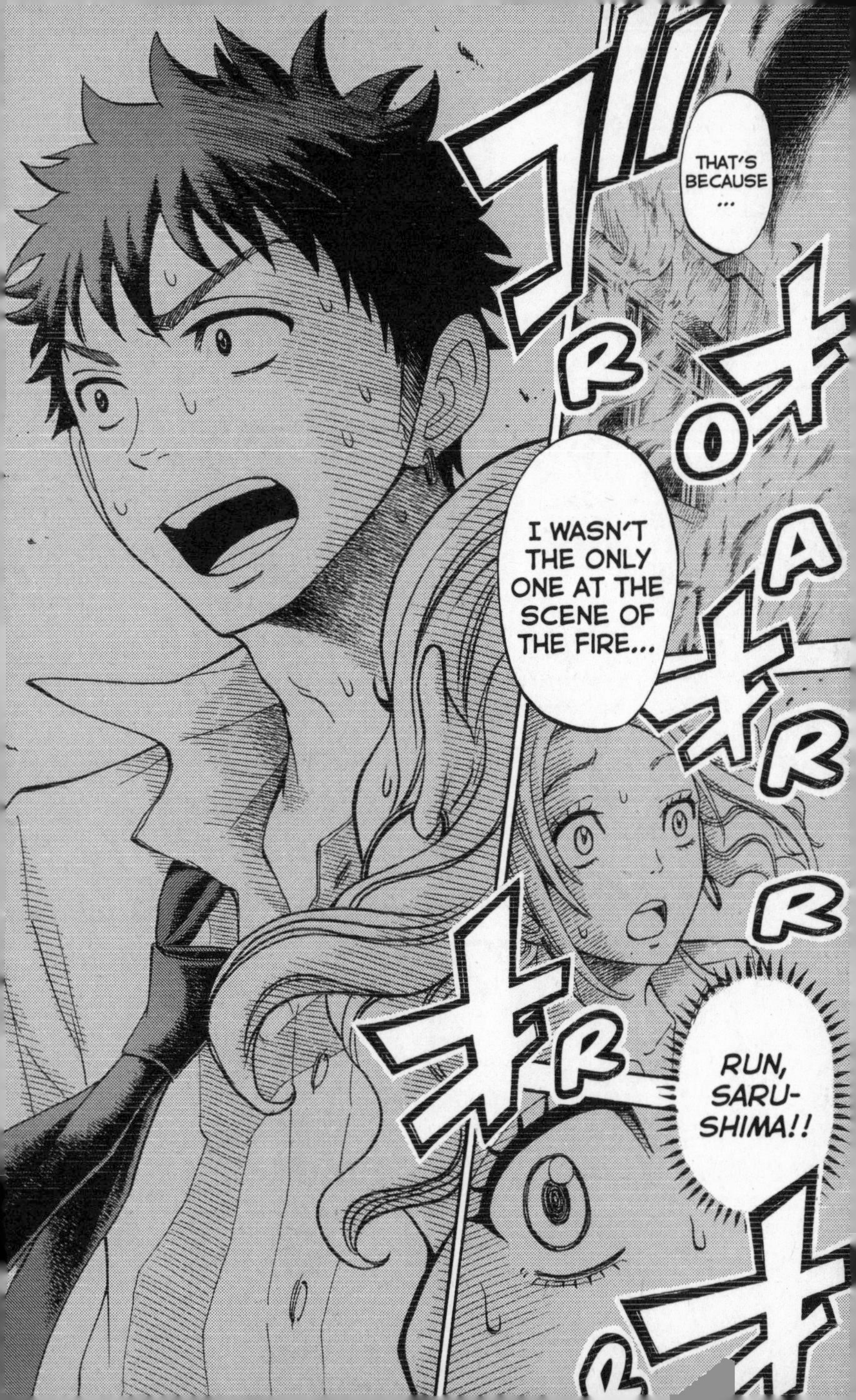
THAT'S BECAUSE ...
ゴオオオオ
ROARRRR
I WASN'T THE ONLY ONE AT THE SCENE OF THE FIRE...
RUN, SARU-SHIMA!!

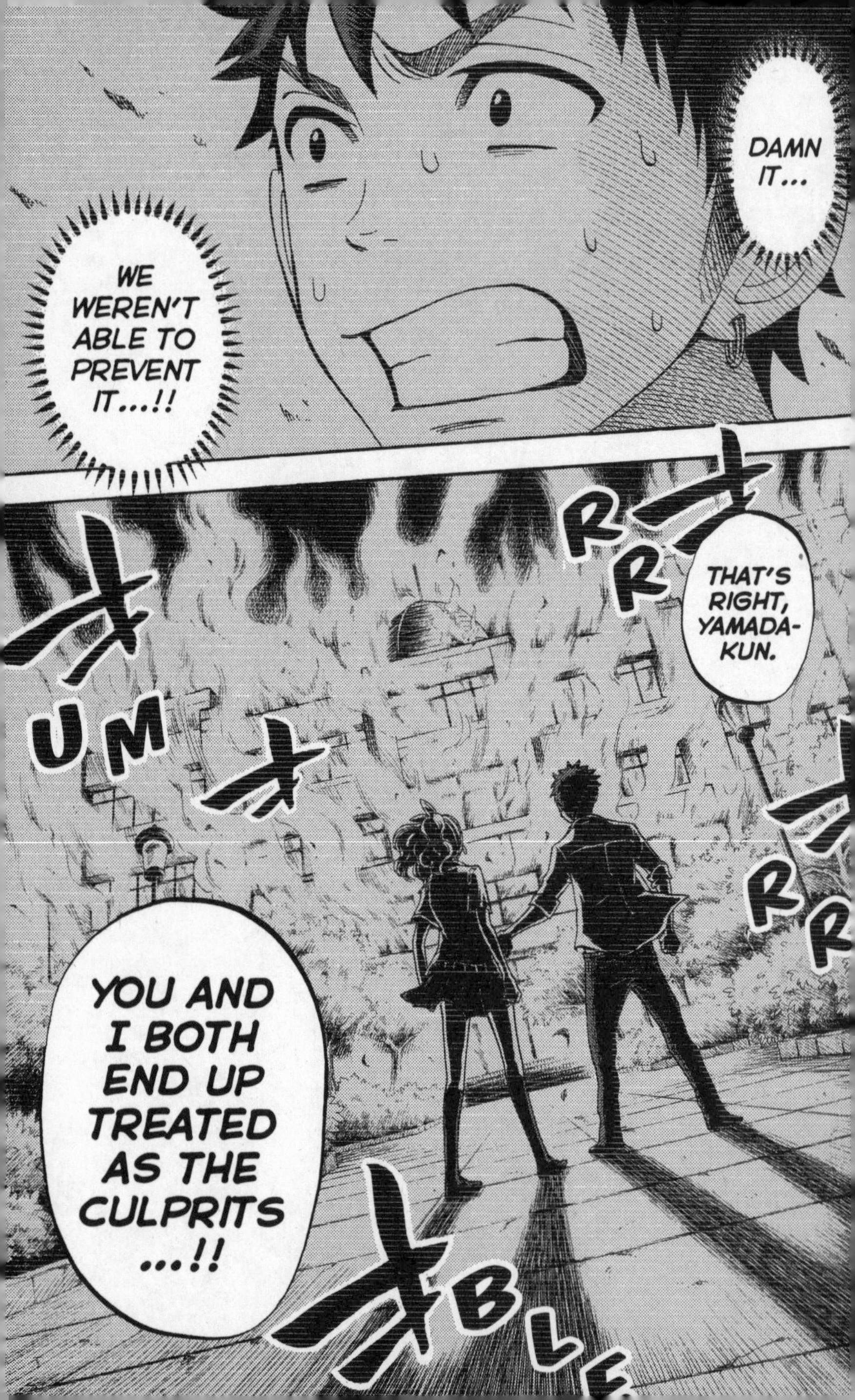
DAMN IT...
WE WEREN'T ABLE TO PREVENT IT...!!
RR
THAT'S RIGHT, YAMADA-KUN.
RR
UM
YOU AND I BOTH END UP TREATED AS THE CULPRITS ...!!
BLE

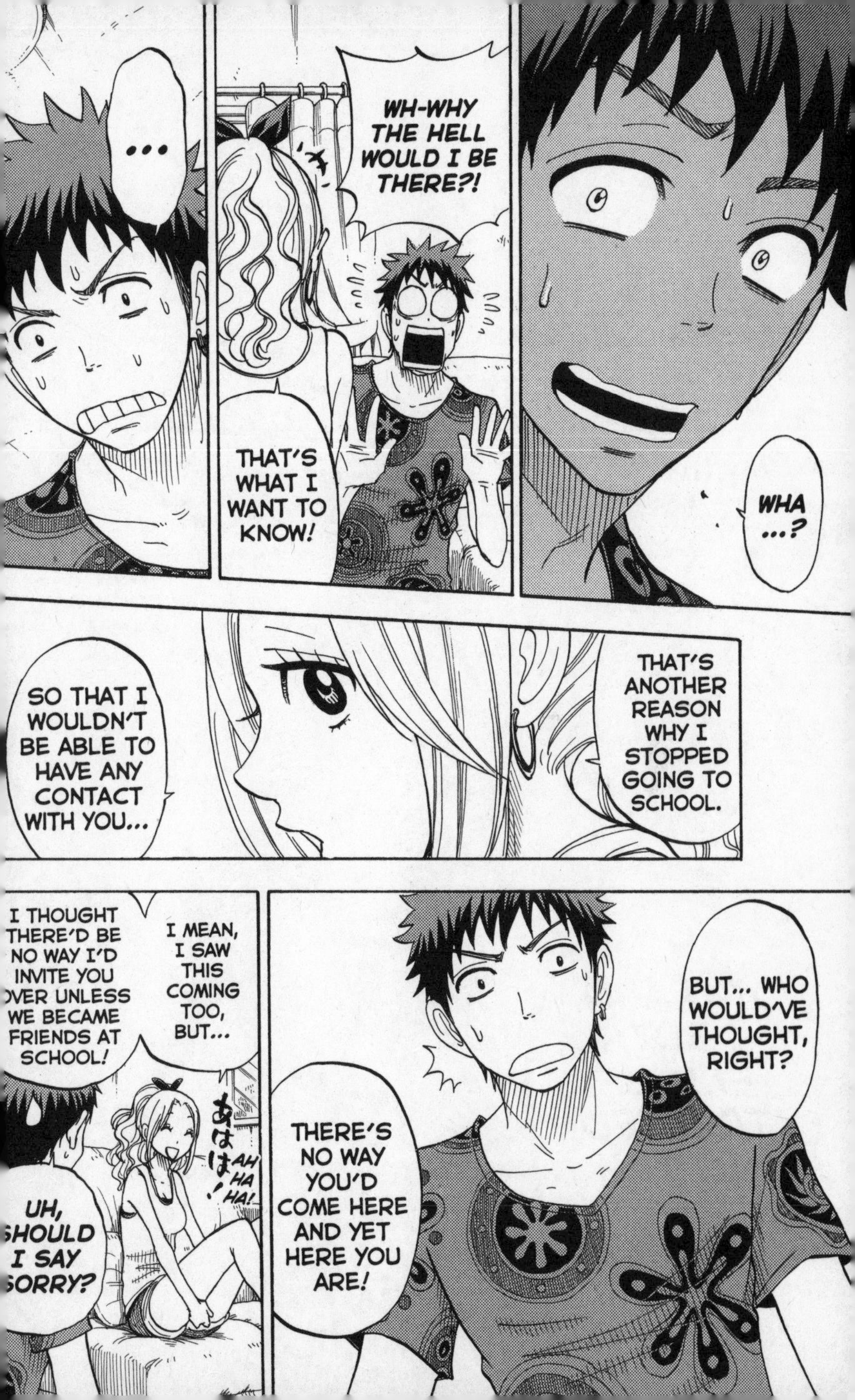
WHA ...?
WH-WHY THE HELL WOULD I BE THERE?!
THAT'S WHAT I WANT TO KNOW!
...
THAT'S ANOTHER REASON WHY I STOPPED GOING TO SCHOOL.
SO THAT I WOULDN'T BE ABLE TO HAVE ANY CONTACT WITH YOU...
BUT... WHO WOULD'VE THOUGHT, RIGHT?
THERE'S NO WAY YOU'D COME HERE AND YET HERE YOU ARE!
I MEAN, I SAW THIS COMING TOO, BUT...
I THOUGHT THERE'D BE NO WAY I'D INVITE YOU OVER UNLESS WE BECAME FRIENDS AT SCHOOL!
あはは! AH HA HA!
UH, SHOULD I SAY SORRY?

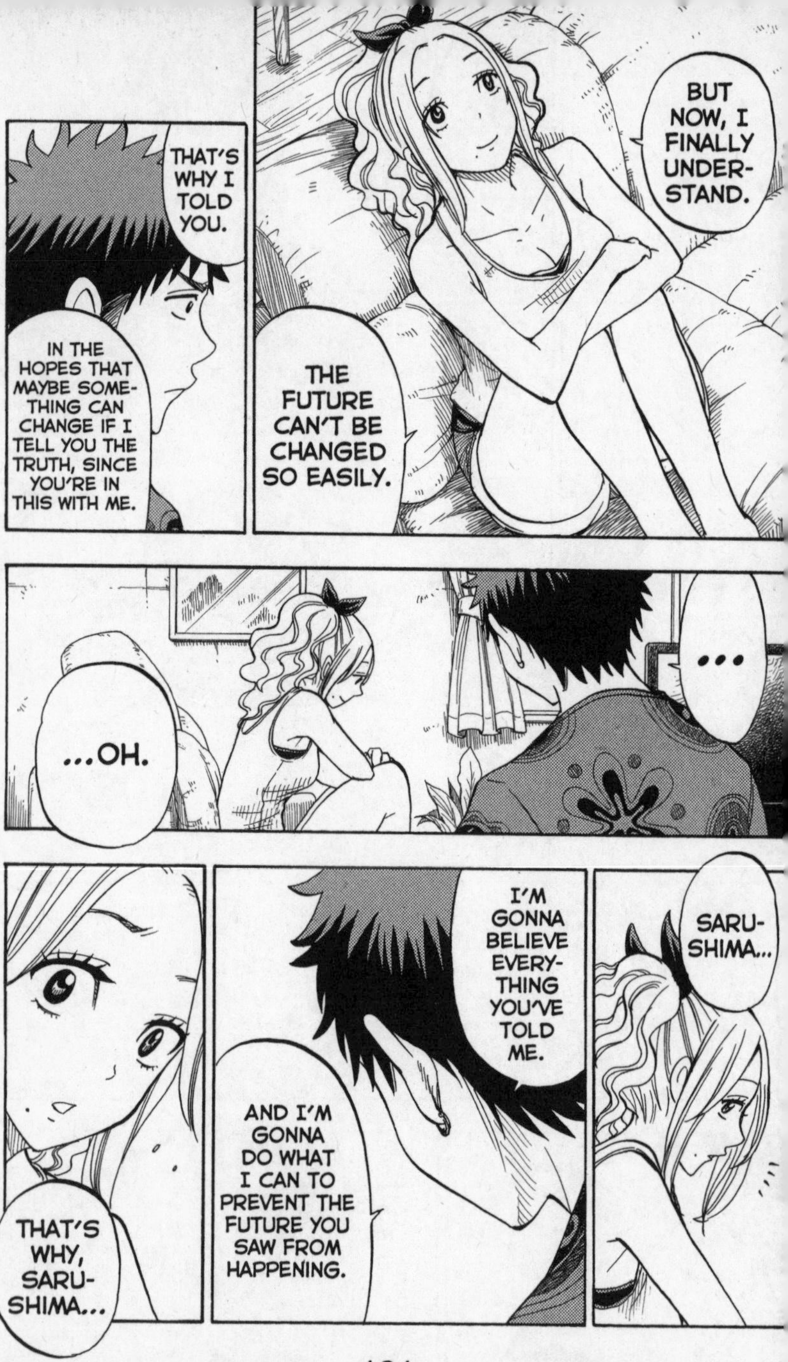
BUT NOW, I FINALLY UNDERSTAND.
THE FUTURE CAN'T BE CHANGED SO EASILY.
THAT'S WHY I TOLD YOU.
IN THE HOPES THAT MAYBE SOMETHING CAN CHANGE IF I TELL YOU THE TRUTH, SINCE YOU'RE IN THIS WITH ME.
...
...OH.
SARUSHIMA...
I'M GONNA BELIEVE EVERYTHING YOU'VE TOLD ME.
AND I'M GONNA DO WHAT I CAN TO PREVENT THE FUTURE YOU SAW FROM HAPPENING.
THAT'S WHY, SARUSHIMA...

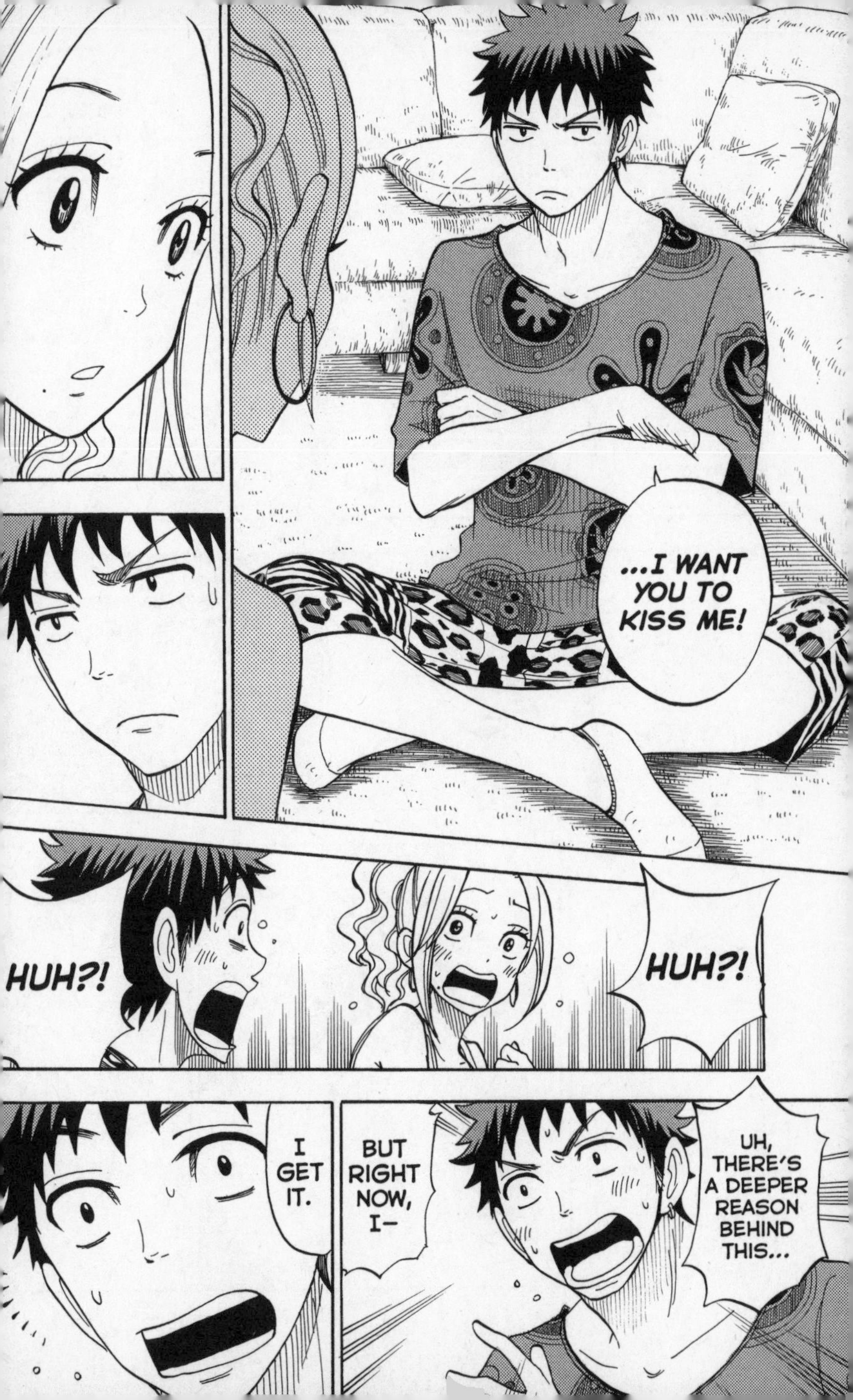
...I WANT YOU TO KISS ME!
HUH?!
HUH?!
UH, THERE'S A DEEPER REASON BEHIND THIS...
BUT RIGHT NOW, I–
I GET IT.

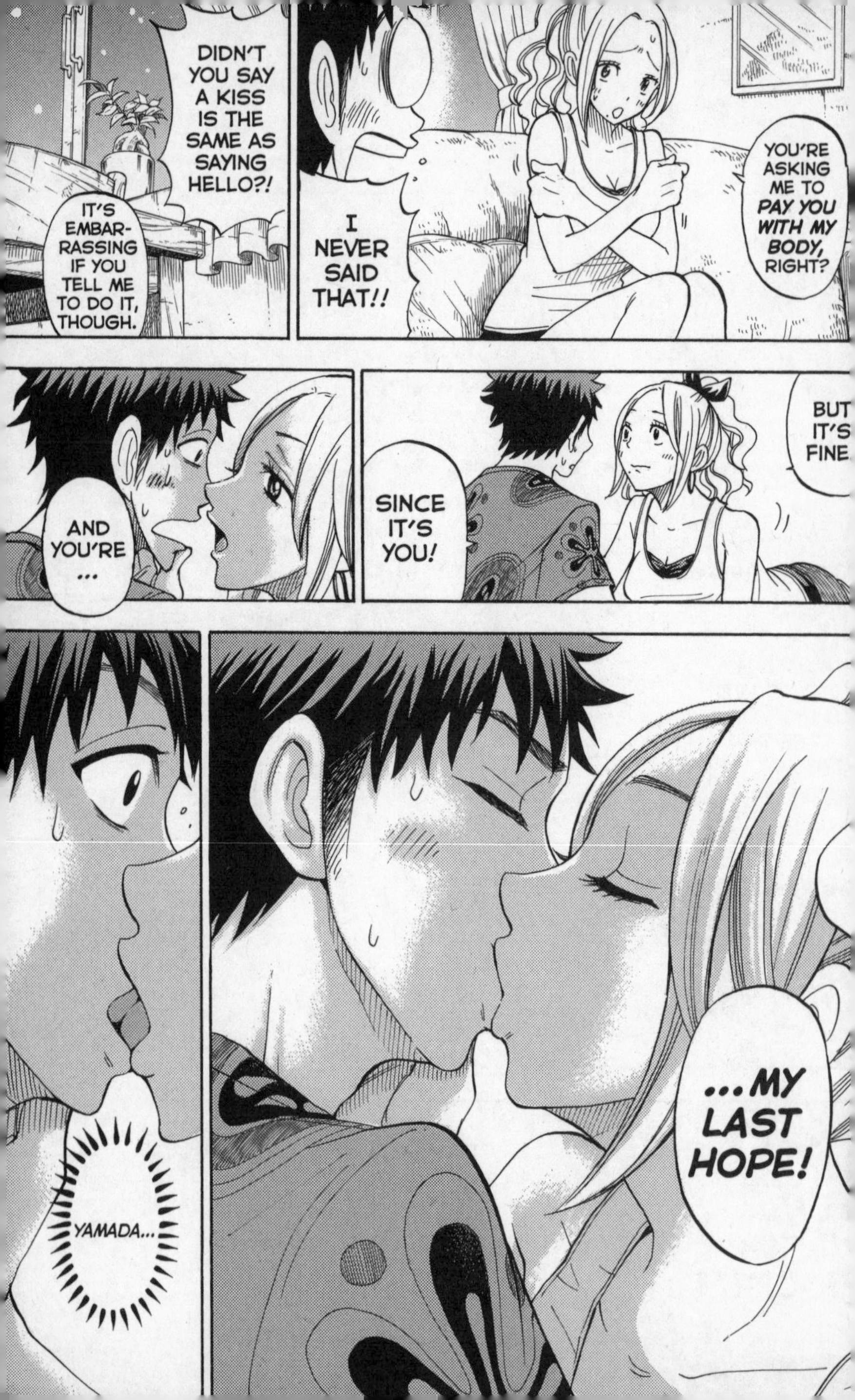
YOU'RE ASKING ME TO PAY YOU WITH MY BODY, RIGHT?
I NEVER SAID THAT!!
DIDN'T YOU SAY A KISS IS THE SAME AS SAYING HELLO?!
IT'S EMBAR-RASSING IF YOU TELL ME TO DO IT, THOUGH.
BUT IT'S FINE
SINCE IT'S YOU!
AND YOU'RE ...
...MY LAST HOPE!
YAMADA...

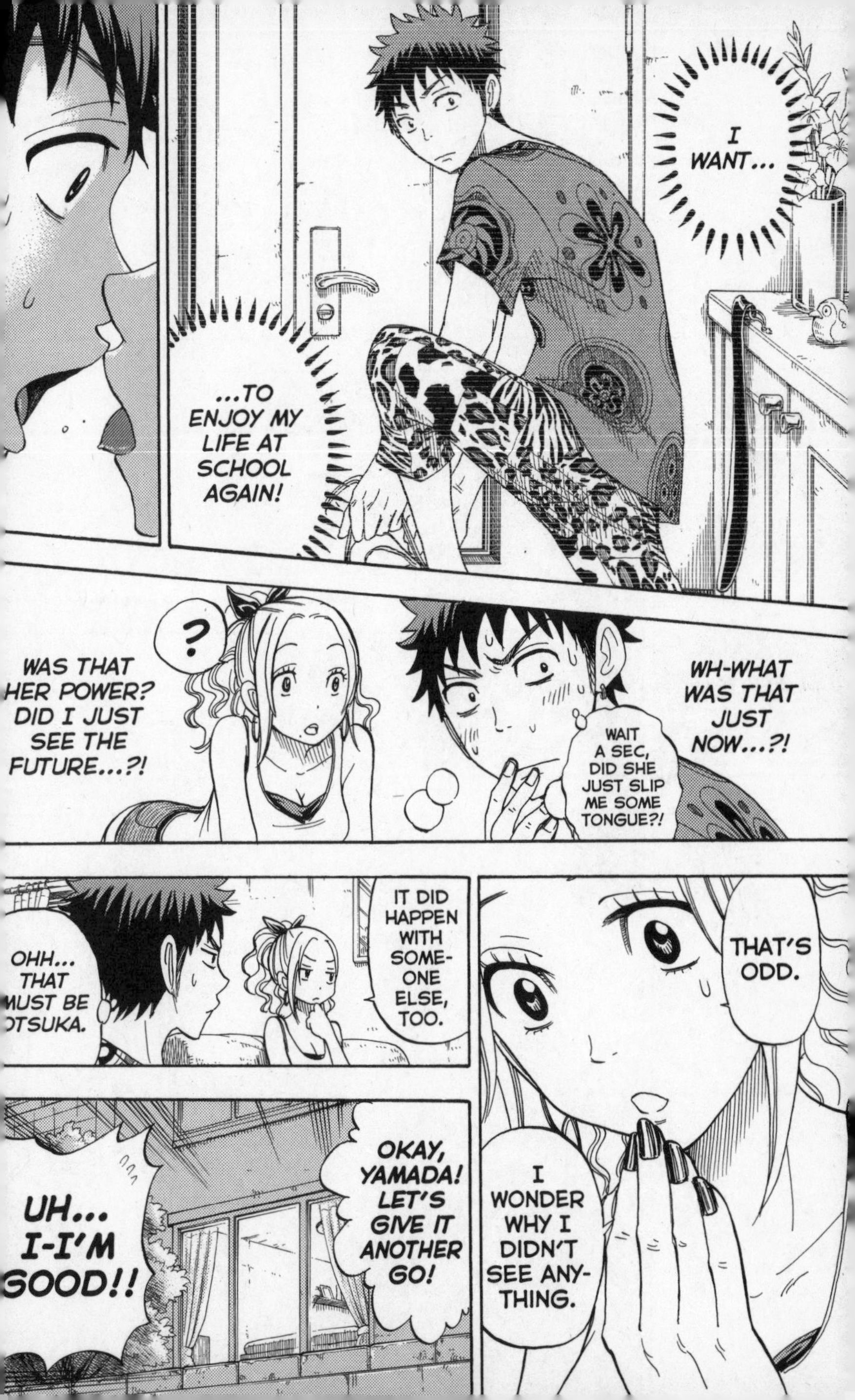
I WANT...
...TO ENJOY MY LIFE AT SCHOOL AGAIN!
WH-WHAT WAS THAT JUST NOW...?!
WAIT A SEC, DID SHE JUST SLIP ME SOME TONGUE?!
?
WAS THAT HER POWER? DID I JUST SEE THE FUTURE...?!
THAT'S ODD.
I WONDER WHY I DIDN'T SEE ANYTHING.
IT DID HAPPEN WITH SOMEONE ELSE, TOO.
OHH... THAT MUST BE OTSUKA.
OKAY, YAMADA! LET'S GIVE IT ANOTHER GO!
UH... I-I'M GOOD!!

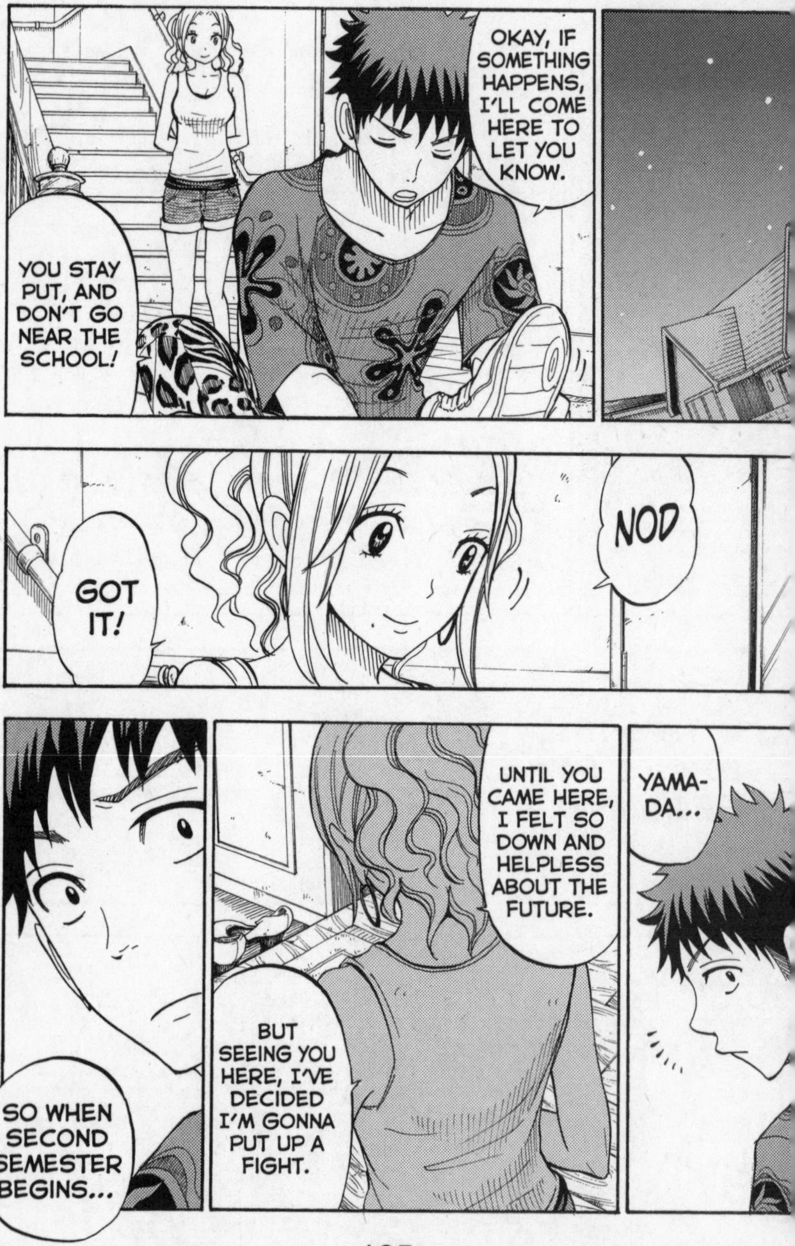
OKAY, IF SOMETHING HAPPENS, I'LL COME HERE TO LET YOU KNOW.
YOU STAY PUT, AND DON'T GO NEAR THE SCHOOL!
NOD
GOT IT!
YAMA-DA...
UNTIL YOU CAME HERE, I FELT SO DOWN AND HELPLESS ABOUT THE FUTURE.
BUT SEEING YOU HERE, I'VE DECIDED I'M GONNA PUT UP A FIGHT.
SO WHEN SECOND SEMESTER BEGINS...

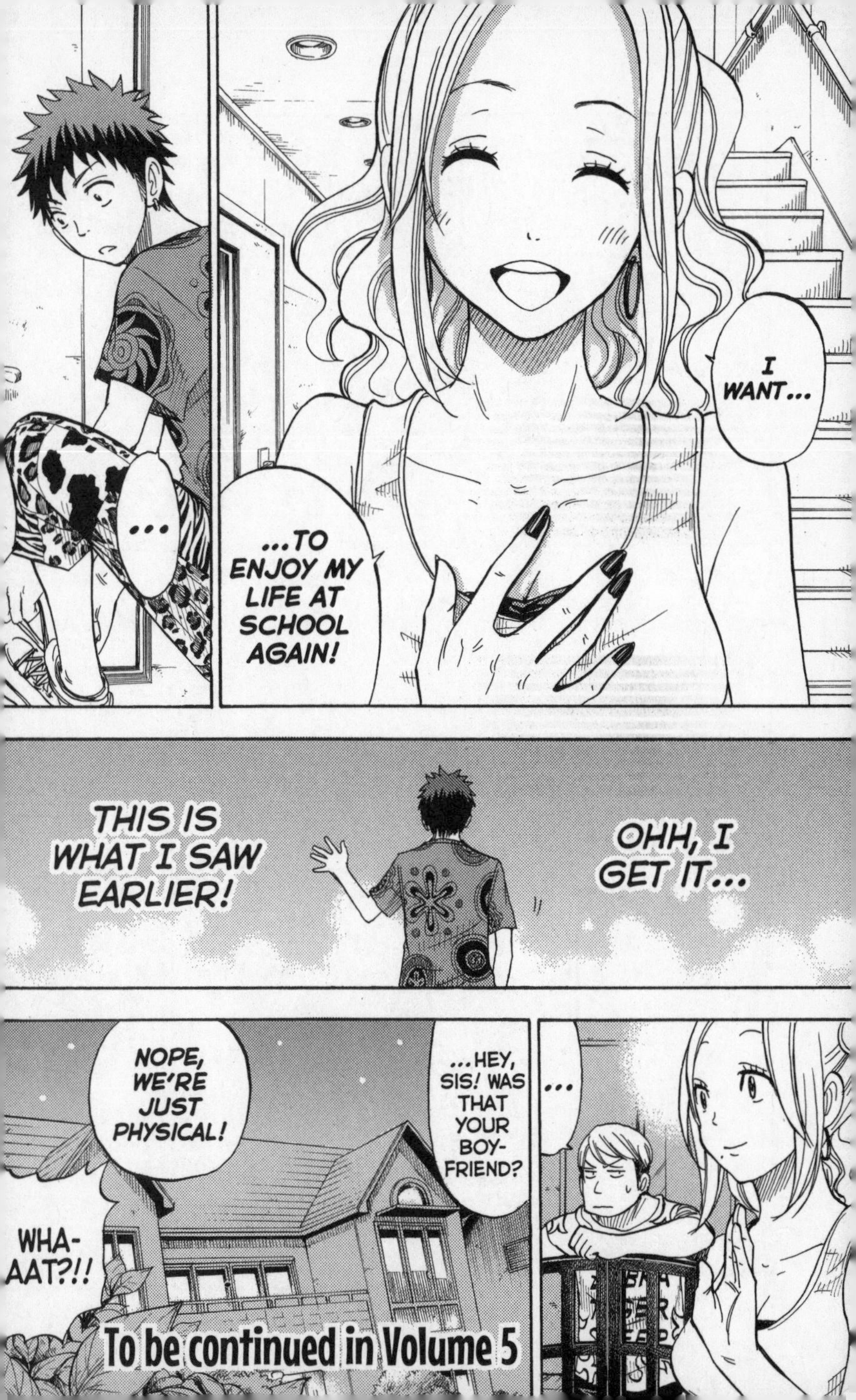
I WANT...
...TO ENJOY MY LIFE AT SCHOOL AGAIN!
...
OHH, I GET IT...
THIS IS WHAT I SAW EARLIER!
...
...HEY, SIS! WAS THAT YOUR BOY-FRIEND?
NOPE, WE'RE JUST PHYSICAL!
WHA-AAT?!!
To be continued in Volume 5

朱 雀 高 等 学 校
裏ホームページ
SUZAKU HIGH SCHOOL UNDERGROUND WEBSITE

We're back with the column for our second round!

This time we got a lot of messages. It's a real struggle to pick the best ones.

All right, let's get right into it.

Q1. I have an issue. Itou-san was in shock at first when she saw Yamada and Shiraishi kissing, but now she kisses Yamada like it's nothing. As a fan of Itou this makes me sad. H.N. (handle name) Akari-san (as well as many others)

N-no...you got it all wrong...!!

What's wrong Itou? You're acting strange.
You really have been actively going for kisses with Yamada lately, haven't you?

You're the last person I want to hear that from! Anyway, that's not how it is! I'm only doing that in order to thoroughly test the witch powers. I'm doing it out of obligation! It's not like I'd ever want to actually kiss Yamada or anything. But come to think of it, Miyamura, you're also kissing Yamada without much hesitation...

Yeah, it's fun, isn't it?

...(THAT'S NOT THE POINT...)

On the school camping trip, the Yakisoba that Shiraishi had was something she prepared herself, right? It looks like it was really something…

H.N. Koshiri-san

I wonder about that. We're in class C, so we were in a different group.

As far as I could see, it looks like Urara-chan was making it with some other girls in her class.

I'm sure that with all the fun she had while making it, even that burnt-up Yakisoba must've been delicious. But as for Yamada…

Oh, Miyamura, I guess you have something nice to say every now and then, don't you?

Q3. In the fourth panel on page 114 of volume 3, there's a sign that says, "Do not thoughtlessly get depressed." That's hilarious.

H.N. Tigernon-san

Huh?! There's graffiti like that in the boys' bathroom?

If you scope things out in the bathroom, you can get a grip on most of what's happening within the school, right?

Wipe that smirk off your face… But now that you mention it, there sure are a lot of rumors flying about in the girls' bathroom! If you like gossip, you should definitely check out the bathroom!! Please send your correspondence here ↓

Yamada-kun and the Seven Witches: Underground Website
c/o Kodansha Comics
451 Park Ave. South, 7th Floor
New York, NY 10016

※ **Don't forget to include your handle name (pen name) and measurements!**

We're also accepting confessions of love to yours truly! But only from girls.

Those won't be coming!

Miyabi Itou's Witch Research Notes

File.2 Page 1

★ Witch and Joker Character Collection!

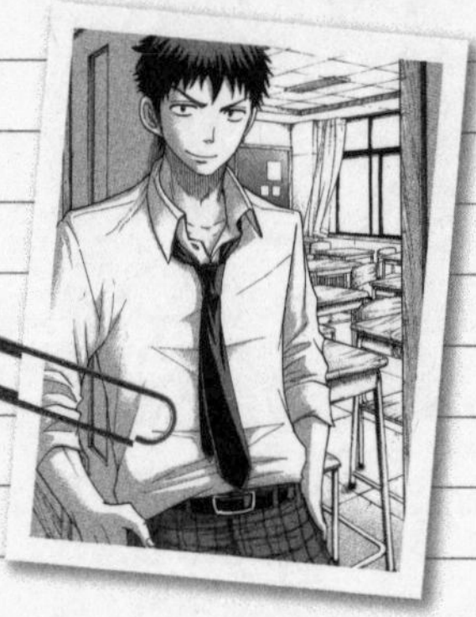

Ryu Yamada

Joker power

Copy!

A former bad boy (!) and Supernatural Studies Club member number two.

(I'm number one!)

He's the most hated person in school (tears).

He has the ability to copy the powers of whomever he kisses.

Thanks to his power he was able to make friends, which is great!

Urara Shiraishi

Body swapping witch power

Change!

President of the Supernatural Studies Club.

She's super smart and cute and stylish, and I'm so jealous of her!

She has the ability to instantly swap bodies with whomever she kisses.

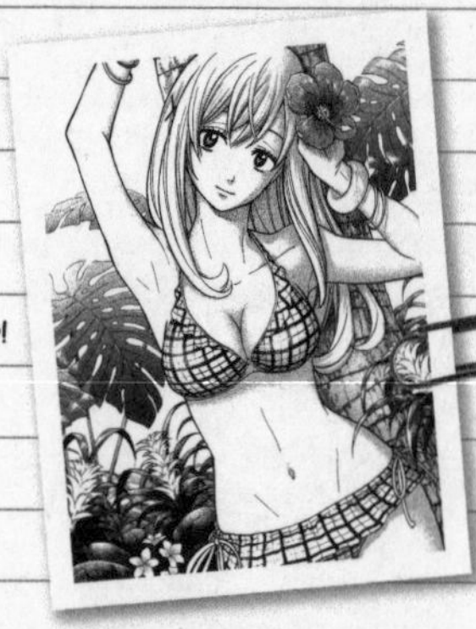

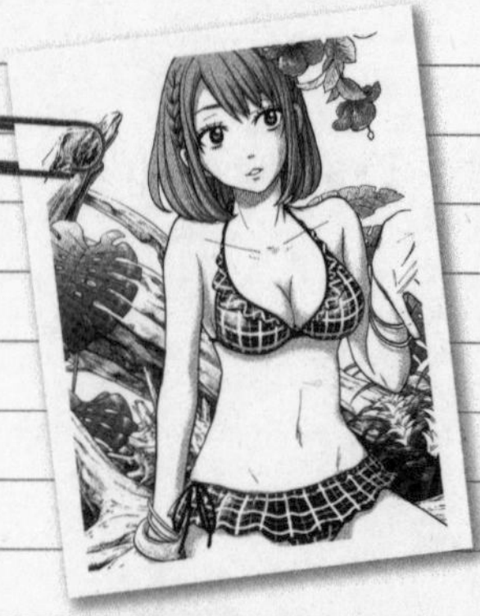

Nene Odagiri

Charm witch power

Charm!

The mean and nasty Vice President of the Student Council.

She has the ability to charm whomever she kisses.

Being put under the charm spell can become a habit...

Meiko Otsuka

Telepathic witch power  Telepathy

She's a super quiet girl who's in the manga club.

She can send and receive telepathic messages from

whomever she kisses.

It seems that you have to have a clear image of the person you're

sending messages to or else the telepathy won't work, so this power

isn't really made out for someone with a poor imagination like Yamada...

Maria Sarushima

Prediction witch power   Precognition

She used to live abroad.

She can see the future of whomever she kisses.

Putting your tongue in someone's mouth when you kiss isn't how

you greet your friends, is it?

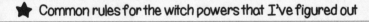

★ Common rules for the witch powers that I've figured out

* One person, one power

* If a person under a witch's spell is kissed by another

  witch, the person being kissed will not be affected

* A witch cannot put another witch under their spell with a kiss

Translation Notes

Fireworks, page 137
When thinking of a summer night in Japan, nothing creates a more picturesque scene than fireworks. Fireworks in Japan can be witnessed in many forms but are usually seen as large aerial fireworks at festivals and individually-held sparklers with groups of friends and family.

Papico, page 151
The ice cream that Yamada-kun's little sister is eating probably looks more like a freeze-pop than anything else, but this is likely an ice cream product called Papico. Papico is manufactured by the confectionary giant, Glico, and comes in a container that resembles a soda bottle, out of which the ice cream inside is sucked out. It comes in an assortment of flavors, but the most common ones are chocolate-coffee and vanilla shake. Each packet comes with two servings, making it great for sharing.

Sugi-chan, page 158
Sarushima appears to be watching a comedy show with someone resembling famous Japanese comedian, Sugi-chan. He can be identified by his denim vests and shorts and for always carrying a bottle of cola that's missing its cap. The reason for the missing cap is that he's such a badass that he throws the cap away as soon as he buys the bottle. Like many Japanese comedians, Sugi-chan became popular from his catchphrase, which is "Wairudo da ze" or "Wairudo darou." This translates to something like, "That's badass, ain't it?" Most of his jokes are him talking about how badass or "wild" he is on account of his silly, devil-may-care attitude with everyday actions and activities.

Puyo Puyo, page 160
The game that Miyamura and Sarushima seem to be playing is Puyo Puyo, a famous series of puzzle games from Japan. In North America, these games were first released under different names such as Dr. Robotnik's Mean Bean Machine on the Sega Genesis and Kirby's Avalanche on the Super NES. The "Oh no!" said by Sarushima's character is specific to a certain character in the Puyo Puyo series by the name of Arle Nadja. In Japanese, she says Batan Kyuu, which is an onomatopoeic phrase that imitates the sound of collapsing from fatigue, or in the case of the game, defeat.

Futon drying, page 161
In Japan, many people sleep on a futon, which is thick bedding that is placed on the floor. Japan can be drastically humid in the summer and futons tend to retain a lot of moisture, so proper futon care involves regularly airing them out. Most people will place their futon out on a veranda or balcony, let them dry out in the sun, and use a carpet beater to get out the dust and clean the futon.

Yamada-kun and the Seven Witches vol

Names, characters, places, and incidents are the products of the author's imagination or are used fictitiously. Any resemblance to actual events, locales, or persons, living or dead, is entirely coincidental.

A Kodansha Comics Trade Paperback Original.

Yamada-kun and the Seven Witches volume 4 copyright © 2012 Miki Yoshikawa
English translation copyright © 2015 Miki Yoshikawa

Published in the United States by Kodansha Comics,
an imprint of Kodansha USA Publishing, LLC, New York.

Publication rights for this English edition arranged through Kodansha Ltd.,
Tokyo.

First published in Japan in 2012 by Kodansha Ltd., Tokyo, as *Yamada-kun to Nananin no Majo* volume 4.

ISBN 978-1-63236-071-7

Printed in the United States of America.

www.kodanshacomics.com

9 8 7 6 5 4 3 2 1

Translator: David Rhie
Lettering: Sara Linsley
Editing: Ajani Oloye
Kodansha Comics Edition Cover Design: Phil Balsman